APPALACHIANS AND RACE

Appalachians and Race

The Mountain South
from Slavery to Segregation

Edited by John C. Inscoe

THE UNIVERSITY PRESS OF KENTUCKY

Publication of this volume was made possible in part
by grants from the E.O. Robinson Mountain Fund
and the National Endowment for the Humanities.

Scholarly publisher for the Commonwealth,
serving Bellarmine College, Berea College, Centre
College of Kentucky, Eastern Kentucky University,
The Filson Club Historical Society, Georgetown College,
Kentucky Historical Society, Kentucky State University,
Morehead State University, Murray State University,
Northern Kentucky University, Transylvania University,
University of Kentucky, University of Louisville,
and Western Kentucky University.

Editorial and Sales Offices: The University Press of Kentucky
663 South Limestone Street, Lexington, Kentucky 40508–4008

01 02 03 04 05   5 4 3 2 1

Library of Congress Cataloging-in-Publication Data

Appalachians and race : the mountain South from slavery to segregation / edited by John C. Inscoe.
    p. cm.
Includes bibliographical references and index.
ISBN 0-8131-2173-6 (acid-free paper)
    1. Afro-Americans—Appalachian Region, Southern—History—19th century.
2. Afro-Americans—Appalachian Region, Southern—Social conditions—
19th century. 3. Slavery—Appalachian Region, Southern—History—19th
century. 4. Appalachian Region, Southern—Race relations. 5. Appalachian
Region, Southern—Social conditions—19th century. I. Inscoe, John C., 1951-

E185.912 .A67 2000
974.004'96'073—dc21   00-028311

This book is printed on acid-free recycled paper meeting
the requirements of the American National Standard
for Permanence of Paper for Printed Library Materials.

Manufactured in the United States of America

CONTENTS

ILLUSTRATIONS

FIGURES

MAPS

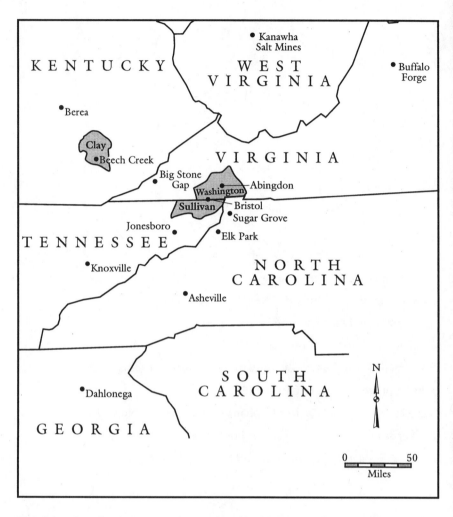

Key sites referred to in essays. (Map produced by University of Georgia Cartographic Services)

INTRODUCTION

JOHN C. INSCOE

The very first issue of the *Journal of Negro History*, published in 1916, included an essay on slavery in Appalachia. It was written by Carter G. Woodson, the journal's founder, who would go on to become one of the most distinguished African American historians of the first half of the twentieth century. Woodson was himself a product of Appalachia; though born in 1875 in piedmont Virginia, he followed his older brothers into West Virginia at the age of seventeen, where he laid railroad ties and mined coal before heading west again for an education at Berea College in Kentucky. He graduated in 1904, only a year before the Kentucky legislature prohibited the enrollment of blacks there. Woodson went on to the University of Chicago, where he became the nation's second black Ph.D. (following W.E.B. Du Bois) with a dissertation on Virginia's secession movement and the creation of West Virginia.[1]

Thus one of America's first great scholars of the African American experience began his career as a scholar of Appalachia, a region he had come to know intimately during his formative years. In his 1916 essay, certainly the most thoughtful and comprehensive treatment of the subject of race and racial attitudes in the mountain South up to that time, Woodson explored the various facets of Appalachian distinctiveness on such issues, many of them well established in popular conceptions about the region. He gave credence to the long-standing impression that southern highlanders were as a whole "a hardy race of European dissenters" of very different stock from other southern colonists, Germans and Scotch-Irish, along "with a sprinkling of Huguenots, Quakers, and poor whites who had served their time as indentured servants in the East." As backwoodsmen and highlanders, they opposed slavery formally, through abolitionist organizations, newspapers, or institutions of higher education (notably Berea and Maryville Colleges), or more informally, through a base, often unarticulated resentment of and estrangement from the slaveholding class that had driven them into the hills. While not denying a black presence in the mountains (he conceded that the mountaineers' attacks on slavery were "not altogether opposition to an institution foreign" to them), Woodson's emphasis was much more on the topographic, economic, and ideological impediments to slavery's existence in the highlands and to the religious and ethnic makeup of those who first shunned the institution in their midst.[2]

Woodson's essay remains a landmark in Appalachian historiography. It represents the first scholarly assessment of an aspect of southern mountain life and culture that, well before and well after its appearance, continued to be perceived as one of its most distinguishing characteristics—its racial innocence. Yet it hardly inspired any further scrutiny by historians or other scholars. The subject of race and Appalachia was raised only sporadically for the next fifty to sixty years. Only with the explosion of scholarship on the region that has taken place in the century's final decades have scholars again given serious attention to the presence of African Americans in Appalachia and the implications of that presence—socially, politically, economically, and culturally—on the region and beyond.

These essays represent a cross section of this recent work. Yet this is not the breakthrough work that an earlier such volume was. In 1985, the University Press of Kentucky published a volume titled simply *Blacks in Appalachia*. Edited by two of the foremost African American scholars then working on and in the region, William H. Turner and Edward J. Cabbell, that book was a rich compilation of new, old, and even "classic" works on the subject. Its purpose was, among other things, to challenge what was still legitimately seen as the "black invisibility" factor in Appalachian Studies, as Cabbell termed it. It was multidisciplinary in makeup and included historical, sociological, demographic, and bibliographic assessments of the topic, along with more intimate writings by and about black residents of the region, in the form of oral interviews, memoirs, and personal reminiscences.[3]

After the appearance of that book, it would be difficult to argue that blacks, past or present, are invisible in the region.[4] The African American presence in the mountain South is now a given, and we have moved on to explore the implications of that presence in more particular and increasingly sophisticated ways. The sheer range of scholarship on the black experience in the mountain South and on white responses to it suggests that race relations there were no less complex (and often perplexing in their contradictions and ambiguities) than anywhere else in the South or the nation.[5] We are now much more attuned to the variety of circumstances that brought blacks, slave or free, into the southern highlands and to the variety of circumstances under which they lived and worked there.

This volume is more traditionally historical in its approach, and represents for the most part work produced since the publication of *Blacks in Appalachia*.[6] While in many ways it expands upon the themes raised in that earlier volume, these essays also reflect new concerns and new questions about race relations in the region over the course of the nineteenth century. The dynamics and diversity of slave labor in the mountains—who owned slaves and how they used them—have been central to this new scholarship. Closely related are new explorations of the shifting demographics of Appalachia's African American presence: questions of how and why blacks were moved by others into and out of the region before the Civil War, and how and why they did so of their own accord (a shift from passive to active voice) afterward.

We are also becoming more aware of the extent to which race relations and the biracial demographics of the mountain South were functions of various forces of modernization. Kenneth Noe notes the apparent paradox in the fact that most such enterprises in antebellum Appalachia were so dependent on that most "unmodern" of institutions—slavery. And yet, as he and others in essays that follow clearly demonstrate, the ways in which black labor (or as Nina Silber demonstrates, the *lack* of a black presence) contributed to the economic development of the region say as much or more about the qualified nature of the term "modernization" when applied to Appalachia, or for that matter, to the South in general.

While we still lack a comprehensive treatment of Reconstruction in Appalachia, several essays here suggest considerable variation in the emancipation experience of highland freedmen and freedwomen throughout the region and equal variation in how historians have approached that era and those experiences. By century's end, what has been termed the "nadir" of southern race relations was in full swing, as racial violence and political and legal setbacks to civil rights began to undo the gains of the postemancipation decade. The mountain South was not immune from the setbacks of Jim Crow, but they coincided with other developments as well: new economic opportunities that drew a significant new black presence into parts of the region; and the so-called "discovery" of Appalachia, in which outside interest in, perceptions of, and a mission impulse toward the region intensified. The implications of these simultaneous, if often contradictory, trends are explored in several essays here as well.

This collection opens with a much discussed and often cited essay by Richard B. Drake, arguably the first historian since Woodson to fully embrace the themes that the latter laid out in 1916. Seventy years later, Drake, a professor of history at Berea, Woodson's alma mater, produced a more hard-hitting and less romanticized analysis of the proslavery and antislavery impulses evident in southern Appalachia. Like Woodson's essay, Drake's is wide-ranging in its coverage. He documents the extensiveness of the peculiar institution's presence throughout the region and establishes a much more realistic context for the emergence of abolitionist sentiments and the various forms it took. In his arguments and in the source material from which he draws them (particularly the WPA exslave interviews of the 1930s), Drake foreshadows much of the multifaceted work on the subject that is represented here.

The essay following his, however, takes a very different tact from any other work in this volume. Cecelia Conway's work is unique in that she explores the impact of African Americans on the mountain region, not so much in social, economic, or political terms, but rather as biracial cultural transmissions that first shaped and continue to be evident in the techniques, styles, and repertoires of Appalachian banjo playing. Though the multigenerational connections she makes span the eighteenth to early twentieth centuries, the heart of her argument rests on the correlation she establishes between antebellum black migration patterns and the emergence of banjo playing by whites in certain communities of northwest North Carolina and southwest Virginia. Conway argues that African traditions were among the earliest and most obvious transmissions that underlay this most distinctive of mountain musical forms. Among several notable implications to her extraordinary, yet well-documented, claims is that even the transitory presence of African Americans had the potential for making a significant and lasting impact on the cultural distinctiveness of the region through which they passed.

Much of the recent scholarship on mountain slavery has focused on ways in which a black labor force was made useful, and profitable, in highland regions devoid of large-scale plantation agriculture. Four essays here reflect the very different contexts in which slave labor operated in "industrial" enterprises in this otherwise most "preindustrial" of times and places. All are drawn from book-length treatments of antebellum economic activity in different parts of the southern highlands.[7]

David Williams chronicles the visible, even central, role played by African Americans in a gold rush that brought thousands of opportunists, white and black, into Georgia's Blue Ridge Mountains in the late 1820s and early 1830s. For slaves and free blacks, the turbulent times in and around the boomtowns of Dahlonega and Auraria presented both limitations and opportunities. For slaves, some opportunities were created or condoned by the owners that brought them into the hills as mining hands; in other cases, slaves themselves took advantage, often through subversive means, of a situation that availed them the chance to gain their freedom by purchase or escape.[8] The impact of that relatively brief surge of activity was felt in a number of ways, one of which was a far more substantial black population base than was evident anywhere else in Georgia's highlands. (The long-term effects of that demographic reality, with somewhat different implications in a second, postemancipation generation of that community, are explored in a later essay by Jennifer Lund Smith.)

John Stealey provides a comprehensive analysis of how slave labor fueled perhaps the most profitable of Appalachia's extractive industries before the Civil War: the salt mines and furnaces of Virginia's Kanawha Valley (which, during the war, would become West Virginia). The demand for salt in antebellum America and the vast supplies available in southwestern Virginia made it the earliest and most extensive industrial operation in the mountain South, with factories established on the Kanawha River by 1810. Slave labor followed quickly, and in this selection from his book on that operation and the markets it served, Stealey's work joins that of Ronald Lewis, Robert Starobin, and Charles Dew, in particular, in demonstrating the extent to which mining enterprises of various sorts in Appalachia took full advantage of the manpower provided by the "peculiar institution" and adapted it—in some ways efficiently and effectively, in others with considerable risk—to serve the demands of their own peculiar labor needs and functions.[9]

Dew's essay examines similar trends in another antebellum industry, an ironworks in western Virginia, and does so at a far more intimate level, from the perspective of a single slave life. Sam Williams belonged to William Weaver, who owned Buffalo Forge and the slaves that worked it. Dew reconstructs in remarkable detail the life of Williams, an exceptionally able and ambitious bondsman; through that life he provides in the most personalized of terms a vivid sense of the antebellum iron industry and how it shaped master-slave relationships, slave family and slave community, and the transition from slavery to freedom. Dew sets this story more within the context of southern industrial slavery than within its Appalachian setting. Yet this rich portrait of these men, their work, and their relationship with each other takes on new meanings when juxtaposed with the other essays here that deal with black miners and master-slave interaction in the nonplantation, nonagricultural environment where so many highland blacks found themselves.

Kenneth Noe's first book focused on another aspect of modernization in the mountains: the economic and political impact of the Virginia and Tennessee Railroad on southwest Virginia. In a chapter from that book reproduced here, Noe traces the peculiar institution's emergence in this vast region of some two dozen counties (a third of which would later become part of the new state of West Virginia) from its early settlement onward. He gives particular emphasis, though, to the several ways in which the construction of a railroad through the heart of this region in the mid-1850s reinforced slavery's economic value, from providing a major new outlet for hired labor as construction workers to facilitating the movement of slaves bought and sold within and beyond this section of the state.

Noe is among the first historians to deal substantively with the movement of slaves into and out of the mountains as a central component of the economic and political dimensions of Appalachian slavery. More recent work by Wilma Dunaway is causing us to rethink the implications of that movement in other ways as well. Her focus, too, is on the economic impact of slavery on the region, but less in terms of their labor than on their marketability as exported commodities. In her essay, Dunaway documents the movement of African Americans into, out of, and through the mountains; she views such activity as part of the vast commercial network by which upper South markets supplied the lower South's seemingly insatiable demand for slave labor. Given the pervasiveness of the lucrative trade in slaves through much of the region, white Appalachian residents of all classes took advantage of the opportunities that such trafficking in human property offered, as slaveholders, as slave traders, even as slave catchers or bounty hunters.[10] Thus, like Cecelia Conway, Dunaway suggests that even the transitory presence of African Americans could have significantly impacted, in direct and indirect ways, those areas through which they moved.

One of the major unexplored areas of highland race relations before the Civil War remains the place held by its free black residents.[11] Thus, Marie Tedesco's portrait of a southwest Virginia slave who emerged as a free black man in northeastern Tennessee in the early nineteenth century offers an insightful introduction into the implications of such status within the region. Tedesco meticulously reconstructs the lineage and the life of Adam Waterford, whose many business transactions in Sullivan County included his own purchase of slave property. One of those slaves was his own brother, whose status as slave or free remained unresolved at Adam's death and thus the basis of continuing legal battles. In tracing the financial and legal entanglements of the Waterford brothers, one owner, one owned, Tedesco reveals much about the business of slavery in Appalachia; at the same time, Waterford's extraordinary interactions with the white elites of the Sullivan County community of which he was a part raise even more intriguing questions about the opportunities, economic and social, available to an ambitious African American in this particular time and place.

My own contribution here is an examination of one of the earliest conscious attempts to analyze the racial attitudes of white mountaineers, that made by the most effective investigative journalist of the slave South, Frederick Law Olmsted. We have many nineteenth-century travelers' accounts of the southern highlands, but no one else moved through the region with so specific an agenda as Olmsted. His aim was to observe and to report on the racial realities, demographically, economically, and ideologically, that made the highland experience different from those of the lowland South, through which he had already moved and written about extensively. His attempt to capture what white mountaineers thought about blacks, whether or not they knew any, gets at the heart of the region's perceived "racial innocence" that later generations of Appalachian observers would find so intriguing and that Nina Silber, in a later essay here, explores.[12]

Community studies have been among the most valuable means by which recent scholarship has come to terms with the intricacies and the variables in the Appalachian experience. No single community in Appalachia has received more scholarly attention over a wider span of time than the Beech Creek community of eastern Kentucky. As part of their own multifaceted analysis of nineteenth-century Beech Creek and of Clay County, within which it fell, sociologists Kathleen Blee and Dwight Billings address what has been until now an unexplored issue for that area or elsewhere: race and its impact on economic opportunity and the lack thereof. In the broadest chronological span covered in this volume, Blee and Billings utilize a variety of statistical data to trace the routes to wealth and poverty taken by black and white residents of Clay County over the course of the last half of the nineteenth century and the different strategies devised by members of each race to cope with the consequences of their economic deterioration as it became more chronic over the course of six decades.

While the antebellum era and the Civil War in the mountain South have become prevalent topics of historical exploration in recent years, Reconstruction remains among the major gaps in Appalachian historiography. Other than Gordon McKinney's *Southern Mountain Republicans*, there is no book-length work devoted to the postwar era and the adjustments, political, social, or economic, with which southern highlanders, like southerners elsewhere, were forced to cope. And yet there are, as demonstrated here, several enlightening studies of the emancipation and Reconstruction experiences of blacks and whites in several highland settings.

John Cimprich looks at the impact of slavery's disintegration in East Tennessee. Drawing from a larger study of the peculiar institution's wartime demise in Tennessee,[13] Cimprich examines how the upheaval in the eastern part of the state undermined the relationship between master and slave, a phenomenon similar to that experienced most intently in areas of the Confederacy occupied by Union forces. What made that process unusual for this area were the relatively few slaves and masters in the region, which, by war's end, allowed a more assertive black populace to demand entry into the postwar political arena. By the same token, the predominant Unionist sentiment among white East Tennesseans led to a more ambivalent stance on emancipation than was true for many other parts of the Confederacy.[14]

Gordon McKinney also addresses the latter issue and pushes it into the postbellum era as highland Unionists became Republicans. His article, one of the first set in Appalachia ever to appear in the *Journal of Southern History*, remains the fullest treatment we have of the political activism of Appalachian African Americans and the larger forces that drove it. While at first there seemed to be less support for black suffrage in parts of Appalachia other than East Tennessee, the political realities of black voters in bolstering Republican candidates and agendas soon changed the minds of highland party leaders. Just as Cimprich demonstrates a new assertiveness among East Tennessee blacks at war's end, so McKinney notes the extent to which freedmen elsewhere in the region became increasingly aggressive as voters and as candidates once their value to the party was apparent. That story hardly ended when Reconstruction did, and McKinney traces the deteriorating relationship between mountain Republicans and their black constituents through the end of the century, as Jim Crow ushered in that "nadir" of southern race relations from which highlanders were by no means exempt, either politically, as McKinney demonstrates, or in more violent fashion, as Fitzhugh Brundage's later essay makes painfully clear.

Education was a high priority for Appalachian freedmen and freedwomen just as it was for blacks throughout the Reconstruction South. That quest for schools and schooling was often central to the dynamics of race relations at the local level, as Jennifer Lund Smith demonstrates was the case in a north Georgia community. Drawn from a dissertation in which she compares how four different Georgia communities struggled with the issues of freedmen's education during Reconstruction, Smith's essay describes the distinctive strategies with which an Appalachian black community negotiated the terms of its independence.[15] Like David Williams earlier, Smith looks at gold-rich Lumpkin County and tells the story of how a second generation of this unique group of freedpeople worked closely with the local white elites to obtain property, resources, and teachers to establish schools. In contrast to the lowland Georgia settings Smith studied, these black highlanders achieved their ends largely without the support or sponsorship of the Freedmen's Bureau or other federal or state intervention.[16]

Conrad Ostwalt and Phoebe Pollitt chronicle a very different scenario in the education of mountain blacks. Unlike the Reconstruction dynamics between local blacks and whites that drove the quest for schools in north Georgia, a different set of impulses led to the establishment of the Salem School and Orphanage in a remote North Carolina Blue Ridge community toward the end of the century. It was the much more pervasive movement by Protestant denominations to establish mission schools for southern highland children that led to the establishment of Elk Park's Salem School. A Connecticut-born woman, five Ohio missionaries, and a group of Russian emigrant Mennonites from Kansas all converged there to establish a school specifically for the few African American children in a three-county area. In telling their story and that of the school over the course of its brief duration, Ostwalt and Pollitt illuminate an unusual experiment in multicultural, biracial, and ecumenical interaction to educate native blacks in circumstances quite unlike those efforts to meet the same needs in Lumpkin County, Georgia.

So much of our understanding and misunderstanding of Appalachia has come from those outside observers whose writings shaped national perceptions of this "strange land and peculiar people." This was particularly true of the region's racial "purity," that is, the widespread assumption that the mountain South distinguished itself from the rest of the region by its whiteness. In a seminal essay James Klotter demonstrated the practical implications of that assumption in arguing that it was the lack of a black presence among southern highlanders that so appealed to northern philanthropists, social workers, and missionaries in the aftermath of the setbacks in their efforts toward freedmen and freedwomen elsewhere in the Reconstruction South.[17] In her essay in this volume, Nina Silber also sees southern Appalachia's racial purity as central to the fascination with which so many Americans, particularly outside the South, viewed the region toward the end of the nineteenth century, but she explains the reason behind that outside interest in different and rather provocative terms. Rather than an all-white section of the South reinforcing the pejorative "otherness" in outside eyes, she suggests that it was the lack of a black presence that gave the highlands a sense of commonality with the North. And rather than the philanthropic impulses that Klotter sees as driving this new attention to the region, Silber sees sectional reconciliation and economic investment as the greater motive on the part of northerners.[18] The mountain South is uniquely suited for such efforts, as Silber demonstrates through a wide range of writings celebrating the many positive, "all-American" attributes of southern highlanders, not the least of which were their racial purity and their detachment from slavery and from the other southern sins committed in its name.

If whiteness was an integral factor in northern capitalist investments in postwar Appalachia, as Silber contends, a black labor force was as central to the implementation of those investments as it had been to similar ventures before the war. Ronald Lewis and Joe Trotter are among the foremost historians of the most extensive Appalachian industry resulting from those investments—coal mining—and what it meant for regional race relations as played out over the late nineteenth and twentieth centuries. In the selection of Lewis's work included here, he examines the use of African American convict lease labor, a form not as closely associated with highland settings as with other parts of the South. Even as applied to the coalfields, convicts worked in such operations in southernmost Appalachia, in Georgia, Tennessee, and Alabama, rather than in the mines of Central Appalachia. Lewis details the extent to which coal companies conspired with the prisons, court systems, and governments in each of those states to implement one of the more egregious forms of racial exploitation imposed on postemancipation blacks. The blatant abuses in working conditions and in the criminal justice system rendered prisoner-workers even more vulnerable than slaves. Lewis's grim chronicle of this most extreme of the "New South's moral failures" offers a revealing basis of comparison with its Old South counterparts, black labor forces that fueled Appalachian industrial enterprises in that earlier era, as laid out earlier in this volume. Such a comparison makes even more apparent the extent to which the monetary worth of slaves shielded them from the extremes of danger and cruelty to which convicts, without any market value, were regularly exposed.

Joe Trotter looks at a very different facet of the same economic phenomenon: the social and political implications of black migration into the coalfields of southern West Virginia. The selection from his book, *Coal, Class, and Color*, focuses on the institutional elements, churches, fraternal orders, and party politics, that contributed to the strong sense of community and racial solidarity that evolved as increasing numbers of blacks moved into the region. Despite inherent class tensions between this black leadership and the workers they served, such tensions were submerged under a growing group consciousness that made itself felt through a revitalized Republican party at state and local levels. Interestingly, the development in the coal communities coincided with the deterioration of the strong Republican-African American alliance elsewhere in the mountains, as Gordon McKinney has documented.

Finally Fitz Brundage, though more than ready to move beyond his well-deserved reputation as our leading scholar of southern lynching,[19] extends his astute analyses of racial violence into the mountain South. Expanding on his study of lynching in Georgia and Virginia, Brundage documents numerous instances of mob violence inflicted on black victims throughout Appalachia, from the late nineteenth through the early twentieth centuries. In causal factors, means of implementation, and the racial identities of their victims, highland violence was little different from that enacted throughout the South. As do other authors here, Brundage sees modernizing tendencies as directly affecting the region's racial dynamics. In only one respect does he suggest a significant diversion from lynching patterns elsewhere in the South: in the mountains, it was more an urban than a rural phenomenon. As such he raises an important issue not addressed elsewhere in this volume: the extent to which Appalachia's town and city residents, all too often overlooked by nineteenth-century historians of the region, experienced very different racial dynamics than did its predominantly rural populace.[20]

Together these explorations of race in the southern highlands address, though often in contradictory ways, the age-old question around which so much of Appalachian scholarship still centers: its distinctiveness. As Brundage and Lewis demonstrate most directly, and others do more by inference, the exploitation of black labor, slave and free, along with the racial violence and political manipulation of the post–Civil War era, all seem to chronicle patterns and trends very much like those elsewhere in the South. Variations were more of degree than of kind, based simply on the demographic reality of a significantly smaller black populace. Other essayists, however, detect significant distinctions between highlander and lowlander—differences in racial attitudes (abolitionist or rabid racist), in the types of work that African Americans performed, and in the extent to which perceptions of whiteness shaped how outsiders understood the region and acted toward it. Still other essays document situations that must have been anomalies as much within Appalachia as in any other part of the South. For example, a Mennonite mission for blacks in a remote Blue Ridge community; the legal, financial, and kinship entanglements of free black Adam Waterford; the transmission of banjo music making from black to white—all of these suggest unusual scenarios that may or may not have been shaped by the mountain environment in which they took place.

The cumulative effect of all of this work then is, first and foremost, a realization of the diversity within the broad and varied region. If challenging myths and stereotypes remains a central thrust of Appalachian scholarship, an equally important facet or, perhaps, by-product of this work has been complexifying the region's historical past by particularizing its various components. We can no longer make blanket generalizations about Appalachia or Appalachians as a whole. Its racial dynamics, as much or more than other issues, should sensitize us to the extent to which the region and its residents often operated in different ways, at different paces, and with different priorities and agendas, depending on time, place, people involved, and other variables. Historian Barbara Fields has warned us of the dangers of according race "a transhistorical, almost metaphysical, status," noting that "ideas about color, like ideas about anything else, derive their importance, indeed their very definition, from their context."[21] The authors in this collection have been particularly sensitive to context in their explorations of racial attitudes, race relations, and black experiences.

With several significant exceptions, one finds relatively little African American agency reflected in these essays. Despite the considerable advances Appalachian scholars have made in our understanding of race relations and black highlanders, it seems that we still lag behind so much of the history of African Americans elsewhere, during and after emancipation, in that we still see that history primarily from a white perspective. Much of our understanding of race relations has to do with white actions and attitudes. Here, as elsewhere, it is white highlanders who hold center stage, but in very different ways. As slaveholders, as slave traders, as employers and labor recruiters, as teachers and mission workers, as politicians, and as lynch mobs and rioters, whites within and beyond the region had much to do with creating and shaping the black presence in the southern highlands and in defining the status they held once there. Most of the essays here reflect that reality and draw from that dominance in terms of agency and source material.

Yet the exceptions are significant, and provide valuable counterpoints to the white-driven stories in whose midst they are set. Whether the implied agency of slaves as culture brokers in the distinctive musical imprints they imposed on white mountain residents, as Cecelia Conway demonstrates, or as politically active coalitions or more subtle, behind-the-scenes negotiators determined to have a voice in shaping their futures through politics, churches, schools, or other institutions, Appalachian blacks take center stage in a variety of places and in a variety of ways in several essays. Richard Drake and Wilma Dunaway demonstrate that black Appalachian voices do exist and have much to tell us on a range of issues for that seemingly distant past. Drake and Dunaway are among the few who have effectively tapped the WPA ex-slave narratives to provide among the most immediate and most emotional testimony we have of the treatment slaves received at the hands of the white highlanders who owned them.

Two other authors, Charles Dew and Marie Tedesco, have met one of the most difficult challenges of nineteenth-century historians—the detailed reconstruction of the very lives of obscure individual blacks, even when their own voices or perspectives are not among the resources that they as historians have to draw upon. These biographical essays provide inspiration and models for the rest of us, not only in the challenging detective work it took to piece together those stories, but also in viewing the region's black populace as fully engaged individuals who managed to better their lives and their families' lives and those of their families within the considerable limitations of the oppressive antebellum regime under which they lived.

Such contradictions become equally apparent through the juxtaposition of the works brought together here. John Cimprich, Gordon McKinney, Jennifer Lund Smith, and Joe Trotter demonstrate that black highlanders were quick to grasp the new opportunities for collective action in the postemancipation era in political, civic, and economic terms; other essayists, particularly Ron Lewis and Fitz Brundage, chronicle the equally oppressive environments within which mountain blacks had to endure, as new forms of unfree labor emerged to replace slavery and other forms of racial abuse before the war.

As vast as the range of issues and experiences chronicled here is in terms of how southern highlanders, white and black, interacted with each other, the field of Appalachian race relations remains wide open. It is hoped that this sampling of current scholarship in that field will stimulate further work and fill many of the glaring gaps. The free black experience in antebellum Appalachia, for example, remains one of the most intriguing of such topics. Several essays document the demographics of black mobility into and out of different parts of Appalachia and the impact that such movement had on the locales where they lived and those that they abandoned. Like much of the best work on the region, the linkages between highlands and lowlands that were so integral to this movement offer rich opportunities for further study.

Gordon McKinney, John Cimprich, and Joe Trotter have provided us with a range of issues and frameworks from which we can glean much more about the political dimensions of a black presence and the impact of such activism at local and regional levels. By the same token, we have barely scratched the surface, it seems, in our attempts to understand the nature of highland white attitudes toward blacks. Other than Frederick Law Olmsted, few have made any systematic attempt to chronicle the beliefs, prejudices, and fears of white highlanders in terms of race, either before or after the Civil War, though the assumptions and stereotypes are rampant. The fact that Appalachians engaged in more abolitionist activity than did other antebellum southerners and also demonstrated some of the most virulent racism in keeping a black presence at bay suggests contradictions that cry out for more serious analysis than they have yet received.[22]

The list of areas still unexplored goes on and on. Other than the teachers who taught at the Salem School, women, individually or collectively, black or white, play remarkably little role in these essays, pointing up yet another void that needs to be addressed: the ways in which gender roles impacted race relations. The distinctive nature of the black experience in Appalachia's few urban areas also remains underrepresented here, with only a few exceptions. The vantage point of community study theory and methodology applied to towns and cities would add a great deal to our understanding of the socioeconomic complexities of the region that have for so long been so easily overlooked.

But it is not just for a greater understanding of Appalachia that the essays here have value. In an essay titled "The Edges of Slavery in the Old South: Or, Do Exceptions Prove the Rule?" historian Peter Parish argues that by a close examination of the less conventional outlets for slave labor, especially those in urban and industrial settings, and the anomalies of slave status, we can better understand the institution as a whole. Reasoning that "the typical, the average, the majority, are not necessarily nor always the same as the most significant, the most dynamic, the most influential—or in terms of historical study, the most illuminating," Parish urges us to pay more attention to the deviations and the peripheries. Such exceptions, he argues, "may serve to illuminate many features of slavery and of southern society generally—its racial attitudes and compromises, its internal pressures, its readiness sometimes to subordinate economic to racial and social priorities, its combination of inflexible rules and flexible application, and not least the ability of slaves to exploit the weaknesses or loopholes of the system in their own interest."[23]

I would suggest that the same holds true not just for slavery but for race relations in general and that Appalachia serves as a particularly interesting "edge" of the South, Old and New, in which the "exceptions" do enlighten us on the "rules" of race in all of its varied manifestations over the course of the nineteenth century: slavery, emancipation, Reconstruction, or, toward century's end, the implementation of Jim Crow and its grim side effects. The essays here include examples of all of the "features" that Parish lists above, along with others, that not only contribute to a greater understanding of the complexities of Appalachian society, economics, politics, and demographics, but also, by extension, tell us much about the commonalities and variables that characterized southern race relations in all of its forms.

In another recent collection of essays on nineteenth-century Appalachia the editors made much the same point. "Unlike a long tradition of Appalachian regional studies," wrote editors Mary Beth Pudup, Dwight Billings, and Altina Waller of the essays in *Appalachia in the Making*, "none claim that the patterns described were necessarily unique to the southern highlands or general to the whole mountain region."[24] I hope that the same might be said of this collection as well and that these essays reflect ways in which the broader themes of southern and American race relations are "nuanced by geographical difference."[25] As such, they should further challenge the long-standing assumption of Appalachian distinctiveness while acknowledging the centrality of regional context as an explanatory force in terms of how black and white Americans interacted with each other over the course of a turbulent century.

NOTES

1. Jacqueline Goggin, *Carter G. Woodson: A Life in Black History* (Baton Rouge: Louisiana State Univ. Press, 1993), chap. 1. See also August Meier and Elliott Rudwick, *Black History and the Historical Professions, 1915–1980* (Urbana: Univ. of Illinois Press, 1986), chap. 1. On Berea College's shift away from black education, see Paul David Nelson, "Experiment in Interracial Education at Berea College, 1858–1908," *Journal of Negro History* 59 (1974): 13–27; and William H. Turner, "Between Berea (1904) and Birmingham (1908): The Rock and Hard Place for Blacks in Appalachia," in *Blacks in Appalachia*, ed. William H. Turner and Edward J. Cabbell (Lexington: Univ. Press of Kentucky, 1985), 11–22.

2. Carter G. Woodson, "Freedom and Slavery in Appalachian America," *Journal of Negro History* 1 (April 1916): 132–50, quotes on pp. 133, 144.

3. Turner and Cabbell, *Blacks in Appalachia*.

4. Since the publication of *Blacks in Appalachia*, both of its editors have edited special issues of regional journals devoted to the black experience. Ed Cabbell edited a special issue on "Black Appalachians" in *Now and Then* 3 (winter 1986), and Bill Turner edited a special issue of *Appalachian Heritage* 19 (fall 1991) called "Blacks in Appalachia." Both consisted of oral histories, individual and community profiles, literary analyses, short stories, and poetry by and about African American highlanders, with the focus primarily on the twentieth century.

5. For a discussion of these complexities, see John C. Inscoe, "Race and Racism in Nineteenth-Century Southern Appalachia: Myths, Realities, and Ambiguities," in *Appalachia in the Making: The Mountain South in the Nineteenth Century*, ed. Mary Beth Pudup, Dwight B. Billings, and Altina L. Waller (Chapel Hill: Univ. of North Carolina Press, 1995), 103–32.

6. The one pre-1980s exception is Gordon B. McKinney's essay, "Southern Mountain Republicans and the Negro, 1865–1900," which appeared in the *Journal of Southern History* in 1975. It is included here because it remains one of the only fully political assessments of race in the region. In fact, despite the wealth and diversity of new scholarship on almost every other aspect of the region, nothing has superceded McKinney's book, *Southern Mountain Republicans, 1865–1900: Politics and the Appalachian Community* (Chapel Hill: Univ. of North Carolina Press, 1978), on post–Civil War politics in the mountain South.

7. David Williams, *The Georgia Gold Rush: Twenty-Niners, Cherokees, and Gold Fever* (Columbia: Univ. of South Carolina Press, 1993); John E. Stealey III, *The Antebellum Kanawha Salt Business and Western Markets* (Lexington: Univ. Press of Kentucky, 1993); Charles B. Dew, *Bonds of Iron: Master and Slave at Buffalo Forge* (New York: W.W. Norton, 1994); and Kenneth W. Noe,

Southwest Virginia's Railroad: Modernization and the Sectional Crisis (Urbana: Univ. of Illinois Press, 1994).

8. On the role of slaves in an earlier gold rush in western North Carolina, see Edward W. Phifer Jr., "Champagne at Brindletown: The Story of the Burke County Gold Rush, 1829–1833," *North Carolina Historical Review* 40 (October 1963): 489–500; and John C. Inscoe, *Mountain Masters: Slavery and the Sectional Crisis in Western North Carolina* (Knoxville: Univ. of Tennessee Press, 1989), chap. 3.

9. See Ronald L. Lewis, *Coal, Iron, and Slaves: Industrial Slavery in Maryland and Virginia, 1715–1865* (Westport, Conn: Greenwood Press, 1979); Lewis, *Black Coal Miners in America: Race, Class, and Community Conflict, 1780–1980* (Lexington: Univ. Press of Kentucky, 1987), chap. 1; Robert S. Starobin, *Industrial Slavery in the Old South* (New York: Oxford Univ. Press, 1970); and Dew, *Bonds of Iron*.

10. See also Dunaway, "Diaspora, Death, and Sexual Exploitation: Slave Families at Risk in the Mountain South," *Appalachian Journal* 26 (winter 1999): 128–49.

11. Another recent venture into the topic is Kathryn Staley, "Between Two Worlds: African Americans in Antebellum Wilkes County, North Carolina" (Master's thesis, Appalachian State University, 1999), in which she documents several free black families and neighborhoods in this Blue Ridge foothill county.

12. One of the more fertile areas of recent scholarship that is not directly reflected in this volume is the role of abolitionism in Appalachia. Among the most valuable is Durwood Dunn's *An Abolitionist in the Appalachian South: Ezekiel Birdseye on Slavery, Capitalism, and Separate Statehood in East Tennessee, 1841–1846* (Knoxville: Univ. of Tennessee Press, 1997). Birdseye was a Connecticut-born abolitionist whose extensive correspondence and reports on his activity in East Tennessee tell us much not only about the opportunities and limitations of antislavery efforts in that region, but also about the nature of slavery and slaveholders there. Other work has focused on two of the academic bases for antislavery sentiment and biracial education in the region before and after the Civil War: Berea and Maryville Colleges. See especially Richard D. Sears, *A Practical Recognition of the Brotherhood of Man: John G. Fee and the Camp Nelson Experience* (Berea, Ky.: Berea College Press, 1986); Sears, *The Day of Small Things: Abolitionism in the Midst of Slavery* (Lanham, Md.: Univ. Press of America, 1986); and Lester C. Lamon, "Ignoring the Color Line: Maryville College, 1868–1901," in *The Adaptable South: Essays in Honor of George Brown Tindall*, ed. Elizabeth Jacoway, et al. (Baton Rouge: Louisiana State Univ. Press, 1991): 64–89.

13. John Cimprich, *Slavery's End in Tennessee, 1861–1865* (Tuscaloosa: Univ. of Alabama Press, 1985).

14. On the relationship between Unionism and slavery in East Tennessee, see Robert Tracy McKenzie, "The Parameters of Unionism in Parson Brownlow's Knoxville, 1860–1863," in *"Enemies of the Country": New Perspectives on Unionists in the Civil War South*, ed. John C. Inscoe and Robert C. Kenzer (Athens, Ga.: Univ. of Georgia Press, forthcoming). For a different perspective on the war's impact on slavery in the mountains, see John C. Inscoe, "Mountain Masters as Confederate Opportunists: The Profitability of Slavery in Western North Carolina, 1861–1865," *Slavery and Abolition* 16 (April 1995): 85–110; and John C. Inscoe and Gordon McKinney, *The Heart of Confederate Appalachia: Western North Carolina in the Civil War* (Chapel Hill: Univ. of North Carolina Press, 2000), chap. 9.

15. Jennifer Lund Smith, "'Twill Take Some Time to Study When I Get Over': Varieties of African American Education in Reconstruction Georgia" (Ph.D. diss., University of Georgia, 1997).

16. The role of the Freedmen's Bureau in Appalachian settings is another example of a topic that has inspired several revealing studies but is not represented here. See, for example, John E. Stealey III, "The Freedmen's Bureau in West Virginia," *West Virginia History* 39 (January/April 1978), 99–142; Paul D. Escott, "Clinton A. Cilley, Yankee War Hero in the Postwar South: A Study in Compatibility of Regional Values," *North Carolina Historical Review* 68 (October 1991): 404–26 [Cilley served as a Freedmen's Bureau agent in Caldwell County, North Carolina]; and Denise Wright's dissertation in progress at the University of Georgia on the Bureau's relief efforts to poor whites and blacks in north Georgia.

17. James C. Klotter, "The Black South and White Appalachia," *Journal of American History* 66 (March 1980): 832–49. This essay is also reproduced in Turner and Cabbell, *Blacks in Appalachia*, 51–67.

18. This is the theme of the larger work from which her interest in Appalachia stems. See Nina Silber, *The Romance of Reunion: Northerners and the South, 1865–1900* (Chapel Hill: Univ. of North Carolina Press, 1993).

19. W. Fitzhugh Brundage, *Lynching in the New South: Georgia and Virginia, 1880–1930* (Urbana: Univ. of Illinois Press, 1993); and Brundage, ed., *Under Sentence of Death: Essays on Lynching in the South* (Chapel Hill: Univ. of North Carolina Press, 1997).

20. A useful exception to this void, along with several cited in Brundage's notes, is Eric J. Olson, "Race Relations in Asheville, North Carolina: Three Incidents, 1868–1906," in *The Appalachian Experience: Proceedings of the Sixth Annual Appalachian Studies Conference*, ed. Barry M. Buxton (Boone, N.C.: Appalachian Consortium Press, 1983).

21. Barbara J. Fields, "Ideology and Race in American History," in *Region, Race, and Reconstruction: Essays in Honor of C. Vann Woodward*, ed. J. Morgan Kousser and James M. McPherson (New York: Oxford Univ. Press, 1982), 144, 146.

22. For further exploration of those contradictions, see Inscoe, "Race and Racism in Nineteenth-Century Southern Appalachia," 103–31.

23. Peter Parish, "The Edges of Slavery in the Old South: Or, Do Exceptions Prove Rules?" *Slavery and Abolition* (September 1983): 106–25, quotes on pp. 106–7, 124.

24. Billings, Pudup, and Waller, "Taking Exception with Exceptionalism: The Emergence and Transformation of Historical Studies of Appalachia," introduction to *Appalachia in the Making*, 3.

25. Ibid. This essay's final sentence is a loosely paraphrased version of the same idea expressed in "Taking Exception with Exceptionalism," 9–10.

1

SLAVERY AND ANTISLAVERY IN APPALACHIA

RICHARD B. DRAKE

One of the least understood periods of Appalachian history is the period be-tween the end of the War of 1812 and the beginning of the Civil War. By 1815 the "backwoodsmen" of Appalachia were becoming strongly identified with the federal experiment in government known as the United States. Those in Tennessee and Kentucky especially had helped Andrew Jackson in 1813 re-move the last real Indian "threat" in eastern America in the Creek War. Then, many were with "Old Hickory" when the American army turned back the British at the Battle of New Orleans, the War of 1812's most significant victory over the British on land. Appalachians furthermore generally supported Andrew Jackson's rise to the presidency, and by the 1830s and 1840s the South's backwoodsmen were clearly loyal to the Union and identified with its for-tunes. The Appalachians enthusiastically supported the Mexican War in the mid-1840s, which added greatly to the territories of the United States. But the acquisition of these territories raised the question of slavery before the Ameri-can people in ways that could not be solved short of a tragic civil war.

Historians have approached this period of the Appalachian experience from 1815 to 1860 with very different attitudes. Forty-five years ago one of the most prominent historians of the Old South, Thomas Jefferson Wertenbaker of the University of Virginia, claimed that one of the most significant struggles in American history was played out within southern society as Appalachian backwoodsmen—"Cohees," as he called them and as they called themselves—attempted to stop the march of plantation society across a line that proceeded southward from Winchester, Virginia, to Chattanooga, Tennessee. Had the Cohees been able to stop the spread of slave society, Wertenbaker suggested that the Civil War might not have been necessary.[1]

But not all historians agree with Wertenbaker's assessment of the impor-tance of the Appalachian backwoodsman within antebellum southern society. One of Appalachia's most widely read modern historians, Ronald D Eller, is not impressed with the story and has called antebellum Appalachia a "quiet backwater of the Old South."[2] Furthermore, a 1985 issue of *Appalachia*, a 108-page "apology" for the Appalachian Regional Commission, goes to great pains to argue that "slavery was not the root cause of the division between the high-land and the lowlands" that developed in the pre–Civil War years. Rather, according to the editors of *Appalachia*, it was the result of a "political and social structure vastly different from the interdependent and relatively prosperous society of the flatlands."[3]

Which of these approaches comes closest to the truth? Was the pre–Civil War Appalachian South a society that played little or no role in the struggle over slavery? Was it only a less prosperous society in a "different South"? Or did this society struggle mightily with the proslavery forces of the plantation South, only to lose that struggle, thus making the larger struggle with an anti-slavery North inevitable? A study of slavery and antislavery in Appalachia in the years between 1820 and 1860 can shed some useful light on this intriguing question. It seems clear that the Appalachian South in the pre–Civil War decades was a quite different "South" from the plantation South that so dominated the region from 1820 to 1860 and that led eleven of its states to secede and create a new nation.

Another South did challenge this dominant "Old South" in the days before the Civil War. The Germans and Quakers especially, within Cohee society, tended to take a strong and consistent antislavery position. In the largely mountain-centered debate over slavery within the South, Hinton R. Helper, author of the strongly antislavery and influential *The Impending Crisis of the South* (1857), reflected the views of his German, up-country ancestry. And the southern Quakers kept up their quick and consistent witness against slavery in the Shenandoah Valley of Virginia and in the North Carolina up-country.[4]

Of course, slavery existed in all of the Appalachian South. It was a legal institution, and it gave an economic advantage to those willing to own slaves. Slavery existed in every Appalachian county south of the Mason-Dixon line. Most southern mountain county populations, however, were less than 10 percent slave. But by 1820 large slave concentrations were emerging in Boyd County, Kentucky, and Madison County, Alabama; in Kanawha and Greenbrier Counties in western Virginia; and in certain areas in the Shenandoah Valley and the Tennessee Valley around Knoxville.[5] By 1860 slaveholding had spread so that more-than-50-percent-black populations existed in most of north Alabama (Madison, Morgan, Limestone, Lawrence, Franklin, Colbert, and Lauderdale Counties), and a proportion of blacks of up to 25 percent existed in a few foothill counties of north Georgia and western North Carolina and in the Shenandoah Valley.[6] There were, however, counties in Appalachia where slavery was nearly absent. In the mountain counties of Madison and Haywood in North Carolina, the slave population was about 4 percent, and in Jackson County, Kentucky, blacks were less than 1 percent of the population.[7]

There is no reason to believe that slavery was particularly mild in Appalachia as compared with other areas in the Old South. Probably slavery was harshest in the lower reaches of the Mississippi River simply because the work in sugar-growing areas was much more difficult. Slaves certainly feared being sold downriver, thus indicating a recognition of slavery's harshness there. But a few stories of slavery in Appalachia should suffice to give something of slavery's condition in the southern mountains.

Sophia Ward was born a slave in 1837 in Clay County, Kentucky. Clay

County reported a slave population of 349, with 262 free blacks and 6,041 whites in the county in 1860. She said of her life in eastern Kentucky, "I wuz a slave nineteen yeahs and nine months, but somehow or nuther I didn't belong to a real mean set of people. The white folks said I was the meanest nigger that ever wuz. One day my mistress Lydia called for me to come in the house, but no, I wouldn't go. She walks out and says she gwaine make me go. So she take and drags me into the house. Then I grab that white woman when she turn her back, and shook her until she begged for mercy. When the master comes in, I was given a terrible beating with a whip but I didn't care for I gave that mistress a good 'un too."

Aunt Sophia, who was interviewed in her ninety-ninth year, continued, "We lived off to the back of the master's house in a little log cabin that had one winder on the side. We lived tobly well and didn't starve for we had enough to eat. We didn't have as good as the master and mistress had. We would slip into the house after the master and mistress wuz sleeping and cook to suit ourselves. . . . My master wuzn't as mean as most masters. Hugh White wuz so mean to his slaves that I know two gals that kilt themselfs. . . . One nigger gal . . . he whipped . . . most to death for fergittin to put onions in the stew. Next day she went down to the river and drowned herself."[8]

The conditions under which slaves lived varied greatly. Not only were there "good" masters and "mean" masters, but the economic situation of the slaves varied according to the wealth of their master. Even in Appalachia prosperous plantations emerged with their communities of one hundred or so slaves, like the place where Callie Elder lived in Floyd County near Rome, Georgia. The plantation house was a "whoppin big place," and there were "too many slaves on that plantation for me to count." The slaves lived in log cabins daubed with mud inside and furnished only with beds held together by cords. Food was largely "cornbread, and meal with plenty of vegetables." Sundays, she remembered, they had "wheatbread." Her master was "just as good to us as could be," but the men had to be in the fields at sunrise and the women by 8 A.M.[9]

In Madison County, Alabama, one of the state's most prosperous counties and a county where the plantation system was firmly established, a white man who worked with the blacks reported that slave "dwellings are log huts, from ten to twelve feet square often without windows, doors or floors. They have neither chairs, tables nor bedsteads. These huts are occupied by eight, ten, or twelve persons each. Their bedding generally consists of two old blankets. Many of them sleep night after night sitting upon their blocks or stools, others sleep in the open air. Our task was appointed, and from dawn til dark all must bend to their work. Their meals were taken without knife or plate, dish or spoon. Their food was corn pone, prepared in the coarsest manner, with a small allowance of meat. . . . For punishing in the field [the overseer] preferred a large hickory stick."[10]

Mrs. Amelia Jones of Clay and Laurel Counties, Kentucky, was owned by a small planter-farmer named Daw White. "He was a Southern Republican and was elected as a congressman . . . from Manchester, Kentucky," she recalled. "Master White was good to his slaves. He fed us well and had good places for us to sleep, and didn't whip, only when it was necessary. But he didn't hesitate to sell his slaves. He said, 'You all belong to me, and if you don't like it, I'll put you in my pocket,' meaning of course that he would sell that slave and put the money in his pocket."

Mrs. Jones continued, "The day that he was to sell the children from their mother, he would tell that mother to go to some other place to do some work, and in her absence he would see the children. It was the same way when he would sell a man's wife . . . when he returned his wife would be gone. The master only said, 'Don't worry, you can get another one.'"[11]

Another slave narrative in this same vein, set again in Appalachian Alabama, tells of how a slave, Diana Wagner, was induced by her mistress to "go down the road a piece" with her: "She went with her, and they got to a place where there was a whole lot of people. They were putting [slaves] up on the block and selling them just like cattle. She had a little nursing baby at home, and she broke away from her mistress and them and said, 'I can't go off and leave my baby.' And they had to git someone and throw her down and hold her to keep her from going back to the house. They sold her away from her baby boy."[12]

Slaves could be sold at any gathering of people, but regular slave markets existed throughout the southern mountains. Slave markets existed at Winchester, Staunton, Lexington, and Bristol in Virginia and at Knoxville, Chattanooga, and Jonesboro in Tennessee. Even in the much poorer Cumberland Mountains of Kentucky, regular slave auctions were held in London, Pikeville, and Manchester. Of the Manchester slave market, Amelia Jones noted that her father was sold at auction: "There was a long line of slaves to be sold and a good price was paid for each. They were handcuffed and marched away South." The auction block in Manchester was built in an open space from "rough made lumber" and had a few steps, then a platform on which the slave stood. "He would look at the crowd as the auctioneer would give a general description of the ability and the physical standing of the man. He heard the bids as they came wondering what his new master would be like."[13]

The threat of sale or harsh treatment often led slaves to attempt to escape the system, sometimes by death, sometimes by other means. A slave owner in western Virginia bought a thirteen-year-old black girl at an auction. When this girl was taken to his home she escaped, and after searching everywhere without finding her, he decided that she had been helped to escape and gave her up for lost. About two years later, as a neighbor on a nearby farm was in the woods feeding his cattle, he saw what he thought was a wild boar running into the thicket among his cows. Getting help he rounded up the cattle and, searching the thick woodland, finally found that what he had supposed was a wild boar was the long lost fugitive black girl. She had lived all this time in caves, feeding on nuts, berries, wild apples, and milk from cows.[14]

Nor were many of the barbaric aspects of the slave trade absent from southern Appalachia. A traveler at Rowley's Tavern, twelve miles west of

Lewisburg in Greenbrier County, Virginia, reported on what he witnessed there in the winter of 1833–1834.

> A drove of 50 or 60 negroes stopped at the same place that night. They usually camp out, but as it was excessively muddy, they were permitted to come into the house. So far as my knowledge extends, droves on their way to the south eat twice a day, early morning and at night. Their supper was a compound of potatoes and meal, and without exception the dirtiest, blackest-looking mess I ever saw. . . . They slept on the floor of the room which they were permitted to occupy, lying in every form imaginable, males and females. There were three drovers. . . . Each of the latter took a female from the drove to lodge with him, as is the common practice of the drovers. . . . Six or eight in the drove were chained. . . . In the autumn of the same year I saw a drove of upwards of a hundred, between 40 and 50 of them were fastened to one chain, the links being made of iron rods, as thick in diameter as a man's little finger. . . . They generally appear extremely dejected. I have seen in the course of five years, on the road where I reside, 12 or 15 droves at least, passing to the south. They would average 40 in each drove. Near the first of January, 1834, I started about sunrise to go to Lewisburg. It was a bitter cold morning. I met a drove of negroes, 30 to 40 in number, remarkably ragged and destitute of clothing. One little boy particularly excited my sympathy. . . . Although he was shivering with cold and crying, the driver was pushing him up to a trot to overtake the main gang. All of them looked as if they were half frozen.[15]

By all indications slavery was expanding in Appalachia even as it was in the Old South throughout the antebellum period. In Burke County, North Carolina, the percentage of slaves in the county population rose from 7 percent in 1790 to 27 percent in 1850, and 26 percent in 1860. The number of heads of families owning no slaves in 1790 was 1,091, and in 1860 it was 1,007. The number of heads of families owning one to ten slaves was 152 in 1790, and 153 in 1860. And the number owning more than ten slaves was 12 in 1790 but 60 in 1860. The population of Burke County, on the eastern edge of Appalachian North Carolina, grew only slightly from 8,110 in 1790 to 9,239 in 1860, though the area of the county was much smaller in 1860 than it had been in 1790. Such data seem to suggest that a larger number of slaves were being held by a small but growing elite. In Burke County a strong nine-family slaveholding elite had developed, and most of those families had English or Scotch-Irish names.[16]

Yet with this Appalachian slaveholding and its typical slaveholding practices, the American antislavery movement was in part born in the southern backcountry areas of the Appalachians. Before 1830, the vast majority of antislavery societies in the United States were in the mountain South, not in the North. In 1827, of the 130 antislavery societies in the nation as a whole, 106 were in the South—and most of these in the southern highlands.[17] Antislavery advocates in the South were, after all, much more immediately challenged by the immoralities of slavery than were those in the North, where the effects of the American Revolution had led to slavery's demise. By 1820, each state north of the Mason-Dixon line, the boundary between Pennsylvania and Maryland, had either abolished slavery outright or had set in motion a scheme for the gradual emancipation of the slaves within that state.

For a time it seemed that this spread of "emancipationism" might reach southward into Virginia, Kentucky, and even Tennessee. Virginia had seriously debated emancipation as late as 1830–1831. In Kentucky, antislavery advocates were hopeful that slavery could be done away with from the first constitutional convention in 1791 until the constitutional convention of 1849. But all antislavery moves were countered by strong proslavery forces. In Tennessee, however, the eastern mountain portion of that state became the nation's center of antislavery activity for a time.

A clarification of terms might be helpful at this point. "Antislavery" is the larger, more inclusive term that refers to all those who took a position against slavery. Antislavery adherents, then, can be divided into three smaller groups. Some were "colonizationists." Such persons generally operated through the American Colonization Society, founded in 1817, and included among its supporters many prominent planters in the South. Bushrod Washington, the first president's adopted son and an associate justice of the Supreme Court, was an early vice president of the Colonization Society. So were Henry Clay and Andrew Jackson. Colonizationists took the position that the tragedy was the introduction of blacks into American society in the first place. The way to solve the slave problem from this perspective, then, was to make arrangements to remove blacks from American society and to send them elsewhere, to a colony in the Caribbean or back to Africa. The American Colonization Society spent its major energies establishing Liberia in Africa as a protectorate of the United States for a haven for the deported American blacks. The inadequacy of the colonization "solution" was not clear until the 1830s, when it became obvious that despite the society's massive efforts the few thousand blacks induced into migration were dwarfed by the massive natural increase in population among American slaves.

A second antislavery position was "emancipationism." This position held that a scheme should be set in motion to do away with slavery on some gradual basis. Owners would be compensated, and slaves born after a certain date would be freed. Others on reaching a certain age at a given time would also be freed. The varieties that this type of antislavery action could take were infinite; its flexibility was its strength and its weakness. Although New York and Pennsylvania had done away with slavery in this manner, the ambiguity of the emancipationists' answer made it a difficult program to sell. In the 1849 Kentucky constitutional debates, for example, probably the major reason for antislavery's failure was the flabbiness of the emancipationist answer.

Finally there were the "immediate abolitionists." At least the answer was clear: end slavery immediately and unequivocally. Clearly, this was the most radical solution to the problem and the hardest for southerners to accept. There were, needless to say, very few southern abolitionists.

East Tennessee until 1830 was the major center for antislavery activities in the United States. The antislavery base in East Tennessee had been laid by the founders of Presbyterianism in that state: Samuel Doak, Hezakiah Balch, Samuel Carrick, and others. Most of these ministers preached the "New Light" gospel of a socially aware evangelicalism. Several of them were prominent in the establishment of the State of Franklin and in the late eighteenth century established the roots of antislavery in East Tennessee. The mountainous areas of Virginia, in what would become West Virginia and the Shenandoah Valley, also had antislavery groups. But in Virginia, antislavery sentiments were aimed mainly at either sustaining a minority antislavery witness, as with the Mennonites in the Shenandoah, or at sustaining the movement, which reached its near-success in the constitutional debates of 1830–1831. With the failure of the antislavery efforts in 1830–1831, the movement subsided in Virginia and trailed off into a sectionalism that was to lead to the birth of West Virginia during the Civil War. In East Tennessee, the firm religious base for antislavery built by Doak, Balch, and others attracted abolitionist Quakers driven from the piedmont of North Carolina by increasing persecution by the proslavery elite.

In the 1820s, for a time, Jonesboro, Tennessee, became the capital of the nation's antislavery crusade. Jonesboro was a remarkable Tennessee Valley town. It had been the seat of the State of Franklin, was one of the first "laid out" towns in the "West," and served briefly as the capital of Tennessee. It was the home of Martin Academy, an early "log cabin" Presbyterian school, and it had a strong Presbyterian church. It became the county seat of Washington County, and in the 1820s, it contained an antislavery printing establishment, which published the leading antislavery journal of the time, Benjamin Lundy's *Genius of Universal Emancipation*, between 1821 and 1825. In some of these years the paper included on its staff the young William Lloyd Garrison. More important, perhaps, was the *Emancipator*, a paper edited by a Quaker, Elihu Embree, published in Greeneville, Tennessee, during 1819, and the first paper published in the United States that took an open and clear abolitionist position.

More important even than this temporary journalistic bastion for antislavery within the southern Appalachians was the educational system begun by Samuel Doak and other pioneer Presbyterians. These "log cabin colleges"— the school alongside the Presbyterian church, both being served by a seminary-trained minister—almost universally taught a strong antislavery doctrine. And when it became too dangerous to continue to teach or preach antislavery in the slave state of Tennessee, these ministers and their students migrated to the Midwest and the West, where they became significant abolitionist leaders. John Rankin, Gideon Blackburn, David Nelson, James and William Dickey, and Samuel Carothers were among the many Tennessee-born leaders of western abolitionism.[18]

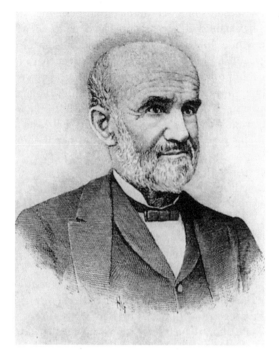

John G. Fee. (Courtesy of Berea College)

In the 1850s, furthermore, a corner of Appalachian Kentucky became the locale for a "radical" abolitionist witness. This was the aggressive abolitionist witness established by John G. Fee in Madison County, Kentucky. Fee had been invited to the area by Cassius M. Clay, a remarkable Kentucky aristocrat who had been converted to emancipationism while a student at Yale University. Clay had heard Garrison speak and went back to Kentucky to try to build a political career on an antislavery base. He ran for the state legislature on several occasions, winning only during his earliest tries. Once he ran for governor and was defeated soundly. Ultimately he was one of the founders of the Republican party in Kentucky. In his try for the governorship he had gained only a little over 3,500 votes of the 100,000 cast,[19] but he had developed a small, loyal constituency, largely in Kentucky's mountain areas.

Fee was also a Kentuckian, from the Ohio River county of Bracken. He had been schooled at Augusta College in Bracken County and also at Miami University in Ohio; he then trained at Lane Seminary in Cincinnati to become a Presbyterian minister. While at Lane he became an abolitionist and pledged to return to Kentucky to preach against slavery. This led to his removal from Kentucky's proslavery presbytery and to his ultimate support by the aggressively antislavery American Missionary Association. Fee was a dedicated abolitionist, and on Clay's invitation he came to "the interior of slavery" in southern

Madison County to establish a community that he named "Berea" (see Acts 17:10–11). Here he established several antislavery churches as well as a school. When the excitement of John Brown's raid in Appalachian Virginia at Harper's Ferry led to a "great fear" in Madison County, the fear that the abolitionists of the county were about to encourage a slave insurrection, the proslavery majority of the county with its leading citizens rode to Berea and insisted that the Bereans leave the state. They returned only fitfully until the issues of the Civil War were pretty well settled in 1863. After the Civil War, Berea became a major force in linking mainstream, evangelical, former abolitionist forces with post–Civil War mountain needs.[20]

The citizens of "Coheedom," however, did not as a whole take a clear antislavery position. Elites in virtually every mountain community owned slaves and were strong supporters of the institution. But a majority of the mountain population, especially in Appalachian Kentucky, Virginia, and Tennessee, probably were antislavery. In traveling through western North Carolina in 1854, Frederick Law Olmsted wrote of a local resident he encountered:"I asked him if the people here preferred Iowa and Indiana to Missouri at all because they were free states. 'I reckon,' he replied, 'they don't have no allusion to that Slavery is a great cuss, though, I think, the greatest there is in these United States. There ain' no account of slaves up here in the West, but down in the east part of the State about Fayetteville, there's as many as in South Carolina. That's the reason the West and the East don't agree in this State. People out here hates the eastern people."[21] The sectionalism that emerged in the mountain area of each southern state appears to have had at least in part an antislavery base.

Through the 1830s, 1840s, and 1850s, slave society became more and more sensitive to a defense of the "peculiar institution." From a "necessary evil," which was the position taken by most apologists of slavery in the days of Jefferson and Madison, southerners increasingly took the position that slavery was a "positive good." The phrase was John C. Calhoun's, himself a product of the fringes of Appalachian Carolina. This "positive good" argument was generally based upon a range of basic rationales, ranging from an organic view of society to an emulation of classical history and a literal reading of selected portions of the Bible. As southern society sold itself on slavery's validity— while convincing few others—it became more and more insistent upon a uniformity of opinion within its borders. Thus in North Carolina, Tennessee, Kentucky, Georgia, and Virginia, where substantial antislavery sentiment had existed, particularly in the "Cohee" mountain sections of these states, antislavery sentiments were either driven out or hushed into silence. In the mountain town of Barbourville, Kentucky, for example, so solid a citizen as Dr. Samuel Freeman Miller was induced to leave the state following the frustrations of the failure of antislavery in the constitutional debate of 1849. Miller, an antislavery man, left for the free state of Iowa, where he first became governor, then was appointed by Lincoln to the U.S. Supreme Court, where he served brilliantly from 1862 to 1890. By 1845, slavery was not a debatable subject inside the slave states, and any significant group within a slave state, like Cohee mountaineers, held their antislavery sentiments at great peril to themselves and to their way of life.[22]

Cohee leadership should have been able to see the emerging division within American society that ultimately tore the Federal Union to pieces. It appears, however, that the reason that most mountaineers were so surprised when the political fabric tore apart in 1860 was that, in the past, politics had always been able to heal such issue-oriented divisions. Furthermore, the Union seemed to be such an effective mechanism in gaining control of the continent for the mutual benefit of Yankee, Cohee, and "Tuckahoe" that it was hard to believe that any one group would tear it apart. But the war among brothers did come. And as the section least prepared for it and the one most divided by it, it was also Coheedom that probably suffered most when the war came.

NOTES

An earlier version of this essay was published in *Appalachian Heritage* 14 (winter 1986): 25-33, and is printed here with the permission of *Appalachian Heritage*.

1. Thomas Jefferson Wertenbaker, *The Old South: The Founding of American Civilization* (New York: Scribners, 1942), 168.

2. Ronald D Eller, *Miners, Millhands, and Mountaineers: Industrialization of the Appalachian South, 1880–1930* (Knoxville: Univ. of Tennessee Press, 1982), xix.

3. "A Region of Contradiction," *Appalachia* 18 (March 1985): 7.

4. Clement Eaton, *Freedom of Thought in the Old South* (New York: Harper, 1964), 239, 242, 251.

5. See Clifford L. Lord and Elizabeth H. Lord, *Historical Atlas of the United States* (New York: Holt, 1953), maps 141–44, pp. 90–91.

6. Joseph G.C. Kennedy, *Preliminary Report on the Eighth Census, 1860* (Washington, D.C.: Government Printing Office, 1862), 260–61.

7. Ibid., 261.

8. Works Progress Administration, *Slave Narratives*, 1938, microfilm, no. 119, Kentucky, 66–67.

9. Ronald Killian and Charles Waller, eds., *Slavery Times Down on Master's Plantation* (Savannah: Beehive Press, 1973), 61–62.

10. Theodore Dwight Weld, *Slavery as It Is: Testimony of a Thousand Witnesses* (New York: American Antislavery Society, 1839), 48.

11. W.P.A., *Narratives*, 38–39.

12. B.A. Botkin, ed., *Lay My Burden Down: A Folk History of Slavery* (Chicago: Univ. of Chicago Press, 1945), 155.

13. W.P.A., *Narratives*, 39.

14. Ibid., 5. This section was reported from Boyd County.

15. This was the testimony of a Mr. Hall, a student at Marietta College, in Weld, *Slavery as It Is*, 69–70.

16. Perhaps the finest countywide study of slavery in the Old South is Edward W. Phifer, "Slavery in Microcosm: Burke County, North Carolina," *Journal of Southern History* 28 (May 1962): 137–65. The statistics used here are taken from the tables on pp. 160–65.

17. See Avery Craven, *The Coming of the Civil War* (New York: Scribners, 1942), 153–54. See also Dwight Lowell Dumond, *Antislavery: The Crusade for Freedom in America* (New York: Norton, 1966), 90–95, 133–38.

18. Dwight Lowell Dumond, *The Crusade for Freedom in America* (New York: Norton, 1961), 134–36.

19. David L. Smiley, *The Lion of Whitehall: The Life of Cassius M. Clay* (Gloucester, Mass.: Peter Smith, 1969), 43–54, 147, 153–54.

20. For the most widely available accounts of Berea's place in Kentucky antislavery, see Elisabeth S. Peck, *Berea's First Century* (Lexington: Univ. Press of Kentucky, 1955), 2–20; and Lowell H. Harrison, *The Antislavery Movement in Kentucky* (Lexington: Univ. Press of Kentucky, 1978), 70–78.

21. Frederick Law Olmsted, *The Slave States*, ed. Harvey Wish (New York: Capricorn, 1959), 226. This account was written in western North Carolina and dated July 13, 1854.

22. On this view of the "plantation mind," see especially Eaton, *Freedom of Thought*, 222, 234–37.

2

Appalachian Echoes of the African Banjo

Cecelia Conway

Today the banjo still sounds throughout Appalachia and has become an emblem for white mountain folk. But this has not always been so. Blacks actually brought the banjo with them from Africa in the 1740s or earlier. Even today, certain elderly and little-noticed black musicians in the North Carolina piedmont continue to play old-time, five-string banjo in much the same compelling style as did white mountain players, and southern black and mountain white repertoires overlap in surprising ways.

When and where white mountain musicians initially acquired the banjo and their playing styles have remained obscure and controversial. The initial formation of white mountain banjo playing likely resulted from southern black influence before the Civil War. By 1840, whites had begun to "catch" banjo styles from African American slaves and to play solo banjo. Some soon blacked their faces and became traveling minstrels. They had opportunities for imitating blacks, from whom they acquired repertory and techniques, and they were utterly dependent upon African Americans as a source for the banjo itself. Only later did they begin to play the banjo in combination with their familiar fiddle.

Some scholars believe that because of the widespread popularity of traveling blackface shows, white minstrels influenced the formation of mountain banjo playing in the nineteenth century. Certainly the traveling shows were influential. And yet it was blacks rather than white minstrels who provided this formative influence. Although their stories are less documented than those of the popular minstrels, several white highlanders in this early period were already playing the downstroking style known to blacks. Before 1840, a man named Ferguson from western Virginia was already playing banjo. The Cincinnati Circus hired Ferguson, a roustabout, for ten dollars a month when it passed through the mountains in the late spring or summer of 1840. By the time the circus reached Lexington, Kentucky, that fall, the manager was willing to say that the banjo-playing Ferguson was "the greatest card we had."[1] Joel Sweeney and his two brothers of Buckingham County, Virginia, played banjo and fiddle to entertain local crowds on court days as early as 1831. These men became well known locally and regionally. During his summer touring with the circus, Ferguson served as a mentor to Dan Emmett, who would later become one of the earliest and most prominent minstrels.

Like many of the early northern minstrels, southern white banjo players actually learned from blacks. The three Sweeneys learned from slaves, with "Negro melodies" remaining an important part of their repertoire, while Ferguson's outspoken circus boss, who described the lively musician as "nigger all over except in color," counted him as Emmett's teacher.[2] Joel Sweeney became the leader of the Virginia Minstels (which included Emmett) when the band became wildly popular in London and Ireland. Their influence was such that it could be argued that mountain whites, as well as blacks, influenced the formation of minstrelsy. Minstrels, then, were irrelevant to the initial transmission of African American banjo playing to mountain folk musicians.

This different explanation of how mountain whites first acquired the banjo appeared in 1973 in the remarks of fiddler Alan Jabbour, then head of the American Folklife Center. "Little is known about this style . . . 'thumping,' . . . the old downstroke style of the Upper South," he wrote, "but there is a smattering of evidence that, like the banjo itself, it came originally from black musicians in the Virginia and North Carolina Piedmont, when it spread southwestward into the Appalachians and beyond."[3] Although overlooked by some, Jabbour's explanation has the virtue of being the simplest. This theory also offers the earliest beginning for this cross-cultural exchange and thus the longest duration. His claim, moreover, does not depend on river routes and schedules or occasional overland southern tours by minstrel shows and circuses, as does the minstrel theory. The acquisition of banjo techniques by whites could easily have occurred even in the piedmont, where many African Americans were living as slaves in close and frequent contact with whites. The white settlers themselves could then have helped carry the banjo and its playing styles with them into the mountains as they moved west.

Historical data supports the likelihood that blacks in Maryland, Virginia, and North Carolina were the initial transmitters of the downstroking style. The eighteenth- and early nineteenth-century written record compiled by Dena Epstein and other scholars established that the earliest and strongest tradition of banjo playing by blacks was located in the upper South.[4] Moreover, a report that indicated that there were black banjo players in Knoxville by 1798 supports the claim that banjo playing spread "southwestward into the Appalachians and beyond" and that blacks themselves carried it into the mountains. Furthermore, Joel Sweeney, among the first whites known to have played the banjo, learned his downstroking style by 1830 and thus even before Ferguson. Indeed, even the Hammonses, a family of mountain musicians from more remote western Virginia (later West Virginia), had access to black traditions in these areas. In the last thirty years of the eighteenth century, the family resided in the Virginia piedmont, somewhat south of the Sweeney plantation, and at the turn of the century, they lived near Cumberland Gap, about fifty miles northeast of Knoxville.[5] Both locations are contiguous with Ferguson's territory and were linked with it by pioneer and circus travel routes.

Banjo playing by blacks reached the far-flung region of the Mississippi River Valley before 1840. The diffusion of this tradition from the upland South through Appalachia to western river routes was accelerated by the presence of

A Pastoral Visit, by Richard N. Brooke, 1881. (Author's collection)

banjo players in New Orleans by the beginning of the nineteenth century. Even mountain whites had an opportunity to hear blacks playing the banjo along the Mississippi. Many of those west of the eastern continental divide, like those who lived near Coe Ridge on the Tennessee-Kentucky border, traveled downriver on rafts to sell their goods in New Orleans, where they might well have seen and heard black musicians performing. In sum, white mountaineers had contact with black musical traditions, including banjo playing, in the piedmont, in the mountains, and on the river routes to New Orleans, all well before the advent of minstrelsy.

A second argument in favor of black transmission of banjo music and techniques to mountain whites lies in Alan Jabbour's observation that "groups with strong musical traditions may be expected to exert an influence out of proportion to their numerical strength." This argument helps refute the doubts of those who consider the relatively small slave populace of the southern highlands less likely to play a significant role. But blues researcher Tony Russell believes that the small number of blacks actually may have enhanced their influence: "Racial antipathy, of course, hampered the free exchange of musical ideas, and it will become clear . . . that interaction was more fertile in areas where blacks were scattered" and thus less feared.[6] Furthermore, since most white mountain settlers tended to be small, independent farmers, they were often Scotch and Irish folk musicians and not above learning banjo by ear and by imitating blacks. Like the Sweeneys, Emmett, and others who eventually won acclaim as minstrel performers, they seemed eager to learn new music from blacks.

Many sources, including the commercial minstrel and medicine shows, influenced mountain music, but apparently even small numbers of blacks initially transmitted downstroking banjo to mountain whites, some of whom became minstrels. Later, opportunities for banjo exchange between blacks and whites and other musical exchange increased during the upheaval of the Civil War and again during the railroad construction and mining operations that drew so many more African Americans into the mountain South late in the nineteenth century.

One means of further examining this crosscultural transmission is to study the patterns of musical continuity and change in three highland crossroad communities in which they are especially evident—two in northwestern North Carolina and one across the state line in southwestern Virginia. All three areas—Sugar Grove in Ashe County, North Carolina, Big Stone Gap, near Norton, Virginia, and Round Peak in Surry County, North Carolina—counted among their residents in the early twentieth century accomplished white banjo players who had contact with black musicians living in or traveling through their communities.

SUGAR GROVE

Where the state lines of Virginia, North Carolina, and Tennessee converge is a mountain crossroads that I call the "Sugar Grove region." I chose this area for discussion because its past is better documented than that of many other sections of the Appalachians and because of its strategic location as an early trading center. This region is the mountainous center of a large area that reported white and black banjo players in the first forty years of the nineteenth century. The northwest border of the region is the earliest migration route westward through the Appalachians, and its southwest border is the Watauga River Valley. Within this region, Johnson County, Tennessee, is separated from Ashe and Watauga Counties in North Carolina by "the crest of the little-known Stone Mountains . . . a ridge, albeit a low and sometimes indistinct one, broken by passable gaps."[7] The region is bounded on the northeast by the New River Valley in North Carolina and includes portions of Grayson and Washington Counties, Virginia. On the southeast, the region is bounded by the Blue Ridge Mountains, which run parallel to the migration route.

The heart of this area, Ashe County, was called the "Lost Province" by North Carolinians. From its establishment in 1799 until the first usable road connected it with the east in 1849, Old Ashe County (which then included what are now Alleghany and Watauga Counties as well) remained rather secluded from the Carolina piedmont but connected with the rest of Appalachia due to its geographical and historical connections to western Virginia, connections that proved significant to the nature of the musical exchange there.

It is more than coincidence that several of the early banjo players lived near the migration route that passed by the Sugar Grove region. The white Virginian Ferguson, Joel Sweeney, and Sweeney's brothers lived northeast of the Sugar Grove area. The Knoxville (1798) and Asheville (1867) black banjo players were southwest of the region, and the travels of the ancestors of the white West Virginia Hammonses overlapped and crossed this main migration route.

Although by the beginning of the twentieth century some blacks were passing through the region with the railroad or on their way to work in the mines, others had settled there in earlier days. Before the Revolutionary War, as "Royal and Proprietary oppressions became more distasteful, migration into Ashe increased and by 1775 was in a steady stream. North Carolinians . . . came over Low Gap into Virginia, then south via the Old Warrior's trail into Ashe." Some of the early white settlers brought black slaves with them, and this route gave them extensive access to the mountains. The 1790 census listed ten slaves in the area that would become Ashe County in 1799. When the 1830 census was compiled, the number of slaves had increased to 492. By 1850, 8,096 whites, 595 slaves, and 86 free blacks were living in the area, giving Old Ashe "a percentage of slaves somewhat lower than the rest of the mountains."[8]

Whites in this region and in most other mountain areas had mixed feelings about the approaching Civil War. This attitude arose in part because many had never been wealthy landholders or slaveholders and tended to favor state rights without necessarily supporting slavery. There was "such a strong Union sympathy in Ashe," for example, "that it remained Republican for a long time."[9] In addition to these political attitudes among the majority of residents, some in Ashe County demonstrated racial tolerance toward free blacks. They were permitted to remain in the area, and runaway slaves sometimes found refuge with local residents. Two mountains, Nigger Mountain (now called Mount Jefferson) and Mulatto Mountain, were named for African Americans. Nigger Mountain, according to local tradition, was named for the fact that fugitive slaves hid there and that it actually served as a station of the Underground Railroad.[10] This tradition reveals that at least some residents were not only Union sympathizers but were working actively for the abolition of slavery. From Ashe County's earliest settlement, then, blacks were present. And before the Civil War a number of whites demonstrated political and presumably cultural open-mindedness toward them.

More specifically, just before the Civil War the ancestors of black banjo player Dave Thompson arrived in Ashe County from the North Carolina piedmont. Dave's grandfather, Archibald Thompson, is known to have been in Chatham County in 1851 and in Guilford County in 1856, the same section of the piedmont where John Snipes, Dink Roberts, and Odell Thompson, all twentieth-century banjo players, lived in the 1980s. Sometime after 1856, Archibald, his son Avery, and other family members moved from that area toward the free lands of Indiana. Because Archibald was a freeborn black traveling in still dangerous times, he carried with him two letters of recommendation from notable white men in the piedmont. Before his family reached Tennessee, according to Dave's cousin, Mrs. Addie Moore, the ox cart broke down on the last mountain in northwest North Carolina. As Quakers were numerous in the piedmont counties where the Thompsons had lived, Archibald probably knew of their Underground Railroad activities and may have already known that this area was not unfavorable for southern blacks. The family settled there, and Archibald Thompson registered his title to land at the county courthouse. The mountain where he settled came to be known as Thompson Mountain, the third one named after an African American.[11]

Archibald Thompson's family was notably musical. Banjo players included his grandson Dave Thompson and Dave's first cousin William. They each had one sister who married local banjo players. One of these men, Frank McQueen, died as a young man in the Virginia coal mines. Dave traveled north sometimes into Tennessee to work on the railroad and other times to the Kentucky coal mines. His son now lives across the West Virginia line, where he works in the mines at Yukon. This family network suggests the extensive travel that occurred throughout Sugar Grove's black community in the late nineteenth and early twentieth centuries. Their work patterns reflect the fact that the mines, like the railroad, accounted for increased contact between whites and blacks. Moreover, frequent string music gatherings, especially at Christmas, provided the Thompsons with opportunities for musical exchange with whites like Frank Proffitt, Doc Watson, and others who attended these gatherings.

This history of a single family in North Carolina is evidence of a strong black banjo tradition to which white mountain banjo players remained exposed during the early twentieth century. Two of the best known white mountain musicians from this district, Tom Ashley and Hobart Smith, were from old families who had brought, acquired, and developed their own musical traditions. In 1905, at the age of eight, Clarence (Tom) Ashley learned black-derived downstroking banjo from his two aunts, although he never fully mastered his Aunt Daisy's unorthodox style of picking up, instead of down, on the fifth string.[12] His Aunt Ary played "standard clawhammer,"[13] and Ashley's mastery of that style earned him a job in a medicine show. He was so accomplished that before he was eighteen his boss, Doc Hower, assigned him the responsibility of training a new recruit, Roy Acuff. Although Acuff was best known as a fiddler and a singer, he also played clawhammer and rememberd his early work with Ashley.[14] Ashley remained an intermittent but widely accessible banjo source on the medicine-show circuits until at least 1943.[15]

Hobart Smith is yet another musician whose career reflects the vigorous local rather than minstrel-style tradition that was crucial to the transmission of clawhammer banjo-playing to the mountains. Smith called his playing "the old-timey rappin' style," which he learned from his father. He also noted that John Greer, "a feller I was raised up with," was a strong influence. He "came along . . . double-notin', and he was the best man I ever heard on the banjer. And I patterned after him."[16] Later Smith described his musical history during the depression, saying that he "had a band" and performed with Tom Ashley.[17]

These men traveled more than we might expect and, in so doing, transmitted their own strong local traditions to other mountain musicians. The variations in banjo playing styles that Ashley (born 1896) and Smith (born 1897) picked up suggest how well established the white folk banjo tradition had become in the northwestern North Carolina mountain region between 1840 and 1880.

Furthermore, Ashley and Smith had contact with black musicians. Hobart Smith, whose ancestors came from Britain in the mid-eighteenth century, grew up in Saltville, Virginia, quite close to the overland migration route on the northern border of the Sugar Grove region. By 1915, when Hobart Smith was eighteen years old, he was playing the fiddle and had been playing the banjo for eleven years. He liked to tell a story that appears in the repertory of tales of many guitar players. He said that a few years earlier, "Blind Lemon Jefferson came through, and he stayed there about a month. He stayed with the other colored fellows and they worked on the railroad there; he'd just sing and play to entertain the men in the work camp. I think that right about there I started on the guitar." Jefferson's influence appears in Smith's "Six White Horses" and "Railroad Bill," both of which he said he learned from Jefferson, and in "Grave-yard Blues."[18] From a black musician, then, and as the result of the arrival of railroads in the mountains, Smith acquired a repertoire and an initial instrumental style.

Even before the arrival of the railroads, a black introduced Smith to the fiddle: "The first fiddle I ever heard in my life was when I was a kid. There was an old colored man who was raised up in slave times. His name was Jim Spencer. He played 'Jinny, Put the Kettle On' and all those old tunes like that. And he would come up to our house and he'd play."[19] During Smith's boyhood, at least three black banjo players lived in the Sugar Grove region, according to a local resident.[20] Though there is no direct evidence of his contact with them, Smith's account demonstrates his appreciation of African American musicianship, style, and repertory, and his eagerness to borrow from blacks.

Tom Ashley also had opportunity for contact with black banjo players. Although his taped recollections make no reference to African American influence on his music, his repertory reveals strains of black tradition, for example, "Red Rocking Chair" and "Walking Boss." His family, who came from Ireland, had access to black music from before 1800, when they settled in eastern Virginia. They moved to Ashe County sometime before the Civil War, and Ashley grew up in Mountain City, Tennessee. Ashley's own travels, even when he was not working medicine shows, probably put him in contact with black musicians. He and the fiddler G.B. Grayson used to go north to play in the West Virginia coalfields, and he met Hobart Smith when he played at a week-long carnival in Saltville.[21]

Although both Smith and Ashley learned their banjo styles from members of their own families, they were able and eager to acquire more inaccessible music from African Americans. Their musical inquisitiveness suggests that they had already incorporated the local black styles into their own banjo playing. This attitude among talented white musicians in the Sugar Grove region during the early twentieth century is important, for it suggests the probable openness of their ancestors to borrowing from African Americans before the Civil War, when banjo playing initially took hold in the mountains.

Big Stone Gap

What happened in Sugar Grove recurred in other Virginia and North Carolina mountain regions to the west and east. To the west, Dock Boggs, like the Sugar Grove whites, was influenced by blacks. His hometown, Norton, Virginia, is about fifty miles northwest of Abingdon, on the migration route that forms the northern boundary of the Sugar Grove area. Norton is also about fifty miles northeast of Cumberland Gap and much closer to Big Stone Gap, both of which are mountain passes on major travel routes from Virginia to Kentucky. This nexus of frontier migration routes near Big Stone Gap was settled by whites and African Americans before the end of the eighteenth century.

The style of banjo playing used by the older members of Boggs's family was, as one would expect, the old downstroking method first learned by whites from blacks. Dock's eldest brother, John, born about 1870, "played fiddle or banjo, either one."[22] "All about the banjo players played that knock-down way, or whatever you want to call it."[23] Although Dock Boggs, born in 1898, was fascinated by his brother John, he did not follow the "knock-down," "clawhammer" style used by John and others in his family and in the area. "I had never heard any man play any kind of blues on a banjo," Dock recalled. "But I had seen two colored men who picked the banjo with one finger and a thumb, or with two fingers. I said to myself never telling anyone, that was the way I was goin' to learn. I started to learn when I was 12 or 13."[24]

Thus at least two banjo-playing methods were available to Boggs when he learned the banjo: the "knock-down" method of his older brother and the two-finger method of these particular African American players. Although he played some tunes in two-finger "picking" style, he developed his own unorthodox three-finger style based on the diverse sounds, rather than methods, to which he was exposed. Musician Mike Seeger has described his unique performance style as "a highly individual synthesis of old mountain and blues styles," whose picking "is as unorthodox as his use of vocal and instrumental melody."[25]

African American influences turn up not only in Boggs's performance style but also in at least two repertory items on his third album. He learned "Turkey in the Straw" and "Sugar Blues" from blacks. Of the latter, he said, "Well that was accompanied by piano, I think sung by Sara Martin . . . some colored lady in New York, it must have been 45–48 years ago," in the early 1920s. Boggs indicates that, although he knew the words to this song for years, he did not work it out where he "could sing it and play it on the banjo" until the 1960s. His translation of such material to the banjo illustrates the process that inspired his personal banjo style. Early and late, Boggs was more responsive to musical sounds than performance techniques, and those sounds that were most formative were African American.

ROUND PEAK

Another section of the Blue Ridge Mountains, one county to the east of Sugar Grove, was also the scene of black influence upon mountain whites. This community, called Round Peak, lies in Surry County, North Carolina, just over the line from Virginia on the eastern slope of the Blue Ridge. This tiny region is northwest of the piedmont, beyond Pilot Mountain on the southern slope of Fisher's Peak. Low Gap is the pass beside Fisher's Peak that North Carolinians used after crossing the southern slope of the Blue Ridge to migrate on toward Ashe County before the Revolutionary War. The twenty or so families in the Round Peak region were self-sufficient and enjoyed their space and freedom. The old-fashioned flavor of rural life in Round Peak that persisted into the early years of this century emerges in Corinna Bowdon's recollections of her childhood. Her grandfather Pet McKinny, for example, made shoes with wooden pegs. The musical traditions of the community were strong, and Corinna was directly connected with them, for she was a regular participant at the local dances, and her grandfather, known as "Old Man Pet," was a prominent fiddler.

In those days "one colored family" lived on Pine Ridge some eight or nine miles away. They were also a part of the community, and folks "didn't even think of them as being black." By the late 1920s, a black band played for white dances down in Mount Airy. At least one dance was held at a warehouse to raise money for the March of Dimes, but most dances were at the Moose Hall. The dancers used the circular formation favored at Round Peak, and the black band played familiar tunes, although they did "change" some of them. The band consisted of a fiddle, a banjo, one big drum,—the first Corinna had seen—and sometimes piano.[26] Born near the turn of the century, the black guitar player Jim Raleigh also documents banjo tradition in Mount Airy at this time by his recollection of several black banjo players who were his contemporaries.

One of Round Peak's foremost white musicians was Tommy Jarrell, born in 1901. He learned to play banjo at the age of ten from Boggy Cockerham, a white man hired to help on the Jarrell family farm. A few years later, about 1915, Jarrell took up the fiddle from his father and uncle and began to acquire repertory from even older members of the community. He learned "Sail Away Ladies," for example, from Corinna's grandfather. But even in this somewhat isolated community he had contact with African American music. Before he learned to play banjo, he remembers that a black man who picked rather than downstroked, came up from Mount Airy to buy whiskey from his father. Although Tommy remained uninfluenced by the black man's picking method, this incident verifies the existence of a banjo tradition among blacks in Mount Airy and his access to it. Later, as a young man, Tommy went with his brother Fred to a tent show where he heard a "yellar gal" sing "Bo Weaval" and accompany herself with tambourine. Tommy and Fred paid their money again to listen to the song a second time. From this hearing Tommy learned to sing and fiddle a beautiful, full version of this song. After he moved to Mount Airy in the 1920s, Tommy also learned another African American song, "Rylan Spenser."[27] Tommy learned to fiddle the tune from his brother-in-law, who had learned to play it on guitar from Jim Raleigh, the black guitar player who lived down the road from Tommy. Tommy caught the words, however, directly from Raleigh at an earlier time. He used to lie in bed and listen to Raleigh sing the song as he walked home from parties about daybreak on Sunday mornings.

Underlying these historical facts concerning the white acquisition of African American repertory and playing styles is an important truth about traditional musicians: good musicians tend to be musically receptive to new influences. The old-timers in Round Peak, Big Stone Gap, and Sugar Grove were not merely back-porch pickers, but exceptional musicians. It is also significant that many of these banjo players and fiddlers are descendants of the Scots and the Irish. A variety of ethnic groups, of course, contributed to the settling of Appalachia. But Celtic American banjo players and fiddlers have influenced American music disproportionately in relation to their small numbers.[28] Likewise, many of the early minstrels who learned banjo or other music directly from slaves, such as Rice, Sweeney, Emmett, and others, were Irish and Scots-Irish. The father of one such minstrel, Dan Emmett, for example, was "an Irishman who lived in Staunton, Virginia, and about 1806 moved to Mount Vernon, Ohio, where he was a blacksmith."[29]

All of the mountain white musicians discussed above played several instruments and became well recognized beyond their own communities. Although the Celtic American mountain banjo players retained the old downstroking style of early black musicians, they were inquisitive, but not unselective, in their search for new, often African American, material, whether by direct contact, recordings, or radio.

This tendency was also true for the preceding generation. The foremost community musicians were usually the first in their areas to own record-playing devices. Tommy Jarrell's father, Ben, bought the first record player in the Round Peak community. In Kentucky, Jean Ritchie's father was the first to own such a machine in his mountain community some twenty miles from Cumberland Gap and not so far from Big Stone Gap. He even made a little extra money carrying it around to play for his neighbors. A photograph of the West Virginia Hammons family ancestors shows one holding a fiddle, one holding a shotgun, and the third holding an Edison player. Although acquisition of new repertory and stylistic techniques was guided by principles of tradition and personal taste, the musicians of both generations were receptive to new material.

The lasting impact of direct and initial contact with strong African American musical traditions also reveals striking diversity. In Big Stone Gap, black traditions were interwoven with a great variety of other influences. As a crossroads of several early migration routes and later of mining traffic, Big Stone Gap was exposed to more diverse cultural and regional traditions than either

Sugar Grove or Round Peak. The family of Dock Boggs alone included brothers who played downstroking (John), two-finger (Roscoe and Dock), and three-finger banjo (Dock). Dock's banjo repertory ranges widely from archaic banjo pieces ("Cumberland Gap" and "Davenport"), to recorded blues ("Sugar Blues"), to fiddle tune ("Turkey in the Straw," as learned from blacks), to topical songs ("Cuba"), to traditionally unaccompanied ballads ("Loving Nancy").

Although the Sugar Grove region also reflects considerable diversity, the white and black banjo players remained focused on African American downstroking and the full complement of techniques associated with this method. The repertory in the relatively more isolated Sugar Grove region emphasized old songs rather than fiddle-tune or fiddle and banjo material. It included a number of banjo pieces of strong African American influence and uncertain origin.

In the Round Peak region, banjo playing was less varied and more specialized. Jarrell, Cockerham, and many others are famed primarily for their extraordinary playing of banjo-fiddle duets. The banjoists played downstroking with a driving rhythm that includes as many notes as possible. The effect of the heavy noting sustained the rhythm as well as produced the fully developed melodies. Although Jarrell and Cockerham were fine singers and knew banjo songs and an unusual number of fiddle-tune verses, their banjo-fiddle arrangements influenced most of their pieces.

This intense merging of the fiddle and banjo in the Round Peak region is not surprising given the information about the early black-white exchange. The old-time string band tradition, an ensemble that reenacts and symbolically honors democratic interaction between the white fiddle and the African American banjo tradition, is one of the especially important results of blacks bringing the banjo to this country.

The contrasting methods, repertory, and ensembles preserved in these three Appalachian regions hold another implication worth exploring. Round Peak players have evolved the most integrated instrumental traditions from the interplay of banjo and fiddle. Sugar Grove offers the greatest variety of banjo song material derived from the solo banjo tradition. Big Stone Gap offers the most diverse traditions. In each of these mountain sections a correlation exists between the preservation of old African American banjo traditions and proximity to the piedmont. Mountain whites, physically closer to the traditions of the piedmont blacks, preserved the older styles. The merging of the Celtic fiddle tradition and the African American banjo tradition into old-time southern music reached its peak in the early decades of this century and represents some of our best American music and vision.

Notes

An earlier version of this essay was published in the *Appalachian Journal* 20 (winter 1993): 146–61, and is reprinted here with the permission of the *Appalachian Journal*.

1. C.J. Rogers (circus manager) to editor of *New York Clipper*, June 20, 1874, cited in Hans Nathan, *Dan Emmett and the Rise of Early Negro Minstrelsy* (Norman: Univ. of Oklahoma Press, 1962), 111.

2. Ibid., 110–11.

3. Carl Fleischhauer and Alan Jabbour, eds., *The Hammons Family: A Study of a West Virginia Family's Traditions* (Washington, D.C.: Library of Congress, 1973), 28.

4. Dena J. Epstein, *Sinful Tunes and Spirituals: Black Folk Music to the Civil War* (Urbana: Univ. of Illinois Press, 1977); see also Epstein, "The Folk Banjo: A Documentary History," *Ethnomusicology* 19 (Sept. 1975): 347–71.

5. Fleischhauer and Jabbour, *The Hammons Family*. The Hammons family lived in Pittsylvania County, Virginia, in the late eighteenth century and, from 1802 to 1833, in Hawkins County, Tennessee, near the migration routes that led to Cumberland Gap, where they lived at about the time that black banjo players were reported in Knoxville.

6. Tony Russell, *Blacks, Whites, and Blues* (New York: Stein and Day, 1970), 10.

7. Bill Sharpe, *A New Geography of North Carolina*, 2 vols. (Raleigh: Sharpe Publishing, 1954), 2: 535.

8. Ibid., 2: 539–40.

9. Ibid., 2: 540.

10. Arthur Lloyd Fletcher, *Ashe County: A History* (Jefferson, N.C.: Ashe County Research Association, 1963), 64.

11. Addie Moore, oral interview with author; also a letter from Moore to author. Thompson Mountain is on the North Carolina-Tennessee border, northwest of Sugar Grove.

12. Richard Rinzler and Ralph Rinzler, liner notes, p. 2, for *Old-Time Music at Clarence Ashley's*, Folkways Records FA 2355, New York, 1963.

13. Robert Winans, "The Folk, the Stage, and the Five-String Banjo in the Nineteenth Century," *Journal of American Folklore* 89 (1976), 425.

14. Conversation with Acuff, Nashville, Tenn., fall 1973.

15. Rinzler and Rinzler, *Old-Time Music*, 2.

16. George Armstrong, album notes for *Hobart Smith*, Folk-Legacy (phonodisc and notes, Huntington, Vt., 1964), 4. Smith also said that he had played in a minstrel show for two years, but there is little evidence that such experience influenced his "marvelously clean and complex frailing style on the banjo" (Winans, "The Folk, the Stage, and the Five-String Banjo," 423) nearly as much as his father and his friend did. Rather his experience with minstrel or medicine shows offers specific evidence only for the expanded transmission of folk playing styles.

17. Armstrong, *Hobart Smith*, 3.

18. Russell, *Blacks, Whites, and Blues*, 48. The railroad reinforced the links between Virginia and northwestern North Carolina. It reached from Abingdon, Virginia, into Ashe County, North Carolina. West Jefferson was established in Ashe in 1915 "at the terminus of the new railway from Virginia (now Norfolk and Western)." Sharpe, *New Geography*, 2: 540.

19. Russell, *Blacks, Whites, and Blues*, 49.

20. Conversation with Joe Wilson, director of the National Council for the Traditional Arts.

21. Rinzler and Rinzler, *Old-Time Music*, Folkways FA 2342, phonodisc and notes.

22. Mike Seeger, ed., *Dock Boggs*, vol. 3, liner notes, p. 4, quoting Boggs, for Asch Records AH 3903, New York, 1970.

23. Ibid., liner notes, 8.

24. Ibid. In 1964, Boggs emphasized the importance of this same, or perhaps a different, event: "There was a colored string band playing for a dance in Norton. I stuck my head in at the door and I liked the way the banjo-player played, so I said to myself, I am going to learn to play that way" (Russell, *Blacks, Whites, and Blues*, 51.)

25. Seeger, *Dock Boggs*, liner notes, 8.

26. Oral interview with Corinna Bowdon by author, 1976.

27. Bowdon interviews, 1976 and 1978. This spelling is Tommy's correction of other titles, such as "Raleigh" and "Spencer."

28. Ashley's family, for example, came from Ireland, and Tommy Jarrell's family was Scots-Irish. See Alan Jabbour, ed., *American Fiddle Tunes from the Archive of Folk Song*, Folk Music of the United States, AFS L62, album and notes, Washington, D.C., 1971, for additional information about the influence of these groups on fiddling.

29. Nathan, *Dan Emmett*, 99. The 1840 rise of minstrelsy correlates with the increase of immigrants due to the great potato blight that starved the poor in Ireland. These new arrivals provided appreciative audiences and sometimes performers for the older Celtic musicians who had created the newly popular entertainment of minstrelsy.

3

GEORGIA'S FORGOTTEN MINERS

African Americans and the
Georgia Gold Rush of 1829

DAVID WILLIAMS

In 1935, an article titled "Georgia's Forgotten Industry: Gold Mining," by Fletcher M. Green, appeared in the *Georgia Historical Quarterly*.[1] The title was indeed appropriate, for this was the first scholarly investigation of the gold rush since it began in 1829, more than a hundred years earlier. In subsequent years the history of gold mining in Georgia has received more attention, but only slightly. A short book by E. Merton Coulter on the gold rush town of Auraria appeared in 1956, and in the past decade two books have been published on the Dahlonega Mint, which coined over $6 million in gold between 1838 and 1861.[2] However, to date, no comprehensive scholarly treatment of Georgia's gold rush era has made it to print.[3]

As little attention as the gold rush has received, one aspect has been almost completely ignored. Nearly everyone with an interest in Georgia history is to some degree familiar with the state's gold rush and the resulting conflict between the state of Georgia and the Cherokee, ultimately leading to Cherokee removal on the "Trail of Tears" during the winter of 1838–1839. But a third group, though not as numerous and largely overlooked, contributed some of the most engaging and extraordinary tales associated with the gold rush era: the African Americans, slave and free. They are, one might say, Georgia's forgotten miners.[4]

Despite numerous claims to the contrary, no one knows for sure when or where the first discovery of gold was made in Georgia. There is even greater uncertainty about who made it.[5] Yet from the very outset, blacks played a prominent role in stories dealing with the origins of Georgia's gold rush. According to one account, in 1828 a slave owned by a man named Logan found gold in a branch of the Nacoochee River in what is today White County. Logan and his servant were returning from the gold fields of Rutherford County, North Carolina, when the slave noticed a similarity between the soil of the Nacoochee Valley and that of the gold region to the north. He tested a sample and discovered that it did indeed contain gold.[6] At about the same time another black man is said to have found gold on Bear Creek near the present site of Dahlonega.[7]

Whatever the origins of the gold rush, there is no question that by the autumn of 1829 it was well under way. The sudden influx of thousands of miners into the Cherokee Nation was known even then as the "Great Intrusion." The natives protested loudly against this obvious infringement on the part of the whites. The *Cherokee Phoenix* noted, "Our neighbors who regard no law and pay no respects to the laws of humanity are now reaping a plentiful harvest. . . . We are an abused people."[8] But there was little the Cherokee could do. It seemed the more vehemently they protested, the more eagerly the miners came.

In 1831, surveyors entered the area and began partitioning the new lands in preparation for a lottery in which the Cherokee Nation would be distributed to Georgia citizens. By September 1832, the surveys were complete and all across the state people were flocking to their respective county seats to register for the drawing. The names were sent to the state capitol at Milledgeville, where they were deposited in a large wooden drum from which they would be drawn. Tickets identifying individual land or gold lots were placed in another drum. Nearly everyone who had been a Georgia resident for a certain number of years was eligible to participate in the lottery, with one major exception: Persons with even a trace of African ancestry were excluded. These people were defined by state law not as citizens but as "free persons of color," and only "citizens" were eligible for the lottery.[9] Nonetheless, there were those of mixed racial background who attempted to get around the restriction. In one instance a man from Tattnall County named Allen Summerall registered for a chance in the lottery as a single white male. Only later did the authorities discover that his mother was black. According to Georgia law, this made Summerall a "free person of color" and as such ineligible for the drawing.[10]

The lottery was not the only activity from which blacks were barred. Life and labor in the gold region was spartan at best, and the miners sought diversion at every opportunity. But free blacks, because of their social status, and slaves, because of their bondage, could not join in recreational pastimes taken for granted by other miners. When the miners were not in the countryside digging for gold, they could usually be found in town looking for ways to spend it. According to one account, "Gambling houses, dancing houses, drinking saloons, houses of ill fame, billiard saloons, and tenpin alleys were open day and night."[11] The men were nearly matched in number by women, who were, wrote a citizen of Dahlonega, "equally as vile and wicked."[12] Wrote another eyewitness, "I can hardly conceive of a more unmoral community than exists around these mines; drunkenness, gambling, fighting, lewdness, and every other vice exist here to an awful extent." It appears that as a group, in the words of this contemporary, "generally the most moral" people were those denied an opportunity to participate in these festivities—the blacks.[13]

If recreation was difficult to come by for the black miners, such was not the case with hard work in the mines. Most were slaves and had less choice in the matter than free blacks. More to the point, they had no choice. Soon after the discovery of gold in Georgia, mining quickly proved to be very popular as an off-season activity among yeoman farmers and planters. After the fall harvest, many headed for the hills to try their luck in the gold fields, taking their slaves with them to work the mines. Those who were residents of the gold country often operated mines on their own lands to supplement their incomes.[14] This practice was so common in some areas that the nineteenth-century mining engineers Nitze and Wilkens commented, "Farming and gold-digging went, in many cases, hand in hand. When crops were laid by, the slaves and farmhands were turned into the creek-bottoms, thus utilizing their time during the dull season."[15] One such man from Augusta, named Phinizy, brought a large group of slaves to the gold region each year to work in the mines.[16] Thomas Lumsden, a Nacoochee mine owner in what is today White County, recorded that his slaves produced thirty thousand dollars in gold during a single season.[17] At one point, Sen. John C. Calhoun of South Carolina had twenty slaves working in his mine just south of Dahlonega in Lumpkin County. Over a two-year period between 1833 and 1835, the mine produced around five hundred dollars per hand annually, and Calhoun saw "no reason why it should not continue to yield at the same rate."[18]

There were also planters who leased gold lands and worked slaves in the mines seasonally or throughout the year. Others gave up "King Cotton" altogether and devoted their energies completely to gold mining.[19] As one writer put it, "Where mining proved more profitable than planting, the former superseded the latter entirely."[20] In most cases, however, when the price of cotton was high farmers and planters abandoned the gold fields and then returned to the mines when the price of cotton again fell off.[21]

Slaves were also purchased strictly for work in the mines or leased from low-country planters for the purpose. Advertisements in Georgia newspapers gave notice to slave traders, "Liberal prices will be given for Negroes."[22] Such ads also announced that "Strong Negro Men are in demand at the Mines, at $10 per month."[23] The money, of course, went to the slave's owner.

The slaves quite naturally resented not profiting from their labor. Some sought to compensate themselves by concealing what gold they could from the overseer. They hid it in the seams of their clothing and even placed gold dust and small nuggets in their hair. One mine proprietor surprised his slaves one evening by ordering that they be shaved before going to their quarters. When the hair was shaken out, several ounces of pure gold were recovered.[24] Sometimes, while working the mines, slaves attempted to secretly bury small gold nuggets and to retrieve them at a more opportune time. One Gilmer County slave maneuvered a large nugget from his shovel and worked it into the dirt with his foot when no one was watching. That night he escaped and tried to find his treasure, but the mine was pitch black. The unfortunate slave found it impossible to locate the spot where he had buried the nugget. While vainly searching for what might literally have been a ticket to freedom, his absence was detected, and he was severely beaten for his insolence. The nugget was later found and estimated to be worth over six hundred dollars.[25]

When slaves were successful in concealing gold from their owners, they

Slaves mining gold, ca. 1830s. (Courtesy of the North Carolina Collection, University of North Carolina at Chapel Hill)

either saved it or tried to sell it to any convenient buyer. This was risky business for the buyer and the seller. In 1833, the Lumpkin County grand jury brought charges against Jefferson Witherow, Alfred Witherow, and Frances B. Bulfinch for buying ten dollars worth of gold from the slaves of James H. Poteet, Jacob Page, and Leander Smith.[26] In Habersham County, a white man named Andrew Johnson was charged with "trading with a slave." Johnson pleaded guilty and was fined five dollars. The slave's punishment was not recorded.[27]

There were at least a few slaves who did not have to conceal gold from their masters. Some mine owners allowed their slaves to keep a portion of the gold they discovered, while others rented out slaves and let them have a percentage of the proceeds. Jacob Scudder permitted his slaves to keep all the gold they found after sundown at his placer mine. It was, of course, no easy task to find tiny bits of gold while panning in the dark by pine torches, but Scudder placed no limit on the amount of gold they could pan. However, he did insist that they sell their findings only to him. At least a few of his slaves saved enough gold from their nightly workings to purchase their freedom.[28]

Besides hard work and often brutal treatment, the mines also presented a danger to life and limb for the slaves. Many tunnels were hastily dug and haphazardly braced by inexperienced workers. Not surprisingly, such tunnels were subject to cave-ins without warning. This was a constant danger to all mine workers, slave or free. An entire work crew of slaves was once killed when supporting timbers gave way and the roof collapsed at the Franklin Mine in Cherokee County.[29]

Some slaves found their treatment and the dangers of mining so unbearable that, like many slaves in the antebellum South, they decided to run away. A few slaves used the gold they had hidden to help them get out of the South once they made a break for it. Area newspapers carried numerous advertisements calling for the return of runaway slaves, sometimes offering handsome rewards. A Cass County mine owner, Charles Cleghorn, announced in the *Western Herald* that a slave named Jack had escaped from his Allatoona mine. Cleghorn offered fifty dollars for the slave's return or "twenty-five dollars if lodged in any Jail." Jack was a blacksmith by trade and described as heavy-built and "light complected, but a full blooded negro." He had "a down look when spoken to," spoke "slow and somewhat stammering," and was "very fond of spirits."[30]

Another slave named Henry, apparently unhappy with his treatment, escaped from a gold mine near Auraria to which he had been leased. Nathan Cook, the mine owner, thought the eighteen-year-old slave might be headed for North Carolina, where he had lived before being brought to Georgia by a speculator. Henry was described as a tall man and, like the slave Jack, had "rather a down look, when spoken to." A reward was offered to anyone who could capture and hold Henry.[31] "A Negro Fellow by the name of John," who had worked in Auraria as a cook in the taverns of William Rogers and Robert A. Watkins, ran away from the mining operations of a man named Pinchback in October 1833. It is hardly surprising that John was more fond of cooking than of mining. Pinchback offered a ten-dollar reward for John's return.[32]

There were also advertisements announcing the capture of blacks thought for one reason or another to be escaped slaves. Typical of these is the following item from an April 1833 issue of the *Southern Banner*:[33]

NOTICE

Brought to Clayton Jail, Rabun county, on Tuesday the fifth instant, a mulatto fellow who says he is a free man, and was hired to P. Caldwell at the gold mines in Lumpkin, and was raised by James Campbell of Iredell county, North Carolina. The owner is requested to come and pay charges, and take him away.

T. M. HENSON, Jailer

It is not known what cause the jailer had to doubt this man's claim to freedom other than the color of his skin. In antebellum Georgia, where less than 1 percent of the black population was free, that was usually enough.[34]

However, not all blacks in the gold region were slaves. Though few in number, there were free blacks in the area who farmed or worked in the mines. A good many did both. This was the case with Dan and Lucinda Riley of Cherokee County, who bought their freedom from Jacob Scudder. After their emancipation the couple worked as sharecroppers and panned for gold in the vicinity of the Franklin Mine to supplement their income.[35]

Perhaps the most remarkable black man in north Georgia during the gold rush was an entrepreneur, gold miner, and part-time preacher named James Boisclair, or "Free Jim," as he was known to the residents of Dahlonega. At the height of the gold rush, Boisclair arrived in Dahlonega from Augusta and set up a small cake and fruit shop. Like other merchants before him, he quickly became interested in mining and soon began to pan for gold. Luck was with him, and he discovered a rich vein of gold ore on lot 998, just east of town. He wanted to buy the property, but as a black man the law permitted him neither to buy nor sell real estate. Dr. Joseph J. Singleton, the first superintendent of the Dahlonega Mint, agreed to serve as Boisclair's "guardian," and it was through Singleton that he bought the lot.[36]

Boisclair worked the mine successfully for nearly a decade, making enough money to establish the largest dry goods and general merchandise store in Dahlonega. He also built an icehouse, where he stored natural ice and sold it throughout the year. Located where the Dahlonega Baptist Church now stands, it was one of the most popular businesses in town, especially during hot mountain summers. Another popular Boisclair establishment was his saloon, which was so popular that he was expelled from the Baptist church "for selling spiritus liquors on the Sabbath." It is not known what sort of penance he was required to undergo, but about a year later he was "restored on recantation."[37] Another problem involved with his saloon was the difficulty he encountered in obtaining a liquor license. By state law, a "free person of color" could not hold such a license. To get around the restriction, a white person was authorized to sell liquor at the saloon "for Boisclair." The license had to be renewed on an annual basis.[38]

Despite the ability of some blacks to buy their freedom and the success of a few like James Boisclair, it is important to note that most blacks in the antebellum gold region were taken there as slaves and remained slaves. There is considerable doubt concerning the number of slaves used in the mines. Because most were transient labor, this is and must remain an open question. It can be said, however, that although some mine owners found it profitable to use slaves, this practice was not nearly as common in the gold mines of north Georgia as it was on the cotton and rice plantations of the coastal plains. Local white residents were uncomfortable with the presence of a large slave population in the vicinity, and mining companies often preferred white labor anyway. It was cheap and did not incur the responsibilities of food, clothing, and shelter associated with slavery.[39]

The use of slaves in gold mining decreased sharply in the early 1840s as the gold began to play out. Within a few years, scarcely any slaves were left in the mines. Then, in 1849, word of the great California strikes reached the gold-hungry miners of Georgia, and singularly and in groups they began a mass exodus westward. Dr. Matthew Stephenson, a geologist and assayer at the Dahlonega Mint, called for a meeting at the town square in a futile attempt to keep the miners in Georgia. Mounting the courthouse steps to address a crowd of about two hundred miners, Stephenson chastised them for allowing their heads to be turned by tall tales of gold in California. Waving his hand toward Findley Ridge, just south of Dahlonega, Stephenson shouted, "Why go to California? In that ridge lies more gold than man ever dreamt of. There's millions in it!" Despite Stephenson's admonitions, the impatient miners, black and white, left for California in droves.[40]

James Boisclair, too, was caught up by this wave of gold fever and left Dahlonega to pursue his fortune in the newly discovered gold fields of California. In 1850, he contracted with about fifty men to pay their way to the new western "El Dorado" in exchange for half their first year's earnings. Such an arrangement might have doubled or tripled his already substantial wealth, but it was not to be. When Boisclair arrived in California, he found not fortune but fate. He soon became involved in a heated argument over a claim. The quarrel turned violent, and Boisclair, age forty-six, was shot to death. But his memory lives on around Dahlonega, where the mine he worked for ten years is still known as the "Free Jim."[41]

More fortunate than James Boisclair were Dan and Lucinda Riley, the free black couple who farmed and panned for gold on the side. Though they did not strike it rich in California, they at least made a few thousand dollars and lived to return home. However, they were nearly prevented from making the journey at all. As the story goes, it was only chance that made it possible for them to try their luck in California. Like other Georgia miners, Dan and Lucinda caught gold fever in 1849 and yearned to go west, but they were much too poor to make the journey for the moment. Shortly after hearing of the California gold strike, Dan made a find of his own while panning for gold along the stream adjacent to the property of Jacob Scudder, his former master. At a certain point along the stream Dan noticed that the gold was "coarse and ragged," indicating the presence of a nearby vein. He traced the gold to its source and, on a hill bordering the stream, dug down about three feet and hit a rich quartz vein. Dan scooped up a pan of dirt from the top of the vein, panned it out, and found so much gold that, as he later said, "it looked like [I] had dug into a yellow jacket's nest."[42] His first thought was that perhaps now he and Lucinda could go to California. His second was to keep the find a secret. While digging he noticed a few of Scudder's slaves working in the distance on the other side of the river and was afraid that they might have seen him. He quickly filled in the hole and erased all trace of his work. The following day Dan sold his findings for seventy dollars, and he and Lucinda were shortly on their way to California. In their later years, after the California gold played out, they returned to Georgia with the intention of locating the rich vein that Dan had discovered so long ago. They searched the area for years, digging holes all along the stream, but they could never find the old vein. Dan told his story to Richard Carnes, a local farmer and part-time miner, who often helped the old couple in their searches. Even after Dan and Lucinda passed away, Carnes continued to look for the mine, but to no avail. The tale has been passed down for over a century, and to this day Cherokee County residents still enjoy telling the story of the "Lost Negro Mine."[43]

By the time Dan and Lucinda Riley came home, the heyday of gold mining in Georgia had long passed. Though the introduction of hydraulic mining in the 1850s resulted in a brief revival of gold fever, the coming of the Civil War saw the final collapse of gold mining as a notable industry in Georgia.[44] The miners went off to war, the mint closed, and emancipation brought freedom to the few slaves still working the mines. So scarce did blacks become in north Georgia following the war that an 1886 issue of Dahlonega's newspaper noted that there were people living in the mountains who had never seen a black person.[45] Even now there are few blacks living in what was Georgia's bustling gold region 150 years ago.[46] Aside from the traditional neglect of African American history before the 1960s, perhaps this is one reason why the role of blacks in the Georgia gold rush has been generally ignored for so long. In any case, considering the significance of their participation, voluntary and involuntary, Georgia's forgotten miners should not remain so.

NOTES

An earlier version of this essay was published in the *Georgia Historical Quarterly* 75 (spring 1991): 76–90, and is printed here with the permission of the *Georgia Historical Quarterly*.

1. Fletcher M. Green, "Georgia's Forgotten Industry: Gold Mining," *Georgia Historical Quarterly* 19 (1935): 1–19, 210–28.

2. E. Merton Coulter, *Auraria: The Story of a Georgia Gold-Mining Town* (Athens, Ga., 1956); Clair M. Birdsall, *The United States Branch Mint at Dahlonega, Georgia* (Easley, S.C., 1984); Sylvia Gailey Head and Elizabeth W. Etheridge, *The Neighborhood Mint: Dahlonega in the Age of Jackson* (Macon, Ga., 1986).

3. Editor's note: This statement was rendered outdated with the publication of the author's book, *The Georgia Gold Rush: Twenty-Niners, Cherokees, and Gold Fever* (Columbia, S.C., 1993).

4. Green and Coulter each included in their respective works some mention of African Americans, but only brief mention. Certainly the dearth of material was a factor. Even now it is difficult to make definite pronouncements or come to firm conclusions on Georgia's black miners. Documentation is fragmentary at best, and much of the evidence is little more than oral tradition. For information on slaves and gold mining elsewhere in the antebellum South, see Fletcher M. Green, "Gold Mining: A Forgotten Industry in Antebellum North Carolina," *North Carolina Historical Review* 14 (Jan. 1937): 12, 15; Fletcher M. Green, "Gold Mining in Antebellum Virginia," *Virginia Magazine of History and Biography* 45 (July 1937): 361–63; Edward W. Phifer Jr., "Champagne at Brindletown: The Story of the Burke County Gold Rush, 1829–1833," *North Carolina Historical Review* 40 (Oct. 1963): 489–500. See also John C. Inscoe, *Mountain Masters: Slavery and the Sectional Crisis in Western North Carolina* (Knoxville, Tenn., 1989), 72–79 passim; Robert S. Starobin, *Industrial Slavery in the Old South* (New York, 1970), 23–24, 214–19; Brent D. Glass, "Midas and Old Rip: The Gold Hill Mining District of North Carolina" (Ph.D. diss., Chapel Hill: University of North Carolina, 1980), 133–43.

5. A detailed discussion of this question can be found in David Williams, "Origins of the North Georgia Gold Rush," *Proceedings and Papers of the Georgia Association of Historians* 9 (1988): 161–68.

6. W.S. Yeates, S.W. McCallie, and Francis P. King, *Gold Deposits of Georgia*, Georgia Geologic Survey, Bulletin 4–A, 1896, 33.

7. Green, "Georgia's Forgotten Industry," 99.

8. *New Echota Cherokee Phoenix*, May 27, 1829.

9. *Acts of the General Assembly of the State of Georgia*, 1831 (Milledgeville, 1832), 165.

10. Mary Bondurant Warren, *Alphabetical Index to Georgia's 1832 Gold Lottery* (Danielsville, Ga., 1981), xiii-xv.

11. William Price, *Sixty Years of the Life of a Country Village Baptist Church* (Atlanta, 1897), 44.

12. Ibid.

13. *Niles' Register*, May 21, 1831.

14. "Mining Interest at the South," *Russell's Magazine* 3 (1858): 442.

15. H.B.C. Nitze and H.A.J. Wilkens, "The Present Condition of Gold Mining in the Southern Appalachian States," *Transactions of the American Institute of Mining Engineers* 25 (1895): 681.

16. "Reminiscences of Miss Fanny Wood," in *History of Lumpkin County for the First Hundred Years, 1832–1932*, ed. Andrew W. Cain (1932; reprint, Spartanburg, S.C., 1984), 53.

17. Green, "Georgia's Forgotten Industry," 218.

18. John C. Calhoun to James Edward Calhoun, Sept. 23, 1835, in *The Papers of John C. Calhoun*, vol. 12, ed. Clyde N. Wilson (Columbia, S.C., 1979), 555.

19. *(Milledgeville) Georgia Journal*, Dec. 14, 1833; William P. Blake and Charles T. Jackson, *Gold Placers in the Vicinity of Dahlonega, Georgia* (Boston, 1859), 7.

20. Nitze and Wilkens, "Gold Mining in the Southern Appalachian States," 681.

21. *Augusta State Rights' Sentinel*, Feb. 16, 1836.

22. *Auraria Western Herald*, Jan. 31, 1834.

23. Ibid., April 9, 1833.

24. *Niles' Register*, Aug. 7, 1830.

25. George G. Ward, *The Annals of Upper Georgia Centered in Gilmer County* (Nashville, Tenn., 1965), 105.

26. Minutes of the Superior Court of Lumpkin County, Aug. 22, 1833, Georgia Department of Archives and History, Atlanta (hereinafter cited as GDAH).

27. Mary L. Church, *The Hills of Habersham* (Clarksville, Ga., 1962), 11.

28. Forest C. Wade, *Cry of the Eagle: History and Legends of the Cherokee Indians and Their Buried Treasures* (Cumming, Ga., 1969), 79.

29. Roy E. Bottoms, "History of the Franklin Gold Mine," *Northwest Georgia Historical and Genealogical Society Quarterly* 5 (Oct. 1973): 4; Lloyd G. Marlin, *History of Cherokee County* (Atlanta, 1932), 147.

30. *Western Herald*, Sept. 21, 1833. This description of slave mannerisms is revealing in that the mannerisms described are typical of the way slaves were encouraged to behave. Blacks quickly learned to assume a posture of submission when spoken to by any white person. For a slave to speak back in a quick and lively manner was considered "uppity," and any violation of this slave society etiquette resulted in severe punishment. Alcohol served as a temporary, if infrequent, escape from the slaves' harsh existence.

31. Ibid., Sept. 28, 1833.

32. Ibid., Oct. 26, 1833.

33. *Athens Southern Banner*, April 13, 1833.

34. Kenneth Coleman, ed., *A History of Georgia* (Athens, Ga., 1977), 185.

35. Wade, *Cry of the Eagle*, 79.

36. Price, *Sixty Years of a Country Baptist Church*, 18; Yeates, McCallie, and King, *Gold Deposits of Georgia*, 439; Head and Etheridge, *Neighborhood Mint*, 33.

37. *Dahlonega Nugget*, June 1, 1917; Price, *Sixty Years of a Country Baptist Church*, 18; Yeates, McCallie, and King, *Gold Deposits of Georgia*, 439.

38. Liquor Selling Licenses, Court of Ordinary, Lumpkin County, Georgia, GDAH.

39. George W. Paschal, *Ninety-Four Years: Agnes Paschal* (1871; reprint, Spartanburg, S.C., 1974), 277.

40. *Dahlonega Nugget*, Feb. 19, 1897; Yeates, McCallie, and King, *Gold Deposits of Georgia*, 274–75. The miners did not take Stephenson's advice, but they took his impassioned phrase with them. "There's millions in it" became a well-known saying among the California miners, and it kept them digging there even if it did not inspire hope on Findley Ridge. This phrase, which was

eventually picked up by Mark Twain and attributed to his character Mulberry Sellers, gave rise to the more widely known cry, "Thar's gold in them thar hills."

41. "Dahlonega, Georgia," *Engineering and Mining Journal* 99 (Jan. 16, 1915): 170; Price, *Sixty Years of a Country Baptist Church*, 11; Yeates, McCallie, and King, *Gold Deposits of Georgia*, 439. There is some uncertainty concerning Boisclair's age at the time of his death. The 1850 census gives an age of forty-six, but the "Register of Free Persons of Color" in Lumpkin County two years earlier reads "about fifty-three years of age." GDAH, microfilm roll no. MC 166–27. The latter would place his age in 1850 at fifty-five.

42. Wade, *Cry of the Eagle*, 79.

43. Ibid., 79–80.

44. Georgia did experience a second gold rush at the turn of the century, but it lasted less than a decade.

45. *Mountain Signal*, Aug. 6, 1886, in Cain, *History of Lumpkin County*, 343.

46. Blacks constitute less than 10 percent of the population in Georgia north of Fulton County. See Thomas W. Hodler and Howard A. Schretter, *The Atlas of Georgia* (Athens, Ga., 1986), 201.

4

SLAVERY IN THE
KANAWHA SALT INDUSTRY

JOHN E. STEALEY III

In the first years of the nineteenth century, a great salt lick in far western Virginia became the site of one of the most significant premodern manufacturing operations in antebellum Appalachia—the Kanawha salt industry. Located along a ten-mile stretch of a major Ohio River tributary, the Great Kanawha, at Kanawha Salines, two or three miles above Charleston, Virginia (later to be West Virginia), it accounted for an almost unparalleled enterprise that served the seemingly insatiable demands of an expanding western market for a commodity that was essential for life, processing, and preservation. Although other sources of salt existed, none rivaled the Kanawha brine in ensuring the emergence of large-scale economic development, rural and urban, in the Ohio River basin. Agricultural prosperity in the West and the growth of the pork-packing industry at Cincinnati, Louisville, and other river towns could not have happened without the salt extracted from the Kanawha Salines.

Only in 1808, after a decade-long series of legal disputes over the property their father had acquired and several years of experimentation, did Joseph Ruffner's sons first successfully establish a drilling operation to excavate the brine that they found concentrated along the river's northern bank. At the same time they constructed the first of what would become many salt furnaces to process the brine into usable and marketable salt. Their operation expanded so dramatically that by 1810 the salt factories on the Great Kanawha constituted the nation's largest salt production area.

From the War of 1812, Kanawha manufacturers, not having sufficient white labor available, relied primarily on slaves for their workforce. The phenomenal growth of the salt industry and its economic opportunities attracted slave owners as furnace proprietors and lessors of chattels. The resultant slave society that emerged there was unusual in the antebellum South: bondsmen located in the Appalachian Mountains produced an extractive commodity for interstate commerce.[1] Initially, slaves came to the Great Kanawha Valley from Kentucky and piedmont Virginia, but as time passed, most slaves came from eastern Virginia.[2] The western Virginia salt industry drew labor from the commonwealth's tobacco economy, which was in decline.[3] Most slaves were hirelings, as some large eastern slaveholders had leasing agents on the Kanawha, and many salt companies annually sent representatives to the piedmont to rent slaves.[4] Legal agreements between eastern Virginia entrepreneurs who entered the salt business often provided for shared furnishing of slave labor.

Keeping pace with the growing demands of the salt industry between 1810 and 1850, the slave population of Kanawha County grew rapidly. From 1810 to 1820 the number of slaves in the county more than tripled, growing from 352 to 1,073. In succeeding decades the growth rate was slower. From 1820 to 1830 slave numbers increased 60 percent to 1,717. The 1830s and 1840s saw growth rates of 49 and 22 percent respectively. In 1850 the slave population reached its peak at 3,140 slaves. The rate of demographic increase of slaves was more impressive when compared with the growth of the white citizenry, which was much slower: from 1810 to 1820, the population grew from 3,468 to 5,297, a 53 percent increase; the 1820s and 1830s saw a 42 and 44 percent increase, respectively; in the 1840s the rate slowed to 10 percent, with 12,001 white residents recorded in the county in 1850.[5]

Although slave numbers were substantial, the slave population numbers are not absolute: the numbers of slaves associated with the Kanawha industry far exceeded fixed census figures. Slaves were often transient, passing in and out of the valley individually and in groups. Many furnace operators moved their owned or leased chattels at will, usually on an annual basis, by redeployment to other occupations, nonrenewal of leases, or sale. When Harry Heth, a well-known Manchester, Virginia, coal operator, his son-in-law Beverley Randolph, and Samuel G. Adams entered the salt business with high hopes in December 1814, Heth and Randolph agreed to furnish thirty-six "Negroe men," and Adams would augment the number as required.[6] Within four months, Randolph, who acted as resident manager and overseer, saw that the partnership had entered an economic quagmire and started to extricate it from the business. The slaves who had been reluctant to come to the Kanawha were eager to return to the Richmond area. In reply to Heth's expressed desire for a group of ten to remain and for the others to return, Randolph warned, "No 10 will be more willing to stay than any other 10. They all despise this place as much as I do, & more they can not." However, in January 1814 William Dickinson and Joel Shrewsbury, a piedmont Virginia partnership, moved slaves they owned and leased to their salt property; many of those slaves and their offspring remained there until the Civil War.[7] Although hired slaves could be transferred quickly, many remained on the Kanawha for years or even decades, usually with several different manufacturers.

Salt makers employed slaves in all phases of the manufacturing process and in all subsidiary activities necessary to support a salt furnace. Most tasks performed by hired and company-owned slaves were routine, but some required a high degree of skill. One completely integrated salt furnace operation that did not contract for coal and barrel deliveries required twenty-three to thirty-three slaves. A two-furnace factory needed approximately double that number. In 1854 James Cowey, a manager of two salt furnaces, deposed that of sixty-four laborers under his control, fifty-eight were slaves. Testifying in 1853, veteran salt maker Richard C.M. Lovell estimated the employment of hands at

View of the salt works on the Kanawha. (From Henry Howe, *The Historical Collections of Virginia* [1845])

two salt furnaces as fourteen coal diggers; five wheelers, who wheeled coal from the interior of the mine to its mouth; four haulers, who hauled coal by team on the railroad tramway from the mine mouth to the furnace; three kettle tenders; one or two "cat-hole" cleaners, who cleaned the coal ash repository; six engineers, who ran steam engines to pump brine from the well; two salt lifters and wheelers, who lifted the salt from the pan after evaporation and wheeled the product to the packing shed; seven "jim arounds" and packers, who served as general laborers and firemen and who placed salt into barrels for shipment; two blacksmiths; one "negro man sort of manager"; and one cook.[8]

To attain optimum production capabilities and return on plant investment, salt makers ran their furnaces twenty-four hours per day and, if they chose to incur the risk of arrest and overproduction, seven days per week. Although police regulations forbade labor on Sunday and established six days as the legal length of the work week, producers usually disobeyed this laxly enforced prohibition. At times, depressed salt prices occasioned by overproduction forced Kanawha manufacturers to agree mutually to "blow out" their furnaces on Sunday. In these periods, community pressure caused the justices of the peace to enforce the law. In 1841 Nathaniel Hatch, a justice who held court in the Terra Salis Presbyterian Church, fined a number of producers for breaking the Sabbath by working and by forcing their slaves to work.[9]

Salt manufacturers offered monetary incentives to factory slaves (except coal diggers) to work without days of rest, and these payments became recognized by custom. The firms paid hired and owned slaves an extra amount for Sabbath labor. The manager carried the accumulated amounts on the books during the year and paid the whole sum to the slave on Christmas Day. A former coal-bank manager noted, "The coal diggers generally dug their coal for Sunday's run on Saturday; but it was paid for extra. It was generally hauled to the furnace on Sunday. The other hands . . . were actually employed on Sunday." Over a five-year period Thomas Friend paid between $1,200 and $1,482 annually for extra Sunday work to thirty-five to forty hands.[10] When Joel Shrewsbury returned leased slaves to Bedford County, Virginia, in 1816, he asked his partner to furnish the slaves certain items of clothing. He also instructed, "You will let Reuben & Frank have the amt set against each of their names in Store goods it being for Cord Wood cut by them of Nights & C." Shrewsbury expected one and a half cords of wood per slave per day. In 1818, Shrewsbury made similar requests to his Bedford partner: "Please pay the negroe boys in Store Goods as follows Viz Spence Nine & half Dollars Tom Six & half Dollars & Abram Four Dollars for labour of Sunday & Christmas &c." Manufacturers frequently operated their furnaces during the Christmas season. Slaves received direct extra payment for this holiday work.[11]

Owners and managers could project the production of a furnace for a certain operating period, barring breakdowns and accidents. They knew the amount of fuel and the number of barrels that were needed for efficient operation, and they could set production goals for labor. A stable and predictable labor supply and work system met these requirements and goals. Kanawha manufacturers universally adopted the task system in the Salines to measure production and to reduce managerial costs. John D. Lewis, who had manufactured salt since 1832, testified in 1854 in a court case that, on the Kanawha, "we operate a furnace by task work, a coal digger has a prescribed quantity of coal to dig, a hauler, a salt packer a prescribed quantity to pack, and engineer, and kettle tender a certain time to be on watch."[12]

Despite the use of the task system, owners maintained a managerial hierarchy. In an integrated salt manufacturing facility, a manager (overseer), boss kettle tender, coal-bank manager, and, in some cases, a well tender composed the supervisory personnel. Resident owners acted as general superintendents and handled sales but left the active management to overseers. Managerial personnel were responsible for meeting the goals of production and for repairing the machinery and equipment.[13] Usually white men occupied supervisory positions, but there is evidence that slaves sometimes performed managerial functions. In the furnaces operated by Thomas Friend, two slaves held the important positions of boss kettle tender and overseer. In an inventory of hands, Tom, the boss kettle tender, was adjudged as very skillful in maintaining and repairing the furnace. Simon, age thirty-three, was appraised: "Kean, stout; salt well tuber, engine repairer, salt-maker and overseer experienced, skilful, and industrious."[14]

Slave ownership and leasing reached a high point in the Kanawha salt industry in 1850, according to the census that year.[15] The census schedule listing products of industry gives thirty-three salt companies, but only twenty-seven appear as possessors of slaves in the schedule of slave inhabitants in

Making salt at Saltville, Virginia. (From Edward King, *The Southern States of America*, vol. 3 [1875])

Kanawha County. The six missing companies, Kleason and Downward, C.W. Atkinson, Norton and Kline, William and Jones, Shrewsbury and Fitzhugh, and Warth and English, reported a combined average monthly total of 133 male workers. We can assume that at least a hundred of these workers were slaves because the proportion would be consistent with the number of slaves in the total workforce of other enumerated firms. The census schedules of slave inhabitants also do not denote whether the slaves in the possession of salt companies were leased or owned. The accuracy of the reporting of the slaves' ages in the census returns cannot be assured, although experienced hirers and users who enumerated slaves in their possession would be approximately correct. Nor were factors such as physical condition and work skill of slaves recognized or recorded. For example, a fifty-year-old slave who was a kettle tender or blacksmith might have been more desirable for a salt company to retain than a twenty-five-year-old laborer.

Generalizations about prime hands are hazardous, but it could be conceded that slaves between fifteen and thirty-nine years old were in greater demand, as most labor around the salt furnace was physically rigorous. In trans-

Allegheny Virginia, Kanawha County had the highest slave population in 1850: 3,140 persons. Of this total, 1,902 were male, and 1,238 were female. Salt firms controlled and possessed at least 1,497 of the total. Adding the one hundred slave hands presumed to have been controlled by the six salt companies mentioned above, one can conclude that over one-half of all slaves in Kanawha County were controlled by the salt industry centered at Kanawha Salines. Based on 1850 census data, salt manufacturing firms retained 60 percent of all male slaves and 29 percent of all female slaves in Kanawha County. Of the slaves owned by salt firms, 76 percent were male. Of all male slaves held by the salt manufacturers, 34 percent were between the ages of twenty and twenty-nine, and 21 percent were from thirty to thirty nine. Hence, 55 percent of all male slaves were in the prime labor age category. If one extended the prime male slave category to include the group aged fifteen to nineteen, 64 percent of all male slaves held by salt companies would be considered prime workmen. Of the total number of slaves, male and female, retained by the salt companies, 49 percent were males between the ages of fifteen and thirty-nine.

Slave family units did exist to some extent. Female slaves had limited use in the domestic establishment of the enterprise: some worked as cooks. Women over fifteen years numbered only 186 and comprised 51 percent of the female slave population in the salt business. Of the total number of slaves held by the salt companies, 364, or 24 percent, were males and females under fifteen. As in the southern slave population as a whole, the numbers of males and females in the under-fifteen group on the Kanawha were approximately equal. The male-to-female ratios in the other age groups differed markedly: fifteen to nineteen, 3.5:1; twenty to twenty-nine, 5.5:1; thirty to thirty-nine, 6.8:1; forty to forty-nine, 5.3:1; fifty to fifty-nine, 4.1:1; and over fifty-nine, 1.9:1.[16] There is a definite correlation between the largest salt firms and manufacturers, measured both in total production and in total slave possession, and the control of slave women and children. The largest salt companies, which included the oldest in the industry, held most of the slave women and children. The top seven firms in slave possession controlled 57 percent of all slaves held by salt manufacturers in 1850 and 50 percent of the males over fourteen. These same firms held 69 percent of all females and 71 percent of the slaves of both sexes under the age of fifteen. Operators of single furnaces could not support many slaves under fifteen or many family units. Newer companies and short-term entrepreneurs had not been in operation long enough, nor had they the resources, to accumulate slave families. Firms or manufacturers on leased property would rent prime labor in order to maximize profits, to maintain annual flexibility, and to withdraw easily upon expiration of the lease. For example, James S.O. Brooks leased a furnace from Luke Willcox in 1845 for an eight-year term.[17] In 1850 he possessed forty-nine male and four female slaves, and all the females were between fifteen and thirty-nine years old.

In 1850, Dickinson & Shrewsbury, one of the two oldest salt manufacturing companies, was the largest slave user, holding 232 slaves, 195 males and 37 females. In 1855, when the partnership dissolved, it owned or had an interest in 128 slaves, 93 males and 35 females. The relatively constant number of female slaves suggests that family units existed. The 104 fewer slaves, almost all male, displayed the level of slave leasing in 1850 and some attrition by sale and death. Analysis of the 1855 Dickinson and Shrewsbury slave inventory reveals the existence of family units. The list gives ages for only one group of sixteen slaves and does not indicate male kinship ties, only noting relationships between mother and child and between grandmother and grandchild.[18]

Of the 128 slaves held by Dickinson and Shrewsbury in 1855, 68 were associated with nine separate common female ancestors; 55 were single men, though several may be related to one or more of the common female ancestor groups; and 5 were single women. The best-documented family group descended from a woman named Fann. The partnership had purchased a half interest in Fann on April 14, 1814, from John Lacy of Franklin County, Virginia. Joel Shrewsbury traveled to Guilford County, North Carolina, where he individually purchased the other half interest. He noted that "the wench is heavy with child."[19] Fann bore ten children, six boys and four girls, who in 1855 ranged in age from twenty-five to forty-five. The two oldest were described as "mulatto," and the remainder "black." The oldest female was sold, and the youngest male had died. Two daughters, Rachel and Elija, had borne respectively two and four grandchildren, aged from a few months to eighteen years. Of Fann's descendants living in 1855, ten were male and four were female. Of the remaining eight maternal ancestors, three women account for thirty-five of the fifty-four slaves in family groups. Four of the women had surnames: Jane Turner, Lucinda McCommas, Marcella Sharpe, and Sally Burke (deceased). Few other slaves on the list had last names. Of the 128 Dickinson and Shrewsbury slaves in 1855, at least thirty-eight males and twenty females were part of the nine family groups.

Most salt firms exclusively employed their chattels in the salt furnace and allied activities. Dickinson and Shrewsbury's effective integration of manufacturing with an extensive agricultural enterprise, however, probably made it the most efficient user of slave labor of all the salt companies. From the time of Joel Shrewsbury's arrival in the Salines in 1814, the firm acquired some of the best agricultural land in the valley. Besides vertically integrating its own furnace operations by cutting its own wood and later mining its own coal, it sold its surplus to others. It constructed its own factories, buildings, barns, outbuildings, and houses.

It established a blacksmith shop (with slave labor) that performed all the firm's work and much for other producers. Its slaves cleared land, raised livestock (the firm speculated in hogs and cattle), and engaged in extensive cultivation of the bottomlands. After a few years Dickinson and Shrewsbury annually raised four thousand bushels of corn. Management shifted its slaves from factory to farm as needed. In 1820 Shrewsbury wrote that he ran two salt furnaces, five or six plantations, a sawmill and gristmill, and a blacksmith shop.[20]

Many slaves held by the Kanawha salt industry were hirelings, but the exact number cannot be determined. In his pioneering work on industrial slavery, Robert S. Starobin concluded that four-fifths of industrial bondsmen in the Old South were company-owned. On the Kanawha, the proportion of owned slaves was much lower, as demonstrated by Dickinson and Shrewsbury, which controlled 232 slaves in 1850 but owned only 128 in 1856, when the partnership was dissolved. One could assume that about a hundred slaves were leased, as Dickinson and Shrewsbury was an active producer until its dissolution. Frequently 30 to 45 percent of a salt company's slave labor force was leased, and in some cases the proportion was as high as 90 percent. One physician-manufacturer stated, "The larger proportion is hired, taking all the furnaces."[21] Leased slaves in the Kanawha salt industry would exceed 50 percent of all slave labor controlled by manufacturers in any given year.

Hire or lease agreements between bailor and bailee in the leasing of slave labor in the salt industry were as diverse as the desires of the contracting parties and reflect the adjustment of the institution to an industrial situation.[22] In the typical hire agreement, verbal or written, the bailee agreed to treat the property humanely, to provide a certain standard of clothing and medical attention, and to pay all taxes. Slaves were usually hired for the period from January to December 25. Hired slaves, by custom, were usually returned to their owners on Christmas or the day before with a blanket and winter clothing. A general slave holiday lasted from Christmas to New Year's Day.

Some slaveholders enhanced their investment by arranging for the instruction of their slaves in trades or occupations useful in the salt industry. Samuel Hannah hired a young slave to a blacksmith for a four-year term for a yearly rent of fifty dollars. The blacksmith bound himself "to teach & learn the said Boy Preston to the best of his skill & judgment the Blacksmiths trade in all its various branches of business and to keep the said boy employed at no other business of work." Three slaves were hired to salt maker Samuel H. Early "to be allowed a Reasonable time to learn to cooper." If they could not become coopers, the slaves could be employed at other labor. A slave named Tom was hired by his master to a producer "to spend part of his time learning the Coopers trade."[23]

One of the safest and most common employments for slaves at the Salines was in the manufacture of barrels for packing salt. The standard slave task was the assembling of seven barrels per day, or 2,142 barrels in a year.[24] William H. Alpin hired two slave coopers, Henry and Ananias, on an incentive basis from the trustees of the estate of L.C. Lett. In addition to paying for medical bills, clothing, taxes, and food, Alpin promised to pay the slaves "ten cents for each and all barrels they shall have made over forty two each week." Several bailors prevented the overexertion of their slaves in manufacturing barrels by inserting restrictive provisions in the lease agreement. Richard, a cooper owned by Samuel B. Brown, was required to assemble only six barrels per day. Of course, such a provision could be interpreted as a requirement for a minimum level of performance. John Waid agreed not to demand hired slaves "when they labor to make more than six barrels per day each."[25] Many lease contracts specified that certain slaves would be employed only in the cooperage trade, so that owners or managers of salt furnaces could not force the slave cooper to work in a more dangerous job.[26]

With the exception of coopering, occupations in the salt industry were hazardous. Coal mining was the most dangerous of all nineteenth-century employments. Slaves were the laborers in the coal banks that supplied the fuel for salt furnaces, and many black coal miners met savage accidents and deaths. In 1844 Luke Willcox wrote in his diary that his slave Isam had his "Arm Broke by Slate and coal falling on him." The master immediately sent for medical aid, but he later tersely noted the outcome: "Isam died about 7 o'clock in the Evening." In a court case in which a doctor was suing a salt manufacturer for a medical fee, a physician's assistant related a gruesome accident. The slave treated was injured in a roof fall, "a very bad one." His thigh was broken, his arm was fractured in two places, one above and one below the elbow, and crushed, and one hand was mangled, with two fingers removed.[27]

Aware of the inherent dangers of mining, some slaveholders stipulated that a lessee could not work the valuable property in coal mines. George W. Summers forced the salt company that leased his slave Jim to agree to several prohibitions: "The negro man Jim is not to be worked in Coal Bank or as a kettle-tender, nor to be compelled to work on Sundays."[28] Prohibitions forbidding slaves from working in unsafe pursuits did not restrain salt makers or managers. A woman sued Lewis Ruffner for eight hundred dollars in damages when her slave was killed in a roof fall in Ruffner's mine. The plaintiff contended that Ruffner had agreed not to employ the slave in his coal mines. On January 1, 1832, Charles G. Reynolds hired two slaves, Lewis and Harry, from Ann Pollard for one hundred dollars apiece. During the term of bailment, the slave Lewis was "suffocated, crushed, and killed" in Reynolds's coal bank. Pollard said that her slave was killed in September 1832. She asserted that Reynolds had promised that he intended to use the slaves to tend kettles. Lewis was appraised at seven hundred dollars, and as a result of being deprived of "divers great gains and profits" by his death, the plaintiff sued for one thousand dollars in damages. The defendant entered a general demurrer to each count of the declaration and pleaded *non assumpsit*.[29]

In a separate case, Pollard again sued Reynolds, this time for the two hundred dollars in rent for Lewis and Harry. Reynolds showed that Lewis was killed in the coal mine on January 18, 1832, seventeen days after his hiring, without any fault on the defendant's part. Declaring that he was willing to pay for the hire of Harry, the defendant claimed a credit for ninety-five dollars for the loss of services caused by the death of Lewis for the remainder of the term of hire. The jury upheld the claims of Reynolds and awarded Pollard $105 and costs.[30] Although this case leaves much unsaid, it is instructive. The distance between owner and slave when the bondsman was hired to a salt manufacturer is apparent. Pollard, though she lived in Kanawha County, did not know when her slave was killed or the circumstances of his demise.

The machinery and highly heated brine of a salt furnace provided many inherent dangers for the unwary novice and the careless workman. Loss of balance around the grainer pan could result in a fall into the nearly boiling water. One of Luke Willcox's slaves, Mid, was so severely scalded and burned in such an accident that he died.[31] Boiler explosions around the steam engines occurred frequently. In 1845 James Cowey and Company hired a slave named Frank to haul coal from its mines to its salt furnace. When the company later used the slave in tending a steam engine, the boiler exploded and killed him. The owner, Edward C. Murphy, sued for the value of the slave plus damages, contending that the boiler was defective. The accident occurred on Sunday, when the slave was working contrary to law, as salt evaporation was not a household duty "of daily necessity." After litigation lasting from 1848 to 1852, the jury in the circuit superior court found for the plaintiff, awarding him $739.75 in damages plus interest from December 4, 1852.[32]

Wiley P. Woods, the hiring agent for the plaintiff, stated that he had hired the slave, Frank, to Stuart Robinson of James Cowey and Company during the Christmas holidays of 1844 for one hundred dollars a year. The agent had never seen this particular slave before, and Frank was the last slave hired by the agent in the Kanawha Salines that year. Woods understood that the slave had been in Kanawha County only one year and had been employed by George Warth as a car driver in his coal banks. Warth had refused to give the agent the full price of the hire for the young man because he considered him an inexperienced hand. In the lease to James Cowey and Company, Woods secured no written contract but understood that Frank would be used as a driver of a coal car. The agent described the slave as a young Negro of small size, "rather below ordinary . . . delicate looking." He estimated his value at $500-550 in 1847.[33]

Edward Turnbull, a native of Great Britain and a "practical Engineer of Locomotive & Stationary Engines," managed James Cowey and Company manufacturing operations from 1845 to 1848. He controlled all slave labor at the furnace. Turnbull employed Frank at hauling coal, packing salt, and wheeling salt, but he found him too weak to perform these tasks efficiently. The manager then placed Frank on the steam engine as an operator, where the work was lighter. He attended the steam engine until the boiler explosion. On Sunday morning, March 7, 1847, at four or five o'clock, the steam engine was stopped because Frank's slave partner, John, had boiled the boiler dry, melting the lead rivets in the bottom. Turnbull worked from the time that the engine stopped until one o'clock in the afternoon replacing the rivets. He then started the engine again. Turnbull ran the engine for one hour before placing John on duty, as it was his turn. (John and Frank had alternate six-hour shifts through a twenty-four-hour period.) Turnbull remained with John for five minutes and then left. Fifteen minutes after his departure, the boiler exploded. In the interval before the explosion, John had left the scene, and Frank had entered the engine house, where he was killed by the blast. The manager, upon hearing the explosion, ran back to the site and saw Frank dead, but he did not find John immediately. Turnbull testified that the slaves stayed in a cabin 100 feet from the engine when not on duty but that the company did not confine them there.[34]

The location of the salt industry on the Great Kanawha River, which furnished so many advantages for transportation, was a mixed blessing for slave owners. The westward-flowing Kanawha River furnished the bondsman an avenue of escape to the free state of Ohio, and accidental drowning was an ever-present threat, as the manufacturing center straddled the Kanawha River. Ann and Martin P. Brooks hired a slave named Lewis to Hewitt, Ruffner, and Company to be used as a blacksmith, kettle tender, or coal digger or in any other work connected with salt manufacture. The company promised to use Lewis in a "reasonable and moderate manner." The Brooks family alleged that the company forced the slave to board a steamboat to labor "without the knowledge or consent of the owners." After completing blacksmith work aboard the *Tuckahoe*, Lewis became intoxicated, fell overboard, and drowned. His owners sued the company. John Hays, a clerk of the steamboat, maintained that Lewis was not on the boat when he became intoxicated and drowned. Upon being cross-examined by the plaintiff's counsel, Hays could not definitely establish the departure of the slave from the boat, as thirty blacks, whom he could not identify, were working around the steamer. This point determined the decision of the jury, which awarded the owners one thousand dollars in damages for the full value of the slave.[35]

The overland flight of slaves from the saltworks to Ohio occurred frequently. In 1827 Joel Shrewsbury surmised that a slave belonging to William Brooks, Isaac, had received advice and provisions from a bondsman of James Gilbert's. Both slaves, he guessed, had fled to Ohio. He thought that two discreet men could capture them if they spent enough money, but he warned that "neither fools nor Misers will ever be able to get runaway Negroes in the corrupted S[tate of] Ohio." After the holiday season in 1834, there was a rash of escapes. Judge Lewis Summers reported to his brother in January 1835 that "there seems to be some restlessness among the slaves of the salt works, and I thought more uneasiness in relation to that species of property than usual." Two slaves had fled from a Mr. Fitzhugh. "On the happening of this occurrence, he shipped all the residue of his slaves to Natches and the lower markets." Moses M. Fuqua "lost three of his black boys," but two were recovered and "pretty efficient measures adopted for the recovery" of the other one. In 1844 Lewis Ruffner advertised the escape of Gatewood, "supposed to be 25 or 26 years old, about 5 feet 7 inches high, tolerably black, speaks gruff when spoken to." Gatewood had run away from Ruffner's coal mine. "There is reason to suppose that he is lurking about in the neighborhood, but may if not soon taken up, make for Ohio." A Monroe County, Virginia, resident advised the law firm to which he was sending a slave to be sold to meet legal expenses to lodge the bondsman "in jail for greater Security and that no notice Should be given him as I think he will be disposed to run."[36]

Salt maker John J. Cabell experienced much difficulty with one slave who desired to secure his freedom by escaping to Ohio. Black Jack ran away from the Cabell furnace to Ohio, but he was captured and placed in jail at Point Pleasant. After paying seventy dollars in expenses to retake Jack from the Mason County jail, Cabell tried to sell him on the Ohio River, but no one wanted to buy a slave who was likely to flee. On the first night of the journey back to the Salines, Jack escaped again. He was soon captured a second time in Ohio. After expending another eighty-five dollars, Cabell lodged Black Jack in the Kanawha County jail, "awaiting an opportunity to Selling him to be carried to New Orleans."[37]

One slaveholder in Kanawha County protected his property from drowning or escape by water by inserting a restrictive clause in lease agreements. Salt producers who leased his slave promised "not [to] suffer s[ai]d Negro or go on the river in any kind [of] Craft for employment." Other slave owners were not so cautious. Francis Thompson leased a slave girl for service on the steamboat *Daniel Webster*.[38] The steamboat, the primary vehicle of transportation of people and goods other than salt, was a corrosive influence on the institution of slavery at the Salines. Steamers frequently employed slaves as stewards and cooks. Such slaves enjoyed a degree of freedom unavailable to laborers at salt furnaces. The steamboat transported ideas as well as merchandise. Contact with "liberated" slaves who transferred knowledge of distant Ohio ports could erode discipline. To fleeing slaves, boats furnished the possibility of quick mobility that overland flight did not. The presence of steamboats provided another motive for owners to keep their chattels away from river craft.[39]

The Great Kanawha that so advantageously carried the produce of the Salines down its current brought an ascending, unwelcome visitor when the steamship eased two-way intercourse with Ohio River towns. The unwelcome visitor was Asiatic cholera, a dreaded scourge in the nineteenth century. Caused by the bacterial toxin *Vibrio chlolerae*, the waterborne, infectious disease inflicted upon its victims violent diarrhea and spasmodic vomiting, muscular cramps, dehydration (often cyanosis), and eventual collapse, and was a serious threat to life. Its effects ranged from extreme illness to death within a few hours or days.[40]

The first major epidemic of Asiatic cholera occurred in the United States and in the Kanawha Salines in 1832. The disease was introduced into Atlantic seaports and passed to the Ohio River via the Great Lakes and the Ohio Canal.[41] Diary and manuscript accounts indicate that slaves were more affected by the epidemic than white residents of the Salines. In October 1832 a Charleston newspaper reported that three slaves had died of the disease. Joel Shrewsbury reported the same three deaths at the same furnace. He had heard that three steamboats had attempted to land with cholera victims at Charleston and that municipal authorities had refused to permit them to stop. Commenting on the presence of cholera in mid-November, John Cabell, salt maker and physician, lamented the loss of one of his slaves and reported that the effect of the disease was abating somewhat; the new cases appeared to be milder and many slaves were recovering. At the end of the month he wrote that there had not been any new cases for several days.[42]

In the summers of 1833 and 1834 cholera again arrived at the Salines. In July 1833, Dr. Cabell, who would himself succumb to the disease in a later year, wrote to his wife in Lynchburg, Virginia, that "the people dying around us everyday more or less with that fatal Epedimic the Cholera." Business was suspended at the saltworks and the towns along the Ohio. Over half of the salt furnaces had stopped production because of the desertion of the labor force. Cabell reported that five or six of his slaves, including his carriage driver, had the disease. In the summer of 1834 the *Kanawha Banner* noted that cholera had killed a number of Negroes at the Salines.[43]

The most serious epidemic of Asiatic cholera spread to Kanawha County in 1849. This attack claimed an estimated three hundred lives in the county between April and August 1849. During May, diarist and salt producer Luke Willcox counted forty-five deaths in the Salines alone. Willcox departed for a timely vacation at Blue Sulphur Springs on June 22, and in a seven-day interval between his departure and his receipt of a letter from home, thirty people had expired. In mid-July, Willcox estimated that approximately one hundred people had died from cholera just in the Salines.[44]

During the 1849 epidemic, a clerk in the John R. Smith and Company store in Malden kept a cholera death register in which he recorded all expirations that occurred on the Great Kanawha from Elk River to the upper saltworks, about a ten-mile stretch. He noted that the first phase of the scourge began on May 1 at Tinkersville and lasted four weeks. Thirty-nine deaths resulted. His register encompassed the second phase, which began on June 19 and ended on August 23 with the death of prominent salt manufacturer Levi Welch. The clerk recorded the place of death, sometimes the victim's name or occupation, the victim's race, whether the victim was an adult or a child, and the sex of adults only. Including Charleston, seventy-eight people died, thirty-one whites and forty-seven blacks. Excluding Charleston, where no salt was made and sixteen whites and four blacks died, all other deaths occurred in the salt manufacturing district. Of these fifty-eight deaths, fifteen of the victims were white, and forty-three were slaves.[45]

The existence of cholera and its effects caused some litigation and adaptation of slave-hire agreements. On behalf of Zalinda L. Davis, agent John McConihay hired a slave named Jack to Crockett Ingles, a salt maker, for the year 1849. Ingles had agreed to return the slave to his owner in the event of a cholera epidemic. When the disease struck the locality in the late spring of 1849, Ingles refused to surrender Jack. Jack contracted cholera and expired on July 10. Upon this slave's death, Ingles's other hired slaves fled to their homes in eastern Virginia. Jack's owner successfully sued Ingles in the circuit court because of noncompliance with the verbal agreement.[46]

After the 1849 outbreak, agreements for hire almost invariably contained provisions for slave safety in case of a cholera epidemic. Martha Stone of Bedford City, Virginia, hired out two slaves, Jim and John, for $325 for the year 1850 with a reservation: "It is further understood that if the cholera should reappear in the salt works during the present year that Mrs. Stone or her agent has permission to withdraw the said negroes deducting for the time so lost at the rate of $325 a year." Warth and English promised to remove a hired slave "should the cholera prevail," with the owner's deducting the time lost from the rent.[47]

In the summer of 1850 Asiatic cholera again struck the Salines. During ten days ending on July 5, a salt maker recorded that eighteen people died in the Salines. The clerk who kept the 1849 register kept an identical tabulation in 1850. Between June 27 and September 2 he recorded sixteen deaths, all in the Salines: five white males and eleven slaves, of which eight were men and three were women. Again slaves suffered more. During the brief visitation, Green, a slave belonging to a John Potter of Franklin County, Virginia, ran away to his home from the salt firm of Warth and English. Advising the owner to retain Green because of the possibility of future flight to Ohio, the firm minimized the alarm of disease as a motive by asserting that the runaway "only used it as a pretext to make a call on his old friends in Franklin."[48]

In all phases of slave life on the Kanawha, what the individual slave thought is difficult to determine. We can consider only acts. No words have survived. Correspondence among the salt makers reveals that owned and hired slaves from piedmont Virginia who did not wish to move from their homes to the Kanawha resisted however they could. In 1819, when Harry Heth marched a coffle from Manchester under the care of an overseer to hire to salt makers, three slaves escaped their chains in Buckingham County.[49] Resistance was usually more subtle. William Dickinson warned his partner, who in 1814 was gathering hired slaves in Franklin County for the trek to the Kanawha, that his father was willing to lease two "if they are Wiling to go, but they don't seem quite Wiling to go, but perhaps you could influence them." Having difficulty convincing another group that he had hired from William Terry, Shrewsbury commented that they "were very loath to go but have had no trouble with them." In 1820 Dickinson wanted to send more of his slaves to the Kanawha, but he had to arrange to overpower one slave who objected. The owner observed, "Jim & Will concluded to frustrate the design & seem to fein them sick, first one & then the other—& Will has hinted that [he] would not go. I have had pr hand Cuffs made & shall put Will & Washington together." Dickinson and Shrewsbury always had an overseer with owned or hired slaves when they traveled westward from the piedmont, but when hired slaves were to return at the end of their hire periods to Franklin or Bedford Counties, the firm often allowed them to travel unaccompanied. At Christmas in 1819 Shrewsbury sent Tom, Spencer, and Abram home with a pass and expense money. "As they are sensible negroes & desireous to get home," Shrewsbury wrote, he "thought it not necessary to be at the expense of hiring a hand to go with them."[50]

A subtle system of control imposed discipline upon the slaves in the Kanawha salt industry. Most tasks, including skilled ones, could be routinized, thus minimizing management costs and establishing a common discipline. Goals for production of coal, barrels, and packed barrels were easily set. Slaves in positions requiring skill and attention, such as kettle tenders and machine operators, worked on a time basis.

If slaves met measured work requirements, they enjoyed considerable freedom to roam at large, although the task size restricted this possibility to some degree. Owners and managers tendered incentives to encourage production. Payments for Sunday and holiday work caused slaves to endure continuous daily labor. Deferring payment until year's end discouraged misbehavior and flight because the slave had accumulated something of value that was possessed by the manager and subject to his whim. A recalcitrant slave who refused to meet production goals could be employed in a wet room in the coal mine and subjected to the ridicule of fellow workers. Salt makers fostered a sense of pride and rivalry among the workforce of the different furnaces. Veteran salt manufacturer Henry H. Wood observed that overestimation of furnace output was quite common, "particularly by the hands," because they try "to excel other furnaces and to gain reputation."[51]

The goals of production had priority over the interests of the slave. At most furnaces, a superintendent or manager oversaw operations. Because assessments of his performance were based on production and efficiency, his primary concern was probably not the condition of the labor force unless output was inhibited. Economic self-interest did encourage kindness to the extent that the protection of property required the humane treatment of personally owned slaves. If a hired slave was abused physically or died from an industrial accident, the result would be nonrenewal of the lease, or the operator might entertain the fear of an unsavory reputation and perhaps a costly legal controversy with a distant owner.[52]

The food and clothing of Kanawha slaves were substantial and plentiful. The nature of the work required ample food and durable apparel, and the presence of company stores that regularly traded with Cincinnati ensured the availability of a variety of articles. Clothing, "stout and coarse, suitable for rough work," consisted of summer cloth (pants and shirt), a blanket, one hat, one winter coat and pants, one winter shirt, socks, and three to six pairs of shoes and tacks. Bacon and cornbread were the basic dietary staples, but flour, sugar, coffee, molasses, and vegetables accompanied this fare. Tea and rice were available to the sick. Allotments of food to slaves were not strict. Thomas Friend, operator of two furnaces, tried to give his slaves what they would eat, as "they labored very hard," although he restricted meat to one and one-fourth pounds of side bacon and one and a half pounds of shoulder per day to each slave.[53]

With the extensive employment of hired slaves, the salt producers separated the owners from their chattel. The producer gained the supervision of the bondsmen away from the knowledge and watchful eyes of the owners. Distance would tend to result in the harsher use of the bondsmen. This separation, especially apparent with slaves from eastern Virginia, is revealed by comments entered in the inventories of estates in Franklin County. Before his death, Samuel Patterson leased a slave to a salt company. The appraisers of his estate reported that the "Negro Man Amos (Known to us but now in Kanawha County, Va if in health)" was worth nine hundred dollars. The administrators of another estate represented "that Man Squire who is now hired at the Kanawha that from the best information that we have we suppose to be worth" four hundred dollars.[54]

Although salt makers hired slave labor for skilled and unskilled jobs in their factories, most leased bondsmen were employed in the unskilled, dangerous occupations of coal mining and wheeling. Most labor at a furnace worked in the mine. The manufacturers often owned the skilled slaves, and the higher rents paid for skilled workmen ensured their usage at their trades. Thomas Friend, who owned a higher percentage of his hands than was usual, rented from five to fifteen slaves per year from 1846 to 1850. He employed every leased slave in his coal mine as a digger or wheeler.[55]

Bailors and bailees recognized that higher rents prevailed for slaves employed in the salt industry of the Kanawha Valley than elsewhere in the upper South because of the increased possibility of accident or escape to Ohio. In a court case heard by the Supreme Court of Appeals of Virginia in the 1830s, the fact that slaves taken from Wood County to the Kanawha Salines hired for rates that were 25 to 30 percent higher than elsewhere was introduced as evidence. In 1838 slaves hiring for $90 per year in eastern Virginia could be leased for $150 in Kanawha County. A resident of Louisa County wrote a friend, a salt maker who had inquired about the slave market, that "in relation to hire likely men can be had at $90 & from that downwards but I discover the people of this country don't like to hire to the Kanawha people, it is a long distance & near the state of Ohio." Some Kanawha petitioners to the Virginia General Assembly blamed the high lease prices on the activity of Ohio abolitionists.[56]

Rentals varied greatly with the knowledge and skill of the individual slave in the salt business. Experienced and skilled workmen hired at higher rates than common labor. Age, sex, and physical condition would affect a slave's rental value. A first-rate boss kettle tender or blacksmith would lease for double the amount paid for a common laborer, such as a coal hauler, salt packer, salt lifter, or salt wheeler. A good coal digger would bring a premium of twenty-five dollars over the rent of a common laborer.[57]

Hire rents for slaves, although they were on an upward trend throughout the antebellum period, fluctuated widely and were quite sensitive to the economic condition of the Kanawha salt industry. In 1937 Thomas Senior Berry conducted an important, comprehensive study of commodity prices in the antebellum Cincinnati market. Basing his findings on sources then available, Berry plotted salt prices in that emporium and related these to Kanawha production. Despite the limitations of his sources that marred his narrative about the development of the Kanawha salt industry, Berry's production figures and price charts are accurate. He charted the monthly purchasing power of Kanawha salt using general prices in the Cincinnati market from 1816 to 1860. Chart 4.1 shows the correlation of the hire rates of common slave labor with the annual purchasing power of Kanawha salt in the Cincinnati market for the period 1844–1854. This time period is the only extensive span for which sufficient slave-hire data exist. It should be emphasized that the slaves were

Chart 4.1. Relationship of Average Annual Hire Rates for Common Slave Labor in the Kanawha Salt Industry to the Annual Purchasing Power of Kanawha Salt in the Cincinnati Market, 1844–1854

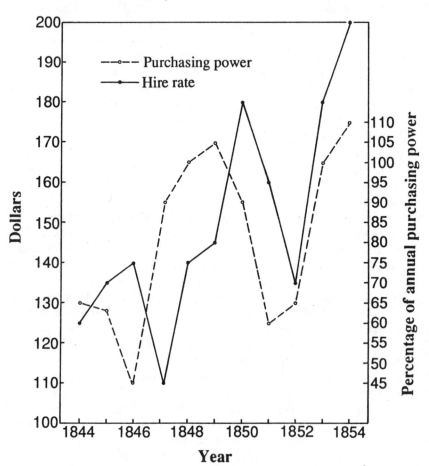

Sources: Berry, *Western Prices,* chart 27, p. 304; Hale, "Salt," 303; deposition of Robert Blaine, [n.d.], in *Early v. Friend* (1857), 1: 222–23; deposition of John N. Clarkson, Feb. 28, 1855, in *Thomas R. Friend v. William J. Stephens, Abraham Williams, et al.,* CSC, MCCR (1853). Luke Willcox Diary, Jan. 1, 11, and 16, 1844, vol. 1, p. 1; Jan. 1, 1845, vol. 1, p. 17; Dec. 5 and 30, 1847, vol. 1, pp. 54[64]–55[65]; Dec. 25 and 26, 1848, vol. 2, p. 10; Dec. 31, 1849, vol. 2, p. 25; Dec. 31, 1851, vol. 2, p. 55; Dec. 27, 1853, vol. 3, p. 5.

hired for common, not skilled, labor. Also, the changes in purchasing power of salt were not as precipitous in fact as on Berry's chart. The abrupt changes are caused by the use of annual percentages.

A close correlation existed between common slave hire prices and the annual purchasing power of Kanawha salt in the Queen City market. This correlation would be even closer if the rent for each year were cast in the preceding year, when the contracts of hire were actually consummated. For example, the rate for the year 1847 could be placed in December 1846, eliminating the lag. The diverse factors affecting salt production are ignored here, although total production affected the annual purchasing power of the commodity. High production begot lower purchasing power, and low production produced higher purchasing power, which in turn affected rents. This is not to suggest that the purchasing power of salt was the sole influence on hire prices. Undoubtedly the cholera epidemic of 1849 had some impact on hire rates for 1850.

Between 1850 and 1860 the salt industry of the Great Kanawha Valley suffered a severe decline unrelated to the labor system. Only nine salt manufacturing establishments existed in 1860. The surviving companies employed only an average of 285 male and 10 female hands in a month of operation. Annual salt production was approximately a third of what it had been a decade before. While Kanawha County's white population increased between 1850 and 1860, to become second only to that of Ohio County in the area of present-day West Virginia, the slave population dropped dramatically because of the demise of the salt industry.[58] The total slave population decreased by 30 percent, and the male and female slave populations decreased by 35 percent and 23 percent, respectively.

Contemporary salt manufacturers believed that slave labor was superior for their industrial needs because of cheapness, supply, and stability. Salt makers who petitioned the Virginia General Assembly asserted, "Slave labor is usually cheaper than free and for the business in which we are engaged it is believed to be the best."[59] A comparison of costs of hired common slave labor and free white labor in the period from 1850 to 1854 (see table 4.1) reveals that slave labor was cheaper than free white, and yet free labor was actually scarce. The operation of the hire system eliminated questions about the cost of rearing slaves and care for the infirm and elderly. The average hire for common slave labor for the period, a time of high rents, was $170 per year. In 1855 John N. Clarkson estimated that board, clothes, taxes, and medical treatment for each leased slave cost a bailee approximately a hundred dollars annually above the rental cost. The major extra cost was board, but furnace operators customarily furnished board to white laborers as they did for slave labor. The slave lease always provided for the rental payment at the end of the hire period. This was, in fact, the loan of capital and labor for a one-year term. The employment of free labor could not be executed with this advantage, and therefore a 6 percent interest rate (a low estimate of the cost of money) on the monthly wage must be charged to free labor in calculating costs. Management costs would be

Table 4.1   Comparative Costs of Hired Common Slave Labor and Free White Labor, Kanawha Salt Industry, 1850–1854

	Hired Slave	Free White
Rent or wage	$170	$450
Board	75	75
Clothing	24	—
Medical care	5	—
Taxes	1	—
Deferred interest on rental (6%)	—	53
Total cost	$275	$578

about the same. John J. Cabell reported to his son-in-law in 1832 that the few white hands that he had hired required more supervision than did all his slaves. On the Kanawha, it was commonly assumed that a salt furnace operated at least three hundred days annually. In 1854 Richard C.M. Lovell deposed that the cost of free labor in the Kanawha Salines was $1.50-$2.00 per day.[60] Taking the lower figure results in a yearly wage of a free white laborer of $450. One can readily see that hired common slave labor was cheaper than free labor. If one assumed the free labor to be skilled, the hire of the common slave can be doubled, as in the case of a boss kettle tender, and a marked differentiation remains. The wage of the free laborer could be reduced to one-half, and the result is the same.

Kanawha salt makers preferred to lease slaves because they could maintain lower costs and flexibility. Less capital could be invested in human property, and manufacturers could adjust their labor needs annually. The payment of rents in December came at a convenient time since the greatest salt sales occurred in autumn, before the slaughtering season. In 1833 John J. Cabell wrote that it was an established rule on the Great Kanawha River that if an able-bodied young male slave could be hired at 20 percent or less of his value per year, then that slave would be cheaper to lease than to purchase.[61] Incompetent workmen could be returned on the basis of misrepresentation, or they could be allowed to find other bailees at the expiration of the lease term. Loss in case of accident could be minimized by leasing slaves because one's own property was not being killed or maimed. The only threat was a lawsuit, but an adverse result could be defeated on appeal, delayed, or avoided when the plaintiff resided in a distant locality.

In light of recent debates of historians concerning the question of the economic efficiency and function of slave labor, the Kanawha salt industry provides an interesting case. Historians usually inquire about the alternative uses of free white or slave labor, a choice not confronted by western Virginia entrepreneurs. In the Salines there never was enough free labor available for employment in all phases of the salt industry. The real choice was between no or insufficient labor and slave labor, and the manufacturers did not hesitate to make the necessary decision. The evidence indicates that Kanawha producers preferred slave labor. There is no sign of ethical opposition or question in the matter. Transient free labor could not be depended upon for salt production. Slave workmanship was adequate in an enterprise where most jobs were routine. Slaves learned to tend kettles, cooper, dig coal, haul and pack salt, load boats, and drive teams as well as free labor. Incentive was not a problem; subtle rewards were provided and production was easily measurable. What was most needed at a salt furnace was a stable supply of workmen, and slaves fulfilled the requirement. In a court case in Mason County in 1853, expert testimony on the cost of erection and operation of salt furnaces was required to settle a controversy between the developers of the West Columbia saltworks. Kanawha salt makers consistently deposed that the Kanawha manufacturing establishments operated more cheaply than did those on the Ohio River because of the lower cost and stability of the slave labor supply.[62] The West Columbia saltworks could not retain free white labor for long periods, as it hired workers by the day or by the month.[63]

Slavery in the Great Kanawha Valley salt industry differed greatly from the institution that prevailed in agricultural or urban situations in the Old South. This microcosmic investigation does not lend itself to extensive, broad generalizations about the larger questions of political economy in the Old South. After all, Kanawha slavery at its peak involved only a few thousand slaves and a few hundred whites, whereas southern slavery as a whole affected millions. On the eve of the Civil War, Virginia's slave population approached a half million. The extractive salt business, depending upon surplus Virginia chattels for its labor and having its product's major market on the Ohio River and its southern and mid-western tributaries, was an exceptional phenomenon resting upon the effective functioning of a hire system. The Kanawha salt industry's rise and fall, essentially unrelated to its labor system, were induced by the market. The institution of slavery did not restrict the entry of entrepreneurs, nor did it inhibit technological progress. The salt enterprise could not have expanded or flourished as it did without slave labor and the hire system. The Kanawha system displayed a remarkable ability to meet the industrial requirements of salt manufacturers. Their success in harnessing the institution for their use suggests what might have occurred in southern Appalachian extractive industries had slavery continued to exist.

NOTES

An earlier version of this essay appeared as chapter 2 in John E. Stealey III, *The Antebellum Kanawha Salt Business and Western Markets* (Lexington: Univ. Press of Kentucky, 1993), and is reprinted here with the permission of the University Press of Kentucky.

1. Several studies of slavery are directly relevant to the present work. Robert S. Starobin produced three: "Disciplining Industrial Slaves in the Old South," *Journal of Negro History* 53 (April 1968): 111–28; "The Economics of Industrial Slavery in the Old South," *Business History Review* 44 (summer 1970): 131–74; and *Industrial Slavery in the Old South* (New York: Oxford Univ. Press, 1970). Also, one should consult Ronald L. Lewis, *Coal, Iron, and Slaves: Industrial Slavery in Maryland and Virginia, 1715–1865* (Westport, Conn.: Greenwood Press, 1979); and James E. Newton and Ronald L. Lewis, eds., *The Other Slaves: Mechanics, Artisans, and Craftsmen* (Boston: G.K. Hall and Co., 1978). The only published volume treating slavery in western Virginia offers a superficial account: Charles Embury Hedrick, *Social and Economic Aspects of Slavery in the Transmontane Prior to 1850* (Nashville: George Peabody College for Teachers, 1927). Hedrick did not recognize the existence of slavery in the Great Kanawha salt industry.

2. Articles of Agreement between Charles Brown and William Cathey, Nov. 14, 1808, County Court, Kanawha County Court Records (hereafter cited as CC, KCCR) (1808); petition of Jesse B. Boone, dated [1812], Legislative Petitions of Kanawha County; Joel Shrewsbury to Col. William Dickinson, Dec. 22, 1815, letterbook, 115 (copy), Dickinson & Shrewsbury Papers, James E. Morrow Library, Marshall University, Huntington, W.Va.

3. Avery O. Craven, *Soil Exhaustion as a Factor in the Agricultural History of Virginia and Maryland, 1606–1860* (Urbana: Univ. of Illinois Press, 1926).

4. *William Cobbs v. David Ruffner, Lewis Ruffner, Daniel Ruffner, and Richard E. Putney, doing business as David Ruffner and Company*, Circuit Superior Court, Kanawha County Court Records (hereafter cited as CSC, KCCR) (1828); *George M. Woods v. Andrew Donnally*, CSC, KCCR (1844); *Martha Stone v. William D. Shrewsbury and Henry H. Wood*, CSC, KCCR (1852); deposition of Jacob Runyon, Feb. 9, 1858, in *George W. Clarkson v. David J.W. Clarkson*, CC, KCCR (1858).

5. Table 2, "Population by Counties, 1790–1870," State of West Virginia, in *Ninth Census of the United States*, vol. 1, U.S. Bureau of the Census (Washington, D.C.: Government Printing Office, 1872), 72. Formations of new counties would affect the growth rate of the white population more than that of the slave population, since few bondsmen were located in portions of Kanawha County territory incorporated into new counties. Most slaves were concentrated in the Kanawha Salines area, which remained within the boundaries of Kanawha County.

6. Memorandum of an agreement between Harry Heth, Samuel G. Adams, and Beverley Randolph, Dec. 3, 1814, Heth Family Papers, Alderman Library, University of Virginia, Charlottesville.

7. Note dated May 25, attached to Beverley Randolph to Maj. Harry Heth, May 23, 1815, Heth Family Papers; "A List of Negros belonging to Dickinson & Shrewsbury, November 1855," in *William Dickinson v. Joel Shrewsbury*, CSC, KCCR (1856).

8. Depositions of Nathaniel S. Brooks, Feb. 23, 1855; John N. Clarkson, Feb. 28, 1855; and James Cowey, Aug. 23, 1854, in *Thomas R. Friend v. William J. Stephens, Abraham Williams, et al.*, CSC, Mason County Court Records (1853). Depositions of R.C.M. Lovell, Oct. 13, 1853, in *Early v. Friend* (1857), 2: 62.

9. *Commonwealth v. Joseph Friend, Commonwealth v. Joel Shrewsbury and William Dickinson, Commonwealth v. Andrew Donnally and Isaac Noyes*, CC, KCCR (1841).

10. Depositions of Obediah Crow, n.d., and Robert Blaine, n.d., in *Early v. Friend* (1857), 1: 276, 245. Coal-bank managers supervised all coal production and supply at furnace operations.

11. Joel Shrewsbury to Col. William Dickinson, Nov. 26, 1816, Feb. 14, 1814, and Jan. 2, 1819, letterbook, 137–39, 61–64, 219 (copy), Dickinson & Shrewsbury Papers; depositions of Robert Blaine, n.d., and Obediah Crow, n.d., in *Early v. Friend* (1857), 1: 245, 277; Luke Willcox Diary, Dec. 31, 1844, vol. 1, p. 17, West Virginia and Regional History Collection, West Virginia University Library.

12. Deposition of John D. Lewis, Aug. 31, 1854, in *Thomas R. Friend v. William J. Stephens, Abraham Williams, et al.*

13. Depositions of James Cowey, Aug. 31, 1854; Nathaniel S. Brooks, Feb. 23, 1855; John N. Clarkson, Feb. 28, 1855; and John D. Lewis, Aug. 31, 1854, in *Thomas R. Friend v. William J. Stephens, Abraham Williams, et al.*; deposition of Robert Blaine, n.d., in *Early v. Friend* (1857), 1: 228.

14. See table 1 in John E. Stealey III, *The Antebellum Kanawha Salt Business and Western Markets* (Lexington: Univ. Press of Kentucky, 1993), 138–39.

15. Table 2, "Population by Counties," 72; table 1, "Population by Counties, Age, Color, Condition," State of Virginia, in *Seventh Census of the United States*, U.S. Bureau of the Census (Washington, D.C.: Robert Armstrong, 1853), 252–56.

16. Carl. N. Degler notes that the ratio between the sexes in the slave population in the United States was approximately equal in the so-called breeding and consuming regions of the South. He asserts that the existence of this ratio was conducive to the development of family units in slave society and eased the exertion of control over slaves. See Degler, "Slavery in Brazil and the United States: An Essay in Comparative History," *American Historical Review* 75 (April 1970): 1017. The disparity between the sexes of slaves in Kanawha County demonstrates the impact of the salt industry in making the local slave system unique in the South. Consequently, if Degler's observations are correct, then one can conclude that in the Kanawha the family unit would not exist to a great extent and that there were obstacles to the maintenance of discipline.

17. Luke Willcox Diary, Aug. 29, Sept. 1, Oct. 27, and Nov. 1, 1845, vol. 1, pp. 27, 30.

18. "A List of Negros belonging to Dickinson & Shrewsbury, November 1855," in *William Dickinson v. Joel Shrewsbury*. This narrative owes much to Herbert G. Gutman's two works: *The Black Family in Slavery and Freedom, 1750–1925* (New York: Pantheon Books, 1976), pt. l, 3–350; and *Slavery and the Numbers Game: A Critique of Time on the Cross* (Urbana: Univ. of Illinois Press, 1975), esp. 88–164.

19. "A List of Negros, the Children and Grand Children of Negro Woman Fann," in *William Dickinson v. Joel Shrewsbury*; Joel Shrewsbury to Pleasant Dickinson, March 14, 1814, letterbook, 33–35 (copy), Dickinson & Shrewsbury Papers.

20. Joel Shrewsbury to Col. Wm. Dickinson, March 7, 1820, letterbook, 270-74 (copy), Dickinson & Shrewsbury Papers.

21. Starobin, "Economics of Industrial Slavery," 132; Starobin, *Industrial Slavery*, 12; *William Dickinson v. Joel Shrewsbury*; deposition of Dr. Spicer Patrick, Nov. 4, 1853, in *Early v. Friend* (1857), 2: 71.

22. For the purposes of this study, a "bailor" is a party who bails or delivers goods, such as slaves, to another under a contract of bailment, expressed or implied. Conversely, the "bailee" is the party to whom personal property is delivered under an expressed or implied contract of bailment.

23. *Samuel Hannah v. Lewis Billings*, CSC, KCCR (1844); *James S. Turner v. Samuel H. Early*, CSC, KCCR (1848); *James A. Lewis v. John C. Ruby and Enos S. Arnold*, CC, KCCR (1857).

24. Deposition of John Waid, Sept. 1, 1859, in *Henry C. Sisson v. John P. Waid*, CC, KCCR (1858).

25. Articles of Agreement between Calvin Armstrong, Spicer Patrick, and R.C.M. Lovell, and William H. Alpin, Dec. 29, 1859 (1859); *Samuel B. Brown v. Thomas Potts and William Tompkins* (1828); *Timothy B. Taylor v. John P. Waid* (1859), all CC, KCCR.

26. *William Cobbs v. John D. Shrewsbury Sr. and John D. Shrewsbury Jr.* (1826); William Gillison, for use of *James Y. Quarrier and Brothers v. William F. Whitteker* (1837); *Joseph Agee Sr. v. Van B. Donnally, Ebenezer Baines, and Andrew Donnally, doing business as V.B. Donnally and Company* (1839); *George W. Summers v. Henry and Robert M. Sims* (1845), all CSC, KCCR.

27. Luke Willcox Diary, Jan. 9, 1844, vol. 1, p. 1; deposition of Arthur Train, Dec. 18, 1852, in *Milton Parker v. William A. McMullin*, CSC, KCCR (1851).

28. William Witcher, administrator of *Charles A. Gill v. Henry Robinson, Thomas Scott, and George Nevels*, CSC, KCCR (1846); *George W. Summers v. John R. Humphries and William Graham, doing business as Humphries and Graham*, CC, KCCR (1856).

29. *Elizabeth Beeson v. Lewis Ruffner*, CSC, KCCR (1846); *Ann Pollard v. Charles G. Reynolds*, CSC, KCCR (spring term 1833).

30. *Ann Pollard v. Charles G. Reynolds*, CSC, KCCR (fall term 1833).

31. Luke Willcox Diary, Sept. 19, 1844, vol. 1, p. 13.

32. *Edward C. Murphy v. James Cowey and Stuart Robinson, late partners in James Cowey and Company*, CSC, KCCR (1853).

33. Deposition of Wiley P. Woods, Sept. 28, 1852, in *Edward C. Murphy v. James Cowey and Stuart Robinson*.

34. Deposition of Edward Turnbull, Nov. 21, 1852, in *Edward C. Murphy v. James Cowey and Stuart Robinson*.

35. Deposition of John Hayes, May 30, 1840, in *Martin P. and Ann Brooks v. James Hewitt et al., doing business as Hewitt, Ruffner and Company*, CSC, KCCR (1839, 1840).

36. *Kanawha Banner*, April 2, 1835; Luke Willcox Diary, June 18, 1848, vol. 2, p. 2; Joel Shrewsbury to Pleasant Dickinson, July 12, 1827, letterbook, 288–89 (copy), Dickinson & Shrewsbury Papers; Lewis Summers to George W. Summers, Jan. 8, 1835, George W. and Lewis Summers Papers, West Virginia and Regional History Collection, West Virginia University, Morgantown, W.Va.; *Kanawha Republican*, July 23, 1844; J.M. Byrnside to Summers and Miller, Dec. 17, 1846, George W. and Lewis Summers Papers.

37. John J. Cabell to Henry Ann Cabell, June 26, 1832, Jubal A. Early Papers, Library of Congress; John J. Cabell to Richard K. Cralle, July 2, 1832, John J. Cabell Papers, Robert A. Brock Collection, Huntington Library, San Marino, Cal.

38. Lindsey Thomas, administrator of *John Thomas v. Matthew Thomas and Levi Welch*, CSC, KCCR (1825); Lindsey Thomas, administrator of *John Thomas v. Van Bibber Reynolds and Robert M. Steele*, CSC, KCCR (1825); *Francis Thompson v. Daniel Ruffner, Lewis Ruffner, Andrew L. Ruffner, Frederick Brooks, and Jefferson Donnally*, CC, KCCR (1835).

39. For an unusual case of an escape by a slave hired out to work on a steamboat on the Ohio River, see Elizabeth Capehart, administrator of *John Capehart v. Moses Norton and Nelson B. Coleman*, CSC, KCCR (1846), in Stealey, *Antebellum Kanawha Salt Business*, 229.

40. The standard work on the subject as the disease affected Virginia slaves is Todd L. Savitt, *Medicine and Slavery: The Diseases and Health Care of Blacks in Antebellum Virginia* (Urbana: Univ. of Illinois Press, 1978), 226–40.

41. Louis C. Hunter, *Steamboats on the Western Rivers* (Cambridge, Mass.: Harvard Univ. Press, 1949), 431; J.P. Hale, *Trans-Allegheny Pioneers*, 2nd ed. (Charleston, W.Va.: Kanawha Valley Publishing Company, 1931), 288. For a national view of the epidemic, see Charles E. Rosenberg, *The Cholera Years: The United States in 1832, 1849, and 1866* (Chicago: Univ. of Chicago Press, 1962), 13–39.

42. *Kanawha Banner*, Oct. 25, 1832; Joel Shrewsbury to Pleasant Dickinson, Oct. 24, 1832, letterbook, 309–11 (copy), Dickinson & Shrewsbury Papers; John J. Cabell to Henry Ann Cabell, Nov. 16 and 25, and Dec. 4, 1832, Jubal A. Early Papers; John J. Cabell to Richard K. Cralle, Dec. 30, 1832, John J. Cabell Papers.

43. John J. Cabell to Richard K. Cralle, July 7, 1833, John J. Cabell Papers; W.S. Laidley, *History of Charleston and Kanawha County, West Virginia* (Chicago: Richmond-Arnold Publishing Company, 1911), 718; *Kanawha Banner*, July 31, 1834.

44. Hale, *Trans-Allegheny Pioneers*, 288; Wyndham B. Blanton, *Medicine in Virginia in the Nineteenth Century* (Richmond: Garrett and Massie, 1933), 241. Luke Willcox Diary, Aug. 21, 1849, vol. 2, p. 20; May 30, 1849, vol. 2, p. 17; June 29, 1849, vol. 2, p. 18; July 13, 1849, vol. 2, p. 18.

45. "Register-Deaths by Cholera in 1849—District Mth of Elk River to Upr Salt Works, Kanawha Salines, Kanawha County, Virginia," West Virginia Department of Archives and History. No discrepancy exists between this register and the Willcox diary. Willcox's total estimate of 300 deaths was for Kanawha County as a whole. His mid-July 1849 estimate for the saltworks only was approximately 100 deaths. Willcox noted in his diary account that his numbers were estimates.

46. *Zalinda L. Davis v. Emiline Ingles*, administrator of Crockett Ingles, CSC, KCCR (1852).

47. *Martha Stone v. William D. Shrewsbury and Henry H. Wood, and John Holland v. George H. Warth and Job English, doing business as Warth and English*, both CSC, KCCR (1852).

48. Luke Willcox Diary, July 5, 1850, vol. 2, p. 33; "Register Deaths by Cholera from 1850

frm [sic] Elk River to Joel Shrewsburys by H.N. Goshorn," West Virginia Department of Archives and History; Warth and English to John Potter, July 24, 1850, in *John Potter v. George H. Warth and Job English, doing business as Warth and English*, CSC, KCCR (1851).

49. For a detailed account, see Lewis, *Coal, Iron, and Slaves*, 13–35.

50. William Dickinson to Joel Shrewsbury, Jan. 2, 1814; Shrewsbury to Dickinson, Jan. 23, 1814; Dickinson to Shrewsbury, Feb. 24, 1820; and Shrewsbury to Dickinson, Jan. 2, 1819, letterbook, 19–20, 21–22, 264–69, 216–18 (copy), Dickinson & Shrewsbury Papers.

51. Deposition of H.H. Wood, April 13, 1857, in *Thomas R. Friend v. William J. Stephens, Abraham Williams, et al.*

52. A Bedford County, Virginia, resident complained to his attorney that everyone in his locality knew that "juries gotten up by Salt Makers and Men of influence at the Salines . . . never fail to hang the Jury or find against a fereighner." Pleasant Purton to Summers & Miller, Oct. 20, 1850, George W. and Lewis Summers Papers.

53. Depositions of Robert Blaine, n.d., and Obediah Crow, n.d., in *Early v. Friend* (1857), 1: 230, 243, 275.

54. Appraisal and inventory of the estate of Samuel Patterson, Nov. 22, 1839, Will Book 5, p. 190; and an appraisal of the personal property of the estate of Philemon Sutherland, Aug. 4, 1848, Will Book 6, p. 379, Office of the County Clerk of Franklin County, Rocky Mount, Virginia, microfilm, Virginia State Library and Archives.

55. Deposition of Robert Blaine, n.d., in *Early v. Friend* (1857), 1: 27–29.

56. *Spencer v. Pilcher*, 8 Leigh 383 (1836); James Michie to William [Tompkins], Nov. 26, 1838, William Tompkins Papers, Roy Bird Cook Collection, West Virginia Univ. Library, Morgantown, W.Va.; petition dated Jan. 27, 1835, Legislative Petitions of Kanawha County.

57. Deposition of Robert Blaine, n.d., in *Early v. Friend* (1857), 1: 222–23, 229.

58. See table 2, "Slave Inhabitants of Kanawha County in 1850 and 1860," in Stealey, *Antebellum Kanawha Salt Business*, 154; Bureau of the Census, Schedule 5, Products of Industry, County of Kanawha, State of Virginia, *Eighth Census of the U.S., 1860*, 214–16; table 2, "Population by Counties, 1790–1870," State of West Virginia, in Bureau of the Census, *Ninth Census of the U.S., 1870*, vol. 1: 71–72.

59. Petition dated Jan. 27, 1835, Legislative Petitions of Kanawha County.

60. *Deposition of John N. Clarkson, Feb. 28, 1855, in Thomas R. Friend v. William J. Stephens, Abraham Williams, et al.*; account of Samuel Watson and Company with Samuel Watson, Nov. 1, 1844–Dec. 25, 1845, in *Charles G. Reynolds v. Samuel Watson*, CSC, KCCR (1847): John T. Cabell to Richard K. Cralle, May 16, 1832, John J. Cabell Papers; deposition of R.C.M. Lovell, Sept. 5, 1854, in *Thomas R. Friend v. William J. Stephens, Abraham Williams, et al.*

61. John J. Cabell to Richard K. Cralle, Dec. 28, 1833, John J. Cabell Papers.

62. Depositions of R.C.M. Lovell, Sept. 5, 1854; Nathaniel S. Brooks, Feb. 23, 1855; and John N. Clarkson, Feb. 28, 1855, in *Thomas R. Friend v. William J. Stephens, Abraham Williams, et al.*

63. See statement of account for evidence of payment of employees for very short terms and of the rapid turnover of personnel in *Thomas R. Friend v. William J. Stephens, Abraham Williams, et al.*

5

SAM WILLIAMS, FORGEMAN

The Life of an Industrial Slave
at Buffalo Forge, Virginia

CHARLES B. DEW

William Weaver was the leading ironmaster in Rockbridge County, and perhaps in the entire Valley of Virginia, when he died at his home at Buffalo Forge
in March 1863. During his eighty-three years he had built up a legendary
fortune that, at the time of his death, included his iron-making facilities and
rich farmlands centered at Buffalo Forge and over twenty thousand additional
acres of land scattered across three western Virginia counties. His accumulated force of seventy slaves (twenty-six men, fourteen women, and thirty children) made him the largest slave owner in the county.[1] The inventory of his
estate provided a detailed listing of his personal property, his "goods and chattels" in the language of the law, and, along with entries for items like feather
beds, rocking chairs, farm implements, and draft animals, a careful enumeration and appraisal of his slave holdings.[2] The lengthy list evaluating Weaver's
slaves included the following brief notations:

> One male slave Sam Williams $2,800.00
> One male slave Sam Williams Senior 0 000.00
> One female slave Sally 500.00
> One female slave Nancy 1,500.00
> One female slave Lydia 2,000.00
> One female slave Caroline and two children 2,500.00
> Two female slaves Mary Caroline and Julia 600.00

These entries constituted one of the rare instances when the name of Sam
Williams and the names of his father, Sam Williams Sr.; his mother, Sally; his
wife, Nancy; two of their children, Lydia and Caroline; and two of their grandchildren, Mary Caroline and Julia, appeared on a legal document. And it is
symbolic of the status of slaves as property that two of Sam and Nancy Williams's
grandchildren, Caroline's "two children" in the appraisal, were not even identified by name on this occasion. The public record, in short, is sparse indeed
on the life of Sam Williams and his family.

As might be expected, Sam Williams did not leave letters, diaries, jour-

William Weaver, ca. 1860. (Author's collection)

nals, or other manuscript materials behind either, the kind of documentary evidence that Weaver and his family left in abundance. Like most slaves in the American South, Sam Williams never learned to read or write; the closest thing we have to a document written by him is an "X" he made over his name on a work contract he entered into in 1867.[3] No member of the Williams family, as far as we know, ever talked to an interviewer from the Federal Writers' Project or from Fisk or Southern University when their invaluable oral histories of slavery were being compiled in the 1920s and 1930s.[4] Yet it is possible to discover a great deal about Sam Williams and his family, and they are, on many grounds, eminently worth knowing. They deserve our attention not only because they were people caught up in the American system of human bondage and thus illustrate something of the nature of the antebellum South's most significant institution. They also warrant our best efforts at understanding because, if we look carefully, we can catch at least a glimpse of them as men and women who lived out human lives despite the confines and cruelties of their enslavement. Their love and affection, their joys and sorrows, their times of trial and moments of triumph come through to us, imperfectly to be sure, but visibly nonetheless, in spite of their inability to speak to us through traditional historical sources. This essay will attempt, in some small measure, to speak for them.

William Weaver became an ironmaster, a slave owner, and a Virginian almost by accident. He was born in 1781 on a farm near Philadelphia, and he spent most of his first forty or so years in and around that city, where he developed a series of successful business enterprises. As a merchant, miller, and textile manufacturer, Weaver began accumulating enough surplus capital to look elsewhere for profitable investments, and the War of 1812 seemed to create some excellent prospects in the Valley of Virginia.[5] The brisk wartime demand for iron prompted him to form a partnership in 1814 with Thomas Mayburry, another Philadelphia merchant, who had several years' experience in the Pennsylvania and Maryland iron business. The firm of Mayburry and Weaver purchased two iron properties in the Valley in the summer of 1814: Union Forge, which Weaver later renamed Buffalo Forge, located on Buffalo Creek some nine miles south of Lexington in Rockbridge County, Virginia; and Etna and Retreat Furnaces, two charcoal blast furnaces approximately eighteen miles southwest of Union Forge in neighboring Botetourt County. Retreat Furnace was abandoned rather quickly, but the firm launched extensive rebuilding projects at Etna Furnace and Union Forge and soon had both properties in full operation.[7]

Weaver did not move to Virginia immediately, however. Mayburry came down to manage the ironworks and supervise renovations at both installations, but Weaver remained in Philadelphia to raise needed capital and to look after his business interests there. Over the next few years, Weaver sank close to forty thousand dollars into the Virginia iron-making venture.[8] Among the more valuable acquisitions made with this money during the early years of Mayburry and Weaver's partnership was a growing force of slaves at Etna Furnace and Union Forge.

The first slaves acquired by the firm were purchased in the fall of 1815. The seller was John S. Wilson, one of the Virginia ironmasters from whom Weaver and Mayburry had bought their furnaces and forge the previous year. Wilson had a number of slaves he wished to dispose of, and Mayburry wanted and needed those hands. In late October 1815, Wilson journeyed north to Philadelphia, and there he and Weaver completed the deal. Weaver paid $3,200 for eleven slaves, divided into two very distinct groups. The first parcel consisted of an ironworker named Tooler; his wife, Rebecca; and her four children, all boys: Bill, seventeen; Robert, seven; Tooler, four; and Joe, two. The father and the oldest son, Bill, promised an immediate return to the firm as their services would be available without delay. It would be several years before Robert, Tooler Junior, and Joe could enter the workforce, but as young males, there was a strong likelihood that they might also be productive furnace or forge hands at some future point.

The second group of slaves that Weaver bought from Wilson, however, included no males. It consisted of a slave woman named Mary and her four daughters: Sally, thirteen; Amey, ten; Louisa, six; and Georgianna, two.[9] In this instance, Weaver appears to have been looking toward a different sort of investment. He was, in effect, seeking to ensure that his slave force could be built up by natural increase. Clearly, Mary seems to have been, in Weaver's eyes, a "breeding woman."[10] The sale papers contain no mention of her husband, and nothing indicates that he was ever acquired by Weaver or Mayburry. He may have lived near Etna Furnace or Union Forge, so the sale of his wife and daughters to Weaver might not have separated the family. Mary had several more children after Wilson sold her, so there is a strong possibility that her husband lived close by. One thing is certain, however: in obtaining Mary and her daughters, Weaver made an investment that was to pay rich dividends. In the years that lay ahead, this slave family would play a monumental role in shaping the fortunes of Weaver's iron-making venture in Virginia.

Mary and her children settled at Etna Furnace. There, probably in 1817 when she was fifteen years old, Sally, Mary's oldest daughter, married a man named Sam Williams, one of the skilled slave ironworkers that Weaver and Mayburry had added to their labor force. Sam and Sally Williams had their first child, a girl, in 1817, and they named her Mary, undoubtedly for her grandmother. Three years later, Sally gave birth to another child, a boy this time, and she and her husband named their new baby after his father, Sam Williams.[11]

Very little is known about Sam Williams Sr. because most of the records dealing with Weaver's early iron-making activities in Virginia have not survived. According to a slave register compiled at Buffalo Forge during the Civil War, Sally's husband was born in 1795, but that date was probably a rough approximation.[12] The appraisal of him at the time of Weaver's death in 1863, "no value," suggests that he was physically or mentally incapacitated and unable to perform useful work at age sixty-eight or so, an assumption reinforced by the fact that other slave men of similar age had values of two hundred to three hundred dollars beside their names on the 1863 estate inventory. Other fragmentary evidence indicates the cause of his disability. In 1832 when one of Weaver's managers was in desperate need of a skilled worker to fill in for a sick hand, he spoke to Sam about taking a turn at the forge. Sam refused; "He objects [because of] . . . his eyes," the manager told Weaver.[13] Ironworkers, black and white, were in constant danger of eye injuries from sparks and flying bits of red-hot metal, and Sam Williams Sr. seems to have suffered such an injury, or perhaps a series of them. Clearly, his eyes were badly damaged while he was still a relatively young man; he would have been in his middle or late thirties in 1832 and, if sound, still in his most productive years as a "prime hand." He may well have been blind by 1863, when the county appraisers examined, itemized, and evaluated "the goods and chattels of William Weaver deceased" and entered a string of zeroes after the name Sam Williams Senior

Toward the end of 1823, when Sam and Sally Williams's son, Sam, was three years old, Weaver took up residence at Union Forge, due to the floundering financial condition of his iron-making enterprise there. Despite the substantial amount of capital that he had poured into the blast furnace and

forge operations since 1814, almost forty thousand dollars, Mayburry and
Weaver had still not returned a profit on their investment.[14] Not long after his
arrival at the forge, he renamed the property after the creek that supplied waterpower to the works. The name Union Forge had not brought much luck to
the two Yankees who made up the firm of Mayburry and Weaver. Perhaps
Buffalo Forge would do better.

A year working with Mayburry on-site apparently convinced Weaver of
something he had suspected for some time—that his partner was incompetent.
As a result, early in 1824 Weaver moved to dissolve their partnership and to
divide the assets of the firm.[15] Prominent among these assets were the "Wilson
negroes," the name that Mayburry and Weaver regularly used to describe the
first slaves bought by the partnership in 1815. Their argument over the ownership of the "Wilson negroes"—Tooler and his wife and children; Mary and
her children (including Sally Williams) and grandchildren (including Sam
Williams Jr.) soon brought to light an interesting fact, one that revealed a
great deal about Weaver and his business practices. When Weaver purchased
these slaves from John Wilson in 1815, he took title to them in his own name,
not in the name of the firm of Mayburry and Weaver. He had done this, he
assured Wilson at the time, only because he feared that Mayburry "might have
some religious scruples" about owning slaves.[16] Mayburry did not discover
Weaver's delicate concern for the health of his soul until Weaver moved to
dissolve their association in 1824, nine years later, and demanded that Mayburry
surrender the entire Wilson slave force. Mayburry, who was living at Etna
Furnace, where a number of these slaves worked, refused to do so on the quite
reasonable grounds that Weaver had duped him in the original transaction.
Their clash over these slaves was one of a series of heated disputes between the
two men that led to Weaver's filing suit against Mayburry and throwing the
entire matter into the tortuously slow machinery of the Virginia chancery
courts.[17] Eleven years passed before the two former partners finally reached an
out-of-court settlement. That settlement brought with it the seeds of bitter
anguish for many of the slaves involved.

In their article of agreement signed on August 3, 1836, Weaver and
Mayburry agreed to a division of the "Wilson negroes." On January 1, 1837,
Mayburry was to turn over to Weaver the bulk of these slaves still in his possession. Because Weaver already had Tooler and his wife and children at Buffalo Forge, that family remained intact under Weaver's ownership. Mary's family
was not so fortunate, however. Mayburry still had Mary and her children and
grandchildren at Etna Furnace, and his share of the human assets of the firm
was to include Mary and three of her younger children. But her two older
daughters, Sally Williams and Louisa, along with their children, were to pass
into Weaver's possession.[18]

The division took place as scheduled at the beginning of 1837. Mayburry
surrendered Sally and Louisa and their children to Weaver at Buffalo Forge;
he retained, as their agreement stipulated, Mary and John, Hamilton, and Ellen,
who he took with him when he moved on to a new iron-making venture in

northern Rockbridge County.[19] As a result, Mary's family was broken in the name of fairness and compromise. But subsequent events were to show that she and the children who went with her were not forgotten by those who were left at Buffalo Forge early in 1837.

Sam Williams would turn seventeen sometime during that year, and this birthday would occur at a new home under a new master. But he could take some comfort from the knowledge that his immediate family was with him. Sam Williams Sr. had been under Weaver's control for a number of years before 1837, and his mother Sally had, of course, come to Weaver in the division, along with young Sam's brothers and sisters. The family had grown substantially and now included at least four children: Sam; his older sister, Mary; a younger sister, Elizabeth, born in 1825; and a younger brother, Washington, born in 1827. The birthplace of Sally's sons was indicated clearly in the Buffalo Forge record as they entered Weaver's workforce: they were listed as "Sam Etna" and "Washington Etna."[20] Sam, at least, knew who he was and resented this place name as his own. It would take him a long time, but he would get his name back.

To be precise, it took sixteen years. On a page in the Buffalo Forge ledgers covering his work for the year 1853, his name appears two ways: as "Samuel Etna" and as "Sam Williams."[21] The most logical explanation for the change is that Sam himself wanted it made. By the 1850s he was important enough to Weaver's operations to get his way. From this point on, as far as the records were concerned, he was "Sam Williams" at Buffalo Forge; his father was "Sam Williams Senior."[22]

Since the early Etna Furnace records have not survived, there is no way to trace young Sam Williams's life before his arrival at Buffalo Forge in 1837. If his youth was spent like that of most slave boys who grew up at iron-making facilities in the South, he probably had no regular duties until he reached age eight or so, when he would have been expected to assume some light chores, such as helping to look after the younger slave children during the day. By age twelve or fourteen, he would have entered the regular workforce, perhaps as a furnace boy doing odd jobs or as a leaf raker at the charcoal pits.[23] The elder Sam Williams's failing eyesight probably prevented him from training his teenage son in his iron-working skills, a method of transmitting knowledge and expertise that occurred frequently at Virginia furnaces and forges in the nineteenth century.[24] He may have been untrained when he arrived at Buffalo Forge as a sixteen-year-old youth on New Year's Day, 1837, but William Weaver could clearly see that Sam Williams's boy had the potential for forge work.

His assets were several. First of all, he came from a family that produced good mechanics. Intelligent southern iron men looking for slave recruits for critical furnace and forge jobs paid close attention to things like heredity, and Weaver was certainly no fool when it came to the iron business. He seemed to feel about black ironworkers the same way he felt about white ironmasters. You had to have "the proper head for it," Weaver once instructed his nephew. "Training alone will not [do] as nature must do something, in order to make a good Iron Master."[25] Nature seemed to have done a great deal for Sam Williams. He had the necessary size and strength; he stood five feet ten inches tall when he achieved his full stature, which made him one of the tallest slave hands at Buffalo Forge. And his color suggested to white southerners of that place and time that he was likely to possess intelligence and good judgment as well. A physical description of him drawn up during the Civil War listed his color as "yellow."[26] He had, at some point in his ancestry, a strong admixture of white blood.

After a year in which the only work recorded for him at Buffalo Forge consisted of field labor with the farmhands, Sam entered the forge in 1838 at the age of eighteen.[27] Weaver undoubtedly had Sam go down to the forge and watch the black refiners and hammermen at their jobs before deciding whether he wanted to train as a forgeman, as was Weaver's usual practice with potential ironworker recruits.[28] It was far better to have a willing apprentice than a surly, rebellious underhand who would turn out poor-quality work, try to escape, or perhaps sabotage the forge machinery. As Sam walked into the stone forge building that stood alongside Buffalo Creek, he would have seen an impressive, even awesome, sight: charcoal fires burning at white heat; slave refiners and their helpers working bars of pig iron in those fires until the iron turned into a ball of glowing, pasty metal, then slinging this semimolten mass of iron onto their anvils, where they pounded and shaped it under the rhythmic blows of their huge, water-powered hammers. Through successive reheatings and poundings, Weaver's refiners removed enough of the impurities in the pig iron to work it into something called an "anchony." Turning out high-quality anchonies was the most important single job in the forge, and that was what Weaver wanted Sam Williams to do.[29]

Weaver himself described an anchony in a court deposition he gave in 1840: It was a piece of malleable iron about six inches square weighing between 80 and 150 pounds, "with a blade of iron about the length of my cane," Weaver noted (his cane measured thirty-two inches); "one end of the blade has what is called the tail end, which contains iron enough generally to make a shovel mould," he added.[30] Producing this rather strange-looking item was no easy task. The key point in the refining process was exactly when the pig iron heating in the refinery fire had reached just the right temperature and consistency for pounding and shaping on the anvil block. Bringing the pig iron "to nature," as this was called, was the most difficult forge skill to learn, and it could be acquired only by many months of apprenticeship to a master refiner.[31] If Sam Williams decided that he wanted to follow in his father's footsteps and became a refiner, he would have to start as an underhand at the fires of men like Phill Easton, John Baxter, or the Hunt brothers, "Harry and Billy," all of whom were skilled slave refinery hands at Buffalo Forge in the late 1830s.[32]

Pounding out anchonies was the most critical part of the forge operation, but it was only the first half of the manufacturing process. The final stage came when a second group of operatives, the hammermen, reheated the anchonies and worked them at another forge called a chaffery. The hammermen produced iron bars of various standardized shapes, sizes, and lengths—"merchant bars," in the language of the iron trade—which would be shipped to market and sold. Merchant bars kept the wheels of agriculture turning. Blacksmiths hammered them into the things needed on (or off) the farm: horse and mule shoes, wagon tires, nails, tools, agricultural implements, and the like.[33] The slave hammermen at Buffalo Forge at the time of Sam Williams's arrival—Tooler, the son of the ironworker of the same name and one of the original "Wilson negroes"; his brother Bob, another "Wilson negro"; and Garland Thompson—were, like the refiners, prize hands worth a substantial premium on the open market.[34]

Weaver was well aware of their value to him. Without his forge and the slaves who ran it, William Weaver would have been just another valley farmer, a prosperous one, to be sure, but a farmer nonetheless. There would have been nothing wrong with that, of course. But Buffalo Forge and his skilled crew of slave hands made him much more. They made him an ironmaster, a person of premier importance in the local economy and someone to be reckoned with, politically and socially, in the Valley. "Some of my Friends in Phila. wondered why I did not reside amongst them," he confided to a friend in Lexington in 1848. "I replied—At home I was but a small person—but that I was somebody—The people knew me—and in crowded Phila. I would be nobody."[35] Weaver was much more than "a small person" in Rockbridge County, and he knew well where the source of his prestige lay. It lay in that stone forge building that stood beside Buffalo Creek, in the massive hammers and charcoal fires and in the black men who worked them so skillfully.

To retain his status, and the wealth that went with it, Weaver had to train and hold good slave artisans and replace those hands who were growing too old, like Billy Hunt, or were too infirm, like Sam Williams Sr., to work. One suspects that when young Sam Williams decided that he wanted to be a forgeman, William Weaver could not have been happier.

The advantage of doing forge work would not have been unknown to Sam Williams. In making himself indispensable to Weaver's iron-making operations, he would be gaining a significant amount of influence over his own fate. There was no sure guarantee against punishment or sale; like all southern masters, Weaver could do pretty much what he wished in the way of punishment, and if he should fall deeply into debt or die suddenly, his slave force could be dispersed either by sale or by the division of his estate. Barring that sort of catastrophe, however, Sam would be in a much stronger bargaining position as a skilled forge hand than in any other occupation at Buffalo Forge. If he trained as a refiner and showed an aptitude for the work, he would have talents that his owner would need and even be willing to pay him for.

Compensation for extra work was almost a universal feature of the labor system at slave-manned furnaces and forges in the Old South, and Buffalo Forge was no exception. Slaves had a daily or weekly task to accomplish, but they were paid for anything they turned out over and above that amount— "overwork," it was called.[36] The task for refiners at Weaver's forge and everywhere else in the Valley was a ton and a half of anchonies per week (the quota required of hammermen was a "journey" of 560 pounds of bar iron per day).[37] These amounts had been the customary tasks for years, and old traditions like this were hard to change. Slaves as well as masters knew what the tasks were, and any attempt by ironmasters to increase work quotas or to abolish compensation for overwork entirely would have been a very risky venture. It did not take much, for instance, to break a hammer "helve," the huge wooden beams that supported the five hundred– to six hundred–pound cast-iron hammerheads in the forge. And every time a helve broke, the forge had to shut down for at least a day or two for repairs. Sabotage of this sort would be relatively simple to accomplish. It was this sort of unspoken threat that gave slave forgemen considerable protection against an increase in their tasks and that helped them to preserve their right to earn compensation for themselves.

Payment for overwork came in several forms, and the option lay with the slave. The slaves at Buffalo Forge could take it in cash; they could take it in credit at Weaver's store and draw against it for items that they wished to buy; they could use their overwork to secure time off from their regular duties; and finally, if Weaver permitted, they could attempt to purchase their own freedom.[38] This last option was almost never granted. In 1830, Weaver allowed an elderly slave forge hand whom he had purchased in the Lynchburg area to buy himself and return to his former home.[39] But this appears to be the only time that Weaver made such a concession to any member of his slave force. Nevertheless, the overwork system had obvious advantages for the slave, as Sam Williams's life at Buffalo Forge illustrates in rich and elaborate detail.

Sam's first year in the forge, 1838, was a year of apprenticeship. He served as an underhand to both John Baxter and Harry Hunt, and under their guidance he sought to master the refiner's art: learning to put up and maintain the special refinery fire, heating the pig iron and bringing it "to nature," and then pounding the red-hot metal under the huge hammer into those oddly shaped anchonies.[40] He undoubtedly cost Weaver some money that year in wasted pig iron and excessive use of expensive charcoal, but the only way to learn was by doing.

Sam had expert teachers. Harry Hunt, for instance, was fifty years old in 1838 and had been a refiner for well over twenty-five years. He, like many other slave ironworkers, had been born to the trade. In his case, this meant birth, youth, and young adulthood at the Oxford Iron Works in Campbell County, not far from Lynchburg. Harry and his brother Billy had been trained in the forge under David Ross, one of the most famous Virginia ironmasters of the Revolutionary and post-Revolutionary eras. Ross's death in 1817 and the subsequent sale of his estate sent a number of his best ironworkers across the Blue Ridge Mountains and into the Valley, where the Virginia iron industry was moving during the early years of the nineteenth century and where ironmasters like William Weaver were eagerly seeking skilled furnace and forge workers.[41]

Harry Hunt knew his job, and Sam learned quickly. Before his first year was out, he had sufficiently mastered the techniques of refining to earn a modest amount of overwork: "1/2 ton over iron 2.00."[42] It was not a great deal of money, especially when compared with what some of the other skilled forgemen were able to put away. But it was a start toward something better, toward a life in which his skills could help make things a little more comfortable and perhaps a bit more predictable and secure. By 1840, he had added reason to be concerned about a more comfortable present and a more certain future.

Sometime during the year 1840, Sam Williams married. His wife was a slave woman named Nancy Jefferson, who was also owned by William Weaver. She was twenty-three years old that year, three years older than Sam, but the difference in age meant little.[43] Sam had finished his forge training by then and was now one of Weaver's master refiners.[44] His future was probably as secure as any slave's could ever be, and he was ready to assume the responsibilities of a husband and, soon, a father. Their marriage was not a legal one, of course. Slave marriages had no standing in Virginia law or in that of any other southern state. But time would clearly show that Sam Williams and Nancy Jefferson viewed themselves as man and wife. The date of their marriage was not recorded in the journals and papers kept at Buffalo Forge, but they knew the year was 1840, and they never forgot it.

The birth of their first child did appear in the Buffalo Forge records, however, and for good reason. The birth of a new baby in the slave quarters meant an addition to the master's wealth and potential workforce. So, when Elizabeth Williams came into the world later that year, note was taken of the event.[45] Elizabeth, or Betty, as she was more frequently called, was undoubtedly named after Sam's younger sister, Elizabeth, who is mentioned in early legal documents dealing with the dispute over the "Wilson negroes."[46]

Sam's marriage and the birth of his daughter gave him added incentive to exploit the possibilities opened up by the overwork system. He had earned some relatively small amounts of money before 1840: $3.00 in 1837, the same in 1838, and just over $4.50 in 1839.[47] He would not be content with earnings of this size in 1840, however. Early in the year, he began to devote a considerable amount of his spare time to "tar burning," as it was called. He would collect the heart of fallen pine trees from the woods around Buffalo Forge, stack it closely on a low, hard-packed mound of earth with gutters running out from the center, cover the resinous pine with dirt, and light it. As the wood smoldered, the gum would flow out as tar through the trenches cut in the earth.[49] Sam would collect this "tair," as it was spelled in the Buffalo Forge books, and sell it to his master. Weaver was willing to pay twenty-five cents a gallon for it—pitch and tar were always needed around installations dependent on waterpower—and Sam's long hours in the woods produced no less than fifty-nine gallons of tar before the year was out.[49]

He also did something else the year he was married that he had not done during his three previous years at Buffalo Forge: he worked through the Christmas holidays. The week between Christmas and New Year's was a traditional period of rest for Weaver's slave hands, as it was for most southern slaves. The forge closed for Christmas, but there were plenty of other things to do: stock to feed and water, roads and walks to shovel if it snowed, ice to cut from the forge pond and haul to the icehouse if a cold snap hit. Sam worked five days out of the seven-day Christmas break in 1840 and earned $2.50 for his labor. (Fifty cents a day was the usual pay for anyone, white or black, who did common labor, so Sam was not paid "slave wages" for his holiday work.) By his tar burning, forge overwork, and Christmas labor in 1840, he earned $22.42, well over four times what he had made for himself in any previous year at Buffalo Forge.[50]

There is no way of knowing why Sam worked so hard in 1840, but it seems safe to assume that his efforts were spurred by a desire to be able to do more for his wife and his new baby. This view is reinforced by the record of his purchases during the year: sugar and molasses (treats all three of them could enjoy), coffee for himself and Nancy, and crocks for her to use for household storage. Several of the larger expenditures that he made in 1840 were not spelled out in the books, like his store "order" of $4.00 on March 7 and a similarly vague entry on September 5 for $9.16.[51] These sizable store purchases probably included items for Nancy and Betty, but we cannot be sure.

Sam and Nancy Williams's family grew steadily. In 1842, a second daughter, Caroline, was born, and she was followed by two more girls, Ann, born in 1843, and Lydia, born the next year.[52] Sam's overwork increased along with the size of his family. He continued his tar burning in 1841 but on a reduced scale. He concentrated more and more on his work at the refinery forge in his effort to earn extra income for himself and his wife and daughters. This made sense. As his skills improved, so did his chance to earn overwork pay by hammering out extra pounds of anchonies. It was now easier for him to make his task of a ton and a half of refined iron per week, and anything he turned out above that amount meant money in his pocket or credit at the Buffalo Forge store. He was paid $8.82 for pounding out over two tons of extra iron in 1841, while his tar production dropped off to thirty-six and a half gallons, which still earned him $9.12. Once again, his purchases at Weaver's store suggest that he was using his overwork compensation to buy things his family could use—items like sugar, calico, ticking, drill, jeans cloth, and trimmings. And a week before Christmas 1841, he spent $1.25 for a silk handkerchief.[53]

Sam's growing prowess as a refiner and his continued support of his family are apparent in his overwork accounts during the next few years. No records have survived for 1842 and 1843, but he made thirty-one dollars in overwork pay in 1844, most of which he earned at his forge. As a master refiner, he was paid for his overwork at the same rate that a white artisan would have been paid for the same job, eight dollars per ton, with three-fifths of that going to Sam, as the refiner, and two-fifths going to his underhand. Sam's five tons of "over iron" in 1844 translated into a credit of twenty-four dollars on Weaver's books.[54]

During the next several years, Sam's overwork earnings continued to mount. By the early 1850s, he was regularly making more than fifty dollars per

Brick slave quarters at Buffalo Forge, with Blue Ridge Mountains as backdrop. (Author's collection)

annum, and in 1855 and 1856, the last two years for which his complete accounts are available, his compensation reached even greater levels. In 1855, his overwork amounted to $92.23, and the next year, for the first time, it exceeded $100. It was $103 to be exact. The first $100 were earned by refining twenty tons of "Over Iron."[55]

There is no need to make a detailed list of his purchases during this ten- to twelve-year period, but some of the things he did with his money suggest a good deal about this man and his attitudes and priorities. He supplemented Weaver's standard rations of pork and cornmeal with regular purchases of flour, sugar, coffee, and molasses, and he frequently bought cloth for Nancy to sew into garments for the family. His overwork kept him, and perhaps Nancy as well, supplied with tobacco. And he continued to give gifts to various family members. His mother received fifty pounds of flour from him in February 1845, and he gave his father a pound of coffee in April 1846. Nancy, as might be expected, received a number of presents: a pair of buckskin gloves at Christmas in 1848, a shawl in May 1849, and nine yards of silk in October 1851. One of his special purchases for his children was eight and three-fourths yards of cloth for a bedspread for Ann when she was ten years old.[56]

The most fascinating items of all that he acquired during these years were the articles of furniture he bought for the cabin that he, Nancy, and the girls shared. His major Christmas gift to the family in 1845 consisted of a table, at three dollars, and a bedstead, at nine dollars, both of which he purchased at the Buffalo Forge store on Christmas Eve. He added significantly to the cabin's furnishings six years later when he apparently attended an estate sale held in the neighborhood. In April 1851, he made two acquisitions "at Blackford's Sale": a set of chairs, for which he paid $7.25, and, probably his most revealing purchase of the entire antebellum era, "1 looking glass," priced at $1.75.[57]

There are many reasons why any family would want to own a mirror, perfectly natural reasons such as curiosity about one's appearance or a touch of vanity perhaps. Sam and Nancy Williams had growing daughters, too. In 1851, Betty was eleven, Caroline was nine, Anne was eight, and Lydia was seven. But a slave's buying a mirror suggests something more. It would seem to indicate a strong sense of pride in one's self and one's family that transcended their status as slaves. Why else would Sam spend that kind of money on such a purchase whose price represented the sweat and sore muscles that went into several hundred pounds of overwork iron? One almost suspects that that looking glass stood as a symbol of Sam and Nancy Williams's feelings about themselves and their children. And there were other signs of pride as well.

In 1849, Sam began fairly frequently making cash withdrawals against his overwork account. Some of this money he undoubtedly used to buy items at rural stores that dotted the nearby countryside, places like Saunder's Store, which stood just across Buffalo Creek from the forge. But he was not spending all of it in this way. Part of the money that he pocketed during these years ended up in a rather remarkable place, as indicated by a letter written by Weaver's young forge clerk in 1855. On February 25 of that year, John A. Rex, a twenty-three-year-old nephew of Weaver's who had come from Pennsylvania to help out at Buffalo Forge, described an incident that had recently occurred there. "I wish to ask you one question," he wrote to James D. Davidson, Weaver's attorney in Lexington: "whether Sam Williams can draw his money from the Savings Bank or if he cannot." Sam, it seems, had made a bet with a man named Henry Nash, a free black cooper who lived near Buffalo Forge and who made the barrels for Weaver's flour. Nash refused to believe that Sam had a savings account in the bank in Lexington, and Sam had bet his watch, another impressive acquisition for a slave, against Nash's watch that he did. "It is my opinion that he can draw his money if he gives the Directors of the Bank 10 days notice," Rex continued. "After he receives the money he wishes to show it to Henry Nash, and then he will return the said money back to the Bank again." Rex closed the letter by assuring Davidson that he "was witness to the said bargain."[59]

James Davidson was an experienced attorney, but it is doubtful that he had ever before had to give an opinion as to how a slave should handle his savings account. The only thing he knew to do was to advise young Rex "to confer with Wm. Weaver" on the business.[60] Perhaps the master could decide how a man who was legally property should deal with his own property, in this case a sizable account in a major Lexington financial institution.

There are several extraordinary things about this incident, not the least of which is the white forge clerk's holding the bet for a slave and a free Negro and serving as a witness to their wager. But everyday life in the Old South was filled with anomalies of this sort, so perhaps this part of the story was not so remarkable after all. That Sam Williams had a savings account was remarkable by any standard, however, and, given the value of the dollar in the 1850s, his account was a large one. We know the size of his savings because just over a year after Rex wrote Davidson about the bet, the lawyer withdrew Sam's money from the bank. It may have been that the bank directors felt uneasy about holding and paying interest on a slave's money, particularly after the wager brought up the subject. Or maybe Weaver decided it would be better to handle these funds in some other way. Whatever the reason, on April 22, 1856, Davidson rode out to Buffalo Forge carrying Sam Williams's savings of $91.31. He also brought with him $61.96 belonging to Sam's wife.[61]

Nancy Williams, it turned out, had a savings account, too, and in her own name. She was in charge of dairy operations at Buffalo Forge and did a good deal of housework at Weaver's residence, so she clearly had had opportunities to earn overwork pay in her own right. The house account books have not survived, so there is no way to discover exactly what she did to make money or to trace the precise amounts of her compensation. But her savings account was two-thirds the size of her husband's, so her earnings must have been substantial. Between them, Sam and Nancy had over $150 in cash.

What were they saving for? No evidence exists to show that Weaver had given the couple the right to buy their own freedom or that of their children, so self-purchase apparently was not the reason. The fact that they were saving anything at all suggests that they felt that their material standard of living was adequate to the family's needs; if it had not been, they probably would have spent much more than they did on various food items and cloth. The most logical explanation for their extraordinary and substantial bank accounts would seem to be that they both had extra overwork funds and that they had simply put their money in a safe place where it would earn interest for them.

William Weaver, in effect, replaced the savings bank as the holder of the Williamses' money and as the payer of interest on their accounts. Special entries were made under their separate names in a private ledger kept at the forge, and Sam and Nancy each placed their full savings with Weaver on April 22, 1856, the day that Davidson brought their funds out from Lexington. The interest rate in both instances was 12 percent.[62]

In the years just ahead, Sam and Nancy would follow quite different courses in handling their savings. In the spring and fall of 1858, Nancy made fairly systematic cash withdrawals of four to five dollars, and in 1859 she used the remainder of her money for substantial purchases at Buffalo Forge and at two neighboring country stores. On October 27, 1859, she closed out her account by spending $4.82 at Saunder's Store. Sam, on the other hand, kept exactly one hundred dollars on deposit throughout these years and into the 1860s. He withdrew the interest each year in either cash or goods but kept the one hundred–dollar principal intact. Weaver regularly credited him with interest on his one hundred dollars, figured after 1860 at 6 percent, and Sam just as regularly drew off his six dollars per year. (For some reason, two interest payments were made in 1862, so Sam took out twelve dollars that year.) His account was not finally closed out until after the Civil War.[63]

The picture that emerges from this story of two slaves with savings accounts is by no means a simple one. On the surface, one might be tempted to argue that their behavior indicated a placid acceptance of their status and condition. They had to complete their required tasks before they could start earning money for themselves, so they obviously were turning out a considerable amount of work for William Weaver, working like slaves, so to speak, and taking the bait that the master offered to do a good deal more than they had to do. Yet they clearly were doing a great deal for themselves as well, and for their children. They were improving the material conditions under which all of them could live, and they were protecting themselves against the fearful threat that hung over them all—the breakup of the family through sale. Weaver would be very reluctant indeed to part with workers like this man and woman, who meant so much to the smooth running and success of his iron-making and farming activities, or to sell their daughters. Through their overwork, Sam and Nancy could help to shield and provide for each other and for their children. The psychological importance of this to them, the added access it afforded Sam to the traditional responsibilities of a husband and father, and Nancy to the role of wife and mother, cannot be overemphasized.

Sam's attitude toward his work need not be left totally to the imagination, however. Thanks to the arrival at Buffalo Forge of a new manager in 1857 and his meticulous record keeping, we can follow Sam at his forge and in the fields for months on end. The insights to be gained from a close look at his daily activities during the late 1850s and early 1860s are revealing.

By the mid-1850s, Weaver was no longer capable of supervising the complex industrial and agricultural operations at Buffalo Forge by himself. He was in his seventies, his health was uncertain, and just moving around the property was becoming more and more difficult for him.[64] As a result, he persuaded his favorite niece and her husband, Emma and Daniel Brady, to move from Philadelphia and to take over the management of day-to-day affairs at the house, the forge, and the farms. Weaver had no one in his immediate family to take over for him; he had not married until 1830, when he was forty-nine, and his wife, only four years younger, had died in 1850. They had had no children.[65] "I am old, all but 75," Weaver wrote to Daniel Brady in 1855, and he was worried about what would happen after his death. "The great object with me is, that my servants shall remain where they are, and have humane masters," he went on. "This point is the only difficulty on my mind in relation to my Estate. Giving them their freedom, I am satisfied, would not benefit them as much as having good masters, and remain where they are."[66]

Late in 1857, the Bradys closed up their affairs in Pennsylvania and moved to Buffalo Forge, with their children, Anne Gertrude, nine, and Charles Patrick, seven.[67] Their arrival was an event of major significance in the lives of the slaves at Buffalo Forge. It must have relieved much of the anxiety that would have been growing in the quarters as Weaver's age advanced and as his health deteriorated. Now there was a clear prospect that the Buffalo Forge slave community would remain intact after Weaver's passing, that families would not be broken and friends separated by a division of the master's estate. Aside from manumission, there was probably nothing more important to these black men and women than the strong probability that they could all "remain where they are," as Weaver put it, after he was gone. The Bradys' coming, and the fact that they already had a son, seven-year-old Pat, who might also inherit the place one day, would have been the cause for some quiet rejoicing in the slave cabins that dotted the landscape around Buffalo Forge.

A historian seeking to reconstruct the lives of these slaves also has reason to celebrate the arrival of the Bradys. Daniel Brady was a remarkably careful and devoted keeper of records. Soon after his arrival, he began a regular daily journal in which he wrote the work routine for each day: what the weather was like, which slaves were doing what jobs, how much work they did, who was sick, who was pretending to be sick. The result is a running description of slave activities at Buffalo Forge that fills three neatly written volumes and covers a span of more than seven years, from March 1858 to June 1865.[68] These years, perhaps the most critical in the entire history of the slave South, are those in which we can follow the life of Sam Williams in the greatest and most elaborate detail.

When Sam was putting in a routine day at his refinery forge, Brady simply noted, "Sam at work," in his journal. And Sam was "at work" most of the time. He and his underhand, a slave named Henry Towles, were the steadiest pair in the forge, but they also had their own ideas about when they had worked long enough and hard enough to deserve a break. The summer of 1860 was such a time. Sam and Henry Towles manned their forge through some very warm days at the beginning of July, but by the middle of the month they had obviously had enough. Henry said he was too ill to work on Wednesday, July 18, and when he failed to show up the next day as well, "Henry Towles sick i.e. loafing" was Brady's assessment. Sam continued to work under very trying conditions, and no one knew it better than he did. He and Jim Garland, a replacement for Henry, finished out the week, however, with "Henry Towles loafing" Friday and Saturday.[69]

On Monday, July 23, it was Sam's turn, and he may not even have made a pretense of being sick. Henry returned to work that day; he could handle Sam's job, with Jim Garland's help. Sam was now "loafing," according to Brady, and he stayed out "loafing" the entire week. Brady realized that he had pushed his hands about as far as he could in the oppressive heat, and he probably was not surprised on Saturday when his two chaffery forgemen, Tooler and Harry Hunt Jr., also took matters into their own hands. "Tooler & Harry drew a few pounds and then broke down to loaf," he wrote. He decided about the middle of the day that there was no sense fighting it any longer: "All hands had a 1/2 [day] holiday."[70] From Brady's vantage point, Saturday, July 28, had been a difficult day. The slaves undoubtedly took just the opposite view.

Sam's vacation was not over yet, though. He did not go back to work for three more weeks. From Monday, July 30, to Saturday, August 18, Brady noted with regularity that Sam was "loafing" each day.[71] Even the appearance on August 7 of J.E. Carson, a Rockbridge County slave trader, did not drive Sam back to his post. If Sam were going to be intimidated into returning to work, the slave dealer's visit to Buffalo Forge should have done it. Carson was no idle threat. In the spring of 1859, he had carried one of Weaver's slaves, a man named Lawson, to New Orleans and sold him, and Carson had purchased a slave woman and her children from Weaver several months later. Lawson had tried to run away; the woman had apparently disrupted the quarters by her licentious behavior.[72] Weaver, as was his custom, simply got rid of unruly slaves. But Sam's extended period of "loafing" was not enough to convince Weaver that he should part with his most valuable forgeman. Carson did buy a slave from Weaver on August 7, a runaway field hand, Bill Greenlee, whom he took away in handcuffs.[73] When Sam returned to his forge on Monday, August 20, he had been off the job four full weeks.[74] Sam returned to work as if nothing had happened. Jim Garland went back into the fields, and Sam and Henry Towles took up where they had left off a month or so earlier. Sam's vacation, if that word fits the occasion, seems to have been something he felt was due him. He had worked hard that year up to his four weeks of "loafing."

Sam had continued to earn overtime payments up until his August vacation. Soon after he returned, he began receiving cash payments from Weaver again, ranging from $2.50 on September 24 to $5.00 on December 1, a strong indication that he was working overtime after he rejoined Henry Towles at the refinery forge.[75] Perhaps most significant of all, his savings account, which Weaver was holding, was not touched during or after his month-long absence from his job.

What this fascinating incident suggests is that Sam was fully aware of the power he possessed and the quite distinct limits of that power. He knew that his skills were critically important to his master and that this gave him a considerable amount of leverage in his dealings with Weaver and Brady. In his view, he deserved some time off, and he chose the hot, muggy dog days of July and August 1860 to take it. It was probably no accident that he did not leave his forge until Henry Towles returned. This kept the situation from assuming potentially dangerous and threatening dimensions. Because they were off one at a time, Jim Garland could come in to spell each one of them temporarily, and forge operations could continue. Iron-making would not grind to a complete and costly stop because Henry was feigning illness and Sam was "loafing" back at his cabin. Sam knew just how far he could go with his resistance, and he was careful to keep the situation under control.

At the same time, he had enough pride in himself to insist, through his actions, that there was a line beyond which he would not allow himself to be pushed. Months of steady labor, followed by forge work in temperatures reaching one hundred degrees, was one step over that line. By tolerating his month-long absence, Weaver and Brady tacitly recognized that Sam had the power to force reasonable, limited, and temporary changes in his work regimen; they also silently acknowledged that, in a certain sense, he was justified in what he was doing. None of this fits the classic definition of what southern slavery was supposed to be: total dominance by the white master and total subservience by the black slave. But social institutions have a way of getting fuzzy around the edges, especially when they are as complex as the institution of human bondage.

Sam Williams won this confrontation, probably because of who he was and because his challenge to the system was guarded and oblique and had a limited objective—rest from work. Bill Greenlee's case was quite a different matter. He was twenty-eight years old and a "prime field hand," but he was, from the perspective of Weaver's labor needs, still only a field hand.[76] Even more important, his defiance of the slave regime was open and direct and had an objective that no slaveholder could tolerate—freedom. Not surprisingly, Weaver brought the full force of the system swiftly and brutally down on him. The example of the unsuccessful runaway's being taken off in chains was immediately before the eyes of Sam Williams and every other slave at Buffalo Forge, and that was undoubtedly the way Weaver wanted it. Even Sam's status as a master refiner probably would not have protected him if he had carried his resistance as far as Bill Greenlee did his.

Bill's attempt to escape and Sam's much more limited protest raise one of the ultimate questions about American slavery. What, in fact, was the better part of valor for a slave? Should one fight, confront, resist openly, run away, do everything one could to bring the system down? Or should one maneuver as best one could within the system, stay with one's family and try to help and comfort them, and attempt to carve out the best possible life despite the physical and psychological confines of enslavement? These were questions that each slave had to decide; they were not easily answered then, and they are not easily answered now. But most, like Sam Williams, chose the latter course. To have done otherwise would have placed almost everything he loved in jeopardy. And Sam—husband of Nancy; father of Betty, Caroline, Ann, and Lydia; and son of Sally and Sam Williams Sr.—had a great deal to lose.

The exact date when Sam and Nancy Williams's oldest daughter married was not entered in the Buffalo Forge records, but it was probably sometime in 1857. Betty was seventeen then, and she and a man named A. Coleman, who apparently belonged to a neighboring slaveholder, became husband and wife.[77] On February 18, 1858, she gave birth to her first child, a boy, and they named him Alfred Elliott Coleman.[78] Sam and Nancy were grandparents now, and Sam had that much more reason to try to shelter his family from the worst aspects of the slave regime.

Perhaps nothing was more indicative of the precariousness of their existence than the events of December 1859. Daniel Brady was away on a cattle drive to Richmond during the first part of the month, but one of the clerks took note of the events that were pressing in on the black men and women there. On Friday, December 2, 1859, "John Brown of Ossawatiamie [*sic*] Noteriety to [be] hung at Charlestown Va. today, for Insurrection," he wrote in Brady's journal.[79] It was also the day before Caroline Williams and Andrew Reid, a slave teamster who lived nearby, had chosen to be married. Caroline, like her older sister Betty, was seventeen at the time of her marriage, and, like her sister, had taken for her husband a man who was not one of Weaver's slaves. Another young slave woman at Buffalo Forge was also getting married at the same time.[80] A double wedding with both grooms coming from off the property meant a large gathering of slaves; and the timing, the day after John Brown was hanged, was undoubtedly why a distinctly unwelcome group of uninvited guests turned up at Buffalo Forge that day. On Saturday, December 3, the Rockbridge County slave patrol went calling.[81]

Something akin to panic had swept over much of the South in the wake of John Brown's October raid on Harpers Ferry, and the Valley of Virginia was no exception. The only way to prevent slave rebellions, whites argued, was an overwhelming show of force and the immediate suppression of the slightest hint of insurrectionary activity.[82] It was not work for the squeamish. We do not know what, if anything, Weaver's slaves said about John Brown, but one of them apparently said or did something the patrol did not like. The hated "paddyrollers," as the blacks called them, left Buffalo Forge after the wedding party broke up on Saturday, but they were back the next day.

Whatever the reason for their return visit might have been, it resulted in an ugly incident that struck close to Sam Williams. The patrol singled out Henry Towles, Sam's helper at the refinery forge, for punishment; the twenty-three-year-old forge hand was taken out, stripped, and whipped.[83] Towles, whose wife, Ann, and three young children lived with him at Buffalo Forge, did not return to work until December 15.[84] It had taken him ten days to recover from the beating administered by the Rockbridge County patrol.

Two weeks later, a much happier event occurred at Buffalo Forge. At eight o'clock in the morning on December 29, Betty Coleman gave birth to her second child, this time a girl. Both mother and daughter were fine.[85] Sam and Nancy Williams now had a granddaughter as well as a grandson at Buffalo Forge.

It had been a month of stark contradictions. The love and hope expressed in the marriage of two young people, followed by the pain and despair brought on by the brutal whipping of one of their own, had been followed by the joy surrounding the birth of a healthy child. Those events spoke eloquently of the pleasure and anguish that mingled together in the lives of these black men and women at Buffalo Forge and throughout the South.

Much of the history of American slavery could also be said to reside in the name of Betty Coleman's new baby. She and her husband called their newborn child Mary Caroline.[86] Her middle name was almost certainly given her in honor of her Aunt Caroline, who had celebrated her marriage just two weeks earlier. The baby's first name, Mary, went back much further in the history of the family, back to little Mary's great-great-grandmother. That Mary, mother of Sally Williams, grandmother of Sam Williams, was the woman taken by Thomas Mayburry when he and Weaver divided the "Wilson negroes" more than two decades earlier. Memories of her, it seems fair to say, were still alive in the minds of her descendants, a family that in 1859 spanned four generations at Buffalo Forge.

John Brown's raid was a prelude to the war that would free them all, although many of them would not be there when emancipation came in 1865. William Weaver also was not there. His final illness set in on a bleak day in mid-March 1863, just over a week after he had celebrated his eighty-third birthday. He died on March 25, 1863, and, true to his word, he left most of his considerable fortune to Daniel and Emma Brady.[87] "As I have kept the great bulk of my estate together partly to provide for the comfort of my servants I desire that they should be treated with kindness and humanity," he had written in his will.[88] The Bradys, from all we can tell, honored his wishes. Only one of his former slaves was put on the block after Weaver's death. Bill Comiskey, a woodchopper, came in from the coal piles with syphilis late in October 1863; a month later he was sold.[89] It was death, not the auctioneer's hammer, that took so many from Buffalo Forge before the day of freedom arrived.

The years of the Civil War were a time of mounting expectations among slaves everywhere in the South, and we can be reasonably sure that such was the case at Buffalo Forge. The Rockbridge Grays, a company in Stonewall Jackson's legendary brigade, had been recruited from the area right around the forge and had drawn off most of the young white men from that section of the county.[90] Even the most isolated slave could see the significance of that fact. Then the refugee families had come streaming past Weaver's place, sometimes spending the night in the big house, while their slaves took their rest in the quarters and undoubtedly passed on the latest news to the black men and women there.[91] In Sam and Nancy Williams's case, however, the joy and hope inspired by the prospect of freedom must have been tempered by the grief and sorrow they had to live with during these years.

By the fall of 1862, their family had grown significantly. Their daughter Caroline had given birth to her first child, Mary Martha Reid (yet another Mary in the Williams family tree), in October 1860, and Betty Coleman had had her third baby, Julia, in November 1861. Less than a year later, in September 1862, Caroline had delivered another healthy child, a boy, William John Reid. (One of Mary's children taken by Mayburry in 1837 had been named John.)[92] But that September was also the month when death began to stalk the Williams family at Buffalo Forge.

Nine days after the birth of Caroline's son, Betty Coleman's four-year-old son, Alfred Elliott, complained of a sore throat. When Daniel Brady examined the boy, he saw unmistakable signs of impending disaster at Buffalo Forge. Alfred had diphtheria. As immunization and effective treatment were not available, it was bound to spread quickly, and no one, black or white, would be safe from its ravages. In rapid succession, Betty, Caroline, and Lydia, three of Sam and Nancy Williams's four daughters, came down with the disease.[93]

When death came to Betty Coleman, it must have been a relief from terrible torment. The first signs of her diphtheria appeared on September 19, and it was clear from the large yellow streaks extending deep into her throat that she had a severe case, much worse than her son's. When a membrane formed at the top of her throat, Brady cauterized it, and she vomited up large, leathery pieces of tissue. She died late in the afternoon on Wednesday, September 24.[94] She was twenty-two years old and the mother of three small children, one of whom, Alfred, was fighting his own struggle against diphtheria. Her father and his forge helper, Henry Towles, dug her grave in the slave cemetery at Buffalo Forge the next morning, and that afternoon, under a clear, cool autumn sky, she was buried. Brady gave all hands the afternoon off so that they could be present at her funeral. Sam was not asked to return to his forge until the following Monday.[95]

For over two months, diphtheria lingered at Buffalo Forge, and before it ran its course, fifteen of Weaver's slaves contracted the disease. Alfred Coleman, Caroline Reid, and Lydia Williams gradually recovered, although the caustic and turpentine with which their throats were treated must have caused them enormous pain. Daniel Brady also was stricken. He was confined to his bedroom for several weeks, but his case was not one of the fatal ones. Three more slaves at Buffalo Forge did die of diphtheria following Betty's fatal attack, however, and before October had ended, her son was also dead. Alfred Elliott Coleman, perhaps weakened by his bout with diphtheria, died on October 31, 1862. Brady listed the cause of his death as an infestation of worms.[96] In the space of six weeks, Sam and Nancy Williams had lost their firstborn child and their eldest grandchild.

More grief was in the offing. Sam Williams was at his forge on May 5, 1864, when news came that his mother was dead. Brady noted that she died of "paralysis," probably a stroke. Sam and a number of the older slaves were released from their duties on the morning following her death, and later that day, Friday, May 6, a beautiful spring day in the Valley, she was buried in the slave cemetery at Buffalo Forge. The cemetery, which stood in a grove of locust trees on a hill behind the mansion, commanded a magnificent view of the Valley: the pale haze of the Blue Ridge, the dense green forests of oak, hickory, walnut, and cedar, the rich fields of wheat, oats, and corn, the waters of Buffalo Creek freshened by the spring thaw. There her wooden coffin was lowered into the earth, and a plain, uncarved shaft of limestone was set up to mark her grave.[97] She had been among family and friends in the last days of her life, and they were doubtless there for her funeral: Sam Williams Sr., in frail health but still alive, her son Sam, her daughter-in-law Nancy, her grandchildren and great-grandchildren, and her friends of many years' standing. Not the least of the comforts that came to the enslaved was represented by that gathering of black men, women, and children on a hilltop overlooking Buffalo Forge in the spring of 1864, the solace and strength that came from family and community in times of trial and sadness.

Sam and Nancy Williams's time of troubles was still not over. Tragedy seemed to haunt them in late 1864 and early 1865 as the end of the war and the moment of freedom drew closer and closer. In the fall of 1864, their twenty-year-old daughter Lydia, who was unmarried, contracted typhoid fever. On October 7, 1864, as her condition worsened, her older sister, Caroline Reid, gave birth to her third child, a girl, and named her Lydia Maydelene Reid in honor of Caroline's stricken sister. Two days later, on Sunday, October 9, Lydia Williams died. Sam's forge was idle on Monday as he spent the day with his family. On Tuesday morning, the black families of Buffalo Forge once again climbed the dirt road behind the big house to the locust grove on the hill. There Sam and Nancy laid their youngest child to rest.[98]

It was not finished even then. By early 1865 it was clear that a third Williams daughter was gravely ill. Caroline Williams Reid had "consumption," or tuberculosis, and there was no cure. She died on Thursday, January 12, 1865, twenty-three years old and the mother of three small children. Sam remained at home that day, and he would have been sorely needed by Nancy, by his one remaining daughter, Ann, and by his grandchildren. Betty Coleman had left two young children behind when she died in 1862, and now there were Caroline's three, all under three years old.[99] If ever there was a time when a man and woman, slave or free, black or white, needed to be with each other and with their own, this was surely such a time. Sam and Nancy Williams were there, together.

They were also there when freedom came to Buffalo Forge in the spring of 1865. Brady's matter-of-fact entries for three days in late May tell the story:

Friday May 26, 1865 Declared free by order of military authorities.
Saturday May 27,1865 All hands quit work as they considered them-
    selves free.
Monday May 29,1865 Commenced work on free labor.[100]

Sam and Nancy Williams were among those who signed three-month contracts on May 29, Sam as master refiner at the forge and Nancy as head dairymaid.[101] Sam continued refining until 1867, when outside competition finally forced Brady to abandon iron-making at Buffalo Forge. Sam shifted to farming on Brady's land in that year and, not surprisingly, became the most successful sharecropper, black or white, on the place.[102] And when he and Nancy finally moved off the property in 1874, they went only a short distance away to an adjoining farm, owned by one of Brady's neighbors, where many of Sam's friends lived and where he found employment as an agricultural laborer.[103]

Space does not permit a full discussion here of Sam and Nancy Williams's life in freedom, but a few points that shed light on their experience in slavery deserve at least a brief mention. Their marriage and their family, so critically important to their survival in former times, were no less vital to them now. We can catch a glimpse of this at two poignant moments. One occurred in 1866 when they entered the office of the Freedmen's Bureau in Lexington. They had come to register their marriage, to legalize that slave union that had taken place twenty-six years before. "Samuel Williams and Nancy Jefferson as man and wife since 1840," the clerk recorded. Sam correctly listed his age as forty-six, Nancy as forty-nine; their only surviving child, their daughter Ann, was twenty-four.[104]

Fourteen years later, in 1880, there is another revealing moment, this one as the census taker was making his rounds in southern Rockbridge County. He reported that Samuel Williams, farmhand, age sixty-one, and Nancy Williams, housewife, age sixty-three, lived in the same household in the Natural Bridge section of the county. Checks placed in the appropriate boxes indicated that neither could read or write. There was a third member of the family, however. Living with them, the census taker noted, was Lydia Maydelene Reid, their granddaughter. The baby who had been only three months old when her mother had died in 1865 was now a girl of fifteen.[105]

How long Sam and Nancy Williams lived on after 1880 is unclear. Lydia married in January 1882 and left the household to begin raising a family of her own. Her husband was a young man named Charles Newman, and their first child, a girl, was born in November 1882; they named her Mary Ann Newman.[106] We do not know exactly when Sam and Nancy died—it was sometime before 1900—but we can be reasonably sure where they are buried.[107] Shortly after the Civil War, the black men and women at Buffalo Forge organized their own church. For a nominal sum, Daniel Brady sold the church trustees a small tract of land just a mile south of the forge. Among the trustees of the Buffalo Forge Colored Baptist Church, soon renamed the Mount Lydia Church, was one Samuel Williams.[108] In 1871, the freedmen erected a wooden church and school-house and laid out a cemetery on this land.[109] The church building has long since disappeared, and today the cemetery site is covered with trees and a heavy growth of underbrush. But if one looks closely enough back among the trees and under the dense carpet of honeysuckle, one can discern small, uncarved, triangular-shaped pieces of limestone. Almost certainly, one of these simple limestone markers stands over the grave of Sam Williams. It is equally certain that a similar stone on the grave nearest his marks the final resting place of Nancy, his wife. The points of all these stones face in the same direction— toward the sky.

NOTES

An earlier version of this essay was published in *Race, Region, and Reconstruction: Essays in Honor of C. Vann Woodward*, ed. J. Morgan Kousser and James M. McPherson (New York: Oxford Univ. Press, 1982), 199-240, and is reprinted here with the permission of Oxford University Press.

1. Weaver's property was located in Rockbridge, Botetourt, and Amherst Counties. On the quantity of land held by Weaver, see his property tax receipts in James D. Davidson Papers, McCormick Collection, State Historical Society of Wisconsin, Madison (hereafter cited as Davidson Papers, McCormick Collection); articles of agreement between William Wilson, and Thomas Mayburry and William Weaver, July 30, 1814, Jordan and Irvine Papers, ibid. (hereafter cited as Jordan and Irvine Papers, McCormick Collection); entries for William Weaver in *Manuscript Census of Agriculture, 1860*, Virginia, microfilm copy, Virginia State Library, Richmond. Weaver's slave holdings at the time of his death are given in "An appraisement of the goods and chattels of William Weaver, deceased," June 1, 1863, William Weaver Papers, University of Virginia Library, Charlottesville (hereafter cited as Weaver Papers, UVA).

2. "An appraisement," June 1, 1863, Weaver Papers, UVA.

3. "Article of agreement . . . between Danl. C.E. Brady . . . and Sam Williams (Freedman)," Jan. 1, 1867, Weaver-Brady Papers in the possession of T.T. Brady, Richmond, Va. (hereafter cited as Weaver-Brady Papers, T.T. Brady). I would like to thank Mr. Brady for kindly granting me access to these papers and for his generous assistance on numerous occasions when I needed help on points relating to Buffalo Forge and the Weaver and Brady families.

4. See Charles L. Perdue Jr., et al., eds., *Weevils in the Wheat: Interviews with Virginia Ex-Slaves* (Charlottesville: Univ. Press of Virginia, 1976), and George P. Rawick, ed., *The American Slave: A Composite Autobiography*, 41 vols. (Westport, Conn.: Greenwood Press, 1972, 1977, 1979).

5. "Weaver Family: Memo and Historical Notes," Weaver-Brady Family Record Book, Weaver-Brady Papers, T.T. Brady.

6. Articles of agreement between William Wilson, and Thomas Mayburry and William Weaver.

7. Mayburry to Weaver, Sept. 15, Oct. 18, 1815, Feb. 4, 1816, in Case Papers, *Weaver v. Mayburry*, Superior Court of Chancery Records, Augusta County Court House, Staunton, Va. (hereafter cited as Case Papers, *Weaver v. Mayburry*).

8. Statement of Thomas Mayburry, Oct. 1, 1821, ibid.

9. John S. Wilson to Weaver, Oct. 24, 1815, ibid. All ages given on the bill of sale were approximations.

10. See deposition of James C. Dickinson, Aug. 15, 1836, in Case Papers, *Weaver v. Jordan, Davis & Co.*, Superior Court of Chancery Records, Rockbridge County Court House, Lexington, Va. (hereafter cited as Case Papers, *Weaver v. Jordan, Davis & Co.*).

11. Bond of Mayburry for the forthcoming of slaves, Dec. 20, 1828, Case Papers, *Weaver v. Mayburry;* "An appraisement."

12. "Names, births & c: of Negroes," Weaver-Brady Papers, T.T. Brady.

13. W.W. Davis to Weaver, July 7, 1832, William Weaver Papers, Duke University Library, Durham, N.C. (hereafter cited as Weaver Papers, Duke).

14. Mayburry to Weaver, Oct. 18, Nov. 10, Dec. 19, 1817, March 29, July 16, 1818, Sept. 22, 1819, Aug. 19, 1821, June 15, Nov. 14, 1822, Case Papers, *Weaver v. Mayburry;* deposition of William Weaver, Dec. 10, 1840, Case Papers, *Alexander v. Irvine's Administrator,* Superior Court of Chancery Records, Rockbridge County Court House (hereafter cited as Case Papers, *Alexander v. Irvine's Administrator*).

15. "Articles of agreement . . . between Thomas Mayburry and William Weaver," Feb. 9, 1825, Weaver Papers, Duke.

16. John S. Wilson to Mayburry, March 1, 1825, Case Papers, *Weaver v. Mayburry.*

17. See deposition of Thomas Mayburry, April 22, 1839, Case Papers, *Weaver v. Jordan, Davis & Co.*

18. "Article of agreement . . . between Thos. Mayburry & Wm. Weaver," Aug. 3, 1836, Weaver Papers, Duke.

19. Ibid.; deposition of Thomas Mayburry, April 20, 1839, Case Papers, *Weaver v. Jordan, Davis & Co.*

20. Bond of Thomas Mayburry for the forthcoming of slaves, Dec. 20, 1828, Case Papers, *Weaver v. Mayburry;* "Names, births & c: of Negroes"; Buffalo Forge Negro Books, 1830–40, 1839–41, 1844–50, 1850–58, Weaver-Brady Records, University of Virginia Library, Charlottesville (hereafter cited as Weaver-Brady Records, Virginia).

21. Buffalo Forge Negro Books, 1830–40, 1839–41, 1844–50, 1850–58.

22. "An appraisement."

23. See Charles B. Dew, "David Ross and the Oxford Iron Works: A Study of Industrial Slavery in the Early Nineteenth-Century South," *William and Mary Quarterly*, 3d ser., 31 (1974): 197–98.

24. Ibid., 197, 210–11; "List of Slaves at the Oxford Iron Works in Families and Their Employment, Taken 15 January 1811," William Bolling Papers, Duke University Library, Durham, N.C. (hereafter cited as Bolling Papers, Duke).

25. Weaver to Brady, March 4, 1856, Weaver Papers, Duke.

26. "Descriptive List of Negroes hired . . . , Confederate States Nitre and Mining Service, 1865," Weaver-Brady Papers, T.T. Brady.

27. Buffalo Forge Negro Books, 1830–40.

28. Weaver to James D. Davidson, Nov. 4, 1849, Davidson Papers, McCormick Collection.

29. See Arthur Cecil Bining, *Pennsylvania Iron Manufacture in the Eighteenth Century*, 2d ed. (Harrisburg, Pa.: Pennsylvania Historical Commission, 1973), 72–73.

30. Deposition of William Weaver, Dec. 10, 1840, Case Papers, *Alexander v. Irvine's Administrator;* Weaver's cane is in the possession of D.E. Brady Jr., Buffalo Forge, Va.

31. Samuel Sydney Bradford, "The Ante-Bellum Charcoal Iron Industry of Virginia" (Ph.D. diss., Columbia University, 1958), 134; Bining, *Pennsylvania Iron Manufacture*, 72–73.

32. Buffalo Forge Negro Books, 1830–40, 1839–41.

33. Bining, *Pennsylvania Iron Manufacture*, 73–74.

34. Buffalo Forge Iron Book, 1831–62, Weaver-Brady Records, Virginia; Moses McCue to Weaver, July 3, 1829, Weaver Papers, Duke; deposition of William Weaver, Dec. 10, 1840, Case Papers, *Alexander v. Irvine's Administrator.*

35. Weaver to Davidson, June 12, 1848, Jordan and Irvine Papers, McCormick Collection.

36. See Buffalo Forge Negro Books, 1830–40, 1839–41, 1844–50, 1850–58. The best general discussions of the overwork system are Robert S. Starobin, *Industrial Slavery in the Old South* (New York: Oxford Univ. Press, 1970), 99–103, and Ronald L. Lewis, *Coal, Iron, and Slaves: Industrial Slavery in Maryland and Virginia, 1715–1865* (Westport, Conn.: Greenwood Press, 1979), 119–27.

37. Depositions of John Doyle, Feb. 5, 1840, Anthony W. Templin, Jan. 24, 1839, John Jordan, July 22, 1836, and Henry A. Lane, Feb. 5, 1840, Case Papers, *Weaver v. Jordan,* Davis & Co.

38. Buffalo Forge Negro Books, 1830–40, 1839–41, 1844–50, 1850–58, and Etna Furnace Negro Book, 1854–61, Weaver-Brady Records, Virginia.

39. Wm. C. McAllister to Weaver, Feb. 22, 1830, Weaver Papers, Duke.

40. See entries for Sam Etna, John Baxter, and Harry Hunt in Buffalo Forge Negro Books, 1839–41.

41. See "List of Slaves at the Oxford Iron Works . . . 1811," Bolling Papers, Duke; Dew, "David Ross and the Oxford Iron Works," 189–91, 222–24.

42. Buffalo Forge Negro Books, 1839–41.

43. Marriage Register for Rockbridge County, Sub-district "A," 6th District, Virginia, Records of the Bureau of Refugees, Freedmen, and Abandoned Lands, Record Group 105, National Archives, Washington, D.C. (hereafter cited as Marriage Register for Rockbridge County, Freedmen's Bureau Records, RG 105, NA).

44. As indicated by his entries in Buffalo Forge Negro Books, 1839–41.

45. "Names, births & c: of Negroes."

46. Bond of Thomas Mayburry for the forthcoming of slaves, Dec. 20, 1828, Case Papers, *Weaver v. Mayburry.*

47. Buffalo Forge Negro Books, 1830–40.

48. For a description of this process, see W. McKee Evans, *Ballots and Fence Rails: Reconstruction on the Lower Cape Fear* (Chapel Hill: Univ. of North Carolina Press, 1967), 95–96.

49. Buffalo Forge Negro Books, 1839–41.

50. Ibid.

51. Ibid.

52. Marriage Register for Rockbridge County, Freedmen's Bureau Records, RG 105, NA; "Names, births & c: of Negroes."

53. Buffalo Forge Negro Books, 1839–41.

54. Ibid., 1844–50.

55. Ibid., 1850–58.

56. Ibid.

57. Ibid., 1844–50, 1850–58.

58. Ibid.

59. John A. Rex to Davidson, Feb. 25, 1855, Davidson Papers, McCormick Collection.

60. Ibid., notation on reverse.

61. D.C.E. Brady Private Ledger, Weaver-Brady Papers in the possession of D.E. Brady Jr., Buffalo Forge, Va. (hereafter cited as Weaver-Brady Papers, D.E. Brady Jr.). I would like to thank Mr. Brady for kindly granting me access to these papers and for his generous assistance on points relating to Buffalo Forge and the Weaver and Brady families.

62. Ibid.

63. One can follow their accounts by tracing the entries under their names in: Buffalo Forge Ledger, 1851–59, Weaver-Brady Papers, T.T. Brady; Buffalo Forge Ledger, 1859–78, Weaver-Brady Papers, D.E. Brady Jr.; Buffalo Forge Journal, 1859–66, Weaver-Brady Records, Virginia; and Buffalo Forge Journal, 1866–78, Weaver-Brady Papers, D.E. Brady Jr.

64. Weaver to Brady, Aug. 27, 1855, March 4, 1856, Weaver Papers, Duke.

65. Weaver family history compiled by D.E. Brady Sr., Oct. 28, 1951, Weaver-Brady Papers, D.E. Brady Jr.; "Weaver Family," Weaver-Brady Family Record Book, Weaver-Brady Papers, T.T. Brady.

66. Weaver to Brady, Aug. 27, 1855, Weaver Papers, Duke.

67. "Brady Family" and "Gorgas Family," Weaver-Brady Family Record Book, and [D.C.E. Brady] to Davidson, July 27, 1867, Weaver-Brady Papers, T.T. Brady.

68. Daniel C.E. Brady, Home Journal, 1858–60, Weaver-Brady Records, Virginia Collection (hereafter cited as Brady, Home Journal, Virginia); Daniel C.E. Brady, Home Journal, 1860–65, McCormick Collection (hereafter cited as Brady, Home Journal, McCormick Collection).

69. Brady, Home Journal, Virginia.

70. Ibid.

71. Ibid.

72. Ibid.; J.E. Carson to Weaver, March 12, May 30, June 27, 1859, Weaver Papers, Duke; Weaver to Carson, July 2, 1859, Buffalo Forge Letterbook, 1858–65, Weaver-Brady Records, Virginia; entries for June 9, July 30, 1859, Buffalo Forge Cash Book, 1849–62, Weaver-Brady Records, Virginia.

73. W.W. Rex to Weaver, Aug. 15, 1860, Weaver Papers, Duke; entry for Aug, 7, 1860, Buffalo Forge Cash Book, 1849–62; Brady, Home Journal, Virginia.

74. Brady, Home Journal, Virginia.

75. Buffalo Forge Cash Book, 1849–62.

76. "Names, births & c: of Negroes."

77. Ibid. Betty's husband's name was given at the time one of their children married in 1876; see marriage registration of Mary C. Coleman and Steward Chandler, July 27, 1876, Register of Marriages, Book IA, 1865–89, Rockbridge County Court House, Lexington, Va. (hereafter cited as Rockbridge County Marriage Register, 1865–89).

78. "Names, births & c: of Negroes."

79. Brady, Home Journal, Virginia.

80. Ibid.; Ch. H. Locher to Weaver, Dec. 3, 1859, Weaver-Brady Papers, T.T. Brady; "Names, births & c: of Negroes"; Marriage Register for Rockbridge County, Freedmen's Bureau Records, RG 105, NA. Caroline's husband's name was given at the time one of their children married in 1882; see marriage registration of Lydia Reid and Charles Newman, Jan. 4, 1882, Rockbridge County Marriage Register, 1865–89.

81. Brady, Home Journal, Virginia.

82. Clement Eaton, *The Freedom-of-Thought Struggle in the Old South* (New York: Harper and Row, 1964), 102–3; Eaton's chapter, "The Fear of Servile Insurrection," provides an excellent discussion of overall white attitudes. See also Charles B. Dew, "Black Ironworkers and the Slave Insurrection Panic of 1856," *Journal of Southern History* 41 (1975): 327–33.

83. Brady, Home Journal, Virginia.

84. Ibid.; "Names, births & c: of Negroes."

85. "Names, births & c: of Negroes."

86. "Names, births & c: of Negroes," Weaver-Brady Papers, T.T. Brady.

87. Brady, Home Journal, Virginia; Last Will and Testament of William Weaver, Jan. 8, 1863, William Weaver Papers, Washington and Lee University Library, Lexington, Va. (hereafter cited as Weaver Papers, W& L).

88. Last Will and Testament, Weaver Papers, W&L.

89. Entry for Oct. 24, 1863, Brady, Home Journal, McCormick Collection; "Names, births & c: of Negroes."

90. Oren F. Morton, *A History of Rockbridge County, Virginia* (Staunton, Va.: McClure, 1920), 126, 425–27; entry for April 20, 1861, Brady, Home Journal, McCormick Collection.

91. Entries for March 7, April 28, 1862, Brady, Home Journal, McCormick Collection.

92. "Names, births & c: of Negroes."

93. Brady, Home Journal, McCormick Collection; ibid., see entries under "Diphtheria & Sore Throat 1862," rear flyleaf, vol. 1.

94. Ibid.

95. Ibid.

96. "Names, births & c: of Negroes"; "Diphtheria & Sore Throat 1862," Brady, Home Journal, McCormick Collection.

97. Brady, Home Journal, McCormick Collection. Mr. D.E. Brady Jr. pointed out to me the site of this cemetery. A number of the gravestones are still there.

98. "Names, births & c: of Negroes"; Brady, Home Journal, McCormick Collection.

99. Brady, Home Journal, McCormick Collection.

100. Buffalo Forge Journal, 1859–66, Weaver-Brady Records, Virginia; Brady, Home Journal, McCormick Collection.

101. See entries under "Sam Williams" and "Nancy Williams," Buffalo Forge Negro Books, 1865–73; "Account Sales Iron made by Rocke & Murrell," Lynchburg, Va., 1865, 1866, Weaver Papers, Duke.

102. "Article of agreement . . . between Danl. C.E. Brady . . . & Sam Williams (Freedman)," Jan. 1, 1867, Weaver-Brady Papers, T.T. Brady; entries for Sam Williams and other sharecroppers in D.C.E. Brady, Home Journal, 1865–76, Weaver-Brady Papers, T.T. Brady (hereafter cited as Brady, Home Journal, T.T. Brady.)

103. The last entries for Sam Williams are dated 1874 in Brady, Home Journal, T.T. Brady; Bureau of the Census, *Tenth Census of the United States, 1880*, Manuscript Population Schedules, Rockbridge County, Va., National Archives Microfilm Publications, T9.

104. Marriage Register for Rockbridge County, 1865–1889, Freedmen's Bureau Records, RG 105, NA.

105. Manuscript Population Schedules, *Tenth Census.*

106. See marriage registration of Lydia Reid and Charles Newman, Jan. 4, 1882, Marriage Register for Rockbridge County, 1865–1889; birth registration of Mary Ann Newman, Birth Register No. 2, 1878–1896, Rockbridge County Court House, Lexington, Va.

107. A search of the index and population schedules for the 1900 Census failed to turn up the names of either Sam or Nancy Williams; Card Index (Soundex) to the 1900 Population Schedules, Virginia, National Archives Microfilm Publications, T 1076; Bureau of the Census, *Twelfth Census of the United States, 1900*, Manuscript Population Schedules, Rockbridge County, Va., National Archives Microfilm Publications, T623.

108. Deed between D.C.E. Brady, et al., and Samuel Williams, et al., Oct. 9, 1871, Deed Book MM, Rockbridge County Court House, Lexington, Va.

109. "Col. Baptist Church of Buffalo Forge, Va.," account with D.C.E. Brady, 1871, Weaver-Brady Papers, T.T. Brady.

6

"A SOURCE OF GREAT ECONOMY"?

The Railroad and Slavery's Expansion in Southwest Virginia, 1850–1860

KENNETH W. NOE

Although officially delineated by the state government only in 1860, southwest Virginia's status as a separate and distinct region within the commonwealth was long-standing and widely recognized. First settled by peoples of Old World descent in the 1740s, southwest Virginia grew steadily in population after the American Revolution. Politically, economically, and socially, the region's residents during the first half of the nineteenth century usually straddled the fence between the tobacco plantation counties east of the Blue Ridge Mountains and the rugged and largely all-white area north of the Kanawha River, northwest Virginia. Well into the 1840s, the two western regions, united by a common desire for improved transportation, more equitable representation in the General Assembly, and a more favorable basis of taxation, cooperated to the degree that most observers spoke simply of "the West."

A series of events in the 1840s and 1850s, however, drove a wedge between the two western regions and drew southwest Virginia closer to the eastern half of the state. Of those, the most dramatic was the construction of the Virginia and Tennessee Railroad (V&T) from Lynchburg to the Tennessee border. Begun in 1850 and completed six and a half years later, the railroad served as the catalyst for dramatic changes in the southwest. Facilitated by more convenient transportation to eastern and southern markets, many southwest Virginia farmers embraced commercial pursuits. Tobacco production in the southwestern counties jumped a remarkable 2020 percent from 1850 to 1860 and, from a handful of counties, spread throughout the region. At the same time the wheat crop doubled. The greater importance of cash-crop agriculture increased land values and taxes, leading to greater economic marginalization among southwest Virginia's white population. Some turned to industrial pursuits, notably the mining of iron, lead, and copper, traditional activities given new impetus by the railroad. Towns grew along the rails, as did a plethora of hot springs catering to well-heeled tourists. Southwest Virginia was better connected with the eastern counties economically, and its political leaders invariably drew closer to their former eastern antagonists as their goals and concerns became more shared, especially after the new state constitution of 1851 alleviated many traditional western grievances that went unanswered by a similar convention in 1830. Among those concerns that were growing more important was the survival of the institution that provided much of the labor force for southwest Virginia's railroad-based commercialism, slavery.[1]

Not all of the southwest Virginia mountaineers affected by railroad-based modernization were white. African Americans also have called southwest Virginia home since the beginnings of settlement. The 1790 census, the nation's first, found 1,787 slaves, about 6 percent of the total population, in southwest Virginia's then four counties. It also identified thirty-nine nonwhite "free persons." The numbers and percentages of slaves in the region grew steadily from 1790 until the Civil War. In 1830, the region's slaveholders held 12,060 bondsmen, 12.3 percent of the population. By 1850, the numbers were 16,442 and 10.6 percent respectively, hardly negligible. The lower percentage was due more to the increase of white population than to any lessening of slavery's importance. Over the same period, in comparison, Virginia's percentage of slave population fell at an even faster rate, from 38.8 percent to 33.3 percent.[2] Looking backward from 1851, the *Richmond Enquirer* not surprisingly found "the relative increase of the slaves in the whole of Western Virginia . . . remarkable."[3]

Black southwest Virginians, though roughly one-tenth of the region's antebellum population, have usually been ignored. Contemporaries played down the presence of slavery in the region for political reasons. In 1830, for example, the eastern opponents of constitutional reform found it useful to depict transmontane Virginia as largely all-white and nearly abolitionist in sympathies. Slavery's opponents, men such as Ossawatomie John Brown and James W. Taylor, then picked up on the image. After the Civil War, influential writers enshrined the stereotype of nearly all-white, antislavery Appalachia.[4]

A few observers, of course, did recognize the "remarkable" presence and importance of slavery in the region. In *A Journey in the Back Country*, Frederick Law Olmsted's negative preconceptions skewed his interpretations; often he saw only what he wanted to see, which in this case was nonslaveholders' resentment of the master class and, occasionally, in East Tennessee, abolitionist ideas. Yet even he had to admit that in southwest Virginia, slaves and slaveholders were much more in evidence as he traveled through the valley subregion and, moreover, that the southwest Virginia whites he met were never openly antislavery.[5]

An additional observer was a native southwest Virginian, George W.L. Bickley. Through a mixture of fact and ideology, Bickley placed slavery even closer to the heart of mountain life. Best remembered as the unstable founder of the notorious Knights of the Golden Circle, a shadow organization dedicated to the expansion of slavery throughout the western hemisphere, Bickley was born in Russell County in 1819. He ran away from home as a youth only to return to the region in the late 1840s to practice medicine in Jeffersonville, Tazewell County. Before leaving again for Ohio in 1851, he registered a notable first, writing the pioneer history of his native region in collaboration with a local historical society.[6]

Considering Bickley's later activities and obvious mental instability, his *History of the Settlement and Indian Wars of Tazewell County, Virginia* remains remarkably useful; it included voluminous information on the region's geography, climate, economy, educational facilities, and customs. The author's real goals in writing the book, however, were largely political and proslavery. Denouncing the eastern Virginia politicians who for most of the century had controlled the state government, Bickley wanted to convince his fellow southwest Virginians to separate politically from Virginia and to form a new state in conjunction with the equally disgruntled mountain residents of eastern Kentucky, western North Carolina, and eastern Tennessee, but not northwest Virginia. Bickley pointedly excluded the heart of the future state of West Virginia from his new state scheme. Because of slavery, he felt, the two regions were much too different. Whereas the northwest increasingly was becoming free territory, slavery occupied a central place in southwestern society. Indeed, he made a point of condemning contemporaries for the common practice of ignoring southwest Virginia and equating "West" with the antislavery "Northwest."[7]

That one of the most notorious advocates of slavery in Civil War–era America was a southwest Virginia mountaineer should have dramatized the differences between northwest and southwest Virginia and the importance of the institution in Appalachia to later observers. Only recently, however, have scholars reaffirmed the importance of slavery in mountain society. That understanding is crucial. If one is to understand why southwest Virginia embraced the Confederate cause in 1861, the centrality of slavery must be acknowledged. With slavery already an important fact of mountain life in southwest Virginia by 1850, the role of the railroad was to provide still greater opportunities for slave-based staple agriculture and, as a result, facilitate the institution's growth through the 1850s, a decade when the institution stagnated elsewhere in the state. Herein lies a seeming paradox, if one fails to recognize the distinctive character of southern modernization or simplistically equates modernization with "progress." In southwest Virginia, as elsewhere in the South, modernization and the expansion of an institution as "unmodern" as chattel slavery went hand-in-hand.[8]

"There are more slaves here than I have seen before for several weeks," wrote Olmsted, outside of Abingdon, as he emerged from East Tennessee to complete his journey in the highlands.[9] It was true. While slaveholding in southwest Virginia was not as extensive as it was in the nonmountain sections of the South, of all sections of the southern mountain region, southwest Virginia was among the leaders in the most slaves and the most slaveholders. Approximately 11.2 percent of sampled householders in 1850 were slave owners. To be sure, most of those masters owned but a few slaves; the median sample holding was three, although the situation varied from county to county. Moreover, there were slave owners in areas such as Washington County who would have qualified as planters anywhere in the South. Washington Countian Eliza White, for example, owned sixty-five slaves in 1850, and her neighbor John Preston held forty-six. Overall, slavery was most extensive in the valley subregion. Three hundred and fifty-two Washington Countians owned slaves, 67 owned ten or more, and 15 owned twenty or more. In contrast, only 112 Floyd Countians belonged to the slave-owning class, and only Joseph Howard owned more than twenty slaves. The contrast was even greater in Raleigh County, where only eight owned slaves in 1850. With six bondsmen, Archibald Walker was Raleigh's leading master.[10] While many of the three counties' leading masters fit Olmsted's description of mountain masters, "chiefly professional men, shop-keepers, and men in office, who are also land owners," most identified themselves as farmers.[11]

As valley subregion slaveholders owned more slaves, they also controlled much more wealth than their peers did elsewhere in the region. Washington County's ten leading masters owned a mean of $28,175 of real property in a county where the overall mean was $761 and the mean of all slave owners was $2,753. In contrast, the mean of Raleigh County's eight slave owners was $2,699. While far above Raleigh's overall mean holding, $453, the figure still was not substantial; indeed, the landholdings of Raleigh's elites were comparable in worth to those of the average Washington County master. Moreover, the gap between rich and poor in the plateau was not as significant. Slaveholding, then, while it approximated the situation of the black-belt elite in the valley, grew more egalitarian as it penetrated the mountains.[12]

This expansion continued numerically and geographically through the 1850s. Most basic was the simple growth of the region's slave population from 1850 to 1860. In 1860, southwest Virginia as a whole contained 20,532 black residents, of whom only 1,506 were free. This meant an increase of 2,584 slaves and 232 free blacks during the decade. Considered as percentages, that translates into a 15.7 percent increase in the number of slaves. This figure does not appear especially remarkable at first. Over the same ten years, for example, Texas's slave population increased 213.9 percent; Arkansas's, 135.9 percent; and Florida's, 57.1 percent. When compared with older states such as Georgia and Tennessee, however, as well as with the rest of Virginia, southwest Virginia's growing slave population takes on new significance. Statewide, slavery grew from 1850 to 1860 at only a 3.5 percent rate. In the Tidewater, growth had stagnated, and in the Valley and especially in the northwest, slavery had de-clined. The rate of growth in the piedmont, while more substantial, was less than half that of southwest Virginia. In short, although the real numbers were comparatively smaller in southwest Virginia, the institution nonetheless evinced a vitality noticeably absent in the rest of the commonwealth. If slavery had peaked in Virginia and entered a period of decline, as William W. Freehling recently implied, it nonetheless showed surprising vigor in the southwest.[13]

Slavery did not grow at a uniform rate across the region. In the Blue Ridge subregion, Carroll County's copper rush led to a sizable increase in the county's slave laborers, from 154 to 262, a 70.1 percent rate of growth. In Floyd and Grayson Counties, however, increases in the white population far outstripped slave population growth. In 1850, for example, 113 Floyd Countians owned 444 slaves. Ten years later, the numbers of both groups had increased roughly by only thirty. The mean and median sample slaveholdings in Floyd were exactly the same as those in 1850, 3.4 and 2.0, respectively. With twenty-two slaves, Joseph Howard remained the county's leading master and the only owner of more than twenty slaves. Meanwhile, the white population had increased by almost 30 percent. In Floyd, very little had changed.[14]

While slavery remained in stasis in the Blue Ridge subregion as a whole, one indicator suggests that future growth was in the offing. The rates of natural increase among slaves, computed from the percentage of slaves under age ten compared with the total slave population, were 35.6 percent and 33.4 percent in Floyd and Grayson Counties, respectively, higher than the statewide average of 30.5 percent. As John Inscoe has noted, a higher-than-average rate of natural increase reflected confidence among slaveholders that slavery was a safe and profitable investment for the future. In other words, the white tide sweeping into Floyd and Grayson Counties did not deter those counties' slaveholders from deepening their involvement in the peculiar institution.[15]

Nor did a lack of substantial growth mean widespread opposition to the institution. Robley D. Evans, for example, a future officer in the Union navy, was the son of one Floyd County master, a physician who owned a dozen slaves. Most of the Evanses' neighbors were nonslaveholders who "as a rule were poor and did their own farm work." Yet all of them carefully maintained the sanctity of the institution in the county, at least according to Evans. "There were two things one must not do," he remembered, "steal horses or interfere with his neighbors' slaves."[16]

A different situation existed in the Valley subregion counties, which together already held half of the entire region's slaves. Two distinct trends may be discerned. Two counties experienced major slave growth. Montgomery County gained 748 slaves, a 50.9 percent increase that far outpaced the county's 21 percent gain in white population. At the opposite end of the Valley subregion, Washington County, southwest Virginia's leading slave county in 1860, added 418 slaves, a 19.5 percent increase. In Washington County, 390 slave owners owned 2,547 slaves in 1860. While the mean sampled holding was 6.5 and the median 4.0, sixty residents of the county owned more than ten slaves, and eighteen owned more than twenty. With seventy-two slaves, Wyndham Robertson now reigned as the county's leading planter. In the other three counties of the Valley subregion, however, slave populations experienced little dramatic change. Pulaski County gained 118 slaves, Smyth County lost 27, and Wythe County lost 23. Again, however, the rates of natural increase in these three counties were higher than Virginia's overall rate.[17]

The counties of the Allegheny Plateau experienced the widest fluctuations. One can simplify analysis somewhat by considering the subregion in 1860 as further subdivided into eastern and western halves, as Paul Salstrom has done. In the more rugged western section of the plateau subregion, Russell and Tazewell Counties' slave populations underwent significant growth. Russell gained 117 slaves in the decade, and Tazewell added 142. Notably, these two counties were those best connected to the railroad through a road network

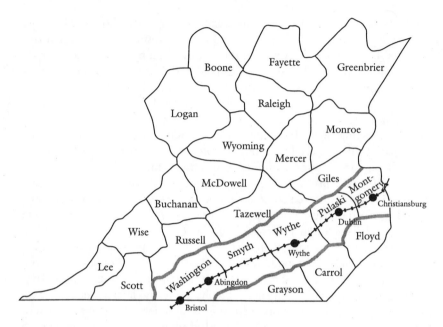

Southwest Virginia, 1860, with the route of the Virginia & Tennessee Railroad. (Map produced by University of Georgia Cartographic Services)

that linked them to Abingdon. As one moved away from the railroad, however, the importance of slavery declined noticeably. The entire remainder of the western plateau gained only 152 slaves in the decade. McDowell County was all-white in 1860, and Buchanan, Wise, and Wyoming Counties were nearly so.[18]

Had the western plateau then become an impenetrable mountain wall against slavery's expansion? The region's slaveholders felt much differently than their neighbors did. Among these slaveholders, one found the highest rates of natural increase among the slave population in all of southwest Virginia. Only McDowell County, with no slaves, and Scott County, with a rate of 25.1 percent, had averages smaller than the statewide average. Elsewhere, the rates varied, from Logan County's 35.8 percent to Buchanan County's whopping 43.3 percent. Boone County's rate of natural increase was 38.0 percent. In those counties, in other words, slavery generated little enthusiasm among most of the rapidly growing white population, many of whom had fled the developing commercial, slave-intensive nexus, but aroused strong faith in the system among the subregion's few slaveholders. More than most of the state's masters, the slave owners of Boone, Buchanan, Logan, and Wise Counties confidently emphasized the breeding or purchase of slave children, human investments whose dates of maturity, literally as well as figuratively, were several years in the future. Clearly, they believed that slavery, not free white labor, would be the wave of the future in the western plateau.[19]

A different situation developed in the eastern half of the Allegheny Plateau subregion. Because of a somewhat gentler landscape, more reliable road and river transportation, and a longer history of settlement and commercial enterprise, some counties in this area already were involved substantially with slave-based agriculture and commerce. In 1850, Greenbrier County held 1,317 slaves, making it the non-upper-valley county with the largest slave population. Only Montgomery, Washington, and Wythe Counties possessed more slaves in 1850. With 1,061 slaves, Monroe County followed close behind. To their west, however, Fayette, Mercer, and Raleigh Counties lagged, together holding only 356 slaves.[20]

By 1860, Greenbrier had added an additional 208 slaves, and Monroe, 53. The rates of slave population growth in these counties were moderate, 15.8 percent and 5.0 percent, respectively. The real story occurred just to the west, where tobacco cultivation captured the economy. Just as in the Tidewater, tobacco meant slave labor. By 1860, Fayette County contained 115 additional slaves, a 73.7 percent rate of growth. Mercer County, with 185 new slaves, exhibited a growth rate of 104.5 percent.[21]

Most interesting of all was Raleigh County. In 1850, only eight slave owners and twenty-three slaves lived there. Ten years later, the number of masters had almost tripled, and the slave population had increased to fifty-seven, a 147.8 percent rate of growth. When calculated with real numbers as small as these, percentages can distort as much as they reveal. Still, when considered along with Fayette's and Mercer's, Raleigh's experience strongly suggests that slavery had started to take a strong hold in the three plateau counties along the New River. To be sure, Raleigh County's twenty-one slave owners had a long way to go to match a Wyndham Robertson. With nine slaves, doctor-farmer John Manser was Raleigh's leading slave owner in 1860. A further indicator that slavery was only in its infancy in Raleigh County was the relatively advanced ages of its slaves. In Floyd County, by way of comparison, the mean slave age was eighteen. In contrast, the mean slave age in Raleigh County was twenty-eight. Moreover, with one exception, Raleigh County's rate of natural increase was the lowest in the region.[22]

All in all, the 1850 and 1860 censuses reveal that slavery in southwest Virginia was spreading out of the counties where the institution had established itself and into the more mountainous parts of the region. It grew at a dramatic rate along the New River, in the line of counties just north of the upper-valley subregion, in Montgomery County, and in Carroll County's mining camps. Ahead of the onrushing tide of piedmont-style, slave-based capitalism, whites unable or unwilling to take part in the new order removed to the more rugged areas of the Blue Ridge and Allegheny Plateau subregions, swelling those counties' white populations. Even there, however, slavery and all that accompanied the institution could not be escaped forever. The elites of the Plateau subregion were increasing their investments in slavery with eyes toward a future expansion of their own. Had civil war not destroyed slavery in the 1860s, it certainly would have continued its march into the southwest Virginia mountains.

If one is to fully comprehend slavery in southwest Virginia, one must do more than count. What was mountain slavery like for the region's expanding slaves? How did the railroad modify the work and lives of slaves? In the absence of slave accounts, one is forced to depend on the biased records of white southwest Virginians, accounts of outside observers, and secondary scholarship. Opinions expressed in these sources vary. W.J. Cash maintained that white mountaineers' treatment of blacks was worse than their treatment in the wider South. Some antebellum travelers, such as the English Quaker abolitionist Joseph John Gurney, found little difference whatsoever in the South's peculiar institution as practiced in its mountain form. Noting slaves' "miserable clothing" in cold weather, Gurney concluded that the institution was just as bad in the springs area as elsewhere. Most observers, however, concluded that mountain slavery was somewhat milder than in the lowlands. Despite his hatred of the institution, Olmsted called mountain slavery "the mild and segregated form" and wrote that mountain slaves' "habits more resemble those of ordinary free laborers, they exercise more responsibility, and both in soul and intellect they are more elevated."[23]

What was the true situation? Just as elsewhere in the South, evidence suggests that the slave experience differed from owner to owner. Some masters seem to have accorded their slaves decent treatment and perhaps even developed bonds of affection. One Lewisburg master asked his brother to purchase "ten Sows big with Pig" in Charleston for his slaves.[24] John Echols trusted two slaves named Dick and George enough to allow them to deliver horses to George Henry Caperton without any white supervision.[25] Most striking of all was the dispute over the treatment of slaves between U.S. Army officer Alexander W. Reynolds and his sister, Sallie Patton. Stationed in Texas in the late 1850s, Reynolds demanded that his sister forward to him his three slaves. Citing his alleged inability to care for them, especially for the slave Jim, Patton refused. Reynolds was furious. "I have never known you to take such heartfelt interest in any thing," he wrote, "as you appear to take in your dear darling negroes. Your brother is but a secondary consideration in comparison to them."[26]

Most slave owners were willing to go only so far, however. Ex-governor David Campbell was known as a kind master who "allowed his servants unusual privileges," including allowing them to sell wood and hogs. When a slave named Page was caught stealing chickens and hogs from neighbors, however, Campbell determined that the "reckless scoundrel" be "taken out of the country, as a matter of safety to the community." Referring to Page's mother, who had helped hide the accused, Campbell added that "I would send old Hannah off but she is too old to treat very harshly." He also approved the whipping of two other slaves who helped hide Page from the authorities.[27] Page was not alone. Three of John Barnes's Tazewell County slaves were jailed for attacking their young overseer as he whipped one of them. Escaping, the three fought another white man and set dogs on others. Their fate too was to be sold to buyers in the Deep South.[28]

The fate of Page and the Barnes slaves demonstrates that the threat of sale "down the river" could be as egregious a punishment as the lash. Such sales would have been easy, as southwest Virginia was an important route in the slave trade. Eastern Virginia and Maryland slaves generally passed through the Valley subregion on the Valley Road on their way to the Deep South. George Featherstonhaugh, traveling in southwest Virginia in the 1830s, encountered the "singular spectacle" of slave drivers shepherding three hundred slaves across the New River from Montgomery to Pulaski County. The slaves forded the river manacled and chained together in double files while being forced to sing to banjo accompaniment. John Armfield, the slave trader, eventually sold the slaves in Natchez, Mississippi, and in Louisiana.[29]

One should note, however, that most sales must have taken place between southwest Virginians. As John Inscoe noted in his study of western North Carolina, that region's higher-than-average rate of natural increase, coupled with a rate of increase in the slave population faster than the state's as a whole, strongly suggests that most regional masters were selling intraregionally. The sale of slaves in these cases usually emanated from the death of the master.[30]

Many southwest Virginia slave owners, of course, expressed discomfort with selling slaves and the resultant tragic effect on the black family. There is little evidence, however, that the discomfort ultimately kept southwest Virginia's masters from breaking up families when it was in their best interests. The heirs of William Preston, for example, coolly divided his eighty slaves among themselves and then swapped and sold to neighbors. Likewise, Monroe County attorney and legislator Allen Caperton took the slaves from one estate across the state to Richmond to sell just as the dead owner's will stipulated.[31] Referring to another estate, also to be disposed of in the state capital, one relative asked Caperton, "Will you sell them to traders or try to sell them privately, that is to persons who are not trading in Negroes?" He then proceeded to suggest good sale prices.[32]

Indeed, price reigned uppermost. When the Panic of 1857 depressed slave prices, the *Abingdon Democrat* reported as encouraging good news that a young woman and her two children had sold in Russell County for $1,905, "pretty well for hard times."[33] Overall, Olmsted reported that "slaves . . . were 'unprofitable property' in the mountains, except as they increase and improve in salable value. Two men . . . spoke of the sale of negroes in the same sentence with that of cattle and swine."[34]

Slaves, of course, could prove profitable to owners in other ways than direct sale. Masters sometimes used their human property as collateral to obtain loans. Planter James P. Strother of Smyth County assured a potential lender in a credit reference that the subject in question had "a tolerably good plantation in Washington [County] & at least one negro man who is young and valuable, perhaps he may have other negroes."[35]

More common was the practice of loaning or hiring out slaves to others: family members, fellow owners, industrialists, and nonmasters unable to amass enough capital to enter the master class. "I believe your Pa hired a negro boy at hillsville," one Wythe Countian wrote in 1851, "gives 50 dollars a year and clothes him."[36] Wythe County slave owner Richard W. Sanders hired slaves for planting and at the same time hired out two of his slaves to neighbors, in one case to a mine operator. Hiring transactions generally occurred at a public place such as a courthouse on the first day of the year. Owners usually agreed to furnish clothing and pay doctor bills, although at times it was the hirer's responsibility. In order to maximize profits, some masters, like Caperton, took their slaves across the state to Richmond to hire them out. Inscoe has noted, however, that most mountain slave owners wanted to keep their property nearby, where they could maintain some control.[37]

Whether working for the owner or hired out, slaves filled a wide variety of roles in southwest Virginia. Like most slaves elsewhere in the South, they toiled as agricultural laborers. On mountain farms, however, that meant a wider array of tasks than on a Deep South cotton plantation. Slaves had to be versatile; they generally tended several crops instead of one staple, herded livestock, constructed buildings and fences, made bricks and shingles, and engaged in various other handicrafts or household industries. Large farmers, such as the Floyds of Tazewell County, used slaves as couriers, often trusted with cash and items of value. Slaves also worked in mines and in industrial operations and served as domestic servants in private homes and hotels. The hot springs, particularly, hired many slaves as cooks and domestics; many ill slaves were provided free of charge in exchange for an anticipated cure. As one southwest Virginian told Olmsted, most whites believed that a white person willing to work as a domestic servant probably was not worth hiring.[38] "In fact," Olmsted added, "no girl hereabouts, whose character was good, would ever hire out to do menial service."[39]

The railroad provided more avenues for slave labor. Its construction provided a new market for slave owners wishing to rent out their human property. Indeed, the completed railroad functioned as a silent monument to the abilities and tenacity of the black laborers who performed most of the line's construction and maintenance. Hired slaves cut wood, graded, broke up stone for ballast, laid track, and cleared snow from obstructed tracks. The skilled toiled as blacksmiths, carpenters, and mechanics. Many also served on train crews as freight hands and brakemen. The railroad generally paid owners two hundred dollars per year for hired slaves, an estimated labor savings of 50 percent. By 1856, 435 of the railroad's 643 workers were hired slaves. Though envisioned by whites, it was black southwest Virginians who made the dream of a mountain railroad a reality.[40]

The railroad hired so many slaves that other hirers had trouble obtaining workers. Olmsted described a conversation with an overseer near Abingdon. The overseer, stick in hand, supervised seven wheat cradlers, five black and two white. He explained that the "niggers had all been hired by the railroad, at $200 a year." Olmsted also accused the railroad of driving its slave laborers hard. Another one of his hosts, an East Tennessee farmer apparently living near the Virginia line, described a railroad contractor "who had some sixty hands which he had hired in Old Virginny. . . . Everybody who saw them at work, said he drove them till they could hardly stand, and did not give them half what they ought to have to eat."[41]

Chief Engineer Garnett found hired slaves "a source of great economy" to the railroad but noted one glaring disadvantage. In 1853, he wrote, "It makes it difficult to collect a force of white laborers on the same work, where a considerable number of slaves are employed."[42] Many of the railroad's hired whites, often Irish immigrants, opposed working side by side with blacks. In cases where the railroad had to choose due to cost or conflict, the white laborers generally lost out. In March 1857, for example, the railroad determined to drop one of its five gangs of freight train hands, as only four had proved necessary. Four crews were black, and one was made up of whites. President and Acting General Superintendent J. Robin McDaniel fired the whites.[43]

Slave laborers cost the railroad less, but they were not without financial liabilities. The railroad, like all hirers, agreed to certain stipulations required by owners. It agreed, for example, to furnish the slaves of a master named Brown four pairs of shoes per slave each year. The railroad, often unwillingly, also bore the responsibility in case of injury or death, frequent occurrences on the line. In January 1857, for example, slaves hired to clear snow off tracks contracted frostbite. Their angry owners required compensation, but the railroad refused to pay. The V&T successfully argued that the slaves themselves were responsible by rushing to a warming fire too quickly.[44]

The Virginia and Tennessee Railroad impacted the state's slave economy in a second manner as well. As had other railroads in the state, it became a carrier of choice in the slave trade. To encourage business among slave traders, the railroad entered into an agreement with several other southern railways, whereby it would carry small slave children free of charge. The railroads used this policy as an incentive to capture the slave trade.[45]

Finally, beyond economics, there were political implications. Virginia governor Henry A. Wise and his fellow nonregional railroad supporters envisioned ideological as well as numerical gains for slavery when they threw their support to southwest Virginia's railroad. Slavery's expansion was a means to a united Virginia and, through that, a united South. With the V&T's crucial link completed, its boosters broadened their vistas. Legislator William M. Burwell, for example, advocated "direct trade" via steamship through the port of Norfolk to Europe. "The supremacy of New York is . . . to be fought with the capital and competition of England, France, and Germany," he wrote. The railroad, by linking Norfolk to the southern interior, had made such a vision possible, Burwell affirmed.[46]

A second, related scheme advocated by Burwell and his friends was a canal across Mexico's Isthmus of Tehuantepec, linking southern ports with the goods and gold of California, weakening New York merchants, and expanding the potential area of slavery expansion, Bickley's "golden circle." Burwell again credited the Virginia and Tennessee Railroad with making the Tehuantepec canal a real possibility. The railroad embraced the two schemes, as it found them good publicity. The names chosen for the line's engines illustrate this.

Most bore the names of regional locales such as Bristol, Holston, Montgomery, Norfolk; of railroad officials; or of swift animals. However, the railroad also gave locomotives names such as El Paso, Mazeppa, San Francisco, St. Nazaire, and Tehuantepec. Thus, the locomotives racing past southwest Virginians constantly reminded them of their southern links and future glories.[47]

Those glories, not incidentally, were to be won as Virginians. While Bickley and perhaps most other white southwest Virginians flirted in 1850 with the idea of state secession, a decade later they had made their peace with the eastern part of the state. Political changes emanating from economic commercialization and slavery expansion had firmly linked southwest Virginia to Richmond by the secession winter of 1860–1861. If the V&T was the medium for such a transformation, it was also southwest Virginia's iron road to secession and civil war.

NOTES

An earlier version of this essay appeared as chapter 4 in Kenneth W. Noe, *Southwest Virginia's Railroad: Modernization and the Sectional Crisis* (Urbana: Univ. of Illinois Press, 1994), 67–84, and is reprinted here with the permission of the University of Illinois Press.

1. Kenneth W. Noe, *Southwest Virginia's Railroad: Modernization and the Sectional Crisis* (Urbana: Univ. of Illinois Press, 1994).

2. *Documents Containing Statistics of Virginia, Ordered to be Printed by the State Convention Sitting in the City of Richmond, 1850–1851* (Richmond: William Culley, 1851), Doc. 13, 1–3; Bureau of the Census, *Seventh Census of the United States, 1850* (Washington, D.C.: Robert Armstrong, 1853), 256–57; Bureau of the Census, *Heads of Families at the First Census of the United States Taken in the Year 1790*, Records of the State Enumerations, 1782–1785: Virginia (Washington, D.C.: Government Printing Office, 1908), 9; James B. Murphy, "Slavery and Freedom in Appalachia: Kentucky as a Demographic Case Study," *Register of the Kentucky Historical Society* 80 (spring 1982): 151–62.

3. *Richmond Enquirer,* Feb. 7, 1851.

4. See, for example, James W. Taylor, *Alleghania: A Geographical and Statistical Memoir* (St. Paul, Minn.: James Davenport, 1862); John C. Campbell, *The Southern Highlander and His Homeland* (New York: Russell Sage Foundation, 1921); William Goodell Frost, "Our Contemporary Ancestors in the Southern Mountains," *Atlantic Monthly* 83 (March 1899): 311–19; Horace Kephart, *Our Southern Highlanders: A Narrative of Adventure in the Southern Appalachians and a Study of Life among the Mountaineers* (New York: Macmillan, 1913); Carter G. Woodson, "Freedom and Slavery in Appalachian America," *Journal of Negro History* 1 (April 1916): 132–50.

5. Frederick Law Olmsted, *A Journey in the Back Country in the Winter of 1853–54* (New York: Mason Bros., 1863); John C. Inscoe, *Mountain Masters: Slavery and the Sectional Crisis in Western North Carolina* (Knoxville: Univ. of Tennessee Press, 1989), 107–12, provides a cogent analysis of Olmsted's depictions. See also Inscoe's essay in this volume.

6. Ollinger Crenshaw, "The Knights of the Golden Circle: The Career of George Bickley," *American Historical Review* 47 (Oct. 1941): 24–26; Frank L. Klement, *Dark Lanterns: Secret Political Societies, Conspiracies, and Treason Trials in the Civil War* (Baton Rouge: La.: State Univ. Press, 1984), dismissed the KGC as a real threat to the North, but James B. McPherson, *Battle Cry of Freedom: The Civil War Era* (New York: Oxford Univ. Press, 1988), 116, 599, 763, 878, disagrees.

7. George W.L. Bickley, *History of the Settlement and Indian Wars of Tazewell County, Virginia* (1852; reprint, Parsons, W.Va.: McClain, 1974), x–xi, 45–48, 118–21.

8. Richard B. Drake, "Slavery and Antislavery in Appalachia," *Appalachian Heritage* 14 (winter 1986): 25–33; Robert P. Stuckert, "Black Populations of the Southern Appalachian Mountains," *Phylon* 48 (June 1987): 141–51; Murphy, "Slavery and Freedom," 151–69; John C. Inscoe,

"Mountain Masters: Slaveholding in Western North Carolina," *North Carolina Historical Review* 61 (April 1984): 143–73; William L. Barney, "Towards the Civil War: The Dynamics of Change in a Black Belt County," in *Class, Conflict, and Consensus: Antebellum Southern Community Studies*, ed. O. Vernon Burton and Robert C. McMath (Westport, Conn.: Greenwood Press, 1982), 146–48; James Oakes, *Slavery and Freedom: An Interpretation of the Old South* (New York: Alfred A. Knopf, 1990), 97; Gavin Wright, *The Political Economy of the Cotton South: Households, Markets, and Wealth in the Nineteenth Century* (New York: W.W. Norton, 1978), 62–74.

9. Olmsted, *Journey in the Back Country*, 273.

10. Noe, *Southwest Virginia's Railroad*, tables 19 and 20, pp. 68–69, tables 21 and 24, pp. 70, 75; Manuscript Census, Virginia, Floyd, Raleigh, and Washington Counties, Schedules I and III, 1850; Charles L. Grant, "An Appalachian Portrait: Black and White in Montgomery County, Virginia, before the Civil War" (master's thesis, Virginia Polytechnic Institute and State University, 1987), 83; Murphy, "Slavery and Freedom," 153–62; *Richmond Enquirer*, Feb. 7, 1851.

11. Olmsted, *Journey in the Back Country*, 253; Inscoe, *Mountain Masters*, 62–68. On professions of slaveholders in sample counties in 1850 and 1860, see Noe, *Southwest Virginia's Railroads*, tables 22 and 24, pp. 72, 75.

12. Inscoe, *Mountain Masters*, 62–68.

13. Noe, *Southwest Virginia's Railroads*, tables 19 and 20, pp. 68–69; *Seventh Census*, 256–57; *Eighth Census of the United States, 1860: Population* (Washington, D.C.: Government Printing Office, 1862), 516–18; Richard Sutch, "The Breeding of Slaves for Sale and the Westward Expansion of Slavery, 1850–1860," in *Race and Slavery in the Western Hemisphere: Quantitative Studies*, ed. Stanley L. Engerman and Eugene Genovese (Princeton, N.J.: Princeton Univ. Press, 1975), 177; William W. Freehling, *The Road to Disunion*, vol. 1, *Secessionists at Bay* (New York: Oxford Univ. Press, 1990), 4, 166–77. The same situation was true in western North Carolina; see Inscoe, *Mountain Masters*, 85–86.

14. Manuscript Census, Virginia, Floyd County, Schedules I, III, 1850, 1860.

15. Noe, *Southwest Virginia's Railroad*, table 25, p. 76; *Seventh Census*, 256–57; *Eighth Census: Population*, 508–15; Inscoe, *Mountain Masters*, 85–86.

16. Robley Evans, *A Sailor's Log* (New York: D. Appleton, 1901), 1–7.

17. Manuscript Census, Virginia, Washington County, Schedules I, III, 1860; *Seventh Census*, 256–57; *Eighth Census: Population*, 508–15; Conway H. Smith, *The Land That Is Pulaski County* (Pulaski, Va.: Edmonds, 1981), 217, 241.

18. *Seventh Census*, 256–57; *Eighth Census: Population*, 516–18; Paul Salstrom, "Appalachia's Path toward Welfare Dependency, 1840–1940" (Ph.D. diss., Brandeis University, 1988), 54–55.

19. *Seventh Census*, 256–57; *Eighth Census: Population*, 508–18.

20. *Seventh Census*, 256–57.

21. Ibid., *Eighth Census: Population*, 516–18.

22. Manuscript Census, Virginia, Floyd and Raleigh Counties, Schedules I, III, 1860.

23. W.J. Cash, *The Mind of the South* (New York: Alfred A. Knopf, 1941), 219; Joseph John Gurney, *A Journey in North America, Described in Familiar Letters to Amelia Opie* (Norwich, Conn.: Josiah Fletcher, 1841), 54; Olmsted, *Journey in the Back Country*, 51–54; Inscoe, *Mountain Masters*, 87–114.

24. G. Wilson, Lewisburg, W.Va., to Nathaniel Wilson, July 22, 1835, Nathaniel V. Wilson Correspondence, West Virginia University Library, Morgantown, W.Va.

25. John Echols, Union, Va., to George Henry Caperton, Jan. 4, 1859, Caperton Family Papers, Virginia Historical Society, Richmond.

26. Alexander W. Reynolds, Indianola, Tex., to Sallie Patton, Nov. 8, 16, 21, Dec. 8, 20, 1859, Jan. 24, Feb. 4, 1860, Alexander W. Reynolds Letters and Papers, Roy Bird Cook Collection, West Virginia University Library, Morgantown, W.Va. (Quote is from the letter of Feb. 4.)

27. J.W. Ross, Abingdon, Va., to William B. Campbell, Nov. 5, 1855, and David Campbell, Murfreesboro, Tenn., to William B Campbell, Nov. 14, 1855, Campbell Family Papers, Duke University, Durham, N.C.

28. *Abingdon Democrat*, Feb. 21, 1857.

29. George W. Featherstonhaugh, *Excursion through the Slave States* (New York: Harper

Brothers, 1844), 36–37. Thomas D. Clark identified Armfield in his edited work, *Travels in the Old South: A Bibliography*, vol. 3, *The Antebellum South, 1825–1860: Cotton, Slavery, and Conflict* (Norman.: Univ. of Oklahoma Press, 1959), 41.

　　30. Inscoe, *Mountain Masters*, 85–86.

　　31. Caroline H. Preston, Wythe Court House, Va., to Maria Preston Pope, June 2, 1828, and Fotheringay, Sept. 18, 1828, Preston Family Papers, Joyes Collection, Filson Club, Louisville, Ky.; A.T. Caperton, Richmond, Va., to D'Sir, July 19, 1850, Caperton Family Papers, VHS; Grant, "Appalachian Portrait," 36–37, and Inscoe, *Mountain Masters*, 82–84, asserted that owners sold to slave traders only as a last resort.

　　32. Lewis E. Caperton, Union, Va., to Allen T. Caperton, Dec. 22, 1847, Caperton Family Papers.

　　33. John Echols, Union, Va., to George Henry Caperton, Dec. 28, 1857, Caperton Family Papers; *Abingdon Democrat*, Feb. 6, 1858; Murphy, "Slavery in Appalachia," 158–61.

　　34. Olmsted, *Journey in the Back Country*, 226.

　　35. James P. Strother, Marion, Va., to Charles W. Christian, Mar. 9, 1841, James P. Strother Papers, Duke University, Durham, N.C.

　　36. H. Sanders, Jackson's Ferry, Va., to John P.M. Sanders, Jan. 9, 1851, Richard W. Sanders and John W. Greene Papers and Notebooks, Duke University, Durham, N.C.; Inscoe, *Mountain Masters*, 76–81.

　　37. Richard W. Sanders, Jackson's Ferry, Va., to John P.M. Sanders, May 21, 1851, Richard W. Sanders and John W. Greene Papers and Notebooks; Lewis E. Caperton, Union, Va., to Allen T. Caperton, Dec. 15, 1847, Caperton Family Papers; Evans, *A Sailor's Log*, 2; Inscoe, *Mountain Masters*, 76–78; John Edmund Stealey III, "Slavery and the Western Virginia Salt Industry," *Journal of Negro History* 59 (April 1974): 119 (see also Stealey's essay in this volume).

　　38. Featherstonhaugh, *Excursion through the Slave State*, 16–26; Frederick Marryat, *Diary in America, with Remarks on Its Institutions*, ed. Sydney Jackson (New York: Alfred A. Knopf, 1962), 236; Olmsted, *Journey in the Back Country*, 226–28, 273–75; David Campbell, Slave Rental Contract, Nov. 11, 1856, Campbell Family Papers; *Wytheville Times*, June 20, 1857; Theodosia W. Barrett, *Russell County: A Confederate Breadbasket* (n.p.: n.d.), 122; Inscoe, *Mountain Masters*, 68–76; Ralph Mann, "Mountains, Land, and Kin Networks: Burkes Garden, Virginia, in the 1840s and 1850s," *Journal of Southern History* 58 (Aug. 1992): 421; Percival Reniers, *The Springs of Virginia: Life, Love, and Death at the Waters, 1775–1900*, 2d ed. (Kingsport, Tenn.: Kingsport, 1955), 184; John T. Schlotterbeck, "The 'Social Economy' of an Upper South Community: Orange and Greene Counties, Virginia, 1815–1860," in Burton and McMath, *Class, Conflict, and Consensus*, 3–28.

　　39. Olmsted, *Journey in the Back Country*, 276.

　　40. V&T Minutes, 1: 37, 99–100, 206, Nov. 12, 1856, n.p., Feb. 2, 1857, n.p.; Board of Directors Minutes, April 8, 1857–Jan. 11, 1866, Virginia and Tennessee Railroad Collection, VPI, 2, 82, 87, 192 (hereafter cited as V & T Minutes, vol. 2); Message of the Governor, 1861, Doc. 17, p. 56; David Campbell to William B. Campbell, May 1, 1854, Campbell Family Papers; Olmsted, *Journey in the Back Country*, 274; Richard O. Curry, *A House Divided: A Study of Statehood Politics and the Copperhead Movement in West Virginia* (Pittsburgh: Univ. of Pittsburgh Press, 1964), 22–23; W. Harrison Daniel, *Bedford County, Virginia, 1840–1860: The History of an Upper Piedmont County in the Late Antebellum Era* (Bedford, Va.: Print Shop, 1985), 110; McFarland, "Extension of Democracy in Virginia, 1850–1896" (Ph.D. diss., Princeton University, 1934), 40; John T. Schlotterbeck, "Plantation and Farm: Social and Economic Change in Orange and Greene Counties, Virginia, from 1716 to 1860" (Ph.D. diss., Johns Hopkins University, 1980), 301–15; Henry T. Shanks, *The Secession Movement in Virginia, 1847–1861* (Richmond: Garrett and Massie, 1934), 6–7; Craig M. Simpson, *A Good Southerner: The Life of Henry A. Wise of Virginia* (Chapel Hill: Univ. of North Carolina Press, 1985), 142.

　　Free blacks served the railroad as well as slaves. In 1856, the directors awarded a free black crewman twenty dollars for remaining on a train nearing a collision after the white crewmen jumped off. See V&T Minutes, 1: Nov. 12, 1856, n.p.

　　41. Olmsed, *Journey in the Back Country*, 271–74.

　　42. *Sixth Annual Meeting of the Stockholders of the Va. & Tenn. Railroad Company* (n.p.: 1853), 16.

43. V&T Minutes, 2: 2.

44. V&T Minutes, 2: 1, Feb. 2, 1857, n.p.; V&T Minutes, 2: 82, 87. The Superintendent's Reports in volume 1 of the minutes constantly note injured or killed workers, several per year. Clearly, constructing and running the line was a dangerous business.

45. Charles W. Turner, "Railroad Service to Virginia Farmers, 1828–1860," *Agricultural History* 22 (Oct. 1948): 242.

46. William M. Burwell, "The Commercial Future of the South," *DeBow's Review* 30 (Feb. 1861): 147–49. See also the Notebook of William M. Burwell, Burwell Family Papers, University of Virginia, Charlottesville.

47. Notebook of William M. Burwell, Burwell Family Papers; V&T Minutes, 2: 349; Governor's Message of 1861, Doc. 17, pp. 98–99.

7

PUT IN MASTER'S POCKET

Cotton Expansion and Interstate Slave Trading in the Mountain South

WILMA A. DUNAWAY

> Master White didn't hesitate to sell any of his slaves, he said, "You all belong to me and if you don't like it, I'll put you in my pocket," meaning of course that he would sell that slave and put the money in his pocket.
>
> —AMELIA JONES, EAST KENTUCKY SLAVE

Since 1600, forced labor migrations have accompanied the expansion of capitalism around the globe. In the New World, European colonists initially enslaved Native Americans, decimating the indigenous populations to one-tenth of their original sizes. From about 1700 onward, the enslavement of African peoples was the principal method by which European societies appropriated foreign labor for their colonies. By the time that transatlantic trade ended, most of these African slaves were deployed mainly in the Caribbean, Brazil, and the U.S. Southeast. In the seventeenth and eighteenth centuries, tobacco production absorbed two-fifths of the slave laborers in the United States. By the end of the American Revolution, however, the three major southern exports, tobacco, indigo, and rice, had declined in profitability on the world market.[1]

Simultaneously, cotton was required to fuel expansion of the English textiles industry, so world prices for that commodity underwent much less disruptive cyclical changes than those of other major southern exports. Between 1810 and 1840, U.S. cotton production increased nearly tenfold as plantations pushed westward to become concentrated in a long belt stretching from South Carolina through Texas. In almost every decade from 1810 to 1860, lower South cotton production expanded three times faster than the agricultural output of the upper South. "A continuation of rising demand for slaves in the West, a new surge of demand in the eastern tobacco region, and a slowdown in the rate of natural increase of the slave population all combined to double slave prices between the mid 1840s and the Civil War."[2]

Between 1810 and 1860, slavery was abolished in most nations of the western hemisphere. In the United States, however, world demand for cotton triggered the largest internal forced migration of slave laborers that has ever occurred in the history of the world. Lower South demand for slaves increased by more than 1800 percent, more than twice the rate of increase in the U.S. slave population. As a result, between 1790 and 1860, upper South slaveholders exported nearly a million black laborers to the lower South. Legislators described the extent to which the border states generated their profits from slave trading rather than from crop cultivation. In a fifty-year period, two-fifths of the African Americans enslaved in the upper South were forced to migrate to the cotton economy, primarily through interstate sales and secondarily though interregional transfers with their masters. This forced labor migration nearly quadrupled the slave population of the lower South, leaving in the upper South only about three-fifths of the slaves who would have been there in 1860.[3]

SLAVE TRADING ROUTES

Southern Appalachia lay at the geographical heart of the forced migration of slaves from the upper South to the lower South. This region was linked by rivers and roads to the coastal trade centers of the Tidewater and the lower South. Across those transportation linkages, southern planters frequented 138 mineral spas scattered throughout the Appalachians, making travel capitalism an important segment of local economies. Furthermore, two major slave-trading networks cut directly through the southern mountains. Out of Baltimore and upper Virginia, slave traders followed a route that cut across western Maryland, utilizing canal and river connections to Wheeling. Seated at the top of the Ohio River, Wheeling grew into a major regional slave-trading hub, an ironic economic role for a large Appalachian town that had so few resident slaves. As western Maryland masters could easily ship their slaves by river, Wheeling also served as a collection point for slaves to be hired or sold to the salt industry. From Wheeling, traders could follow the Ohio River southward to capitalize on major regional slave markets at Louisville, Memphis, Natchez, and New Orleans.[4]

A second major route emanated from Tidewater Virginia, which was served by slave-trading hubs at Alexandria, Danville, and Norfolk. Using river, canal, and overland connections, traders moved southward through Richmond. Virginia masters exported 441,684 slaves to other states across this route between 1810 and 1860. Out of Richmond, traders proceeded southwest through Appalachian counties, triggering a small subregional trading nucleus. Abingdon provided market access for eastern Kentucky, southwest Virginia, and upper East Tennessee buyers and sellers. To attract slave trader business, the East Tennessee and Virginia Railroad implemented a policy to carry small slave children free of charge. Down the route southward through the Tennessee Valley, speculators were served by an East Tennessee trading hub around Knoxville. Further south, near the triangular conjuncture of Tennessee, Georgia,

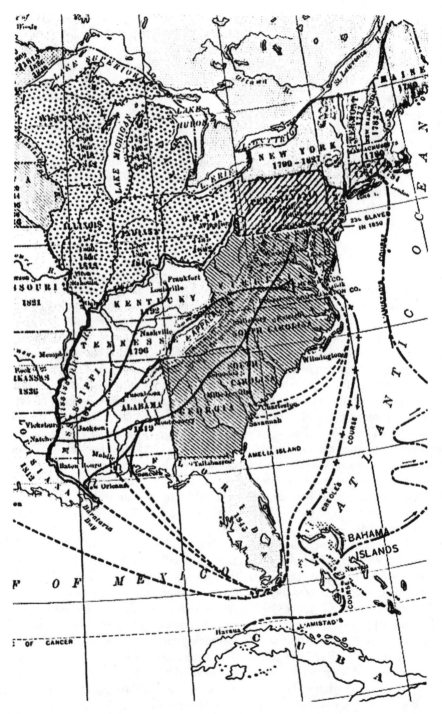

National slave-trading routes. (From Fox, *Harper's Atlas of American History*, p. 42)

and Alabama, they could take advantage of major subregional markets in Chattanooga, Tennessee, and Rome, Georgia.[5]

On the eastern boundary of southern Appalachia, a third significant trading route linked Norfolk inland to Richmond, then south through the North Carolina piedmont via Salisbury. A Jackson, North Carolina, slave recalled that local owners "took hands in droves 150 miles to Richmond to sell them." Because they had been considering "selling property of that description," a Burke County, North Carolinian informed his family that "Negro property has taken a very considerable rise in Norfolk . . . in consequence of the number of purchasers for the Louisiana market." Thus, the counties of western North Carolina were connected to a transportation network that transferred slaves from the upper South through middle North Carolina, to terminate either at Charleston or, via Montgomery, at Mobile or Natchez.[6]

On the western boundary of southern Appalachia, a fourth trading route ran southward from Louisville via Lexington and Nashville to terminate in the Vicksburg and Natchez markets. Because of their geographical proximity, middle Tennessee and eastern Kentucky counties linked into this trading network. When middle Tennessee slaves were not bought by itinerant speculators, they were sent to the "slave yards" at Nashville or Memphis, where they often waited two weeks or longer to be auctioned to Mississippi, Texas, or Arkansas buyers. Secretly financed by prominent elites, Lexington slave dealers circulated throughout the Kentucky mountains, buying up coffles of slaves directly from owners or at local auction blocks. As a result, Kentuckians sold more than six thousand slaves annually to southern markets, occasionally in large lots, like one Lewis County sale of "3 Bucks Aged from 20 to 26, Strong, Ablebodied, 1 Wench, Sallie, Aged 42, Excellent Cook, 1 Wench, Lize, Aged 23 with 6 mo. old Picinniny, One Buck Aged 52, good Kennel Man, 17 Bucks Aged from twelve to twenty." In 1829 a Menefee County, Kentucky, clergyman encountered "a company of slaves, some of them heavily loaded with irons, singing as they passed along." Because they were headed west to be auctioned at Lexington, the traveler was informed by the speculators that the slaves engaged in their march songs as "an effort to drown the suffering of mind they were brought into, by leaving behind their wives, children, or other near connexions and never likely to meet them again in this world." An eastern Kentucky slave remembered that Bluegrass dealers "made a business of buying up Negroes at auction sales and shipping them down to New Orleans to be sold to owners of cotton and sugar cane plantations. . . . They would ship whole boat loads at a time, buying them up 2 or 3 here, 2 or 3 there, and holding them in a jail until they had a boat load. This practice gave rise to the expression 'sold down the river.'"[7]

ITINERANT SPECULATORS

According to Appalachian slave narratives, two of every five of the region's sellers made transactions with slave traders engaged in interstate trafficking,

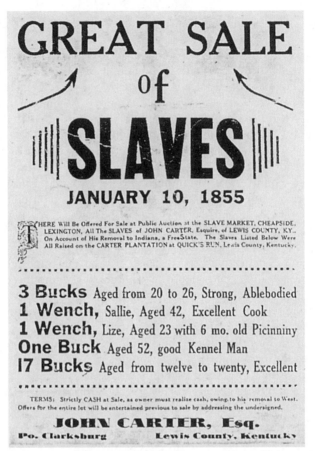

GREAT SALE

of

SLAVES

JANUARY 10, 1855

HERE Will Be Offered For Sale at Public Auction at the SLAVE MARKET, CHEAPSIDE, LEXINGTON, All The SLAVES of JOHN CARTER, Esquire, of LEWIS COUNTY, KY.. On Account of His Removal to Indiana, a FreeState. The Slaves Listed Below Were All Raised on the CARTER PLANTATION at QUICK'S RUN, Lewis County, Kentucky.

3 Bucks Aged from 20 to 26, Strong, Ablebodied
1 Wench, Sallie, Aged 42, Excellent Cook
1 Wench, Lize, Aged 23 with 6 mo. old Picinniny
One Buck Aged 52, good Kennel Man
17 Bucks Aged from twelve to twenty, Excellent

TERMS: Strictly CASH at Sale, as owner must realize cash, owing to his removal to West. Offers for the entire lot will be entertained previous to sale by addressing the undersigned.

JOHN CARTER, Esq.

Po. Clarksburg   Lewis County, Kentucky

Advertisement of slaves to be sold from Lewis County, Kentucky. (From Coleman Papers, University of Kentucky)

many of whom made regular annual or biannual circuits throughout the upper South. Traders tended in their buying "to be semi-itinerant and to rove over one or two counties (and perhaps the fringes of others). They might have a base at a particular town or village and might attend the public auctions at local county-towns, but usually they directly sought out their clients in the country districts. This practice, no doubt, stemmed from the advantages of developing local knowledge and of offering sellers the least troublesome and hazardous way of disposing of their slaves." Itinerant traders also regularly purchased free blacks from state and local governments when they had been sold into "absolute slavery" for offenses "punishable by confinement in penitentiaries."[8]

Winchester, Virginia, attracted several itinerant traders in the 1820s. One newspaper announced that roving slave traders had for several days been wandering the streets of that town "with labels on their hats exhibiting in conspicuous characters the words 'Cash for Negroes.'" John Williamson offered to give cash "for fifteen or twenty likely negroes" to any local slaveholders who sought him out at his base of operation, Bryarly's Tavern. Similarly, Thomas Dyson did business in McGuire's Hotel, where he bought up twenty or thirty Appalachian slaves. In the 1850s, the Baltimore-based Campbell firm employed a regular agent in Winchester, one of the sites selected to keep a steady supply of "large lots of the choicest Negroes" for export to New Orleans. Marshall Mack reported that itinerant traders were a common sight in Bedford County, Virginia; from there, coffles of slaves were "took to Lynchburg, Va. to the block to be sold." The Louisiana-based firm of Franklin and Armisted contracted regularly with J.M. Saunders and Company of Fauquier, Virginia; with George Kephart and Company of Frederick, Maryland; with Newton Boley of Winchester, Virginia; with Thomas Hundley of Amherst, Virginia; and with several smaller traders in western Maryland, southwest Virginia, and eastern Tennessee. These local agents collected slaves for consignment to the distant company that marketed them in New Orleans. Beginning in the early 1800s, one such Warrenton, Virginia, speculator opened business to "purchase slaves for the Southern market"; and he subsequently "made a large fortune" from these activities until the Civil War.[9]

In the early antebellum period, Samuel Carey appeared regularly to buy up slaves in small western Maryland towns. Between 1832 and 1860, an agent for an Alexandria firm frequently sought out buyers by setting up operations at taverns in small Maryland communities. In the 1830s, he offered "CASH IN MARKET. I wish to purchase FIFTY LIKELY YOUNG NEGROES, of both sexes, from ten to thirty years of age. Persons wishing to dispose of slaves, would find it to their advantage to give me a call, as I feel disposed to pay the highest market price." Interested parties could leave messages for him at one of three tavern locations, including the Union Tavern in Frederick County.[10]

Itinerant traders even situated themselves in counties with few slaves. In the 1820s, speculators traveled regularly into the isolated mountains of the Cherokee Nation. In the 1830s, Jeremiah Giddings advertised in Monongalia County to "purchase FIFTY LIKELY YOUNG NEGROES from 12 to 28 years old." Distant commission speculators also employed resident agents who operated in many out-of-the-way Appalachian communities. In eastern Kentucky, which had the region's smallest slave population, "traders came into the county to buy up slaves for the Southern plantations," taking them by boat or overland "down the river or over in Virginia and Carolina tobacco fields." Lexington-based slavers L.C. Robards and William F. Talbott employed local representatives in several eastern Kentucky towns. Betty Cofer "saw some slaves sold away from [her] Wilkes County, North Carolina plantation" to traders who "sold 'em down to Mobile, Alabama." In East Tennessee, local and itinerant traders went from farm to farm buying slaves; the speculator paid a cash deposit and signed a note to complete payment when he resold them to cotton planters in Alabama or Mississippi. Itinerant traders "travel[led] around the country" regularly in middle Tennessee, attaching their handbills to storefronts, jails, courthouses, mills, and churches.[11]

To arrange connections with itinerant traders, Appalachian slaveholders often engaged lawyers in regional trade towns. For example, a Monroe, West Virginia, master sent a slave to the Summers law firm in Charleston for export down the Ohio River. The agent was advised to keep the slave "in jail for greater Security" and not to tell him that he was being sold out-of-state as he would "be disposed to run." Appalachians also maximized their family linkages with lower South and southwestern traders. For instance, the Walkers were urged to rent their slaves in Missouri "at double the Virginia rates." A South Carolinian wrote to his Madison, Virginia, relatives that "the cholera has thinned the Negroes much on the Coast and the South generally and they are then said to be selling very high." In early 1850, a Norfolk trader wrote his Appalachian kin that prime male slaves were "selling in Georgia or Florida at $1,000 to $1,200." A Fauquier, Virginia, owner decided to sell a slave family west after encouraging news from relatives there.[12]

Primarily rural in character, Appalachian slave trading was organized by roving traders who made direct transactions with slave owners. According to regional slave narratives, it was very common in the fall and spring for itinerant traders to appear in the countryside. Penny Thompson of Coosa County, Alabama, remembered that "de speculation waggin (negro traders) come by often. Dey stops 'cross de road f'om de Marster's place an' all de Marsters come dere for to trade." In Jackson County, Alabama, "de speckulaters was white men dat sometimes comes around buyin', sellin' or tradin' slaves jest lak dey do cattle now. . . . Dem speckulaters would put de chilluns in a wagon usually pulled by oxens and de older folks was chained or tied together sos dey could not run off and dey would go from one plantation ter another all ovah de country."[13]

To avoid any threat of runaways, Appalachian masters tried to disguise their plans. When one Floyd County, Georgia, master decided to trade, a twelve-year-old boy "was fooled out of [his] mammy's house by dem speculators wid an apple. When [he] went out, two or three white men grabbed [him]." A Buncombe County, North Carolina, master sent all his slaves to their regular work in the fields. Then "Ole Marse he cum t'ru de field wif a man call de specalater. Day walk round jes' lookin', jes' lookin'. All de [slaves] know whut dis mean. Dey didn't dare look up, jes' wok right on. Den de specalater he see who he want. He talk to Ole Marse, den dey slaps de han'cuffs on him an' tak him away to de cotton country." When the speculator was ready to leave with his purchases, "effen dey [was] enny whut didn' wanta go, he thrash em, den tie em 'hind de waggin an' mek um run till dey fall on de groun', den he thrash em till dey say dey go [wi]thout no trouble."[14]

APPALACHIAN SLAVE TRADERS

Clearly, local Appalachian communities did not censor residents who sold slaves out of state, for towns and counties did not regulate against such business activities. Indeed, slave trading occurred often enough that Appalachian towns passed ordinances authorizing their sheriffs, judges, and constables to collect fees for conducting auctions and for jailing slaves. In addition, most towns and counties charged slave dealers a special business tax. Recognizing the amount of revenue involved in the enterprise, Chattanooga taxed slave traders five hundred dollars annually. Some Appalachian entrepreneurs engaged in the practice of buying up local slaves for export to distant buyers. In reality, about one of every 154 Appalachian households acquired part of its income from slave-trading activities. Nearly half of these Appalachian slave traders were landless, but they averaged $10,890 in household wealth, far above regional averages. Ten percent of them averaged $79,333 in assets, and they reported primary occupations like merchant, land speculator, farmer, or commercial wagoner. Some of these slave traders were among the region's most respected economic elites, such as attorneys and judges who regularly handled slave transactions for distant clients. As a routine service, country stores advanced to bounty hunters the advertised rewards for runaways, then received larger commissions from the slave owners.[15]

Four respected community leaders acted as professional slave traders in Loudoun County, Virginia, often representing large interstate traffickers located in distant port cities. Between 1839 and 1841, William Holland Thomas of western North Carolina bought and resold eight to twelve slaves every year. A Coffee County, Tennessee, master worked on commission for his neighbors to carry "a bunch of the field hands down in Louisiana" every year. Hamilton Brown earned a commission for arranging interstate sales for his neighbors. When prices were lower than he desired, he withheld the laborers for a better profit. In one instance, he advised the owner, "I think the opportunity will be much better for selling them in the fall. I have no doubt but I shall be able to sell for a much better price then than at this time." Over a ten-month period in 1835 and 1836, Floyd Whitehead of Nelson County, Virginia, exported to Mississippi seventy-three slaves. Obviously, Whitehead's slave trading was extensive and continual, for he formed a business partnership with a Lynchburg agent. Moreover, he empowered a trusted slave to seek out, buy, and sell slaves in the countryside. Still, Whitehead's involvement in the "abominable trade" did not prevent him from being elected to positions as county sheriff and representative to the state legislature.[16]

In Wilkes County, North Carolina, the partnership of Gwyn and Hickerson aggressively engaged in land and slave speculation from 1845 through the Civil War. James Gwyn initiated the lucrative business when a Missouri relative proposed a venture in which Hickerson would buy up military bounties, resell the lands to new Missouri settlers, and then procure slaves for resale to those new farms. Within a few months, Gwyn was buying up young male field hands at bargain prices from neighbors who were burdened by debt. In order to accumulate coffles for export, Gwyn and his agents frequented public auctions throughout western North Carolina. Gwyn went so far as to use the courts to have a local widow declared "a fit subject for the Asylum" when she tried to prevent the sale of her slaves to speculators who would "scatter them." Friends testified that "if she had no nigrose, [the traders] would not care what

Slave coffle camped along the New River, Virginia. (From George Featherstonaugh, *Excursion*, vol. 1)

became of her." Still the court declared Gwyn "guardian," giving him legal right to dispose of her property. When they had accumulated enough for export to Missouri, Gwyn sent the slaves off in overland caravans. In one instance, his driver notified him that "tonight we have pitched our tents within ten miles of Knoxville. . . . The negroes all seem to do as well as they know how." In East Tennessee, Gwyn's slaves were put on Tennessee River flatboats for the second stage of their long journey westward.[17]

As the Staunton agent for the Lynchburg Hose and Fire Insurance Company, John McCue wrote policies on the lives of slaves and supervised the required medical examinations. Using this insider information about his clients' property, McCue acted as a commissioned middleman. In one instance, he secretly evaluated the slaves of a client for a third party. He informed the potential buyer that he "had Several Conversations with the parties," but that there could be "no Compromise" unless "all [would] be Strictly Confidential." McCue also reminded the secret buyer that he "could get a fare chance" for him, for which assistance he expected to receive "a Small mite."

Two western Virginia speculators regularly transported slaves, via Charleston, down the Ohio River to Kentucky markets. One of their coffles of seventeen laborers landed at the Maysville steamboat wharf in the spring of 1849. The local newspaper reported that citizens had spotted the cohort "being conducted," in handcuffs and chains, inland to Lexington. Another western Virginian offered to buy up local slaves for resale. He responded to an inquirer, "Negroes always rise in the Spring. It is the time the traders are making out their companies for the South. January and February are the months to make purchase advantageously. . . . It would require some weeks to pick up such negroes as you want at the county about. It would be better to authorize me to purchase them for you."[18]

In addition to Appalachians who dabbled in the business as a sideline, there were many merchants who specialized in "the abominable traffic." A small trader in Knoxville, Tennessee, notified potential Bluegrass buyers that he would "carry slaves on speculation" and that he "intend[ed] carrying on the business extensively." One East Tennessee merchant boasted that he had "bought and sold in [his] day over 600." In what was then the small town of Chattanooga, two companies, F.A. Parham and A.H. Johnston, operated slave exchanges on Market Street near the railroad depot. Frederick, Maryland, slavers Kephart and Harbin invested in a ship to export slaves, and they maintained a marketing agency in New Orleans. Augusta Countian J.E. Carson regularly bought up Shenandoah Valley slaves for export. One of Carson's typical newspaper advertisements declared that he would pay high cash prices for "500 likely YOUNG NEGROES of both sexes, for the Southern market." In addition, Carson searched down runaways and then purchased them cheap from their owners. A flourishing slave trade was centered in the Surry County, North Carolina, area where the notorious slave driver Kit Robbins carried on his operations in a six-county vicinity. Similarly, Tyre Glen was active in slave buying in the counties west of him; he exported laborers to southern Georgia and South Carolina. Calvin Cowles, a Wilkes County, North Carolina, merchant, purchased and hired slaves from whom he earned profits by contracting them out on annual hires. Frank White and William Beasley gathered coffles of slaves from Wilkes County for the Charleston market. In White County, Tennessee, Daniel Clark and W.H. Matlock bought and resold about 150 slaves per year through their dealings in Tennessee, Virginia, North Carolina, Alabama, and Mississippi.[19]

Charlie Merrill, a regular trader in Franklin County, Tennessee, bought up local slaves for export to Nashville and Memphis. North Georgian H.M. Cobb regularly transported slaves from Virginia to auction at his firm in Rome, Georgia. Even in eastern Kentucky local traders were active. Floyd County, for example, had two speculators. County judge Houston and his son-in-law "gathered up all the slaves that were unruly or that people wanted to trade and housed them in an old barn until they had enough to take to New Orleans on a boat." Cherokee elites also accumulated part of their wealth from slave trading. Several Native American dealers, including planter James Vann, made regular trips to New Orleans, Savannah, and Charleston to buy and sell slaves. In addition, the federal agent for the Cherokees collected bounties from masters for slave runaways and arranged transactions between them and whites.[20]

Forty-five percent of the Appalachian slave traders headed middling households, averaging $13,175 in assets. A land and slave speculator of Cass County, Georgia; a Frederick County, Maryland, merchant; and traders of Giles and Randolph counties, Virginia, were typical of this segment. For example, Frank White and David McCoy of Page County, Virginia, engaged in intermittent slave trading as a sideline to farming and livestock. McCoy purchased Bethany Veney from a neighbor, "thinking he could make a speculation" on her at Richmond. Between 1835 and 1845, two local traders, Britton Atkins and William Manor, regularly transported overland coffles to the Mobile market from the small towns of Blount County, Alabama.[21]

Surprisingly, another 45 percent of the region's slave traders resided in Appalachian households with much more limited assets. A sizable segment of those who engaged in the human traffic averaged $244 or less in total wealth, and 15 percent of them owned neither land nor any other personal assets. How, then, could a poor Appalachian speculate in slave trading? First, such a person may have had dreams of future fortunes, like the two "Negro traders" in the sample from Franklin and Tyler Counties in Virginia who invested in cheap slave children in order to earn significant profits when they reached prime marketable age. Second, a landless laborer may have thought of himself as a slave trader because he worked for a commercial speculator, helping to transport coffles or acting as intermediary to buy up local slaves for export. In many communities, Appalachian slaveholders maintained private jails separate from the facilities that incarcerated white criminals. Poor laborers managed the jails that housed runaways and slaves about to be hired or sold at nearby auctions. Customarily, Appalachian slaveholders paid these jailers thirty cents to one dollar per day for each slave housed. In addition, some poor whites were "slave catchers" who trained and used bloodhounds to track and capture runaways.[22]

Poor Appalachians could engage in slave trading in a fourth way. When slaveholders advertised runaways, poor whites acted as "bounty hunters" seeking to profit from the capture of slaves. When they spotted blacks "working about as free men" who fit the description of runaways, they contacted owners and offered their assistance for reward plus expenses. After a Wilkes County, North Carolina, master publicized a runaway, he was contacted by such a slave hunter. "I have noticed him closely since I have seen your reward," he wrote. "He is hired out by the month, and he has every opportunity of running away, if he should suspect a discovery. The man who has him hired has agreed with me to keep him in his employ until you can come and get him." In another instance, B.W. Brooks offered to assist an owner if he came "in the night" to check the identity of a black who was "working about as a free man" who had not "yet obtained any Certificate of freedom from the Court." Brooks thought "it most prudent not to take him up and commit him to jail as he would in that event be certain to break jail and escape." John P. Chester wrote to an owner that "if there is no other hand I will kidnap them." Fearing that someone else would interfere and collect the reward, Chester added, "I am compelled to keep this secret from the world."[23]

Fifth, poorer Appalachians dabbled in the human export business by "blackbirding." Nearly 4 percent of the Appalachian slave narratives describe incidents in which individuals were captured and sold illegally through slave trafficking, and this activity occurred often enough for regional newspapers to coin the term "blackbirding" when they reported such cases. In Wythe County, Virginia, two poor whites in a buggy lay in wait on an isolated country road for fourteen-year-old Benjamin Washington. "One jumped out and tied his hands together," and the pair sped off to sell him to an itinerant speculator who was collecting a coffle for export to Mississippi. In McMinn County, Tennessee, free blacks were kidnapped and sold at Chattanooga. In Grayson County, Virginia, "five white men undertook to take five negroes." When the latter resisted, "two white men and two or three negroes were killed." Free Cherokees were also kidnapped and sold into slavery. Near Lookout Mountain, Tennessee, Sarah Red Bird, "a pureblood Indian," was sold to a Mississippi slaveholder after her family was killed "in an uprising wid de whites" who were "trying to drive dem out." Free Cherokees of mixed-Negro heritage were sometimes captured for profiteering, and free blacks could be kidnapped in the Cherokee Nation and sold to traders. While driving a wagon to an isolated western Virginia field, the teenage Peter Wych "was overtaken by a 'speculator' and brought to Georgia where he was sold." Similarly, two middle Tennessee slave children "wuz stole" and exported to Georgia and Mississippi. Because middle Tennessee children "were often stolen by speculators and later sold at auctions" in Nashville, one Warren County master constructed "a tall lookout on the roof" of his mansion. From that vantage point, a "watchman" kept guard over "the carefree children who played in the large yard of the nearby quarters."[24]

At Lexington, Virginia, an eight-year-old boy "was taken from the lower end of town by kidnappers, and carried off in a row boat." In West Virginia, blackbirders kidnapped slaves who had been hired out to the saltworks, then sold them at Wheeling or Richmond. Promising their captives a march to freedom, Floyd County, Kentucky, "slave rustlers" stole slaves at night and hid them "in Campbell's Cave." When their trail had cooled, the kidnappers exported the black laborers to Clarksville, Tennessee, where they would "sell them again on Mr. Dunk Moore's slave market." Lewis Robards, a Lexington slave dealer, used the services of "slave stealers" in rural eastern Kentucky. Some blackbirders formed regional networks for their illicit traffic. In Rutherford County, North Carolina, for example, William Robbins colluded with poor whites to "rustle" slaves. In one instance, Robbins even convinced a free black that, by "stealing slaves," he could "make money much faster than he was doing" as a blacksmith. In Surry County, North Carolina, "a number of colored people" were "illegally held in bondage" after they were kidnapped and sold by a group of blackbirders. One company of slave and horse rustlers comprised several men scattered through a four-county area along the East Tennessee and northwest Georgia border. "They had stations in various parts of the country, at convenient distances, and when a member of the club succeeded in stealing away a negro or pony, he would pass him on as quickly as he could to the nearest station, from which point he would be forwarded to another, and so on, till the negro or horse was quite safely disposed of." By promising them freedom, another gang was able to attract slaves to leave with them voluntarily. In northern Georgia, Buck Hurd "used frequently to come round to [the] quarters of a night" to "try to entice" slaves away. This kidnapper bragged in his community that he "had got slaves to run from one master, and after selling them to another, would induce them to run from him, and then sell them to a third." In that way, "he had been known to sell the same [slave] three or four times over."[25]

OVERLAND SLAVE COFFLES

The traffic in Appalachian slaves was dominated by "coffles" lasting as long as seven to eight weeks. Antebellum journalists observed that lower South firms preferred overland transport because it was "attended with less expense." Moreover, "by gradually advancing [slaves] into the climate, it in a measure preclude[d] the effect which a sudden transition from one state to the other might produce." The son of a western Maryland slaveholder reported in the 1830s that he had "seen hundreds of colored men and women chained together, two by two, and driven to the South." Western Virginians sent slave coffles overland to the Ohio River for steamboat transport to New Orleans. When a western Virginia master sent twenty-four slaves to the Richmond slave mart, he cautioned his son to "be discreet . . . so as not to excite a runaway slave." Over a five-year period in the 1830s, Samuel Hall spotted twelve or fifteen such coffles, averaging forty slaves each, passing along the road near his home in Greenbrier County. Distant speculators like Franklin and Armisted sent consigned slaves "overland but once a year—in midsummer."[26] One traveler described the organization of such coffles leaving western Maryland for the lower South: "A train of wagons, with the provisions, tents, and other necessaries, accompanies the expedition, and at night they all encamp. . . . Not more than three or four white men frequently have charge of a hundred and fifty slaves. Upon their march, also, they are usually chained together in pairs, to prevent their escape; and sometimes, when greater precaution is judged necessary, they are all attached to a long chain passing between them. Their guards and conductors are, of course, well armed."[27]

In 1830, a West Virginia newspaper documented the frequency with which slave coffles were spotted in regional towns. "During the past year," lamented the *Kanawha Register*, "the roads passing through Charleston have been crowded with travel of every sort. . . . The demon in human form, the dealer in bones and sinew, driving hundreds . . . clanking the chains of their servitude, through the free air of our valley, and destined to send back to us from the banks of the Mississippi the sugar and the cotton of that soil moistened with sweat and blood." Slave traders traversed the same roads as livestock drives through southern Appalachia, and hundreds of camping spots, like those near Bean Station or in Warren County, Tennessee, became well known as intermediate stopping points for coffles.[28]

Such a camp was described by an 1834 traveler who encountered a trading caravan passing through southwest Virginia. Just as they reached New River in the early morning, they came upon

> a camp of negro slave-drivers, just packing up to start; they had about three hundred slaves with them, who had bivouacked the preceding night *in chains* in the woods; these they were conducting to Natchez on the Mississippi River to work upon sugar plantations in Louisiana. . . . they had a caravan of nine waggons and single-horse carriages, for the purpose of conducting the white people, and any of the blacks that should fall lame. . . . The female slaves were, some of them, sitting on logs of wood, whilst others were standing, and a great many little black children were warming themselves at the fires of the bivouac. In front of them all, and prepared for the march, stood in double files, about two hundred male slaves, *manacled and chained to each other.*
>
> [Once the caravan was packed and ready to move], a man on horseback selected a shallow place in the ford for the male slaves; then followed a waggon and four horses, attended by another man on horseback. The other waggons contained the children and some that were lame, whilst the scows, or flatboats, crossed the women and some of the people belonging to the caravan. . . . The slave-drivers . . . endeavor[ed] to mitigate their discontent by feeding them well on the march, and by encouraging them to sing "Old Virginia never tire," to the banjo.

As the traveler proceeded southward by stage coach, he encountered a second coffle encamped north of Knoxville, Tennessee. "Long after sunset," he reported, "we came to a place where numerous fires were gleaming through the forest. . . . There were a great many blazing fires around, at which the female slaves were warming themselves; the children were asleep in some tents; and the males, in chains, were lying on the ground, in groups of about a dozen each. The white men . . . were standing about with whips in their hands."[29]

CONCLUSION

Global demand for cotton spurred in the United States the largest internal forced migration of slaves that has ever occurred in world history. For that reason, slave trading was pervasive throughout the South. As part of the exporting upper South, Appalachia lay at the hubs of the national slave trade routes. Contrary to popular mythology and much scholarly romanticism, southern Appalachia was neither isolated from nor culturally antagonistic toward the interstate slave trade. From poor white to local sheriffs to wealthy elites, numerous Appalachia households participated directly or indirectly in the interstate trafficking. Only a small minority of Appalachians may have exported black Appalachians directly, but local merchants and nonslaveholding farms benefited from the economic spin-offs from that trade. Thus, every courthouse, even in those counties with tiny black populations, sported its own slave auction block, and the movement of slave coffles and speculators is easy to document in regional newspapers. As the introductory quote clues us, black Appalachians were victimized by interstate trafficking frequently enough that fears of export were a shaping force in their family lives. Jim Threat remembered that those with whom he shared slave quarters in Talladega, Alabama, "lived in constant fear that they would be sold away from their families." Maggie Pinkard of Coffee County, Tennessee, described the recurrent trauma most poignantly: "When the slaves got a feeling there was going to be an auction, they would pray. The night before the sale they would pray in their cabins. You could hear the hum of voices in all the cabins down the row."[30]

NOTES

1. The introductory quote is from George P. Rawick, comp., *The American Slave: A Composite Autobiography*, vol. 16, pt. 2 (Westport, Conn.: Greenwood Press, 1972), 38; Immanuel Wallerstein, *The Modern World-System*, vol. 3, *The Second Era of Great Expansion of the Capitalist World-Economy, 1730–1840s* (New York: Academic Press, 1989), 167; Robert W. Fogel, *Without Consent or Contract: The Rise and Fall of American Slavery* (New York: W.W. Norton, 1989), 63–64.

2. James L. Watkin, *King Cotton: A Historical and Statistical Review, 1790–1908* (1908; reprint, New York: Negro Univs. Press, 1969), 195; Fogel, *Without Consent*, 64, 70.

3. Fogel, *Without Consent*, 65, 270; Thomas R. Dew, *Review of the Debate in the Virginia Legislature of 1831 and 1832* (Richmond: T.W. White, 1832); Michael Tadman, *Speculators and Slaves: Masters, Traders, and Slaves in the Old South* (Madison: Univ. of Wisconsin Press, 1989), 58–63; Richard Sutch, "The Breeding of Slaves for Sale and the Westward Expansion of Slavery, 1850–1860," in *Race and Slavery in the Western Hemisphere: Quantitative Studies*, ed. Stanley L. Engerman and Eugene D. Genovese (Princeton: Princeton Univ. Press, 1975), 173–210.

4. For a map of slave-trading routes, see Dixon R. Fox, *Harper's Atlas of American History* (New York: Harper and Brothers, 1920), 42. For a map of the counties included in the region, see Wilma A. Dunaway, *The First American Frontier: Transition to Capitalism in Southern Appalachia, 1700–1860* (Chapel Hill: Univ. of North Carolina Press, 1996), 110; J.R. Commons, ed., *A Documentary History of American Industrial Society*, vol. 2 (Cleveland: Arthur H. Clark, 1910), 341.

5. Charles H. Ambler, *A History of West Virginia* (New York: Prentice-Hall, 1933), 212; Lynda J. Morgan, *Emancipation in Virginia's Tobacco Belt, 1850–1870* (Athens: Univ. of Georgia Press, 1992), 36; Charles W. Turner, "Railroad Service to Virginia Farmers, 1828–1860," *Agricul-*

tural History 22 (1948): 242; Rawick, *The American Slave*, Supp. 2, vol. 9 (Westport, Conn.: Greenwood Publishing, 1979), 3639; ibid., vol. 12, 136.

6. For a description of a Richmond slave yard by an Appalachian slave, see Louis Hughes, *Thirty Years a Slave: From Bondage to Freedom* (1897; reprint, New York: Negro Univs. Press, 1969), 7–12; Rawick, *American Slave*, vol. 11, pt. 1, 167; letter dated Dec. 7, 1821, Thomas Lenoir Papers, Duke University Library, Durham, N.C.

7. Rawick, *American Slave*, vol. 6, page 9, and vol. 16, page 67; Eloise Conner, "The Slave Market in Lexington, Kentucky: 1850–1860" (master's thesis, University of Kentucky, 1931), 49–58; Robert Wickliffe, "Speech on Negro Law," 1840 pamphlet, p. 14, Wickliffe-Preston Family Papers, University of Kentucky Library, Lexington, Ky.; handbill dated Jan. 10, 1855, J. Winston Coleman Papers, University of Kentucky Library; J. Winston Coleman, "Lexington's Slave Dealers and Their Southern Trade," *Filson Club Historical Quarterly* 12 (1938): 19–20; "Journal of the Life, Labours, and Travels of Thomas Shillitoe," *Friends Library* 3 (1839): 461.

8. Content analysis of 280 Appalachian slave narratives. Tadman, *Speculators and Slaves*, 49; Kenneth Stampp, *The Peculiar Institution: Slavery in the Antebellum South* (New York: Alfred A. Knopf, 1956), 216; Slaves Condemned, Executed, and Transported, 1783–1865, Records Group 48, Auditor of Public Accounts, Virginia State Library and Archive, Ellen Afto Manuscript, Handley Library, Winchester, Va.

9. *Virginia Northwestern Gazette*, Aug. 15, 1818; *New Orleans Picayune*, Jan. 4, 1860; Frederic Bancroft, *Slave Trading in the Old South* (Baltimore: J.H. Furst, 1931), 25–26n; Rawick, *American Slave*, vol. 7, pt. 1, 213; Wendell H. Stephenson, *Isaac Franklin: Slave Trader and Planter of the Old South* (Baton Rouge: Louisiana State Univ. Press, 1938), 26–27, 44–50, 103–9, 223; Edward St. Abdy, *Journal of a Residence and Tour in the United States of America, from April, 1833 to October, 1834*, vol. 2 (London: John Murray, 1835), 209–10.

10. *Cumberland Advocate*, Oct. 28, 1826; *Maryland Journal and True American*, Feb. 14, 1832, Jan. 8, 1833.

11. *American State Papers: Indian Affairs* 2:651; *Winchester Republican*, June 23 and Aug. 18, 1826; *Monongalia Farmer*, Feb. 15, 1834; Slave Interviews, 24 and typed working notes, Coleman Papers; Rawick, *The American Slave*, vol. 11, page 20, vol. 5, no. 2, page 321–2, vol. 12, page 257.

12. Letter dated Dec. 17, 1846, George W. and Lewis Summers Papers, West Virginia University Library, Morgantown, W.Va.; these manuscripts at University of Virginia Library, Charlottesville, Va.: letter dated June 6, 1837, Walker Family Papers; letter dated April 22, 1833, Wallace Family Papers; letter dated Jan. 18, 1850, Rives Family Papers; letter dated June 30 (no year), Blackwell Family Papers.

13. Rawick, *American Slave*, Supp. 2, vol. 9, 3872, vol. 3, 800.

14. Ibid., vol. 14, bk. 1, 354–55; Ibid., Supp. 1, vol. 7, 690–91.

15. Other writers have claimed that "no stigma attached to strictly local trades in which buyer and seller were both residents . . . but a local seller who sold slaves to a buyer from another state was often censored." See Edward W. Phifer, "Slavery in Microcosm: Burke County, North Carolina," *Journal of Southern History* 28 (1962): 153–54. Similarly, John C. Inscoe, *Mountain Masters: Slavery and the Sectional Crisis in Western North Carolina.* (Knoxville: Univ. of Tennessee Press, 1989), claims that few western North Carolina masters "violated the community norm of selling slaves only locally." Gilbert E. Govan and James W. Livingood, *The Chattanooga Country from Tomahawks to TVA* (1952; reprint, Knoxville: Univ. of Tennessee Press, 1977), 147. Out of a sample of 3,056 Appalachian households drawn systematically from the 1860 Census of Population manuscripts, 20 reported slave trading as a source of family income. For 1860 Census sampling methods, see Dunaway, *First American Frontier*, 326–27; Wilma A. Dunaway, *Never Safe in the Family Way: Forced Labor Migrations, Household Survival, and Reproductive Exploitation on Small Plantations* (forthcoming), tables 4.6 and 5.7.

16. Brenda E. Stevenson, *Life in Black and White: Family and Community in the Slave South* (New York: Oxford Univ. Press, 1996), 178; Diary and Accounts, 1839–1841, William Holland Thomas Papers, Duke University Library; Rawick, *American Slave*, Supp. 1, vol. 12, 257; letter dated June 5, 1838, Hamilton Brown Papers, Southern Historical Collection, University of North Carolina; Whitehead and Loftuss Accounts and Letters dated March 14, 1837, May 15, 1839, Floyd L. Whitehead Papers, University of Virginia Library.

17. Letters dated May 7, 1845, Feb. 4, 1846, Feb. 12, 1846, Dec. 14, 1846, Aug. 14, 1849, Aug. 19, 1849, May 12, 1858, Aug. 18, 1859, Jan. 25, 1863, June 2, 1859, June 11, 1859, July 4, 1859, Oct. 10, 1857, James Gwyn Papers, Southern Historical Collection, University of North Carolina.

18. Letter dated Feb. 8, 1858, McCue Family Papers, University of Virginia Library; *Maysville Eagle*, Nov. 6, 1849; 1844 letter (date illegible), Wilson-Lewis Papers, West Virginia University Library.

19. Wickliffe, "Speech," 14. George M. Stroud, *A Sketch of the Laws Relating to Slavery in the Several States of the United States of America* (Philadelphia: Henry Longstreth, 1856), 108, 167, 219, 232; *Calendar of Virginia State Papers and Other Manuscripts*, vol. 8 (Richmond: State of Virginia, 1875–1893), 255; John T. Trowbridge, *The Desolate South, 1865–1866*, ed. Gordon Carroll (New York: Duell, Sloan, and Pearce, 1956), 125; *Chattanooga Gazette*, Feb. 16, 1849; *Chattanooga Advertiser*, Jan. 8, 1857; *Washington, D.C., Daily National Intelligencer*, Nov. 7, 1836, Oct. 21, 1837; *Lexington (Virginia) Gazette*, Aug. 2 and 9, 1860; Charles B. Dew, *Bond of Iron: Master and Slave at Buffalo Forge* (New York: W.W. Norton, 1994), 279; *Raleigh News and Observer*, July 26, 1925; many letters between 1835 and 1845, Tyre Glen Papers, Duke University Library; letters dated June 9, 1862, June 25, 1862, Jan. 30, 1863, April 5, 1863, Cowles Family Papers, North Carolina Department of Archives and History, Raleigh; letter dated March 2, 1835, Brown Papers; Monroe Seals, *History of White County, Tennessee* (Spartanburg: Reprint Co. Publishers, 1974), 58.

20. Ophelia Egypt, H. Masuoka, and C.S. Johnson, comps., "Unwritten History of Slavery: Autobiographical Account of Negro Ex-Slaves," Social Science Document No. 1 (1945), mimeographed typescript, Fisk University Archives, Nashville, Tenn., 166; Rawick, *American Slave*, 7: 141; Slave Interviews, Coleman Papers, 34; Kenneth G. Hamilton, ed., "Minutes of the Mission Conference Held in Spring Place," *Atlanta Historical Bulletin* (winter 1970), 36; "Letters of Benjamin Hawkins," *Georgia Historical Collections* 9 (1924): 242, 313.

21. *The Narrative of Bethany Veney: A Slave Woman* (Worcester, Mass.: A.P. Bicknell, 1890), 27; *Huntsville Democrat*, Dec. 30, 1835, April 14, 1841.

22. Letter dated Dec. 29, 1845, Gwyn Papers; Rawick, *American Slave, Supp. 1*, 8: 128.

23. Letters dated Nov. 18, 1835, Dec. 20, 1836, Sept. 13, 1837, Brown Papers.

24. Louise M. Pease, "The Great Kanawha in the Old South, 1671–1861" (Ph.D. diss., West Virginia University, 1959), 198; *Staunton Spectator*, Feb. 3, 1858; Rawick, *American Slave*, vol. 11, bk. 1, 47, vol. 16, bk. 1, 2, vol. 3, bk. 1, 118; James Gwyn Diary, entry dated Aug. 14, 1851, 271, Gwyn Papers; Rawick, *American Slave, Supp. 1*, vol. 9, 1419–20, vol. 5, 461, vol. 10, 2175, vol. 12, bk. 1, 196; Rawick, *American Slave, Supp. 2*, vol. 1, 68; Records of the Cherokee Indian Agency in Tennessee, 1801–1835, National Archives, microfilm, July 29, 1805, Aug. 18, 1805.

25. *Alexandria Gazette and Daily Advertiser*, Aug. 8, 1818; Pease, "Great Kanawha," 198; Eaves narrative, Coleman Papers; J. Winston Coleman, *Slavery Times in Kentucky* (Chapel Hill: Univ. of North Carolina Press, 1940), 211; *Western Citizen*, April 30 and May 3, 1848; *Asheboro Southern Citizen and Man of Business*, May 6 and June 3, 1837; John H. Franklin, *The Free Negro in North Carolina, 1790–1860* (Chapel Hill: Univ. of North Carolina Press, 1943), 54; *Slave Life in Georgia: A Narrative of the Life of John Brown*, ed. L.A. Chamerovzow (Freeport, N.Y.: Books for Libraries Press, 1971), 49–50.

26. Tadman, *Speculators and Slaves*, chap. 3; J.W. Ingraham, *The South-west by a Yankee*, vol. 2 (New York: Harper and Brothers, 1835), 238; letter dated July 1836, Wilson-Lewis Papers; Theodore D. Weld, *American Slavery as It Is: Testimony of a Thousand Witnesses* (1839; reprint, New York: Arno Press, 1968), 69–70, 76.

27. E.A. Andrews, *Slavery and the Domestic Slave Trade in the United States* (Boston: Light and Stearns, 1836), 140, 142–43, 148.

28. *Kanawha Register*, Feb. 5, 1830; Will T. Hale, *Early History of Warren County* (McMinnville, Tenn.: Standard Printing, 1930), 44.

29. G.W. Featherstonhaugh, *Excursion through the Slave States, from Washington on the Potomac to the Frontier of Mexico, with Sketches of Popular Manners and Geological Notices* (1844; reprint, New York: Negro Univs. Press, 1968), 1: 119–23, 169.

30. Rawick, *American Slave, Supp. 1*, vol. 12, 335, 257.

8

A Free Black Slave Owner in East Tennessee

The Strange Case of Adam Waterford

Marie Tedesco

On May 4, 1830, the chancery court at Rogersville, Tennessee, transferred to the United States Court for the Seventh Circuit and District of East Tennessee in Knoxville a transcript of a court record in the case of Adam Waterford, complainant, and Isaac Baker, defendant.[1] A year earlier, Waterford, a "freeman of color and citizen of the county of Sullivan," had filed a complaint in Rogersville against Baker, a citizen of Washington County, Virginia. Waterford sought and received an injunction against Baker to prevent him from evicting Waterford and taking possession of his land in Sullivan County, Tennessee. In November 1829, Baker successfully petitioned for the removal of the case to federal court, as the dispute involved citizens from two states and property was valued in excess of five hundred dollars.[2]

On its most elementary level the case revolved around debts owed by Waterford to Baker, for which the sale of Waterford's lands had become security. A close reading of the case, however, reveals a tangle of trust deeds for hundreds of acres of land owned by Waterford in Sullivan County and in Burkes Garden in Tazewell County, Virginia. Moreover, it became apparent that prominently involved in the case was a "slave Waterford," owned first by white masters in Washington County and then by Adam Waterford. Also central to the case were a number of propertied, white, slave-owning families of Washington County, Virginia, and Sullivan County, Tennessee.

Many questions surround Adam Waterford, his family, and his circumstances. When and how he came to live in southwest Virginia is uncertain, as is the process by which he came to be a landowner whose acreage should have put him in the category of the elite. Highly unusual were Waterford's legal entanglements with wealthy, white landowners. Unusual, though not unheard of, was Waterford's status as a free black slave owner. Focusing on legal documents, foremost among them the *Waterford* v. *Baker* transcript, this essay analyzes Waterford's place in the worlds of slavery and freedom in southern Appalachia. Although his experiences as a free black were unusual because they allowed him to enter a white commercial world usually forbidden to nonwhites, it is possible that Adam's life demonstrates that at least infrequently free blacks and whites interacted as equals in commerce and court.[3] Further, Adam's role as slave owner not only put him in a position that was the very antithesis of his own former enslaved status, but it also allowed him to develop a role prized by many a white master—that of "shrewd businessman." Adam Waterford's date and place of birth are unknown. It is possible that he somehow was related to, was perhaps the grandson of, an Adam Waterford who was a cooper and landowner in later eighteenth-century Williamsburg. That Adam Waterford shows up in tax records of the time: he paid taxes on a town lot from 1782 until 1789, and his estate owed taxes from 1790 until 1803.[4] Given that a 1787–1790 schedule of delinquent taxpayers listed his estate as insolvent and its owner as deceased, it is clear that he died in 1790.[5] The Williamsburg Waterford had lived in the area at least since 1769, when the Williamsburg-James City County Tax Book recorded a debit against Adam Waterford for "2 tithes, 14 lb. tobacco." The next year, according to the accounts of the Botetourt estate, 1768–1771, Lord Botetourt paid Waterford one pound for coopering work. Four years later Waterford "made a bucket for the use of the Public Goal for which the charge is five shillings."[6]

A 1778 reference to Waterford found in the accounts of William Finnie, deputy quartermaster general, calls the cooper "Negro Waterford," not slave Waterford.[7] Adam the cooper evidently was a free person. Legal records later refer to the younger Adam Waterford as an emancipated slave. If the Tazewell Adam was the grandson of the Williamsburg Adam, he and his father had to be offspring of a relationship with a slave woman, as in Virginia there appears to be no exception to the rule that the status of the mother determined the slave or free status of the child.[8]

A 1989 memo by Emma L. Powers of Colonial Williamsburg insisted that there was no evidence that Waterford was married, "much less to the slave woman cited in the [Colonial Williamsburg] *Guidebook*."[9] Yet, Powers's reference to a slave woman introduces the possibility of a liaison between the two. Such a liaison could have produced a son, the David Waterford referred to later in Tennessee court records as the father of the younger Adam Waterford. The younger Adam had a son whom he named David, probably after his father. The pattern of naming sons (Adam-David-Adam-David) suggests possible blood relationships.

How and why the younger Adam Waterford—and perhaps his father as well—came to live in Tazewell County as a slave is a mystery. By the latter part of the eighteenth century, however, slavery and slave trading had become established on the western frontier of Virginia. In 1750, James Patton, the land broker for William Beverley, the Virginia burgess who held a substantial frontier grant, noted the arrival of "several Negroes and Five Norwood horses and meers" to Augusta County, the vast frontier county that then encompassed all of western Virginia. While Patton's statement does not indicate the status of the blacks, the context of his statement indicates that these individuals were probably slaves, who were to be sold in a fashion similar to that of the horses. By 1754 it was clear that Patton himself had become a slave trader, buying and selling slaves for his own profit and for that of his relatives. More than likely, he bought slaves from Beverley, who in 1739 had become involved in the Barbados slave trade.[10]

It is difficult to determine how many persons of African heritage lived on the Virginia frontier, but there is evidence of a free black and a slave presence there. Augusta County court records of the 1740s identify black slaves, while 1750s records refer to free Negroes and mulattoes. In 1753 a Moravian missionary wrote in his diary of a free Negro blacksmith (later identified as Edward Tarr) who lived in Augusta. During the early 1760s, as hemp production expanded in the county, Augusta registered a number of African children as slaves: thirty-two in 1761 and fifteen in 1762. Estate settlements and wills for the decades from the 1740s through the 1780s also testify to the value accorded black slaves.[11]

Lists of tithes also provide evidence for a black presence on the frontier. The 1755 list of 2,313 tithes for Augusta County, for instance, included 40 held by African Americans. Washington County tithable lists for the years 1784, 1785, 1786, covering an area later consisting of Russell, Lee, Wise, Buchanan, Dickenson, and Washington Counties in southwest Virginia, showed an increase in black tithes from 217 in 1784 to 314 in 1785 and 383 in 1786. White tithes for these years were 710, 859, and 1,062, with estimated white population at 3,767, 4,609, and 5,693.[12] By the time of the first census of 1790, Washington and Russell Counties, the two large southwest Virginia counties, had total populations of 5,625, and 3,338, respectively. In Washington there were 5,167 whites, 450 black slaves, and 8 free blacks. Russell County had 3,143 whites, 190 black slaves, and 5 free blacks.[13]

Although it is difficult to ascertain with any certainty when the younger Adam came to live in Tazewell County, it is possible that he came with his father or his mother as a child or an adolescent in the 1780s or 1790s, when the Virginia frontier was developing commercially. If they traveled from the Tidewater region to the western frontier as slaves, there are at least two commonly used routes over which they could have traveled to the Tazewell region. They could have traveled manacled in a slave coffle, trudging on the same roads used earlier by Patton and his associate John Lewis as they led settlers from eastern Virginia through the Blue Ridge Mountains to the region around Staunton. By the 1790s, Staunton had become a lively redistribution center for trade beyond the mountains. It is not unreasonable to assume that Staunton had a slave market, especially considering that Patton's Springhill plantation earlier seemed to have served as a jumping-off point for slaves and indentured servants brought from the east. From Staunton, it would have been relatively easy to move southwestward along the Great Wagon Road and its extensions.[14]

The other route the Waterfords may have taken was one commonly used by white pioneers who settled in the Tazewell region. Many pioneers journeyed from the New River to the Clinch Valley using Indian trails. Crossing the New River, they followed creeks on to a divide six miles east of the present town of Tazewell and then traveled one more mile to the headspring of the

Clinch.[15] If the Waterfords came via this route, it seems likely that they came as slaves of a master who owned only a few bondspersons and who perhaps had bought them on the Richmond market.[16]

In 1799, the Virginia legislature carved out Tazewell County from Russell and Wythe Counties.[17] Rural and lightly settled, Tazewell was a county of small farms with a few towns. Slaves probably served a variety of functions, among them household chores, planting and harvesting, and other outdoor work. Assuming that Adam Waterford was a young slave in Tazewell in the late eighteenth and early nineteenth centuries, he probably performed a variety of tasks for his master, who perhaps also hired him out to neighboring farms.[18]

The first mention of Adam Waterford in Tazewell County records occurred in 1811, when clerk John Perry registered his marriage to Betsy Day: "I certify that on the 26th Day of May 1811 Adam Waterford and Betsy Day people of Colour was bound together according to Law by me."[19] Betsy's status previous to that point is unknown. Although there were many white Days in Tazewell, including early settlers of Burkes Garden, we don't know whether or not any of them owned her. Her surname alone is not sufficient evidence to indicate prior ownership; emancipated slaves often had surnames taken from very early masters or from other sources unconnected to white owners.[20]

Waterford last appeared as a taxpayer in Tazewell County in 1812, but in 1817 he went before the court asking for permission, as a free black, to remain in the county. The court complied: "Adam Waterford, emancepated [sic] slave, made satisfactory proof of his being a man of extraordinary merit [and] was granted permission to reside in the Commonwealth and within this county."[21] The reference to Waterford as a "man of extraordinary merit" indicates that he applied to the court under the provisions of an amended 1806 Virginia law that allowed slaves freed after May 1, 1806, to remain in the state and in the county of their residence, providing courts deemed such slaves to be persons who were emancipated for extraordinary merit.[22]

The unamended statute passed by the General Assembly in January 1806 was part of a piece of legislation titled "An Act to amend several laws concerning slaves," section 10 of which stipulated that any slave who remained in Virginia for more than twelve months after emancipation would forfeit freedom and could "be sold by the overseer for the benefit of the poor."[23] The 1806 statute represented the culmination of political debates on slavery that stemmed from white reactions to the aborted insurrections of Gabriel Prosser in Richmond and Petersburg in 1800 and the failed revolts of Sancho, a riverman who enlisted slaves in Henrico, Charlotte, Nottaway, Amelia, and Dinwiddie Counties in 1801–1802.[24] These attempted revolts caused whites to strengthen controls over slaves and to seek to make manumission illegal. A number of politicians in the General Assembly sought to overturn the 1782 law that allowed manumission by will or by other instrument of writing. Narrowly failing to overturn the 1782 law, which many Virginians viewed as a prerogative of property ownership, opponents of manumission turned their attention to restricting the increase of free blacks in the state as a way of restricting the freeing of one's slaves.[25]

If Waterford received his freedom between May 1806 and 1811, when he legally married Betsy Day, why did he wait so long to apply for permission to remain in Virginia? In his book *The Free Negro in Virginia*, historian John Russell noted that in the initial years after the statute's passage, enforcement was lax. Thus, there remained in Virginia many free blacks who by law should have been forced to leave the state.[26] Yet, land deeds reveal that shortly after the granting of his application to remain in Tazewell County, Waterford left Virginia and moved due south just across the state line into Sullivan County, Tennessee.

Formed in October 1779, when the Tennessee country was still part of North Carolina, Sullivan County, like its Tennessee neighbor to its south, Washington County, in the late eighteenth and early nineteenth centuries had a relatively small black population, free or slave. For example, according to the 1791 census taken in the Southwest Territory, Sullivan County had a population of 4,447 persons, including 297 black slaves and 107 free blacks. Five years later the federal census taken just before Tennessee's becoming a state revealed that Sullivan County's black population totaled 815 (777 slaves and 38 free), while the 1796 county tax list recorded 196 black polls.[27] Waterford's land dealings began in April 1817, when he purchased two hundred acres of land in the Reedy Creek watershed for $2,320 from Adam Miller of Sullivan County. Three years later, Waterford purchased an additional six acres in the Reedy Creek section from John Miller, perhaps a relative of Adam Miller's.[28] In early 1821 Waterford made two purchases of land from William P. Thompson of Washington County, Virginia, one of 160 acres at a cost of $1,000, the other, 480 acres that cost $760.[29] How Waterford obtained the funds to pay for all this land is not clear. There is no indication that he had a skilled trade or that he pursued any occupation other than farming.

By January 1822 Waterford was short of cash, as on the eleventh of that month he borrowed $400 (or $450) from John Baker, a resident of Washington County, Virginia.[30] As security for the debt, Waterford "put into the possession of the said John Baker as a pledge a Negro man a slave for life, named Waterford." The next day, January 12, Waterford purchased a slave named Jefferson from Harrold Smith, also of Washington County, with the money borrowed from Baker.[31] Who were these two slaves, and how did Adam Waterford become a slave owner?

The "Slave Waterford" who Adam mortgaged—or sold—to Isaac and John Baker was his brother, Walter. On January 1, 1822, Adam agreed to purchase Walter from William P. Thompson, who eight months earlier had bought him from his brother, Evan S. Thompson.[32] It is not clear from whom Evan bought Walter, but legal records reveal that on August 16, 1819, Evan entered into a trust deed with James Orr of Washington County, Virginia, in which Thompson sold several slaves, among them one identified as "Waterford." The transaction was dependent on payment of a debt owed to William Byars, also of Washington County. If the debt of $2,064 was not paid, then Orr was authorized to sell the slaves to get the money to cover the debt. Apparently,

Evan Thompson paid the debt, because William Thompson bought Waterford from Evan.[33]

William P. Thompson, Walter's new owner, was a habitual debtor.[34] For whatever reason, Thompson "had become involved in debt" and let Harrold Smith "have several slaves and among them, one he called Jefferson." According to John Baker, when Thompson executed the bill of sale to Adam Waterford for Walter, Thompson "took a writing from the plaintiff declaring that bill of sale to be void if [Waterford] did not procure the said Jefferson for [Thompson]." To procure Jefferson, later described by Smith as a "negro boy slave 17 or 18 years old or thereabouts," Waterford borrowed $450 from Baker in January 1822, and pledged Walter as security for the loan.[35] The next day Waterford purchased Jefferson from Smith. Waterford then went to Thompson and "obtained a writing shewing that the bill of Sale which had been conditional, was then good and valid and never to be revolked [sic]."[36]

A bill signed by Thompson attested to the foregoing. He stated that Adam had executed to him "an instrument of writing" declaring that the sale of Walter would be null and void if "Adam should fail in furnishing Jefferson in ten days from the date of said writing." But, according to this document "said Adam hath this day furnished me with Jefferson agreeable to contract and the Bill of Sale for Waterford is good and valid and never to be revoked."[37]

Waterford thus entered into a triangular agreement with Thompson and Baker, by which he furnished Jefferson to Thompson in order to purchase Walter, whom he then pledged to Baker as security for the money he borrowed. Jefferson, then, was simply the instrument through which Adam Waterford purchased his brother. Jefferson then vanished from the legal record. It should be noted, however, that in a May 1836 judgment on an act of detinue brought by John Baker against George Rutledge charging that the latter illegally held Walter, the judge referred to Jefferson as Adam's son. In ruling against Baker, the judge described the earlier transaction as one in which Adam pledged Walter, his brother, to Baker in order to redeem from bondage his son Jefferson.[38] This assumption that Jefferson was Adam's son was almost certainly in error, as there is no other evidence that suggests such a relationship between the two.

Examination of Adam Waterford's household as recorded in the 1830 census, together with the list of Waterford's children provided by court documents, supports the contention that Jefferson was not Adam's son. In 1830 there were thirteen persons in Waterford's household, with four of them males between ten and twenty-four years of age. Smith, in his 1839 deposition given on behalf of John Baker in a federal case brought against him by David Waterford, said that Jefferson was about seventeen or eighteen years old when purchased from Thompson.[39] Give or take a few years, then, Jefferson would have been of the right age to be included among the males in Waterford's household. But, including David Waterford, later the executor of Adam's estate and referred to numerous times as his son, there were eleven children and heirs of Adam Waterford listed in the case transcript. Jefferson was not one of them. It seems likely that if Waterford bought his son for the purpose of emancipating him from slavery, then Jefferson would be in his household. Also odd is that Harrold Smith never mentioned Jefferson's being Adam's son. Smith said in the 1839 deposition only that Adam desired to buy Jefferson.[40]

Walter Waterford, pledged as security for Waterford's loan from John Baker, became the subject of disagreement between Adam Waterford and the Bakers. According to the terms of Adam's agreement with the Bakers, if he paid back his loan by "February next" (presumably 1822), then possession of Walter would pass back to Adam. But Adam did not repay the loan. Subsequently, in early 1823 James Orr of Washington County, Virginia, as assignee of William P. Thompson, brought suit against Waterford for a debt of two hundred dollars.[41] On January 28, 1823, Waterford entered into a trust deed with Andrew Russell of Washington County for the 206 acres of Sullivan County land on which Adam lived. For one thousand dollars, Waterford sold the land in trust to Russell. But, if Waterford secured the Bakers through "the undisturbed title and possession of a certain slave named Waterford," and protected them from "all costs and damages which they may sustain by any adverse claim being set up to the said slave Waterford," and indemnified them from court costs, then the deed would be null and void. The Bakers claimed in their answer to Waterford's complaint that the jury decision against him in the Orr case, together with court costs and other expenses, cost them seven hundred dollars.[42]

Waterford continued to entangle himself in trust deeds and to obligate himself to the Bakers. As June 1823 approached, he realized that he would not be able to pay a $620 debt incurred to Francis Smith of Sullivan County. Waterford had entered into a deed of trust on his Burkes Garden land, and Smith was preparing to have the trust closed by sale of the land. Again, Adam called on the Bakers, who agreed to take over the Smith obligation, which, with interest accrued, in May 1823 totaled $704.83. Another deed was executed for the Burkes Garden and Sullivan County land. Waterford agreed to pay the debt to the Bakers by November 12, 1824.[43] Subsequently, Waterford was unable to pay the Bakers, and trustee Campbell went ahead with the sale of the lands in the spring of 1825. The Burkes Garden and Sullivan County properties were sold to Isaac Baker for $550. Because Tennessee law stipulated that the complainant had two years to redeem land so sold, title was not transferred to Baker until 1827.[44]

During the next two years Baker attempted to evict Waterford from his Sullivan County land, but failed to do so. In 1829 Waterford successfully beseeched the chancery court for an injunction to prevent the Bakers from evicting him from his land. This decision—characterized by Clarke as "capricious"—left the Sullivan County lands in the hands of Waterford and his heirs for the next eleven years as litigation moved from chancery to federal court.[45] Waterford claimed that no real sale of the lands ever took place because Baker had engaged in fraud when he had had the title of the land transferred. Furthermore, Waterford charged, Baker had no legal right to the Sullivan

County lands because trustee Russell had no authority to transfer the title to Campbell. Waterford also accused the Bakers of underselling forty head of cattle that he had driven to the Bakers' farm to help pay his debt to them. The cattle were "sacrificed" for $15, when they actually were worth $350.[46] In short, Adam contended, the Bakers sought to prevent his meeting of his debt obligation so that they could acquire his land.

In his 1829 complaint Waterford also accused the Bakers of duping him in regard to Walter. According to Adam, some time after the original 1823 trust deed was drawn up, James Orr pretended to have had a claim on Walter. John Baker therefore asked Waterford to insert a clause in the original deed stipulating that Baker "should not be disturbed in the possession of said slave Waterford by reason of the claim of the said James Orr, until the said slave should be redeemed by Your Orator [Waterford]." Waterford agreed to this. But, Adam later claimed that he was "an illiterate person who, unfortunate for himself, can neither read nor write," and if the deed now says that he sold Walter to the Bakers, then the deed "does not speak the language it was intended to speak when your Orator consented that said addition should be made to it, for Your Orator positively states that he never made any contract with . . . Isaac Baker of any kind respecting said Negro slave nor did he ever sell said slave to either of the Bakers, nor was it so understood between Your Orator and either of the Bakers, nor was it understood on the part of Your Orator that any thing should be added to said Deed of Trust respecting said slave except that Baker should be indemnified from all claims to said slave while he should continue as a pledge of . . . John Baker."[47]

From Adam Waterford's perspective the Bakers did not own Walter and thus were not entitled to the $100-120 received annually for hiring him out. On the contrary, Adam insisted that he was entitled to sums accumulated from Walter's hiring out in the years from 1822 until the time in 1834 when Walter "went out of possession" of the Bakers and came into Adam's.[48]

The case dragged on through the legal system, surviving Adam Waterford, who died in the spring of 1835, and Isaac Baker, who died in the fall of 1830. Waterford's interests were looked after by his son and administrator, David, while Isaac Baker's son, John, continued the case on behalf of the estate of his father. The eleven children of Adam Waterford became his heirs.

On October 23, 1840, judges John Catron and Morgan Brown handed down their decision in the case of *Adam Waterford* v. *Isaac Baker*. They ruled that at the time of the sale of the Sullivan County land by trustee Campbell under the deed of trust executed on May 23, 1823, the legal title actually was vested in Andrew Russell, to whom the land previously had been entrusted on January 28, 1823. Thus no legal title passed by sale of the land from Campbell to Isaac Baker, and the title to the land was "too much embarrassed because of said outstanding deed to bring a fair and full price." Furthermore, Russell's relinquishment of the deed to Baker in 1827 was not legal, as Russell had exceeded his authority as trustee. The judges ruled that the complainants were entitled to redeem the land but that the defendants were entitled to $1,356 from debts owed the Bakers by Waterford. If these debts were not paid within three months, the county marshal would sell the lands at public auction and give remaining proceeds after court costs to John Baker. Until further order, title to the land remained with John Baker. The court did not rule on the status of the Virginia lands but said only that the defendant was "left to his own remedy" in regard to these lands.[49] The court also declined to rule on the status of Walter Waterford. Dissatisfied with the decision, David Waterford requested an appeal to the U.S. Supreme Court for the term to be held January 1841, but there is no evidence that anything came of that effort.[50]

In March 1837, almost two years after Adam Waterford's death, Walter Waterford, then living with George Rutledge of Sullivan County, filed a case in equity in chancery court against David Waterford, administrator for his father Adam's estate. Filing through Lewis Garner, a local free black man, Walter claimed that he should be freed immediately because he fulfilled the terms of an 1826 contract in which Adam agreed to emancipate his brother once Walter reimbursed him for the purchase price. Walter first asked that David Waterford "and any others" be restrained by an injunction from removing or in any way interfering with him. The court granted the injunction in April 1837.[51]

Walter recounted to the court the arrangement under which William P. Thompson, a citizen of Virginia, transferred "all right and title which he had as master to your Orator to one Adam Waterford who was the brother of your Orator, and also a man of colour," for either $450 or $500.[52] Walter further testified that David Waterford "who was the father of the said Adam and also on an express agreement with your Orator that as soon as said Adam should have refunded to him the sum of money which he had expended on the purchase," he would emancipate Walter. Walter went on to say that in these activities his brother was "prompted by love and natural affection as . . . by other considerations herein after to be mentioned."[53] Apparently Walter knew nothing of Jefferson, the slave used by Adam to purchase Walter from Thompson. But Walter knew that Adam had borrowed money from the Bakers and that "by some arrangement" with them Adam had placed him in the Bakers' possession. Walter then testified that he remained with the Bakers for many years.[54]

To support his claim of Adam's intention to free him, Walter referred to "an instrument of writing" dated March 28, 1826, and agreed to by Adam as evidenced by his mark. In this document Adam said he had a bill of sale on "my brother named Waterford, now living with Isaac Baker of Washington County and State of Virginia," and that he had from Walter two sums of money, eighty dollars and sixty-four dollars. Walter, Adam said, had sued him over the disposition of these sums, and as a result Adam agreed to place these sums toward Walter's emancipation. A separate sum of thirty-five dollars, with interest from 1822, also was to be placed in Walter's emancipation fund. Adam further agreed that all the wages earned by Walter were to be credited toward his emancipation.[55]

Although the document to which Walter referred was dated 1826, internal evidence from it indicates that he and Adam must have entered into this contract in 1822. By 1826 Walter had had the opportunity, by hiring himself out, to earn wages that he applied to his purchase price.[56] It is highly unlikely that Walter would have had the opportunity, in addition to the work he did for the Bakers, to earn $144 in 1826 alone. Moreover, the $35 sum that the court ordered Adam to credit to Walter's emancipation carried with it interest from 1822. But Walter claimed that the amounts mentioned in the 1826 document represented only a fraction of the money that he turned over to Adam and his father, David. To support this assertion Walter presented a February 1826 document from Sullivan County that detailed the disagreements between Adam and David over the amounts entitled to Walter. Adam and David submitted their dispute to arbiters, who awarded the latter, as the agent for his son's emancipation, $659. This amount included separate sums of $80 and $64, which Walter said he had turned over to Adam; $35, with interest accruing from 1822; and $480 for work performed by Walter. Walter charged in his April 18, 1837, request for an injunction that not only had Adam failed to "perform the contract," but also that David Waterford [the son] had failed to "perform the contract."[57]

In his answer to Walter's complaint against him, David contended that he knew little of the facts of the case. David admitted, however, that Walter and Adam may have made an arrangement as stated in the complaint and, moreover, that it may be true that the complainant "has paid or refunded to said intestate the sum he was bound to do." But David pleaded that he was only a "young man who knew little of his father's affairs." David insisted that his father had the "kindest feelings" toward the complainant and a "deep interest in his freedom and any thing that concerned his interests." His father, David said, incurred great expense in counsels, loss of time, and great trouble trying to save Walter from "those who would have doomed him to endless servitude."[58]

David Waterford claimed to know little of his father's affairs, but his response to Walter relied on more than a superficial knowledge of Adam's legal affairs, especially as they related to Walter. David noted that Adam had two suits against the Bakers: one recently decided in Abingdon against Adam and the other (the basis for much of this essay) pending in federal court in Knoxville. David insisted that he and his father had incurred great expenses in cases that involved Walter and that he [David] was entitled to court costs and reimbursement for such trouble and services. Furthermore, David maintained that "under these circumstances compl[ainan]t has not, and could not be entitled to emancipation, and Resp[ondan]t is informed that compl[ainan]t never did apply to said intestate to be emancipated—nor did said intestate ever refuse to comply with his agreement made with compl[ainan]t, but on the contrary was always ready and willing to comply therewith, and in laboring to secure the freedom of compl[ainan]t perhaps hastened his death."[59]

Although David informed the court that the charge that Walter had overpaid Adam his purchase price was without foundation, he said he would abide by the court's decision if it freed Walter. In such a circumstance, David stated, Walter should then be assessed court costs; he even added that, "if strict accounting be made by the court of services and court costs, the court would find that the complainant owed money to the respondent."[60]

On November 6, 1838, the chancery court issued a decree in the case of *Waterford* v. *Waterford*. It did not, however, settle the issues raised concerning Walter's freedom. Questions of law, the decree stipulated, were to be deferred until the coming in of the clerk and master's report, neither of which unfortunately are included in the court record.[61]

Walter Waterford also sought and received an injunction in 1840 against John Baker, Isaac's son and executor, to prevent him from seizing Walter and taking him to Virginia as a slave. The following year Walter initiated an action against Baker and David Waterford to prevent them from securing his services as a slave.[62] Walter continued to seek his freedom in court actions against both men through May 1844. In that year Walter's appeal bond against Baker was recorded in chancery court in Jonesborough, Tennessee.[63]

Although the chancery court apparently found for Baker in 1840, the Tennessee Supreme Court must have granted Walter's appeal and awarded him his freedom sometime between 1844 and 1860, because the 1860 census shows that Walter resided as a free man in Greene County, Tennessee, with his wife and five children, the oldest of whom was twenty-three. In that year Walter was seventy years old and possessed two hundred dollars worth of personal property, but no real estate. No occupation was given for him, but his wife's occupation was washerwoman. Walter's birthplace was given as Tennessee.[64]

The legal actions involving Walter and the question of his freedom revolved around two questions: first, whether or not Walter and Adam had a contract entitling Walter to his freedom upon reimbursement of his purchase price; and second, whether or not Walter had actually paid Adam or his father, David, the stipulated amount. The cases were all equity cases in which Walter sought his freedom on the grounds of fairness. In no instance was reference ever made to Tennessee's legal restrictions on emancipation and the status of free blacks. Tennessee's laws on emancipation and on rights accorded free blacks in the state were quite lenient until December 1831, when in reaction to "abolitionist agitation" and the fears of insurrection occasioned by the Turner revolt, the General Assembly passed a law forbidding emancipation, except on the express condition that any slave so freed be immediately removed from the state.[65] Two years later the assembly modified that law to exempt from its provisions slaves who had made contracts for their freedom before passage of the 1831 statute.[66] In so doing the Tennessee legislature reaffirmed the right of a slave to make a contract for freedom. This right, as Helen Turner Catterall pointed out in her 1926 history of judicial cases involving slavery, was one that the Tennessee Supreme Court repeatedly upheld. Its decisions, she explained, reflected development of the twofold nature of emancipation: the assent of the master and of the state were required for a slave to obtain freedom. Thus, a person could be a "quasi-slave," if the master had given permission for freedom but the state had withheld its assent in the matter.[67]

Before obtaining the state's consent that he was a free person, evidence suggests that Walter Waterford in essence existed as a quasi-free person. He had a document indicating that his master, Adam Waterford, had consented to his emancipation on condition that Walter fulfilled a particular bargain. Yet, questions concerning Adam's ownership of Walter, together with the equity issues brought up in Walter's and Adam's court cases, obscure the issue of Walter's legal status before his becoming a free person.

What conclusions can we draw from this case and its participants? Were the Bakers guilty, as Adam Waterford claimed, of "gross fraud" in their transactions with him? Were they trying to cheat Waterford, and to deprive him of his lands? Were the Bakers, as a historian of the Clark and Baker families contends, initially motivated by an altruistic desire to help Adam?[68] Did Adam Waterford, as the Bakers charged, reveal himself as a "schrewd, unprincipled man cloaking his cunning and artifice under the garb of ignorance and illiterateness?"[69] Why and how did Adam Waterford, a free black man, become so entangled with affluent white slave owners?

Upon initial examination, it appears that Adam Waterford indeed was, as the Tazewell County court said in 1817, "a man of extraordinary merit." It seems incredible that as an emancipated slave he was able, in a short period of time, to accumulate enough wealth to purchase 846 acres of land, valued at $4,080. J. Merton England, in his study of free blacks in antebellum Tennessee, found that in general most lived on the economic edge and did not earn enough money to accumulate much property. Relying on the 1850 census, England determined that 5,380 free blacks in forty-three counties, out of a total of 6,422 free black persons, held real estate valued at $157,713. A general rise in land prices over the next decade, one characterized by England as prosperous for free blacks and whites, resulted in the value of real estate owned increasing to $450,732 for 5,874 free blacks out of a total of 7,300 in thirty-nine counties.[70]

Waterford's ownership of this land put him in an elite category of not only free black owners of property but also of white property owners. In his study of prosperous African Americans in the South, Loren Schweninger set up a "wealth model," to determine who was prosperous, with two thousand dollars in real estate defining one as wealthy. In the upper South before 1840, Schweninger found fewer than a hundred families who met this mark.[71] Waterford's acquisition of so much land thus made him extremely unusual in East Tennessee and in southern Appalachia.

A significant number of whites in southern Appalachia and East Tennessee owned no property in the years from 1800 to 1840. In her study of capitalistic development in southern Appalachia, Wilma Dunaway made a number of distinctions concerning land-ownership and types of farm labor. She concluded that, beginning with speculation in land, a small elite came to control the best lands throughout the region. The majority of whites with connections to agriculture were not owners but rather laborers, tenants, or croppers. East Tennessee exhibited the same patterns and trends in regard to land-ownership and labor systems.[72]

Adam Waterford's land-ownership, then, becomes even more problematic, especially considering that he was an illiterate man with no known skills. Was he a "man of extraordinary merit" who managed to acquire thousands of acres of land but who in his lifetime compromised that ownership through debts and trust deeds? After his death an inventory of his estate listed only $161 worth of property, excluding the disputed 206 acres of land.[73] Yet others, among them Isaac Baker and Catherine Thompson, William P. Thompson's mother, listed Waterford as a debtor in inventories of their estates.[74]

In addition to questions surrounding Waterford's land deals, there are questions concerning his legal friends and adversaries. As a free black, Waterford frequently had court business with prosperous and influential whites in Sullivan County, Tennessee, and Washington County, Virginia, including the Thompsons, the Bakers, the Rutledges, James Orr, and William Byars.[75] All of these individuals were slave owners who, it can be assumed, to some degree accepted prevalent white attitudes of the social, legal, and intellectual inferiority of blacks as compared with whites. Yet, these men had extensive dealings with a free black person. Perhaps, motivated by malice and greed, these white persons set aside their views on race.

Malice and greed may also have been motivating factors for Waterford as well, especially with regard to his purchase of Walter. Historians typically have categorized slave ownership by free blacks as either "benevolent" or "commercial." Carter Woodson, for example, characterized almost all slave ownership by free blacks as benevolent—that is, free blacks bought family members or friends to save them from sale or continued mistreatment.[76] More recent scholarship casts doubt on the universality of this assumption, as more and more cases have come to light of free blacks who owned slaves, often many of them, and profited by their labor and even their sale.[77] Waterford, perhaps, was a benevolent owner; after all, he did purchase his brother, and in so doing, may have prevented Walter's sale to the lower South. But then Adam entered into an agreement with his brother to make him pay back his purchase price. Although he never traded in slaves or owned a large number of bondspersons from whose labor he profited, Adam nonetheless profited from Walter's hiring himself out to others. Moreover, Adam and his father apparently spent for their own purposes money that Walter turned over to them to be put toward his emancipation.

Adam's benevolence is also called into question as a result of his legal action against the estate of Burke, a free man of color in Washington County, Virginia. Around 1833 Burke died and left a small estate for which John Clarke became the administrator. For unknown reasons, Waterford brought suit against Clarke for the Burke estate. By the time that Judge Benjamin Estill heard the case in 1836, Adam had died and his son David had become party to the suit. In his ruling, Estill noted that Burke had purchased his wife from his former master and that for many years she lived as a freewoman and "would have been legally emancipated . . . had the said Burke known it was necessary to entitle her to her freedom after his death." Estill explained further that Burke's wife was "old and valueless as a slave" and that, in such a doubtful case as this one, it would be "inhuman and against conscience" to deprive her of the "little pittance of property in the hands of the administrator Clarke, which has been acquired partly by her industry." Adam Waterford, Estill ruled, "has wholly failed in shewing right to said property."[78]

Adam Waterford, as a free black master, and Walter Waterford, as a slave owned by his brother, were participants in the slave system of southern Appalachia. Mountain slavery has not received as much scholarly attention as has slavery in the Deep South, but in recent years a few scholars have analyzed the institution. In his path-breaking *Mountain Masters*, John Inscoe discussed the nature of mountain slavery. In many regions of western North Carolina, he wrote, slaves had freedoms and responsibilities not enjoyed by their counterparts elsewhere in the South. For instance, slaves often served as couriers for their white masters and as guides for hunting parties.[79] Writing on slavery in Burkes Garden, Virginia, in the 1840s and 1850s, Ralph Mann agreed that slaves there had freedom of movement, especially to go over the mountains to Wytheville as couriers to buy and sell for their white masters.[80]

To recognize that some slaves had freedom of movement is not to contend that slavery was "easy" in the mountains. Aside from the obvious disadvantage of being unfree, mountain slaves, like slaves elsewhere in the South, lived in fear of being sold away from their families or of being hired away by the master for extended periods of time. In the upper South, especially early in the nineteenth century, when agricultural income from a number of crops declined, selling slaves to planters in the new cotton lands of Alabama, Mississippi, and Georgia and to the sugar plantations of Louisiana was common practice for white masters. Tidewater planters, in particular, saw tobacco profits decrease, so they replaced tobacco profits with income from sales of slaves to the cotton and sugar lands. Mountain masters were not immune to the lure of profit from sales of their "best" slaves, who brought the highest dollar value, to agents of the interstate slave trade.[81]

Hiring out by masters, as opposed to self-hire by slaves, provided additional income for masters attempting to maximize their investments in slaves. Often, masters hired out laborers who they considered "surplus" for as long as a year at a time. While hiring out was beneficial to masters, for slaves it was often a source of disruption and anguish for family members separated from one another by the practice. It was not uncommon for spouses or parents and children to see one another just once a year, perhaps at Christmas, only to be separated again by renewal of the hiring-out contract.[82]

The story of Adam and Walter Waterford, brothers on the opposite sides of freedom—one a free black slave master, the other a slave seeking his freedom—is unique to southern Appalachia and to East Tennessee. Their numerous legal affairs and court battles help us to understand something about relationships among free and enslaved African Americans and slaveholding whites. England contends that the free black "did not participate upon an equal level with whites in any of the activities of the dominant group."[83] Yet the court cases studied here document instances where free blacks and whites interacted as equals in legal and financial undertakings. It is difficult to conclude that the whites in any way took advantage of Waterford in the courtroom. And in terms of their land transactions and their disputes over ownership of Walter Waterford, the principal actors dealt with one another as equals, all pursuing the same goals—profit and control over others.

That Walter's owner was black and that he was his brother seemed not to excite the least bit of concern or consternation. None of the whites, or blacks, for that matter, involved in the Waterford cases indicated in the court proceedings that they thought it unusual for a free black person to own a slave, especially one closely related to the owner. While ownership of slaves by free blacks was relatively rare in antebellum Tennessee, and especially in East Tennessee where there were far fewer slaveholders than in Middle and West Tennessee, it did not elicit moral outrage from either whites or blacks.

The court record tells us much about Adam Waterford, emancipated slave and slave owner, but it omits a crucial part of the human record because it does not tell us why Adam bought his brother or why he failed to free him (though Walter ultimately won his freedom). An illiterate man, Adam Waterford left no diary or letters in which he recorded his innermost thoughts.[84] Whether he was a benevolent master or a shrewd, unprincipled man, Adam Waterford's motivations for his actions must remain a mystery.

NOTES

An earlier version of this essay, titled "The Opposite Sides of Freedom," was published in *Tennessee Historical Quarterly* (spring 1996) and is printed here with the permission of the Tennessee Historical Society.

1. The chancery court at Rogersville heard cases from Sullivan, Grainger, Hawkins, and Claiborne Counties in East Tennessee. The Rogersville chancery was part of the eastern division, as established by the Act of 1827 (Section 58). See John Haywood and Robert L. Cobbs, *The Statute Laws of the State of Tennessee of a Public and General Nature* (Knoxville: F.S. Heiskell, 1831), 175–76. On the establishment of the seventh circuit, see *U.S. Statutes at Large* 2 (1807): 420.

2. *Adam Waterford v. Isaac Baker Case Transcript*, Archives of Appalachia, East Tennessee State University, p. 1, typed transcript (hereafter cited as *Waterford v. Baker*). All page references are to the typed transcription. The laws governing disputes between citizens of different states over property valued at five hundred dollars or more can be found in *U.S. Statutes at Large* 1 (1789): 78.

3. Elizabeth Fortson Arroyo, in her article "Poor Whites, Slaves, and Free Blacks in Tennessee, 1796–1861," *Tennessee Historical Quarterly* 55 (spring 1996): 57–65, discusses the interaction of free blacks with poor whites. She notes that although many of these interactions were antagonistic (e.g., slave patrols made up largely of poor whites often preyed on free blacks), many were not (e.g., liquor drinking, interracial sexual relations). See especially pp. 57, 59, 61–62.

4. Memo from Harold Gill to Earl Soles, Colonial Williamsburg Foundation, Feb. 26, 1969, Archives of Appalachia accession file, *Waterford v. Baker*. In materials sent Edward Speer, Archives of Appalachia, from John E. Ingram, Curator of Special Collections, Colonial Williamsburg, Dec. 1, 1992 (hereafter cited as *Waterford v. Baker*).

5. Clay, Robert, contributor, "Some Delinquent Taxpayers, 1787–1790," *Virginia Genealo-*

gist 22, no. 2 (April-June 1978): 130.There are no Waterfords in Debra L. Newman, comp., *List of Free Black Heads of Families in the First Census of the United States, 1790* (Washington, D.C.: National Archives and Records Service, 1973). The list of free black heads of families compiled from the 1830 census by Carter Woodson lists Adam Waterford of Sullivan County, Tennessee (p. 161), as well as a number of Waterfords in the Philadelphia area (pp. 144, 149, 150). See *Free Negro Heads of Families in the United States in 1830, together with a Brief Treatment of the Free Negro* (Washington, D.C.: Association for the Study of Negro Life and History, 1925).

6. Two unsigned memos about Waterford, n.d., *Waterford v. Baker.*

7. Memo from Earl Soles to Harold B. Gill, Feb. 26, 1989, *Waterford v. Baker.*

8. The Virginia law of 1662 stipulated, "Whereas some doubts have arisen whether a child got by an Englishman upon negro should be free or slave, be it therefore enacted . . . that all children born in this country shall be bound or free according to the condition of the mother." See William Hening, *Statutes at Large: Being a Compilation of All the Laws of Virginia from the First Session of the Legislature in the Year 1619*, vol. 2 (Richmond: George Cochran, 1823), 280. James Hugo Johnston, in his 1937 doctoral dissertation, explained that in Maryland the situation was a little different, at least for a number of years. A 1664 law said that if English women "forgetful of their free condition do intermarry with Negro slaves . . . that all issue of such freeborn English women shall be slaves as their fathers were." This law remained in effect until its repeal in 1715. Johnston, *Race Relations in Virginia and Miscegenation in the South, 1776–1860* (Amherst: Univ. of Massachusetts Press, 1970), 73–74.

9. Memo, Powers to George Dellengill, Feb. 28, 1989, in Johnston, *Race Relations in Virginia.* John Russell, *The Free Negro in Virginia, 1619–1865* (1913; reprint, New York: Negro Univs. Press, 1969), 130–33, discusses marriage between free blacks and black slaves. Herbert G. Gutman, *The Black Family in Slavery and Freedom, 1750–1925* (New York: Vintage, 1977), focuses almost exclusively on the slave family and marriage and only briefly touches on free blacks, especially as they practiced endogamous marriage. See p. 90.

10. Patricia Givens Johnson, *James Patton and the Appalachian Colonists* (Verona, Va.: McClure Printing, 1973), 9, 22. South of the western frontier of Virginia, in the Cherokee country of present-day Tennessee, North Carolina, and South Carolina, slavery and slave trading flourished by the mid-eighteenth century. English traders, in violation of the law, brought black slaves into Cherokee lands. The Cherokee also became involved in slavery by capturing runaway slaves and by selling them back to the English and by enslaving runaways. On Cherokee participation in slavery and the slave trade, consult R. Halliburton Jr., *Red over Black: Black Slavery among the Cherokee Indians* (Westport, Conn.: Greenwood Press, 1977), 4–16; Kenneth Wiggins Porter, "Negroes on the Southern Frontier, 1670–1763," *Journal of Negro History* 33 (Jan. 1948): 70–71; and Theda Perdue, *Slavery and the Evolution of Cherokee Society, 1540–1866* (Knoxville: Univ. of Tennessee Press, 1979), 36–42. Augusta County, officially established in 1738–1739, was one of those huge tracts of land with undefined boundaries that stretched to the Mississippi River. Beverley's grant, called "Beverley Manor," consisted of 118,491 acres, and Benjamin Borden's grant covered another 92,100 acres. See F.B. Kegley, *Kegley's Virginia Frontier, The Beginnings of the Southwest: The Roanoke of Colonial Days* (Roanoke, Va.: Southwest Virginia Historical Society, 1938), 40, 42, 47.

11. J. Susanne Schramm Simmons, "Augusta County's Other Pioneers: The African-American Presence in Frontier Augusta County," in *Diversity and Accommodation: Essays on the Cultural Composition of the Virginia Frontier,* ed. Michael J. Puglisi (Knoxville: Univ. of Tennessee Press, 1997), 160–65. As Simmons notes, Nathaniel Turk McClesky, "Across the First Divide: Frontiers of Settlement and Culture in Augusta County, Virginia, 1738–1770" (Ph.D. diss., College of William and Mary, 1990), identifies the blacksmith of the Moravian diary as Edward Tarr.

12. Simmons, "Augusta County's Other Pioneers," 160, and Gordon Aronhime, "Slavery on the Upper Holston," *Historical Society of Washington County, Va. Publication,* 2d ser., no. 18 (May 1981): 3. Simmons uses a multiplier of two to arrive at eighty as the number of blacks living on the Augusta frontier, while Aronhime uses a multiplier of five for population figures. Aronhime refers to black tithes as slaves. So when he refers to the 1755 list he considers the forty black tithes as slaves. Although most of the black tithes probably were slaves, a few, no doubt, were free.

13. Aronhime, "Slavery on the Upper Holston," 5.

14. Johnson, *James Patton and the Appalachian Colonists*, 55–56; and Wilma A. Dunaway, *The First American Frontier: Transition to Capitalism in Southern Appalachia, 1790–1860* (Chapel Hill: Univ. of North Carolina Press, 1996), 202. Slave coffles were commonly used to transport slaves within the interior. Dunaway discusses early nineteenth-century transportation of slaves by overland coffles through southern Appalachia in "The Incorporation of Southern Appalachia into the Capitalist World Economy, 1700–1860" (Ph.D. diss., University of Tennessee-Knoxville, 1994), 729–34; "Diaspora, Death, and Sexual Exploitation: Slave Families at Risk in the Mountain South," *Appalachian Journal* 26 (winter 1999): 132–37; and in her essay in this volume. Travelers described seeing coffles. In 1844, for example, G.W. Featherstonhaugh, an Englishman traveling in the South, saw a coffle of 300 slaves at the New River in western Virginia. Not long after, near Kingston, Tennessee, he came upon a bivouac of slaves being led on a forced migration, perhaps to the slave market at Louisville. See *Excursion through the Slave States*, 2 vols. (London: John Murray, 1844), 119–23, 168–70. Michael Tadman discusses coffles as they were used in the interstate slave trade from the upper to lower South, 1830–1860, in *Speculators and Slaves: Masters, Traders, and Slaves in the Old South* (Madison: Univ. of Wisconsin Press, 1989), 71–82. On the Great Road and its extensions, see Parke Rouse Jr., *The Great Wagon Road from Philadelphia to the South* (New York: McGraw Hill, 1973), 67–68; and Thomas Speed, *The Wilderness Road* (1886; reprint, New York: Lenox Hill, 1971), 12–13, 26. William E. Myer, "Indian Trails of the Southeast," Forty-Second Annual Report, Bureau of American Ethnology, Smithsonian Institution (Washington, D.C.: Government Printing Office, 1928), 15–26, details the antecedent Indian trails used as the basis for the Great Road and its extensions. The map included with Myer's work is excellent.

15. Louise Leslie, *Tazewell County* (Radford, Va.: Commonwealth Press, 1982), 8.

16. On the Richmond market, see Tadman, *Speculators and Slaves*, 57–65. Slaves purchased, for example, in Staunton would have traveled the Great Road and reached the Tazewell area from the north.

17. Lewis Preston Summers, "Bickley's History of Tazewell County, Virginia, 1856," in *Annals of Southwest Virginia, 1769–1800*, pt. 2 (1929; reprint, Baltimore: Genealogical Publishing), 1433.

18. On renting-out practices in southern Appalachia, see Dunaway, "Diaspora, Death, and Sexual Exploitation, 138. Brenda E. Stevenson discusses renting out in Loudoun County, Va., during the antebellum period in *Life in Black and White: Family and Community in the Slave South* (New York: Oxford Univ. Press, 1996), 184–86, 191–92, 199.

19. *Tazewell County Marriage Register*, bk. 1, Tazewell County Courthouse, County Clerk's Office, Tazewell, Va., p. 20; and Netti Schreiner-Yantis, ed., *Archives of the Pioneers of Tazewell County, Virginia* (Springfield, Va.: n.p., 1973), 203.

20. Schreiner-Yantis's transcription of the 1820 Tazewell County census lists five Days. None at the time were slave owners. See *1820 Census of Tazewell County, Virginia* (Springfield, Va.: n.p., 1971), 5. Pioneer Days are mentioned by Jim and Louise Hoge, "Burkes Garden," in Leslie, *Tazewell County*, 422. On surnames of slaves and emancipated blacks, see Herbert Gutman, "Somebody Knew My Name," chap. 6 in *The Black Family in Slavery and Freedom, 1750–1925* (New York: Vintage, 1977), 230–56.

21. John N. Harman Sr., *Annals of Tazewell County, Virginia* (Richmond: W.C. Hill Printing, 1922), 191; and Schreiner-Yantis, *Archives of Pioneers of Tazewell County*, 236, 284.

22. Jane Purcell Guild, *Black Laws of Virginia: A Summary of the Legislative Acts of Virginia concerning Negroes from Earliest Times to the Present* (1938; reprint, New York: Negro Univs. Press, 1969), 72; and Philip J. Schwarz, "Emancipators, Protectors, and Anomalies: Free Black Slave Owners in Virginia," *Virginia Magazine of History and Biography* 95 (July 1987): 321–22.

23. Guild, *Black Laws of Virginia*, 72; and Samuel Shepherd, *The Statutes at Large of Virginia from October Session, 1792, to December Session, 1806, Inclusive*, vol. 3 (1835; reprint, New York: AMS Press, 1970), 252.

24. On Gabriel's and Sancho's planned revolts, see Douglas R. Egerton, *Gabriel's Rebellion: The Virginia Slave Conspiracies of 1800 and 1802* (Chapel Hill: Univ. of North Carolina Press, 1993); and Joseph Cephas Carroll, *Slave Insurrections in the United States, 1800–1865* (1938; re-

print, New York: Negro Univs. Press, 1968), 47–70. On Gabriel's plot alone, see Herbert Aptheker, *American Negro Slave Revolts* (New York: International Publishers, 1943), 219–28; and Jordon, *White over Black*, 393–94.

25. On the 1782 law, see William W. Hening, *Statutes at Large: Being a Collection of All the Laws of Virginia*, vol. 11 (Richmond: George Cochran, 1823), 39; and John Russell, *The Free Negro in Virginia, 1619–1865* (1913; reprint, New York: Negro Univs. Press, 1969), 59–60. Previous to the 1782 law, manumission occurred by act of the Virginia General Assembly. As Schwarz notes, such manumissions were rare. See "Emancipators, Protectors, and Anomalies," 321. On the political debates during the years 1800–1805, see Egerton, *Gabriel's Rebellion*, 147–62; and Russell, *Free Negro in Virginia*, 66–72. The Gabriel and Sancho plots involved slaves, not free blacks. Nonetheless, white Virginians somehow connected free blacks to the conspiracies. See Jordan's analysis of the debates and Virginians' fear of free blacks, *White over Black*, 574–82.

The 1806 law probably prevented benevolent white and black masters from emancipating their slaves for fear that the newly freed persons would be forced to leave family and friends in Virginia. Whether, as Egerton claims, the free black community became a "closed society" at this time is debatable. Russell found that the free black population increased by approximately ten thousand from the 1800 census to the 1810 census. The real decrease came in the wake of the Nat Turner revolt, in the decade from 1830 to 1840, when the increase was only twenty-five hundred. (See Russell, *Free Negro in Virginia*, 61, 80.) The significance of the 1806 law was, as Jordan claimed, that it marked the reversal of Revolutionary trends toward greater freedom. No longer in Virginia would there be any hope of abolishing slavery. See Jordan, *White over Black*, 574–75.

26. Russell, *Free Negro in Virginia*, 156. Donald Sweig found that Fairfax County registers of free blacks revealed that large numbers of slaves freed after passage of the 1806 law remained in the county. Sweig, ed. and indexer, *Free Negroes Commencing September Court 1822*, registrations of bk. 2, and *Register of Free Blacks 1835*, bk. 3 (Fairfax, Va.: History Section, Office of Comprehensive Planning, Fairfax County, Va., July 1977), 4.

27. On the formation of Sullivan County, see Oliver Taylor, *Historic Sullivan: A History of Sullivan County, Tennessee, with Brief Biographies of the Makers of History* (Bristol, Tenn.: King Printing, 1909), 90–91; and Pollyanna Creekmore, comp., "Early East Tennessee Taxpayers" [Sullivan County], *East Tennessee Historical Society's Publications*, no. 31 (1959), 112. For the 1791 census figures, see Edward Michael McCormack, *Slavery on the Tennessee Frontier* (Nashville: Tennessee American Revolution Bicentennial Commission, 1977), 18; and the 1795 census figures, J.G.M. Ramsey, *Annals of Tennessee* (1852; reprint, Kingsport: Kingsport Press, 1967), 648. Creekmore (p. 121) provides the number of black polls in 1796. By comparison, Washington County, Tennessee, in 1791, had 5,872 persons, with 535 black slaves but only 12 free blacks (McCormack, *Slavery on the Tennessee Frontier*, 18). Lucy Gump, in her 1989 master's thesis, "Possessions and Patterns of Living in Washington County: The Twenty Years before Tennessee Statehood, 1777–1796" (East Tennessee State University), 137, notes that in 1791 there were 535 slaves in the county, and in 1795 that figure had increased to 978. Black polls in 1791 numbered 141, and in 1796, 222. The age range for taxing slaves varied, but it usually was either ten-to-sixty or twelve-to-sixty. Consult Gump, "Possessions and Patterns of Living," 136–37; and Chase C. Mooney, *Slavery in Tennessee* (Bloomington: Indiana Univ. Press, 1957), 25.

28. Sullivan County Deed Books, microfilm, bk. 7, 158–59; bk. 8, 72–73. Unlike other of Virginia's neighbors, most notably Kentucky and Maryland, Tennessee in 1817 had no laws restricting the entry and settlement of free blacks. Later, in 1831, however, Tennessee joined the ranks of those prohibiting the settlement of free blacks within its boundaries. See Jordan, *White over Black*, 575; and William Imes, "The Legal Status of Free Negroes and Slaves in Tennessee," *Journal of Negro History* 4 (July 1919): 260.

29. Washington County, Virginia Deeds, Deed Book 4, Washington County Courthouse, Abingdon, Va., 190–92. There were many Thompsons who lived in southwest Virginia, particularly in the Tazewell area. The Thompsons who Waterford had dealings with were descendants of James Patton, the colonizer, whose daughter Mary married William Thompson. Mary and William had a son, James, who probably fought in the Revolutionary War and who later moved to Washington County, Virginia. James had a wife, Catharine, and two sons, William P. and Evan. It

is this William Thompson from whom Waterford bought land. On the Thompsons, consult Johnson, *James Patton and the Appalachian Colonists*, 20, 73–75, 213; Mary B. Kegley and F.B. Kegley, *Early Adventures on the Western Waters*, vol. 1, *The New River of Virginia in Pioneer Days, 1745–1800* (Orange, Va.: Green Publishers, 1980), 88, 144, 336, 338–40.

30. Isaac Baker Jr. was the son of Isaac Baker Sr., a Pennsylvania native who moved to Maryland and then migrated to the Holston country in 1772 with Evan Shelby. Isaac Senior was one of the purchasers of the Shelby Grove tract. Isaac Junior, one of five Baker sons, received full title to the Sapling Grove tract and eight black slaves in Isaac Senior's will of 1796. See Gerald H. Clark, *From Whence They Came: The Record of a Clark Family* (privately published, 1981), 129, 132, 139; and the will of Isaac Baker Sr., Will Book 2, Washington County, Va., 68–69, typescript at the Washington County, Virginia, Historical Society, Abingdon, Va.

Isaac Junior continued to be a slave owner. According to census records in 1810 he had one slave; in 1820, eleven; and in 1830, eighteen slaves. His will of Feb. 3, 1831, however, included only nine slaves. See Bureau of the Census, *United States Census, 1810, 1820, 1830*, Washington County, Va.; Clark, *From Whence They Came*, 160; and Will Book 6, Washington County, Va., typescript at the Washington County, Virginia, Historical Society, 174.

31. *Waterford v. Baker*, 45, 54. Schwarz, in "Emancipators, Protectors, and Anomalies," 328, notes that free Negroes regularly offered their slaves as security for loans.

32. *Waterford v. Baker*, 53–54. References to Walter as Adam's brother are found on pp. 84, 90, 94, and 96 of the transcript. Exhibit no. 3, p. 59, in the case transcript consists of the bill of sale for Walter Waterford from E.S. Thompson to William P. Thompson. Walter is described as a "mulatto man."

33. Washington County, Virginia Deeds, WCCH, Deed Book 7, 109. But Orr, in a later case against Adam Waterford, made a claim to the "Slave Waterford" [Walter]. See *Waterford v. Baker*, 7.

34. The court minutes of Washington County Court, Abingdon, Va., reveal that William Thompson was in debt to many individuals. See especially Minute Book 2, pp. 200, 218, 274–76. These debts were recorded in 1820.

35. *Waterford v. Baker*, 122.

36. Ibid., 54.

37. Ibid., 59–60.

38. Ibid., 94–95. *[John] Baker v. [George] Rutledge*, Law Order Book "A," 1830–1841, Washington County, Va., 229. Baker filed the detinue action in October 1834, 144.

39. *Waterford* v. *Baker*, 122.

40. Bureau of the Census, *Fifth Census of the United States, Population Schedules*, Sullivan County, Tenn., 334–35; and *Waterford v. Baker*, 94, 97–98, 122.

41. *Waterford v. Baker*, 20. How and why Orr was acting as Thompson's assignee is not known, but one scenario perhaps is that Thompson owed Orr two hundred dollars, which Orr had difficulty collecting. Waterford owed Thompson two hundred dollars, and in order for Thompson to satisfy his debt to Orr, he perhaps authorized Orr to collect the two hundred dollars from Waterford.

42. Sullivan County Deeds, Deed Book 9, Jan. 23, 1823, 328–29; *Waterford v. Baker*, 6-7; 20–21. The Bakers claimed that it was said that William Byars had a claim against Walter Waterford. Byars was the party involved in the trust deed executed by Evan Thompson with James Orr.

43. Sullivan County Deeds, Deed Book 9, May 12, 1823, 325–27; *Waterford v. Baker*, 22–23; and Clarke, *From Whence They Came*, 165. The Bakers also became Waterford's security in a suit brought by Waterford against William Shoemaker. See the trust deed, p. 327.

44. *Waterford v. Baker*, 23–25, 39.

45. Ibid., 1–3, 6; and Clarke, *From Whence They Came*, 165.

46. *Waterford v. Baker*, 2–5.

47. Ibid., 43–44.

48. Ibid., 42–43, 48, 50, 97.

49. Ibid.,77–79.

50. Ibid., 79.

51.*Walter Waterford by next friend Lewis Garner v. David Waterford, administrator of Adam Waterford*, March 4, 1837, Washington County Court Records, Chancery Court, Alphabetical Series, Box 205 (hereafter cited as *Waterford v. Waterford*). Garner is listed in Woodson, *Free Negro Heads of Families in the United States in 1830*, 161. By the time Walter Waterford filed his case the chancery setup had changed as a result of passage of the Act of 1835 (chap. 41). In the eastern division (now one of three, not two, divisions in the state: eastern, middle, and western) chancery cases for Carter, Sullivan, and Washington Counties were heard at Jonesborough in Washington County. See R.L. Caruthers and A.O.P. Nicholson, *A Compilation of the Statutes of Tennessee* (Nashville: James Smith, 1836), 225.

52. *Waterford v. Waterford*, April 1837.

53. Ibid.

54. Ibid.

55. Ibid.

56. According to Mooney, self-hire of slaves in Tennessee was common before 1823 but thereafter was restricted by law. The laws must have been violated because, as Mooney states in 1839, the illegality of self-hire was reiterated and penalties for offenses made more severe. (*Slavery in Tennessee*, 24). See also Imes, "The Legal Status of Free Negroes and Slaves in Tennessee," 269. J. Merton England, in his article "The Free Negro in Ante-Bellum Tennessee," contends that self-hire of slaves added a "considerable number" to the free black population: *Journal of Southern History* 9 (Feb. 1943): 40.

57. *Waterford v. Waterford*, April 1837.

58. Ibid., answer of David Waterford, Sept. 18, 1837, to bill filed against him by Walter Waterford, March 1837.

59. Ibid.

60. Ibid.

61. Ibid., decree, Nov. 6, 1838.

62. *Walter Waterford v. John Baker*, Nov. 7, 1840, Washington County Court Records, Chancery Court, Alphabetical Series, Archives of Appalachia, East Tennessee State University (hereafter cited as *Walter Waterford v. Baker*); *Walter Waterford by next friend Lewis Garner v. John Baker and David Waterford*, 1841(hereafter cited as *Waterford v. Baker and Waterford*).

63. *Walter Waterford v. Baker*, appeal bond, May 10, 1844.

64. Bureau of the Census, *Eighth Census of the United States. Population*. Greene County, Tenn., p. 76. I did not find a marriage record or a will for Walter.

65. Caleb Perry Patterson, *The Negro in Tennessee, 1790–1865* (Austin: University of Texas, Bulletin No. 2205, Feb. 1, 1922), 155; Mooney, *Slavery in Tennessee*, 20; and Caruthers and Nicholson, comps., *Compilation of the Statutes of Tennessee*, 278. The 1801 law permitted any slave to be freed by his/her owner provided that the court "should be of the opinion that acceding to the same would be consistent with the interest and policy of the state," and provided that the petitioner gave bond for damages in case the freed person became a "charge" on the county. See James Patton, "The Progress of Emancipation in Tennessee, 1796–1860," *Journal of Negro History* 17 (Oct. 1932): 75. Consult also pp. 79–81 of the Patton article on 1829 emancipation law.

66. Caruthers and Nicolson, comps., *Compilation of the Statutes of Tennessee*, 278; and Patton, "Progress of Emancipation in Tennessee," 77.

67. Helen Turner Catterall, ed., *Judicial Cases concerning American Slavery and the Negro* (1926; reprint, New York: Negro Univs. Press, 1968), 479.

68. Clark, *From Whence They Came*, 165.

69. Ibid., 53.

70. England, "Free Negro in Ante-Bellum Tennessee," 52–53.

71. Loren Schweninger, "Prosperous Blacks in the South, 1790–1880," *American Historical Review* 95 (Feb. 1990): 33–34, 41. Lee Soltow, *Men and Wealth in the United States, 1850–70* (New Haven: Yale Univ. Press, 1975), only briefly comments on property holding among free blacks before the Civil War. He does note, however, that the "probability of a free colored male's owning property was very small indeed, about one-fourth of that of all free men in 1850" (see p. 54). Also consult Ira Berlin, *Slaves without Masters* (New York: Pantheon, 1974), 44–49. Luther Porter Jack-

son wrote a classic 1942 study on property holding among free blacks in Virginia, *Free Negro Labor and Property Holding in Virginia, 1830–1860* (New York: D. Appleton, 1942).

72. Dunaway, *First American Frontier,* 66–121. See also her dissertation, "Incorporation of Southern Appalachia," 1048, 1051–52. Pages 1054–59, 1062–63, 1070, 1078 focus on land-ownership in 1860. Pages 988–1004 contain explanations of sources and methodology used to analyze land-ownership patterns. (Page 995 concerns Tennessee.) In his study of farming in Tennessee, Donald L. Winters concludes that although tenancy was a common form of land tenure in the state, a majority of farmers owned their land in 1850 and 1860. See *Tennessee Farming, Tennessee Farmers: Antebellum Agriculture in the Upper South* (Knoxville: Univ. of Tennessee Press, 1994), 99.

73. Will Book 2, Tazewell County Courthouse, 57.

74. See, for example, *Adam Waterford v. Catherine Thompson,* May 8, 1832, p. 6; Oct. 8, 1833, p. 27; May 18, 1837, p. 136; Oct. 25, 1837, p. 151, Chancery Order Book "A," 1831–1847, Washington County, Virginia, Courthouse.

75. Census records for 1830 and 1840 document the number of slaves held by the Bakers, the Rutledges, James Orr, and William Byars, while the court actions cited in the *Waterford v. Baker* transcript document the Thompsons' slave ownership. Further information on the Rutledges is available in Richard Rutledge Lewis, *The Rutledges of Vance, Sullivan County, Tennessee* (Knoxville: privately published, 1984); and Robert Thomas Case, "The Rutledges," *The Lookout,* no. 8 (Aug. 4, 1928).

76. Woodson, *Free Black Owners of Slaves in the United States in 1830* (1924; reprint, New York: Negro Univs. Press, 1968), 1–6.

77. Larry Koger, *Black Slaveowners: Free Black Slave Masters in South Carolina, 1790–1860* (Jefferson, N.C.: McFarland, 1985), 1–3, 80–82. See also R. Halliburton Jr., "Free Black Owners of Slaves: A Reappraisal of the Woodson Thesis," *South Carolina Historical Magazine* 76 (July 1976): 129–35.

78. Fee Book, 1823–39, Washington County, Va., 26, Washington County Courthouse, Abingdon, Va.; Chancery Order Book "A," 1831–47, Washington County, Va., 24–25, 59, 119, Washington County Courthouse, Abingdon, Va. In 1833 Hannah Spriggs petitioned that she was entitled to Burke's estate; she dropped her claims in 1834. See Order Book "A," 24–25, 42–43. In 1833 the Literary Fund of the Commonwealth of Virginia, an organization that collected half of the proceeds of the sale of slaves illegally brought into Virginia in violation of the 1806 law or of emancipated blacks who illegally remained in the state for twelve months after emancipation, submitted a legal claim against Spriggs and Waterford to the Burke estate. The fund's cause against Waterford was heard with Clarke's claim in 1836. See Fee Book, 1823–39, p. 36; and Order Book "A," p. 119. I do not know the fund's interest in the Burke estate.

79. John Inscoe, *Mountain Masters: Slavery and the Sectional Crisis in Western North Carolina* (Knoxville: Univ. of Tennessee Press, 1989), 89–90.

80. "Mountains, Land, and Kin Networks: Burkes Garden, Virginia, in the 1840s and 1850s," *Journal of Southern History* 58 (Aug. 1992): 421.

81. Tadman, *Speculators and Slaves,* 5–8; Stevenson, *Life in Black and White,* 177–79; and Dunaway, "Diaspora, Death, and Sexual Exploitation," 132–33.

82. Dunaway, "Diaspora, Death, and Sexual Exploitation," 132, 137; Stevenson, *Life in Black and White,* 184–86; and Inscoe, *Mountain Masters,* 76–77.

83. England, "Free Negro in Ante-Bellum Tennessee," 55.

84. One of the few—perhaps the only—collection of papers that centers on an illiterate free black person who was an emancipated slave in the "Free Frank Papers," a private collection of documents on Frank McWorter, an emancipated slave born in Union County, S.C., and freed in Lincoln County, Tenn. See the introduction and epilogue to Julia E.K. Walker, *Free Frank: A Black Pioneer on the Antebellum Frontier* (Lexington: Univ. Press of Kentucky, 1983).

9

OLMSTED IN APPALACHIA

A Connecticut Yankee Encounters Slavery and Racism in the Southern Highlands, 1854

JOHN C. INSCOE

Outside observers have provided among the richest primary sources for scholars of the antebellum South. Despite the stereotypical assumptions, florid prose, and regional and moral biases that characterized the majority of such travel accounts, their detailed descriptions of the people and places encountered have often been of great value to later chroniclers of slavery and the Old South.

Probably the most valuable of such accounts are three volumes of commentary on slavery and southern society written by Frederick Law Olmsted. These accounts are based on his fourteen months of travel throughout the South from 1852 to 1854.[1] Though it was his later career as a landscape architect, environmentalist, and urban planner for which Olmsted is most widely remembered, his much briefer stint as a journalist and social critic during the 1850s is equally significant. Because his mission to observe and report objectively on slavery and its effects on southern society was so precise, his route so extensive, and his observations so voluminous, historians from James Rhodes and U.B. Phillips to Kenneth Stampp and Eugene Genovese have made Olmsted's work the most cited and quoted of any contemporary source on the "peculiar institution." Yet relatively little attention has been paid to one of the most distinctive and uniquely revealing segments of Olmsted's southern tour: the summer month in 1854 in which he journeyed through the southern Appalachians.

Born in Hartford, Connecticut, in 1822, the product of a comfortable New England upbringing and a Yale education, Olmsted seemed to have been imbued with a sense of wanderlust throughout his youth. After an extensive tour of Europe and the British Isles, which led to the 1852 publication of his first book, *Walks and Talks of an American Farmer in England*, Olmsted was commissioned by two New York newspapers to serve as a roving correspondent in the American South. That assignment led to a series of letters that appeared in the *New York Daily Times* and the *New York Daily Tribune* during and after his trip; the letters were then compiled and expanded into three volumes: *A Journey in the Seaboard Slave States* (1856), *A Journey through Texas* (1857), and *A Journey in the Back Country* (1860).[2]

Though Olmsted, like many of his fellow New Englanders, firmly opposed slavery, he was, early in the decade, almost as offended by the hyperbole
and pious posturing of what he felt were overwrought and ill-informed abolitionists. He saw his southern assignment as an opportunity to provide a more
objective appraisal of slavery based entirely on his firsthand observations. "Very
little candid, truthful, and unprejudiced public discussion," he wrote, "has yet
been had on the vexed subject of slavery." He maintained that the true nature
of southern life, white and black, had thus far proved more impenetrable to
outsiders and thus subject to misconception than was true of most foreign
countries.[3]

Once his trip was under way, Olmsted's concern was not so much the
black labor system's cruelties and injustices to those enslaved. In fact, he found
the physical treatment and quality of the slaves' lives to be somewhat better
than he had anticipated. Rather it was the economic and cultural detriments
that slavery inflicted on southern whites—slaveholders and nonslaveholders—
that made up his most stinging indictment of the system. As a labor force,
slavery proved grossly inefficient, due in part to too much indulgence on the
part of owners and taskmasters. Olmsted concluded that, because of their lack
of incentive and their inherent shortcomings as a race, slaves worked slowly
and poorly. Even worse, they lowered the expectations for white labor output
and locked southern agriculture into crude, backward methods that limited the
progress and the productivity that characterized American farming elsewhere.[4]

A far more serious defect in Olmsted's eyes was the cultural and social
stagnation that the peculiar institution imposed upon the South. Slavery robbed
the region's yeomen of any Calvinistic work ethic or of any incentive for self-
improvement, material or otherwise. But what made Olmsted's commentary
most original was that his descriptions of nonslaveholders—"unambitious, in-
dolent, degraded and illiterate . . . a dead peasantry so far as they affect the
industrial position of the South"—he found almost equally applicable to the
ruling class.[5] Its black property inhibited intellectual activity or interests and
perpetuated among the planter elite crude, primitive living conditions usually
indicative only of frontier society.[6]

In the summer of 1854, toward the end of his second tour, that covering
the "backcountry" or inland South, Olmsted moved into Appalachia. There he
found exceptions to the deplorable conditions of the plantation South and evidence confirming his explanation for those conditions. From late June through
late July, the Connecticut correspondent traveled through the hills of northern Alabama, passed briefly through Tennessee and Georgia, then moved
through western North Carolina across the northeastern tip of Tennessee, and
on into the Blue Ridge Mountains of Virginia. His itinerary included Chattanooga and the nearby copper-mining region of Polk County; the westernmost
string of North Carolina county seats (Murphy, Waynesville, Asheville,
Burnsville, and Bakersville); Elizabethton, Tennessee; and finally Abingdon
and Lynchburg, Virginia.[7]

With the exception of the few substantial towns through which he passed,

Frederick Law Olmsted. (Courtesy of the National Archives)

Olmsted's mountain route took him through areas with among the fewest slaves in the South. In 1850, the total slave population of the ten identifiable counties through which he passed was a little over eight thousand—only 10 per cent of the counties' total populations. Excluding Hamilton, Buncombe, and Washington Counties, with their respective communities of Chattanooga, Asheville, and Abingdon, whose populations were larger, more affluent, and included a higher percentage of slaves, the remaining seven counties were home to a mere 2,446 slaves, who made up only 6.7 percent of the populace.[8]

While moving in and between these highland counties, Olmsted found much to confirm his general conclusions formed after observing other parts of the South. Though the impact of bondage on its black victims was a major concern of Olmsted's throughout his southern travels, he paid little attention to slaves themselves once he moved into the mountains. While he occasionally noted their presence in households or farms that he visited, he related only one specific encounter with a highland slave, a woman he observed while en route through a prosperous mountain valley. But neither her treatment nor her mental state interested him by then. In rounding up a herd of "uncommonly fine cattle," she forced the animals to leap over a four-foot fence rail rather than lower it and beat a pregnant heifer that failed to make the unreasonable jump. Such behavior confirmed to Olmsted his theory that "slavery breeds unfaithful, meritorious, inexact and non-persistent habits of working," habits that are inevitably passed on to white laborers as well, so that they become "even more indifferent than negroes to the interests of their employers."[9] Even though he maintained that the highlanders he observed were much more industrious than their lowland counterparts (no doubt due to the presence of far fewer slaves), this regrettable side effect of the system was nevertheless apparent in the mountains.

But Olmsted was also quick to note the much improved temperaments of those in areas little touched by slavery, which he credited to the absence of black bondsmen and their owners. "Compared with the slaveholders," he generalized about the mountain residents he observed, "these people are more cheerful, more amiable, more sociable, and more liberal. Compared with the nonslaveholders of the slaveholding districts, they are also more hopeful, more ambitious, more intelligent, more provident, and more comfortable" (293). Even the material conditions of mountain life were, he claimed, an improvement over those of plantation society.

Olmsted wasted no time in drawing these conclusions. As he moved north into the Alabama hill country, he passed through a valley he described as having "thin, sandy soil, thickly populated by poor farmers." He added that "negroes are rare, but occasionally neat, new houses, with other improvements, show the increasing prosperity of the district" (220). The journalist would later go to great lengths to reinforce his case for the degenerative effects of slavery on the character and physical well-being of owners. He told of approaching a substantial log house with cabins for blacks, only to be told by its owner that he could afford to spare neither food nor fodder for Olmsted or his horse (233). A lengthy sequence on his visit with a Tennessee "squire" slightly farther along his route stressed the indolence and slovenly lifestyle exhibited by both his host and hostess. The squire slept late and did not change his clothes, and his wife spent most of her time smoking a pipe on the porch, leading their New England guest to exclaim incredulously, "Yet every thing betokened an opulent and prosperous farmer—rich land, extensive field crops, a number of negroes, and considerable herds of cattle and horses. He also had capital invested in mines and railroads, he told me" (236).

In his most clear-cut elaboration of this point, Olmsted described his accommodations on two consecutive nights near Elizabethton, Tennessee. One was the residence of a slaveholder; the other was not. Though similar in size and furnishings—"both houses were of the best class common in the region" (268)—and though the slaveholder was much the wealthier of the two, Olmsted maintained that he lived in much less comfort. His house was dirty, disorderly, and in need of repair; he and his wife were "very morose or sadly silent"; the household's white women were "very negligent and sluttish in their attire";

and the food was badly cooked and badly served by blacks (269). By contrast, Olmsted's next host, a nonslaveholder, lived in much neater, well-ordered, and comfortable quarters. The women were clean and well dressed, and everyone was "cheerful and kind." The food served was abundant and wholesome (the first Olmsted claimed to have had of that quality since Natchez, Mississippi, months earlier), and all work was carried on far more smoothly and conscientiously (269–70).

Though such convenient contrasts may strain credibility, the southern highlands provided the Connecticut Yankee with interesting variations to his theory that the negative effects of a slaveholding society extended well beyond its black victims. But it is his interviews with the region's inhabitants that serve as the most revealing and valuable aspects of his work, for his account gave voice to this ordinarily inarticulate and rarely quoted group. The testimony of these generally inaccessible southerners elicited by their northern guest serves as the most significant body of evidence regarding what has long been a baffling array of opinion, expert and otherwise, on racism in the mountains.

On no other aspect of Appalachian culture has opinion been so divided as on the question of how mountaineers regarded blacks. On the one hand are those who concluded that the lack of contact meant a lack of prejudice as well. Carter Woodson, an African American historian with West Virginia roots, was the first and still one of the few scholars to have dealt seriously with the subject of racial attitudes in the southern Appalachians. He maintained that greater social harmony existed between the races there than elsewhere in the South. "There was more prejudice against the slaveholder than against the Negro," he wrote, and "with so many sympathizers with the oppressed in the back country, the South had much difficulty in holding the mountaineer in line to force upon the whole nation their policies," namely, the continuation of slavery. John C. Campbell agreed, stating that "large sections of the Highland South were in sympathy with the North on the Negro question." Far more recently, Loyal Jones, an Appalachian scholar and native western North Carolinian, asserted that the "Appalachians have not been saddled with the same prejudices about black people that people of the deep South have."[10] Such statements seem to credit mountain residents with a sort of moral superiority, as if being somewhat removed from the harsher realities of the institution enabled them to view it more objectively and to see the slaves' plight more sympathetically.

Other scholars have drawn from the "rugged individualism" and fierce independence associated with early mountain settlers the corollary that their love of freedom led them to repudiate the concept of human property. Those "true democrats" of Appalachia, according to one account, "cherish liberty as a priceless heritage. They would never hold slaves and we may almost say they will never be enslaved." An even more general assessment proposed that bondage and high altitudes were incompatible: "Freedom has always loved the air of mountains. Slavery, like malaria, desolated the alluvials of the globe. The skypiercing peaks of the continents are bulwarks against oppression."[11]

In stark contrast stand those who have posited that the lack of black contact by many white mountaineers resulted in an even more intense hostility toward blacks than that felt by whites in areas with more substantial black populations. This view owes much of its popularity to the oft quoted statement of W.J. Cash in *The Mind of the South:* "The mountaineer has acquired a hatred and contempt for the Negro even more virulent than that of the common white of the lowlands; a dislike so rabid that it was worth a black man's life to venture into many mountain sections."[12] Some of the more secluded pockets of settlement in the southern highlands did have and continue to have reputations for their vehement opposition to a local black presence. A resident explaining the absence of blacks, free or slave, in the Rock Creek section of North Carolina's Mitchell County stated that "colored people have a well-founded belief that if they venture up there they might not come back alive."[13]

These extreme points of view suggest, at the very least, that the degree of racism among antebellum mountain residents ran the full gamut of opinion. But it should be noted that most of the statements quoted above come from twentieth-century secondary sources and are largely conjectural as to how pre–Civil War highlanders would view a race with whom they had little or no contact. Thus Olmsted's testimony is particularly significant, in that it addresses these issues so directly.

Most of the mountain residents with whom Olmsted discussed the topic of slavery seem to have had equal contempt for slaves, their masters, and the system itself. Their objections toward the institution in their own area, however, were far fewer than was their hatred of it in the lowland South. One Tennessee mountaineer summed up the viewpoint held to varying degrees by almost all of those Olmsted interviewed. The journalist reported, "He'd always wished there had n't been any niggers here but he would n't think there was any better way of getting along with them than that they had" (239). One of Olmsted's hosts near Burnsville, North Carolina, said, "Slavery is a great cuss . . . the greatest there is in these United States." But his explanation mentioned only the fact that it allowed eastern planters to dominate state government at the expense of westerners (259). Others expressed very real regional prejudices against the lowland society dominated by a slaveholding elite. Olmsted must have reveled in the chance to quote one mountain resident, whose objections to the system's moral effects on slaveholders and nonslaveholders alike echoed Olmsted's own: "He was afraid that there was many a man who had gone to the bad world, who wouldn't have gone there if he had n't had any slaves. He had been down in the nigger counties a good deal, and he had seen how it worked on the white people. It made the rich people, who owned the niggers, passionate, and proud and ugly, and it made the poor people mean" (263).

But despite their objections to the system, almost none of the highlanders that Olmsted encountered advocated abolition. The only exception was, significantly, a resident of East Tennessee, virtually the only section of the South with an ardent and well-developed antislavery movement.[14] This "man of superior standing" was a merchant and farmer near Elizabethton, whose home Olmsted described as "the pleasantest house I have yet seen in the mountain[s]" (262). Such praise from Olmsted should make it obvious that this man owned no slaves. Never missing an opportunity to belabor a point, Olmsted later noted that the slaveholding neighbors of this nonslaveholder had "houses and establishments . . . much poorer than his" (272).

This East Tennessean was far more outspoken than other highland nonslaveholders about his disdain for the system and the blacks it embraced. Slaves "were horrid things," he said, insisting that he "would not take one to keep if it should be given to him." He maintained that it "would be a great deal better for the country . . . if there was not a slave in it," and advocated sending all blacks to Liberia. Olmsted noted that this "colonizationist" even owned a copy of *Uncle Tom's Cabin* and said that he "thought well of its depiction of slavery and its message" (263–64). In reply to Olmsted's question as to whether most mountain residents felt as he did, the Tennessean replied, "Well, there's some thinks one way and some another, but there's hardly any one here that do n't think slavery's a curse to our country, or who would n't be glad to get rid of it" (264).

But Olmsted found no one else in the highlands with as firm a commitment to ending the system. He was quick to dismiss similar antislavery rhetoric from three young men "of the poorest class," that he overtook on the road a day later. "Let the reader not be deceived by these expressions," he warned. "It is not slavery they detest; it is simply negro competition, and the monopoly of the opportunities to make money by negro owners, which they feel but dimly comprehend" (265).

The relative absence of slaves in the region defused any concern over the threat of black labor as competition. But the fear of a free black populace was very apparent among southern highlanders and accounted for much of their commitment to slavery. One mountain woman, on learning that Olmsted was from New York and that blacks there were all free, said "with disgust and indignation on her face" that "I would n't want to live where niggers are free, they are bad enough when they are slaves. . . . If they was to think themselves equal to we, I do n't think white folks could abide it—they're such vile saucy things" (237).

But even more often it was their belief in the rights of property owners that led most mountaineers to stop their condemnation of the institution short of advocating its abolition. To be deprived of one's possessions, human or otherwise, was an injustice with which they could and did identify. As one highland slave owner reminded his nonslaveholding neighbors, "If they can take our niggers away from us they can take our cows or hosses, and everything else we've got!"[15] Whatever distaste they may have felt for slavery or slaveholders, this argument was one in which most highland yeomen readily acquiesced. Even the seemingly subversive sentiments of the Tennessee "colonizationist" stopped short of infringing upon slaveholders' rights. He admitted, though reluctantly, that he "supposed it would not be right to take them away from those who had acquired property in them, without any remuneration" (263).

Like most other southerners, the peculiar institution remained considerably less offensive to highlanders than did outside interference with either property rights or any other aspect of their or any other southerners' way of life.[16] The backgrounds of the small mountain farmers who Olmsted met also contributed to their attitudes toward black bondage. Some observers concluded that the region's poorer residents bore a strong grudge against slavery because their inability to compete with it as free laborers had forced them from their seaboard or piedmont homes up into the highlands. There, the argument followed, they were insulated from the system but quickly found themselves shut off as well from the economic opportunities that the outside world offered, thus adding to their resentment. As an early twentieth-century missionary to the mountains concluded, "The aristocratic slaveholder from his river-bottom plantation looked with scorn on the slaveless dweller among the hills; while the highlander repaid his scorn with high disdain and even hate."[17] Similarly, another advocate of this thesis explained that southern highlanders "were penned up in the mountains because slavery shut out white labor and left them no market for their skill and strength. . . . It denied those that looked down from their mountain crags upon the realm of King Cotton a chance to expand, circulate, and mingle with the progressive elements at work elsewhere in the republic."[18]

Whatever element of truth there was to those assumptions, Olmsted's interviews provide very real evidence that such displacement, whether actual or imagined, was a source of Appalachians' animosity toward the lowland planter class. But as his narrative also makes quite apparent, an intense racism was far more widespread and deeply rooted in the cultural baggage that mountain settlers brought from the lowlands. That racism in turn carried with it a basic belief in the institution of slavery, regardless of their feelings toward its most prosperous beneficiaries, the slaveholding elite."[19]

In light of the very slim body of evidence of such views from the nineteenth century, much less the antebellum period, the sheer volume of material provided by Olmsted's narrative regarding racial attitudes among mountaineers makes it significant. Equally admirable is the sensitivity with which he conveyed the variety of sentiments toward slaves, slavery, and slaveholders that he witnessed along that route. But one must be wary of accepting the comments of those he interviewed as a thorough or accurate representation of overall regional attitudes. One of the major attractions of the mountains to Olmsted, as he neared completion of his second southern tour, was the contrast that they offered to the rest of the South. Mountain residents were, in effect, a unique control group by which he could test his theories regarding the impact of slavery on southern society; they made up virtually the only group of southerners whose lives were relatively untouched by the institution. Thus his depiction of highland society became far more selective than was his itinerary in the region.

Olmsted visited several of the highlands' more bustling commercial hubs and population centers, such as Chattanooga, Asheville, and Abingdon. These areas supported far larger populations, white and black, and maintained many more vital links with other parts of the South through trade and tourist networks than did the more remote and primitive areas he also visited. The three counties in which these towns were located were home to 5,683 slaves in 1850. Not only did that make up an average of 13 percent of those counties' total populations—almost twice the average proportion of slaves in the seven other mountain counties that Olmsted visited—but these 5,600 slaves also accounted for over two-thirds of the total slave populace in the ten-county area that Olmsted covered.[20]

The conclusions that Olmsted reached based on his observations of those larger and more prosperous highland communities are among his most astute and potentially significant. He noted, for example, that mountain masters were "chiefly professional men, shop-keepers, and men in office, who are also land owners" (226). He also concluded that "the direct moral evils of slavery are less—even less proportionately to the number of slaves," that the habits of those slaves "more resemble those of ordinary free laborers," and that they "exercise more responsibility, and both in soul and intellect they are more elevated" (226–27). The implications of such statements on the issue of master-slave relations are, at the very least, intriguing; yet Olmsted never elaborated on these generalizations or substantiated them with specific examples. He included no interviews with the benevolent and affluent slaveholding businessmen to whom he referred, nor did he indulge in detailed descriptions of their situations as he did so extensively for those more deprived and deeply entrenched mountain residents.[21]

It would be another generation or more before the stereotypical image of the southern mountaineer in all his ignorance, isolation, and crudity emerged, so Olmsted could hardly be accused of giving in to such preconceived notions. Yet by limiting the bulk of his treatment to those he met who did fit that image, he certainly had much to do with laying the groundwork from which those stereotypes grew.

He made much of the ignorance of his mountain hosts, for example, particularly their misconceptions regarding slavery and the sectional crisis in which it was already embroiled. He recorded a conversation with the Tennessee "squire" regarding Irish laborers in New York. His slaveholding host assumed that they were imported from Ireland and purchased just as black labor from Africa had been. He was amazed to learn not only that New York had no slaves, but also that blacks there were free (236–37).

Slaves could become victims of their owners' ignorance, as was the case of a white couple with whom Olmsted spent a night. They thought that Virginia was a cotton-growing state to their south and had sold their three slaves south, largely because of the slaves' desire to be reunited with their mother in Virginia (240). He cited other instances in which highlanders thought coffee was grown in New York (262), confused the locations and proximity of Charleston, Texas, and New York (249–50), wondered if the Mexican War was over yet (266), and speculated about the nature of the "new country [of] Nebrasky," which one old woman "reckoned must be a powerful fine country, they'd taken so much trouble to get possession of it" (235).

But in recording mountaineers' vague and often highly distorted ideas about geography and politics, neither Olmsted's purpose nor his tone was as derogatory or as demeaning as those of later chroniclers of mountain life. His purpose was to demonstrate that mountain residents' statements regarding slavery and slaveholders were rarely thought out and were usually based on little beyond their own limited experience with blacks. Likewise, his descriptions of their crude living conditions and bleak lifestyles served a specific function in regard to his more general theories about slavery's impact on southern society. But there was an inherent contradiction in Olmsted's use of the southern highlands in substantiating his arguments. Olmsted blamed the deprivations of mountain life on the presence of slavery elsewhere and portrayed the highlanders as tragic, and perhaps innocent, victims of the institution. Yet, at the same time, a basic theme remained: mountain residents, free from so many of the shackles imposed upon those southerners with investments in or mere proximity to the system, were happier and better people than those less fortunate lowlanders.

Yet despite discrepancies, inconsistencies, and major omissions in his description and interpretation of racial and sectional attitudes among southern highlanders, the seventy or so pages that Olmsted devoted to the region in his *Journey in the Back Country* remain invaluable as a record of the most extended and substantive foray into an area neglected not only by contemporary travelers but also by historians of slavery and the antebellum era ever since. Much of the strength of Olmsted's overall commentary on the South lay in his determination to understand it at the grassroots level. The mere fact that he gave voice to the southern highlanders, one of the most inscrutable and misrepresented groups of antebellum Americans, is a remarkable indication of the extent to which he succeeded.

NOTES

An earlier version of this essay was published in *Slavery & Abolition* 9 (September 1988): 171–82, and is reprinted here with permission of Frank Cass & Co., London.

1. The fullest treatments of Olmsted's careers are Laura Wood Roper, *FLO: A Biography of Frederick Law Olmsted* (Baltimore: Johns Hopkins Univ. Press, 1973); John Emerson Todd, *Frederick Law Olmsted* (Boston: Twayne Publishers, 1982); and Broadus Mitchell, *Frederick Law Olmsted: A Critic of the Old South*, Johns Hopkins University Studies in History and Political Science, vol. 42 (Baltimore: Johns Hopkins Univ. Press, 1924). The latter provides the best account of Olmsted's antebellum southern travels and writings, along with Charles E. Beveridge, introduction to *The Papers of Frederick Law Olmsted*, vol. 2, *Slavery and the South, 1852–1857* (Baltimore: Johns Hopkins Univ. Press, 1981), 1–39. The author would like to acknowledge the helpful comments of Jane Turner Censer and John Boles.

2. Frederick Law Olmsted, *A Journey in the Seaboard Slave States* (New York: Dix and Edwards, 1856); Olmsted, *A Journey through Texas: or, a Saddle Trip on the Southwestern Frontier* (New York: Dix and Edwards, 1857); and Olmsted, *A Journey in the Back Country in the Winter of 1853–54* (New York: Mason Brothers, 1860). A condensed version of these three books was published in two volumes as *The Cotton Kingdom* (New York: Mason Brothers, 1861). On the circumstances that led to Olmsted's southern assignment and the subsequent publication of his work, see Beveridge, introduction, *Papers of Olmsted*, 9–35; and Mitchell, *Olmsted*, 47–53.

3. Olmsted, *Seaboard Slave States*, 176; Olmsted, *Back Country*, 103–4. See also Mitchell, *Olmsted*, 88–89.

4. Olmsted, *Seaboard Slave States*, 146–48; Olmsted, "The South," nos. 7 and 47, *New York Daily Times*, 17 March 1853, and 26 Jan. 1854, in Beveridge, *Papers of Olmsted*, 2:103–10, 247–54; see also introduction, 13–15.

5. Beveridge, *Papers of Olmsted*, 2:252.

6. Todd, *Frederick Law Olmsted*, 57–58; Mitchell, *Olmsted*, chap. 2.

7. For Olmsted's schedule and route, see Beveridge, *Papers of Olmsted*, 2:309 (map) and 481–82 (itinerary).

8. The ten counties that can be identified along Olmsted's highland route are Hamilton, Polk, and Johnson Counties in Tennessee; Cherokee, Macon, Haywood, Buncombe, Yancey, and Watauga Counties in North Carolina; and Washington County in Virginia. County population figures are derived from Bureau of the Census, *Seventh Census of the United States, 1850* (Washington, D.C.: Robert Armstrong, 1853), table 1 for Virginia, North Carolina, and Tennessee, 256–57, 307–8, and 573–74. For a discussion of the demographics of slavery in North Carolina's mountain counties, see John C. Inscoe, *Mountain Masters: Slavery and the Sectional Crisis in Western North Carolina* (Knoxville: Univ. of Tennessee Press, 1989), chap. 3.

9. Olmsted, *Back Country*, 227. Subsequent quotations of material from *Back Country* are designated by page numbers within the text. Note the contrast in Olmsted's tone and interest regarding the treatment of slaves just six months earlier in "The South," no. 47, 24 Jan. 1854, in Beveridge, *Papers of Olmsted*, 2:247–52.

10. Carter G. Woodson, "Freedom and Slavery in Appalachian America," *Journal of Negro History* 1 (April 1916): 140, 149; John C. Campbell, *The Southern Highlander and His Homeland* (1929; reprint, Lexington: Univ. Press of Kentucky, 1969), 95; and Loyal Jones, "Appalachian Values," in *Voices from the Hills: Selected Readings of Southern Appalachia*, ed. Robert J. Higgs (New York: Unger, 1975), 512.

11. Julian Ralph, "Our Appalachian Americans," *Harper's*, June 1903, p. 37; and James W. Taylor, *Alleghania: A Geographical and Statistical Memoir* (St. Paul, Minn.: James Davenport, 1862), l.

12. W.J. Cash, *The Mind of the South* (New York: Alfred J. Knopf, 1941), 219.

13. Muriel E. Sheppard, *Cabins in the Laurel* (Chapel Hill: Univ. of North Carolina Press, 1935), 60.

14. Among the best discussions of antislavery sentiment in East Tennessee and its political repercussions are Oliver P. Temple, *East Tennessee and the Civil War* (1899; reprint, Freeport, N.Y.: Books for Library Press, 1971); Mary Emily Robertson Campbell, *The Attitude of Tennesseans toward the Union, 1847–1861* (New York: Vantage, 1961); Vernon M. Queener, "East Tennessee Sentiment and the Secession Movement, November 1860–June 1861," *East Tennessee Historical Society Proceedings* 20 (1948): 64; and E. Merton Coulter, *William C. Brownlow: Fighting Parson of the Southern Appalachians* (Chapel Hill: Univ. of North Carolina Press, 1937).

15. Harry M. Caudill, *Night Comes to the Cumberlands: A Biography of a Depressed Region* (Boston: Little, Brown, 1962), 38.

16. For other evidence from Olmsted on the priority of property rights among mountaineers, see *Back Country*, 240.

17. Samuel T. Wilson, *The Southern Mountaineers* (New York: J.J. Little and Ives, 1914), 57. See also Campbell, *Southern Highlanders*, 94; and Edward J. Phifer, "Saga of a Burke County Family," *North Carolina Historical Review* 39 (spring 1962): 145.

18. Ralph, "Our Appalachian Americans," 36.

19. Cratis D. Williams, "The Southern Mountaineer in Fact and Fiction" (Ph.D. diss., New York University, 1961), 379.

20. See note 8.

21. Olmsted did not have the letters of introduction during his backcountry trip that he had for much of the plantation South, where he utilized his own and his brother's various Yale acquaintances. For a fuller treatment of large slaveholders in the highlands and their relations with their slaves, see Inscoe, *Mountain Masters*, chaps. 3 and 4.

10

RACE AND THE ROOTS OF APPALACHIAN POVERTY

Clay County, Kentucky, 1850–1910

Kathleen M. Blee and Dwight B. Billings

Much of what is known about how Appalachians cope with chronic poverty is the result of the landmark Beech Creek studies, a series of investigations of an impoverished, geographically isolated group of neighborhoods in eastern Kentucky.[1] In 1942, James Brown purposefully selected a remote, nonmining area in rural Clay County, Kentucky, to document a way of life that was less deeply affected by the penetration of commodity, labor, and consumer markets than were Appalachian coalfield communities at the time. Brown's detailed ethnographic observations of subsistence farming, social stratification, and family and community life, together with subsequent studies of residents and out-migrants from Beech Creek, provide the best empirical record of the strategies by which Appalachian persisters and migrants have coped with chronic, intergenerational poverty.

By the time studies of Beech Creek began, a postbellum exodus of African Americans from the Appalachian region had left Clay County's population virtually all white. Thus, the Beech Creek studies yield little information on how African Americans coped with persistent poverty in Appalachia or about the interpenetration of race and class factors in that region's poverty. To understand how race influenced the economic conditions and opportunities of Clay County's populace, we examine longitudinal data on blacks and whites in an earlier, more racially diverse period in Clay County.[2] This comparison not only affords information on an understudied population, African American Appalachians, but also makes it possible to understand the different historical trajectories that led blacks and whites into poverty in Appalachia and the diverse strategies by which each coped with poverty and economic marginality. Building on data gathered in prior studies of Beech Creek, we used manuscript census, tax roll, and property records to examine racial differences in migration and persistence, resource accumulation, and household and family structure in nineteenth- and early twentieth-century Clay County.

Background

In the late nineteenth century, when local-interest fiction writers and social reformers began to describe social life in the southern mountains, it became commonplace to describe preindustrial Appalachia as an isolated folk culture.[3] Although largely "mythical,"[4] this treatment of the region contributed positively to a tradition of ethnographic studies of rural Appalachia, including the Beech Creek studies on which we build here, that provides an indispensable twentieth-century viewpoint on social change in the region.[5] However, the treatment of Appalachia as a folk culture also reinforced an image of Appalachians as a "people without history" that diverted scholarly attention from the region's actual history.

In the past twenty years Appalachian scholars have begun to respond to this scholarly neglect, first by devoting attention to the social history of postbellum industrialization.[6] Only recently has attention turned to antebellum Appalachia and to topics such as farming, commerce, and socio-economic development before the modern era of coal and textile industrialization.[7] Even more neglected has been the experience of black Appalachians; and here, too, what little has been published has focused primarily on blacks in the coalfields.[8] The history of slaveholding in Appalachia has only recently begun to be explored,[9] while the postbellum experiences of African Americans in areas of rural Appalachia outside the zones of railroad building and coal extraction have received almost no scholarly attention at all.

By choosing to build our analyses on the prior ethnographic and survey research of James Brown and his associates on the farming community of Beech Creek, we have acquired baseline data on the best-studied twentieth-century white population in the entire region, as well as a vantage point on processes of social stratification and rural impoverishment that are independent of the confounding effects of industrialization. Modern surface mining technology has made coal mining economically important to the Beech Creek vicinity only during the past two or three decades, but until then this section of the Kentucky mountains was remarkably isolated. In 1920, Clay County was the last county in the state to be reached by railroads.

It would be a mistake, however, simply to project Brown's description of Beech Creek twentieth-century social isolation and economic marginality backward onto Clay County's past; our research suggests that the county was more closely incorporated into interregional trade networks and less geographically isolated in the 1840s than were the Beech Creek neighborhoods when Brown first observed them one hundred years later. In the early years, life in Clay County revolved around two very different systems of production: subsistence-oriented forest farming, based predominantly on family labor and practiced by the vast majority of the population, and a smaller, slave-based manufacturing and mercantile economy controlled by a few wealthy families. In 1850, the county's fifty-eight slave owners, representing only 7 percent of household heads, owned 10 percent of the total population (515 slaves),[10] but slave ownership did not directly touch the lives of most farm households in Clay County. The result was a highly stratified community.

Elsewhere we have shown that agricultural production in Clay County and Beech Creek in 1860 was comparable to that of farm regions in the northern United States. The next two decades, however, witnessed dramatic and rapid agricultural decline. Whereas farms in the North, especially but not only in the Midwest, increased the value, productivity, and efficiency of their operations through improvements in transportation, mechanization, specialization, and the use of chemical fertilizers, Beech Creek and Clay County farms decreased dramatically in size and productivity throughout the remainder of the nineteenth century as enormous population growth and family-farm subdivision worsened the inherent limitations of subsistence farming. In the context of these pressures on the farm population, migration and wage labor become important phenomena here and throughout the Appalachian region.[11]

METHODOLOGY

The data for this study consist of linked records from the manuscript decennial U.S. censuses of agriculture (1850–1880), the decennial U.S. censuses of population (1850–1880 and 1900–1910; the 1890 census was destroyed), county deeds and county tax rolls (1871, 1879, 1892), and a one-in-four sample of Clay County households from the 1860 U.S. Census of Population matched to the 1860 U.S. Census of Agriculture. We examined two groups: (1) all nonenslaved African Americans who lived in Clay County in 1850 and 1910; (2) all whites who lived between 1850 and 1910 in the area that later served as the site of the Beech Creek studies.[12]

As the census does not provide identifiable geographic boundaries for rural areas, we demarcated the Beech Creek population in two steps. First, drawing on James Brown's extensive genealogical data on the ancestors of his 1942 Beech Creek study population, we established an inventory of names and family relationships extending back into the nineteenth century. These genealogical data also allowed us to trace women through marital name changes; to establish the lineage of brothers, uncles, and cousins; and to distinguish household members who were extended kin from farm laborers and other unrelated individuals. Second, we located the Beech Creek area over time by identifying ancestors of Brown's study population and by coding all households on census pages in which those ancestral households are clustered. Here, we used a method developed by historians Steven Hahn, Robert Kenzer, and others that takes advantage of consecutive enumeration in the census as an indicator of neighborhood proximity.[13] These methods produced data on blacks and whites over time (see table 10.1). Our analysis of African Americans begins with free blacks, as the federal censuses did not enumerate slaves by name. Any emancipated slaves who remained in Clay County are added to our data files of subsequent census years.

Table 10.1. Population, by Race and Gender, Clay County, Kentucky, 1850-1910

	African American		White	
	Male	Female	Male	Female
1850	82	96	222	206
1860	116	142	258	247
1870	212	269	477	458
1880	324	352	458	441
1900	253	296	244	234
1910	257	238	213	197

Sources: U.S. Census of Population, 1850-1880, 1900-1910.
Note: We include those designated in the census as "mulatto" in the sample of African Americans because the census distinction between the two groups is unreliable.

MIGRATION AND PERSISTENCE

The late nineteenth and early twentieth centuries witnessed tremendous population turnover in the southern Appalachian Mountains, as small-scale farming declined and employment opportunities in mining and lumbering areas expanded. The population of African Americans in Appalachia declined dramatically in the decades after emancipation.[14] In Clay County, African Americans were 15 percent of the population in 1840, of whom 77 percent, or 503, were enslaved. Fifty years later African Americans represented only 3 percent. During these same years, Clay County's once significant salt industry collapsed and local subsistence farming declined in viability, beginning a descent into poverty that would leave the county among the most persistently impoverished areas in the nation.[15]

By linking individual and family records over time from the manuscript censuses of population and agriculture, we can examine racial differences in migration and in the long-term economic conditions of those who remained in Clay County.[16] We compare rates of persistence of Clay County's black household heads with those of whites in the Beech Creek neighborhood, and we compare rates of persistence among landowners with total persistence rates at each period and across race (see table 10.2).

Blacks and whites in Clay County had fairly low rates of persistence, mirroring the pattern found in other southeastern areas.[17] Only one decade, the 1860s,

Table 10.2. Persistence Rates of All Household Heads and Landowning Household Heads, by Race, Clay County, Kentucky, 1850-1910

		1850-1860	1860-1870	1870-1880	1880-1900	1900-1910
African American						
	All heads	.41	.24	.27	.29	.27
	Owners	.38	.60	.48	n/a	.24
White						
	All heads	.29	.27	.34	.15	.40
	Owners	.41	.40	.38	n/a	.41

Sources: U.S. Census of Population, 1850-1880, 1900-1910.
Note: Persistence is the number of household heads from the base year found in the subsequent census divided by the number of household heads in the base year. Owners are defined as those reporting ownership of real property in the 1850, 1860, and 1870 censuses and residing in an owned (not rented) home in 1900 and 1910. The 1880 census did not collect information on property ownership. Because the 1900 and 1910 census instructed enumerators to regard the family as the statistical unit in recording data on home ownership (thus crediting ownership to all members of the family unit), the extent of ownership is inflated overall. This table is restricted to household heads.

saw more than one-half of African American household heads in the county at the beginning of the decade (1860) still there a decade later. Nearly half the time, fewer than one-third of them could be found. Thus the stereotype of early rural Appalachia as stable and isolated is wrong on both counts. Here, as in much of the nation in the nineteenth and early twentieth centuries, communities and neighborhoods underwent frequent and substantial population turnover.[18]

Surprisingly, the persistence rates of blacks and whites were similar, averaging about 30 percent over this period, although the causes of persistence and migration may have been different for them. A decade-by-decade examination of the data hints at racially specific factors. With the exception of 1850–1860, the rate of persistence of African American household heads was stable. White household heads had more variable persistence rates, including a dramatically low rate of 15 percent from 1880 to 1900. Such a racial difference may indicate that whites were more likely than African Americans to respond to the pull of economic opportunities elsewhere, such as the lumbering and mining booms between 1880 and 1900. The decisions of black families may have reflected instead the more constant push of economic instability and racial tension.[19]

Usually, but not always, land-ownership increased the chance that a family would remain in Clay County over time. Among white household heads, property owners were always more likely to persist than the landless. Among black household heads, however, property ownership was associated with higher rates of persistence in only two of the four periods.[20] Further, detailed examination of the census indicates that the occupations of persisters varied across race. White household heads who remained over time were nearly all landowning farmers, reflecting out-migration among white landless households. Black household heads who remained, especially in the late nineteenth century, were nearly as likely to be landless farm laborers as landowning farmers. For African Americans at the end of the nineteenth century, more than for whites, property may have provided the economic means for a family to emigrate from Clay County.

In contrast to Orville Vernon Burton's finding that African American persisters in a lower South community tended to acquire significant amounts of property,[21] African Americans who persisted over time in Clay County began with, but did not continue to accumulate, substantially more property than the average. The few black household heads who were present in 1850 and 1860 had an average real property value of $1,700 in 1850, more than twice the average holdings of $775 for all black landowners in Clay County that year. Ten years later, the economic advantages of persisters had greatly declined. Property owners' worth averaged only $900, just slightly higher than the average of $880 for all African American property owners in Clay County.

Finally, the similar persistence rates across race suggest that it was racial differences in rates of natural increase and of migration *into* (but not migration out of) Clay County that led to the increasing racial disparity in population.[22] Beginning in 1808, Kentucky enacted a series of laws that sought to restrict the migration of free blacks into the state. The effect of these laws is evident in census data on place of birth, which reveal that large numbers of whites continued to arrive until the 1880s, but only negligible numbers of nonenslaved African Americans arrived after 1850. Virtually all free blacks who resided in Clay County, especially after the Civil War, were born in Kentucky.

These patterns of persistence and migration suggest that Clay County had little to offer and much to repel African Americans in search of economic opportunity. Those with the financial means to do so left. Those who did not have such resources were forced to remain in the county, where they faced increasing economic hardship in a declining economy. If geographical stability could brighten the fortunes of landholding whites, it often portended financial downfall for African Americans.

RESOURCE ACCUMULATION

In the emerging market economy of nineteenth-century rural Appalachia, wealth and the ability to accumulate it were based fundamentally on land-ownership. By establishing a pattern of economic opportunity for some whites and economic subordination for nearly all African Americans, disparities in land-ownership etched racial contours of wealth and poverty that would endure into the twentieth century.

Table 10.3. Characteristics of Landowners, by Race, Clay County, Kentucky, 1850-1870

	1850		1860		1870	
	African American	White	African American	White	African American	White
Number of landowners	8	37	10	57	21	120
% of household heads owning land	22	54	24	64	24	64
Mean value of land	$775	$945	$880	$1281	$486	$700
Aggregate value of land	$6,200	$34,962	$9,300	$73,306	$10,200	$86,087
Mean per capita value of land	$35	$82	$36	$145	$21	$92

Sources: U.S. Census of Population, 1850-1870; U.S. Census of Agriculture, 1850-1870.

Property ownership was exceedingly uncommon among blacks in ante-bellum Clay County (see table 10.3), as it was throughout the South.[23] Only ten African Americans in Clay County owned land in 1860 (only eight in 1850), and seven of these came from just three families. This represented 24 percent of free black-headed households in 1860 (22 percent in 1850), compared with 64 percent of white households in 1860 (54 percent in 1850). Together, all free blacks in Clay County in 1850 owned only $6,200 in land (less than 2 percent of the county total), or $35 per capita. By 1860 this had barely increased, to $9,300, or $36 per capita. Whites in Beech Creek owned more than twice as much per capita in 1850 ($82) and four times as much ($145) ten years later. If the 515 slaves in 1850 or the 348 slaves in 1860 (none of whom owned land) are included, the racial disparity in per capita antebellum land-ownership is even more pronounced. There are also striking differences in the value of land owned by whites and African Americans. In 1850 the average African American landowner in Clay County owned $775 of land, compared with $945, or 22 percent more, for Beech Creek whites. Ten years later, the disparity increased significantly. Black landowners owned $880, while Beech Creek whites owned $1,281, or 45 percent more.

African Americans gained little additional land in the postbellum period. In 1870, whites in Beech Creek still owned more than 400 percent of real property per capita than Clay County's blacks. Although the percentage of black households that owned land was slightly higher in Clay County than in the upper South states on average (24 percent versus 19 percent), it was considerably lower than the percentage of local white landowning households (64 percent). The value of property held by Clay County's postbellum African Americans was low, even by the standards of southern states. In 1870 blacks in the upper South averaged real-estate holdings of $746[24]; in the state of Kentucky, $684; in Clay County, only $486.

As Jaqueline Jones found in the Deep South,[25] racial differences in the availability of credit accounted for the difference in land-ownership between whites and African Americans. An analysis of Clay County's deeds indicates that blacks, far more than whites, purchased land with cash, especially in the antebellum period. For example, Nicholas Cotton, one of Clay County's largest African American landowners, used cash for all his land purchases before 1860; only during the Civil War years was he able to secure mortgages. His brother, Nelson, secured a land mortgage in 1857, but only by pledging significant livestock holdings in addition to the land. Whites, with better access to mortgages and other forms of credit, were far better positioned to acquire land in Clay County.[26]

Almost all adult males in the antebellum Clay County census reported themselves to be farmers. But the apparent racial similarity in occupations masked significant differences. Perhaps three-fourths of free black farmers in 1850 were landless tenants, compared with 44 percent of white farmers in Beech Creek.[27] In 1860, sixteen African Americans listed themselves as farmers, seven owners and nine tenants, and an additional thirty were farm laborers. Among Beech Creek whites, there were seventy-four farmers, of whom only twenty were tenants, plus fifty-three farm laborers. Thus, 85 percent of blacks working on farms, compared with 57 percent of whites, worked as sharecroppers, tenant farmers, or hired laborers in 1860. This racial difference is even more pronounced, however, because many white laborers and tenant farmers were sons of farm owners and their status an artifact of life cycle rather than a permanent class position.

Agricultural life in postbellum Clay County remained rigidly defined by race. Increasing proportions of white and black farmers owned the land they farmed, but, just as Burton found in Edgefield, South Carolina, tenant farmers and farm laborers in postbellum Clay County were disproportionately African American. Of the sixty-four black household heads engaged in agriculture in 1870, only eighteen (28 percent) were owner operators; the rest were tenants or farm laborers. Nine years later, only 22 percent were owner operators.[28] Moreover, the farms of most postbellum African American owner operators were tiny, typically yielding fewer than one hundred bushels of corn. Black-owned farms in 1870 produced only slightly more than $200, compared with nearly $400 for the farms of Beech Creek whites. By 1879, this racial disparity widened even further. Black-owned farms generated only $172, compared with $375 for Beech Creek white-owned farms.[29]

If the experience of land-ownership differed substantially for blacks and whites, so, too, did the experience of tenancy. Especially in antebellum Clay

Table 10.4. Farm Equipment and Livestock Holdings of Tenant Farmers, by Race, Clay County, Kentucky, 1850-1870 (number of cases in parentheses)

	African American	White
1850		
Value of machinery	$12 (8)[a]	$13 (27)
Value of livestock	$100 (14)	$162 (34)
1860		
Value of machinery	$10 (5)	$34 (15)
Value of livestock	$285 (5)	$355 (15)
1870		
Value of machinery	$14 (14)	$11 (29)
Value of livestock	$170 (17)	$153 (30)

Sources: U.S. Census of Agriculture, 1850-1870: U.S. Census of Population, 1850-1870.
[a] Number report value > 0.

County, white tenant farmers, although younger on average, owned more farm equipment and machinery and had substantially more valuable livestock holdings than did black tenants. In 1850, there was little racial difference in the average value of farm equipment (twelve dollars for blacks and thirteen dollars for whites), but only 57 percent of Clay County's African American tenants, compared with 79 percent of Beech Creek's white tenants, owned any farm implements at all (see table 10.4). By 1860, all tenants reported some farm equipment, but its value averaged ten dollars for blacks and thirty-four dollars for white tenants.

Livestock holdings showed a similar pattern. In 1850, blacks averaged $100 in livestock, compared with $162 for whites. Ten years later African Americans averaged $285 and whites $355. In 1850, 21 percent of black and white tenants owned no horses, asses, or oxen, animals that were important in farming and that also served as mortgage resources for tenants seeking to acquire land.[30] Fully 50 percent of black tenants, but only another 38 percent of white tenants, owned just one of these animals. By 1860 all tenants owned at least one horse, ass, or ox, but 20 percent of black and 27 percent of white tenants owned no more than one. Virtually all tenants of both races owned either milk cows or cattle in antebellum Clay County.

Postbellum racial differences in tenancy were less pervasive. Although 22 percent of black tenants owned no farm equipment in 1870, compared with only 6 percent of white tenants, they averaged more of it ($14 versus $11) and also more valuable livestock ($170 versus $153) than the younger white tenant farmers. White tenants were more likely than black tenants to own no (26 percent versus 22 percent) or only a single (52 percent versus 44 percent) horse, ass, or ox.

In a rural society, tenancy can represent either a lifelong agricultural class position or a stage in the family life cycle as sons wait to inherit their father's land. With longitudinal data it is possible to distinguish these two forms of tenancy by following tenants over time and linking records across generations. These data show that in nineteenth-century Clay County, life prospects differed radically between black and white tenants. The latter tended to be those awaiting inheritances. They were significantly younger than white owners and more likely than black tenants to live near property-owning family members.[31] Such inheritance, combined with out-migration of the landless, meant that there were few white permanent tenants in Beech Creek. Between 1850 and 1870, only two whites remained as tenants in any two consecutive census years; both owned livestock worth less than the average holdings of white tenants and much less than the average holdings of white owners.[32] In contrast, lifelong tenancy was common among African Americans; in fact, it was not confined to the poorest farmers. Because of the difficulty that even African Americans with substantial farm equipment faced obtaining credit for land purchases, livestock and machinery holdings do not predict which farmers were able to make the transition from tenant to owner. Black permanent tenants in some years had livestock holdings that exceeded those of other black tenants, and even some owners.[33]

In Clay County, personal property ownership was more widespread among blacks and whites than was land-ownership. Farmers were the most likely to possess property—livestock and farm equipment—but small amounts of personal property were reported by men and women of both races in virtually every occupation, including servants, washerwomen, seamstresses, and field hands. Unlike in the Deep South, where Jacqueline Jones has found that African American landowners owned less personal property than did white tenants,[34] in Clay County there was little difference in the amounts that they owned.

Eventually, occupation and education began to supplant land-ownership as the foundations of economic stratification in Clay County. But they, too, were circumscribed by race. In antebellum Clay County, African Americans were almost entirely restricted to service occupations: as servants, washerwomen, seamstresses, and cooks.[35] In contrast, many whites in rural Beech Creek established themselves in retail trade (as grocers, merchants, millers), craft production (blacksmiths, silversmiths, wool carders, well diggers) and semiprofessions (e.g., clerks and preachers). Very few whites worked as servants. This pattern continued in postbellum decades. Blacks found work as cooks, washerwomen, and laborers, while Beech Creek whites secured positions as coopers, physicians, lumber dealers, salesmen, and teamsters, though farming remained the principal occupation.

Educational opportunities for free blacks in Clay County initially were highly restricted. Only two attended school in 1850. Later, as education was opened to both races in postbellum Clay County, African American household heads gained somewhat proportionately to white household heads, but fewer than one-third of them, compared with one-half of white heads, could read by 1880. Further, literacy was possessed disproportionately by men during every time period and for both races, although the gender gap was wider among whites than among African Americans (see table 10.5). The unique advantages, and perhaps the marketable value, of education for white men is evident in the fact that less than one-half of white women, black women, or black men could read or write before 1900, a threshold reached by white men by 1860. Indeed, more than three-quarters of white women were illiterate before 1870, and more than four-fifths of African American women could not read and write before 1900. As expected, literacy and economic advantage were found together in Clay County, although it is not clear whether literacy bestowed wealth or the reverse. For blacks and whites, those who could read and write were much more likely to own land than those who could not. The few African Americans in professional occupations (e.g., clerks and teachers) were literate, but, surprisingly, literacy among African Americans was not confined to particular occupations. Literate blacks worked as farmers, servants, laborers, cooks, and wagon makers. The sole African American recorded as literate in the 1850 census, for example, was a thirty-one-year-old tenant farmer. Ten years later, eighteen blacks were listed as literate; of these, six were farm owner-operators, two were women married to white husbands, one was a woman tenant farmer, and two were male field hands. Four of the eighteen were members of the same family.

Finally, as Loren Schweninger found in his study of southern African American female property owners,[36] barriers of race and gender reinforced each other in Clay County, restricting the property and opportunities of white and black women. White and black women differed not only in the likelihood that they were employed for wages but in the occupations that they held and in the family and household situations that had led them to seek paid work.

Women constituted only 20 percent of Beech Creek whites with occupations in 1860, and most of them were widowed women operating farms. But contrary to stereotypes of Appalachian frontier widows, not all of these women were owners in title only. In 1850, for example, twenty-seven-year-old Nancy Andrews was married to a farmer and raising a young child. Ten years later she appeared in the census as unmarried (presumably widowed, though possibly deserted) and operating a one thousand–dollar farm with the help of her fourteen-year-old daughter.[37] By 1870, now nearly fifty, she had transferred her land (which had increased in value by $800) to her daughter, who was operating the farm. Similarly, Sarah Johnson headed a farm household consisting of several coresident daughters and granddaughters; the value of her farm had

Table 10.5. Literacy, by Gender and Race, Clay County, Kentucky, 1850-1910 (percentages)

	African American		White	
	Men	Women	Men	Women
1850	6	0	39	27
1860	33	11	57	23
1870	29	19	69	47
1880	30	16	57	34
1900	66	56	84	70
1910	75	64	86	77

Sources: U.S. Census of Population, 1850-1880, 1900-1910.

more than doubled (from $130 to $300) between 1850 and 1860. Tenant farming, less common among Beech Creek's white women, mostly consisted of unmarried women supporting minor children.

African American women were much more likely than white women to report paid occupations. In 1860, 42 percent of employed African Americans were women, who held a variety of service and farming occupations. There were two black women farmers; like the white female farmers, both were unmarried (probably widowed) and had coresident minor children. Unlike the white women, however, they were tenant farmers, and neither remained in Clay County for more than a decade. But not all employed African American women in 1860 were widows or household heads. Clay County's three black seamstresses included a nineteen-year-old woman married to a white man, a forty-year-old mother living with her adult children, and a thirty-two-year-old woman heading a household of four minor children. Female farm laborers included three household heads supporting minor children and two young adults living with white farm-owning families.

In postbellum Clay County, black women held a smaller range of occupations than they did in earlier decades. In 1870, thirty-one of thirty-three black women with identified occupations were servants, as were ten of sixteen white women, a pattern that continued in 1880.[38] Three black women (but no white women) owned land and other property in 1870, although none of them was listed in the census as a farmer. Two of these were widows (one a widow of a white man), and both were supporting minor children at home. The other was a forty-year-old single woman who did not appear in earlier censuses because she was either recently arrived or recently freed. The twentieth century saw some opening of occupations to African American women, but again, in very race-segregated occupations: laborers, washerwomen, cooks, and servants. Thus gender and race interacted to shape the opportunity structure for white and black women in Clay County. African American women, who were much more likely than white women to head their own households or to live in households headed by impoverished male laborers or tenant farmers, relied on wage employment for economic survival. Although black women were somewhat more likely than white women to work in agriculture, such pursuits rarely translated into eventual economic security or opportunity, as they often did for white men. Rather, agricultural work, like wage employment, represented a survival mechanism for those severely dispossessed by race and gender.

In Clay County, propertied white men were able to transfer their financial advantages in the earlier, land-based economy into the skills and occupational positions that conferred privilege in a new market-based system. Landless whites and blacks, with few resources in land, had little access to the educational and occupational opportunities of the commercial marketplace. They either left the county or remained as its poor.

HOUSEHOLD AND FAMILY STRUCTURE

Studies of poor populations indicate that kinship networks and household arrangements can either ameliorate or magnify financial hardships over time and across generations. At times, household and family structures provide a margin of security against financial disaster. But family obligations can also deepen financial distress and make economic viability impossible.[39]

In Clay County, household and family structures varied by race, and blacks and whites differed in how they drew upon kinship ties and household living arrangements to cope with poverty.[40] Antebellum African American–headed households were far more likely to be female-headed than were households headed by whites. Of the Clay County households in 1850 that had a free black household head, fully 32 percent were headed by women, compared with only 8 percent of the white-headed households. In 1860, the gap widened: 45 percent of free black households were female-headed, compared with only 6 percent of white households. But ten years later, with emancipation, the race difference in female headship almost vanished: 19 percent of black and 13 percent of white households were headed by women.

The situation of persons living in households headed by nonkin shows a similar pattern but also reveals the extent to which family life was disrupted for many free blacks in antebellum Clay County. Over 20 percent of all free blacks there, but no more than 3 percent of Beech Creek whites, lived in households headed by nonkin in every decade from 1850 to 1870. Thus African Americans were eight times as likely as whites to live with nonrelatives. After 1870 the percentage of blacks who lived with nonkin fell sharply to fewer than 10 percent through 1910, but it remained higher than the very low rate for whites (see table 10.6).

Table 10.6. Persons Unrelated to Household Head, by Race, Clay County, Kentucky, 1850-1910 (percentages)

	African American	White
1850	22	2
1860	25	3
1870	24	3
1880	7	2
1900	3	2
1910	8	1

Sources: U.S. Census of Population, 1850-1880, 1900-1910.

These racial disparities in antebellum patterns may have resulted in part from the manumission of some members of slave families, causing a prior overcount of one-parent and female-headed households in the census of free persons, rather than from more deeply rooted cultural differences in household and family formation. But it is impossible to tell from the census data.

African American women living with nonkin were, on average, older than white women in similar households (see table 10.7). Living in the household of nonkin may have been a life course stage for white females who served as servants or governesses in the late teen and early adult years. For black women, in contrast, living with white nonkin may have been an arrangement of servitude or labor that continued well into adulthood. Among whites, men were more likely to reside in a white nonkin household, primarily as farm laborers. Among African Americans, however, women were more likely to do so, principally as servants.[41] Lifelong servitude in another's household may have been more characteristic of African American females than males. In almost every year, black women living with white nonkin were significantly older, on average, than men. For whites, the sex differences in age were more variable over time, due largely to the smaller number of whites in this situation.

The range of occupations and ages of those living with nonkin further underscores how different this experience was for whites and blacks. Almost all those living with nonkin (except for young children) reported one of two occupations: servants, for women, and farm laborers, for men. Among whites in Beech Creek, those who lived in a nonrelative's household as a farm laborer were typically in their early twenties. The African American farm laborers in that situation were much older, from their late twenties to late thirties. Moreover, white farm laborers living with nonkin were mostly of similar, young ages.

Table 10.7. Mean Age of Members Unrelated to Household Head, Clay County, Kentucky, 1850-1910 (number of cases reported on in parentheses)

	White		African American	
	Male	Female	Male	Female
	Mean age	Mean age	Mean age	Mean age
1850	19 (7)	9 (2)	18 (17)	27 (23)
1860	21 (10)	20 (5)	23 (27)	22 (37)
1870	21 (15)	24 (11)	19 (36)	25 (79)
1880	23 (11)	12 (9)	22 (22)	33 (24)
1900	21 (4)	27 (2)	23 (10)	31 (8)
1910	22 (3)	-(0)	17 (2)	45 (6)

Sources: U.S. Census of Population, 1850-1880, 1900-1910.

African American farm laborers living with white nonkin ranged in age from early teens to over sixty years old. The situation of female servants was similar. African American servants living in a nonrelative's home were much older than comparable white servants, who were in their late twenties to early forties. The few white female servants residing with nonkin tended to be much younger, generally in their early twenties.

A close examination of the living situations of Clay County's most dependent populations, the elderly and children, underlines the extent to which race shaped one's chances of living with family or with nonkin.[42] For elderly persons, racial differences in living arrangements were associated with differential access to land. Property ownership greatly increased one's chances of continuing to head a household in old age.[43] Thus, elderly whites, who were much more likely than elderly African Americans to own property and to own more valuable property, also were more likely to head households in most years. Overall, the majority of white and black elderly persons (except blacks in 1870) lived in their own households as heads or spouses of heads (see table 10.8).

The living situations of older persons who did not head households are also revealing. Daniel Scott Smith and his colleagues found that in the late nineteenth-century South, "co-residence of older southern blacks with their children was less influenced by the motives of production and inheritance" than by concerns of family welfare.[44] This pattern was even more pronounced in

Table 10.8. Race Differences in Landholding and Family Relationships Among the Elderly, Clay County, Kentucky, 1850-1910 (*N* = Number of cases reported on)

	1850		1860		1870		1880		1900		1910	
	A[a]	W[a]	A	W	A	W	A	W	A	W	A	W
N	19	10	17	13	17	17	25	33	40	22	35	20
% who owned land[b]	21	30	12	38	6	41	–	–	32	77	43	92
Average value of land owned ($)	338	583	1,600	2,040	1,999	571	–	–	–	–	–	–
Household Position % head or wife of head	68	70	53	85	47	77	68	70	70	82	80	85
% related to head but not head or wife	0	30	0	15	0	17	20	27	25	18	14	15
% not related to head or wife	32	0	47	0	53	6	12	3	5	0	6	0

Sources: U.S. Census of Population, 1850-1880; 1900-1910; U.S. Census of Agriculture, 1850-1870.
Note: We define "elderly" as 60 years and over, instead of the more conventional 65 years because of a marked pattern of "age heaping" at decade intervals in census data on reported age, especially for African Americans.
[a] A= African Americans W= White
[b] Property ownership figures may be inflated for 1900 and 1910 because the census reported the number of persons who lived in a home that was owned or rented rather than the number who owned property. These figures are reported for assessing race differences, not as absolute levels of property ownership.

Clay County in the mid-nineteenth century. Before 1880, elderly African Americans who did not head their own households were much more likely to be employed as servants or laborers in the households of nonrelatives than to live with children or other relatives. Indeed, substantial numbers of elderly blacks, as many as 53 percent in 1870, avoided dependency on their children by living in households headed by white nonkin. In contrast, elderly whites were often economically dependent upon family members. Few white elderly persons in any year lived in nonkin-headed households. This racial difference reflected the extreme economic marginality of most households headed by free blacks and their consequent inability to absorb additional dependents, as well as perhaps their desire to accept or avoid economic dependence on oth-

Table 10.9. Relationship to Head of Household for Elderly Women, by Race, Clay County, Kentucky, 1850-1910 (distribution by percentage)

	1850	1860	1870	1880	1900	1910
African American women						
Heads of households	22	0	11	8	17	47
Wives	33	43	0	33	33	21
Mothers, grandmothers	0	0	0	43	38	21
Sisters	0	0	0	0	4	0
Servants	0	14	0	0	4	11
Boarders	0	0	0	8	4	0
Unrelated to head	44	43	89	8	0	0
White women						
Heads of households	17	17	44	0	18	25
Wives	50	50	0	53	54	50
Mothers, grandmothers	33	33	44	47	18	25
Sisters	0	0	0	0	9	0
Servants	0	0	0	0	0	0
Boarders	0	0	0	0	0	0
Unrelated to head	0	0	11	0	0	0

Sources: U.S. Census of Population, 1850-1880, 1900-1910.
Note: Some columns do not add up to 100 because of rounding.

ers.[45] Before 1880 not a single elderly African American was living in a household headed by a relative, while significant numbers of elderly whites did.

Elderly women, none of whom owned property in their own names, found living situations that differed greatly by race (see table 10.9). In every decade, all white elderly women lived in their own homes as household heads or wives of heads, with their adult children, or, in one case, with a sister. Elderly black women who did not live in their own homes as heads or wives of heads lived as

Table 10.10. Living Arrangements of African American and White Children, Clay County, Kentucky, 1850-1910 (percentages)

	Live with parent(s)	Live with other family	Head or spouse of head	Live with nonkin
1850				
African American (N=92)	76	0	1	23
White (N=256)	93	4	0	3
1860				
African American (N=142)	76	3	0	21
White (N=299)	94	4	1	2
1870				
African American (N=240)	73	1	2	24
White (N=502)	94	3	1	2
1880				
African American (N=356)	90	6	1	3
White (N=514)	90	7	1	2
1900				
African American (N=271)	84	13	2	1
White (N=228)	84	13	2	1
1910				
African American (N=253)	87	11	1	1
White (N=205)	93	6	1	0

Sources: U.S. Census of Population, 1850-1880, 1900-1910.
Note: Children are those sixteen years and younger. Some columns do not add up to 100 because of rounding.

servants, boarders, or lodgers or with grown children or other relatives. Across the entire South, one-third of African American and one-quarter of white elderly unmarried (single, divorced, widowed) women headed their own households in 1880; but, perhaps due to the scarcity of employment opportunities for elderly women, this was not true in Clay County. In 1880, all unmarried white women lived with adult children. Among unmarried black women, 73 percent lived with their adult children; the other 27 percent lived as boarders, as household heads, or in the homes of white nonkin. Except in 1870, there were substantial race differences in the chances that an elderly woman lived with a spouse. In every census year except 1870, more than half of all white elderly women lived with husbands. For elderly African American women, however, no more than half, and in most years a third or fewer, lived with a spouse.[46]

If the lives of Clay County's adult population differed radically by race, the lives of children did not. In nineteenth-century America, as in early modern Europe, childhood was, for many whites as well as blacks, a period of servitude and labor.[47] There was little consistent racial difference in the percentages of Clay County's children who reported paid employment, which ranged from 26 percent of black and 20 percent of white children in 1870 to 5 percent of black and 11 percent of white children ten years later. One major racial difference stemmed from an 1825 Kentucky state law that allowed for the arbitrary seizure and forced apprenticeship of free African American children, especially those from poor families. Work conditions for these children sometimes differed little from slavery, and economically marginal African American families were deprived of their children's potential contributions to household production.[48] Children worked as farm laborers and as servants. For whites, the labor experiences of childhood constituted a rite of passage to adulthood that often preceded the acquisition of a home and land. For many African Americans, however, labor in the employ and household of another extended throughout a lifetime.

The living arrangements of Clay County's children did differ by race, especially in the early years (see table 10.10). Virtually all white children lived with at least one parent between 1850 and 1870, but nearly one-fourth of the black children lived with someone else, usually as a servant or laborer in a white nonkin household. From 1880 to 1910, though, there was a racial convergence in the living arrangements. The percentage of white children living with at least one parent declined to a low of 84 percent in 1900, while the percentage of African American children living with a parent increased to a high of 93 percent in 1910. The percentage of black children living with nonkin dropped sharply, approaching the negligible level of whites, while the number of black and white children who lived with family members other than parents increased.

These patterns suggest that the common scholarly practice of viewing households and families as universal strategic resources for the poor is problematic.

Among the very poor—Clay County's landless blacks, for example—the combined assets of households or families were simply too meager to sustain additional dependent members. Many, especially dependent elderly and children, were forced to make living arrangements as servants or laborers at their places of employment. Such strategic use of kinship networks required financial stability that was simply inaccessible to African Americans in early Clay County.

CONCLUSION

The comparison of black and white citizens of Clay County in the nineteenth century suggests several conclusions about the relationship between race and poverty, or its reverse, economic opportunity. First, there are racial differences in the relationship between persistent poverty and out-migration. In most research, out-migration has been understood as an individual or family response to chronic regional poverty.[49] Further, large-scale out-migration typically is viewed as heightening overall poverty in the region of origin, as it is typically the very old, the very young, and the unemployable who persist in a poverty region during periods of economic opportunity elsewhere. A comparison of whites and blacks in Clay County, however, suggests a more complex relationship between regional poverty and migration. In the nineteenth century, possessing the means of economic security (i.e., land-ownership) increased the likelihood of persisting in the county among whites but increased the likelihood of leaving during some periods for African Americans. White persisters, often property owners, increased their property accumulation over time, while African American persisters, without an initial base of property, tended to sink more deeply into poverty. Thus the incidence of poverty among whites initially decreased in the nineteenth century due to the out-migration of landless whites. Among African Americans, in contrast, the poorest remained in Clay County, creating a base for significant impoverishment in this group. Economic opportunity outside Clay County, in the coal and timber industries of Appalachia or the emerging industrial centers of midwestern cities, did not operate in the same way across race and thus shaped racially distinct trajectories for those who remained in the county.

Second, resource accumulation in nineteenth-century Clay County was in part a function of age and life cycle stage for whites but not for blacks. For many young white men, a lack of resources, particularly land, was a characteristic of young adulthood as they awaited land inheritance from their fathers. Among blacks, however, age did not often lead to ownership; being without land was likely to be a lifelong condition. Moreover, while whites typically accumulated greater amounts of property over time (often by using small amounts of land to purchase additional land), African Americans typically did not. The ability of an economically marginal household to maintain or increase its financial base was a function not only of its initial holdings but also of racial factors.

Third, as rural Clay County changed from a subsistence-farming economy to an economy based increasingly on commerce and industry, white men were better positioned than African American men or than women to take advantage of new economic, educational, and occupational opportunities. Rather than reducing the economic disparities between whites and blacks (and between men and women) that had been built up in a system of household-based agricultural production, commercialization and industrialization exacerbated inequalities and heightened the advantages of whites and men.

Finally, the ability to expand or contract households provided a means of survival for economically marginal rural whites but not for blacks in nineteenth-century Clay County. Among white Beech Creekers, marginal and below-subsistence farming households were sustained during economic crises by family and kinship networks. Beech Creek farming households producing above subsistence levels shared surplus kin and absorbed additional household members from economically troubled kin households.[50] But such household-based strategies were only possible among kinship groups in which at least some households were economically secure. Among African Americans, kinship ties linked households of similar economic precariousness. In times of economic crisis, therefore, surplus members in African American households (typically the elderly and the young) were forced to live in nonkin, and typically white-headed, households as domestic or agricultural laborers. Household situations adopted only during hard times by whites more often became permanent, impoverishing situations for African Americans.

When James Brown entered Beech Creek on horseback on the eve of World War II, Clay County had become, as it has remained, severely poor. Economic decline throughout Appalachia impoverished nearly all who remained in the region. But the common financial destination of whites and blacks there should not obscure the racially specific historical paths that each group followed into chronic poverty.

Notes

An earlier version of this essay, with the title "Race Differences in the Origins and Consequences of Chronic Poverty in Rural Appalachia," was published in *Social Science History* 20 (fall 1996): 345–73, and is reprinted with the permission of Duke University Press.

1. James S. Brown, "The Conjugal Family and the Extended Family Group in a Kentucky Mountain Farming Community," *American Sociological Review* 7 (1952): 297–305; James S. Brown, "The Farm Family in a Kentucky Mountain Neighborhood," Bulletin 587, Kentucky Agricultural Experiment Station, Lexington, 1952; James S. Brown, *Beech Creek: A Study of a Kentucky Mountain Neighborhood* (1950; reprint, Berea, Ky.: Berea College Press, 1988); Harry K. Schwarzweller, James S. Brown, and J.J. Mangalam, *Mountain Families in Transition: A Case Study of Appalachian Migration* (University Park: Pennsylvania State Univ. Press, 1971); Virginia McCoy, "Solidarity and Integration of Migrant Family Groups" (Ph.D. diss., University of Cincinnati, 1986).

2. There are only a negligible number of persons of races other than white or African American in Clay County.

3. John C. Campbell, *The Southern Highlander and His Homeland* (1921; reprint, Lexington: Univ. Press of Kentucky, 1969); Horace Kephart, *Our Southern Highlanders: A Narrative Adventure in the Southern Appalachians and a Study of Life among the Mountaineers* (1913; reprint, Knoxville: Univ. of Tennessee Press, 1976).

4. Henry D. Shapiro, *Appalachia on Our Mind: The Southern Mountains and Mountaineers in the American Consciousness, 1870–1920* (Chapel Hill: Univ. of North Carolina Press, 1978).

5. Kathleen M. Blee and Dwight B. Billings, "Reconstructing Daily Life in the Past: A Hermeneutic Approach to Ethnographic Data," *Sociological Quarterly* 27 (1986): 443–62.

6. Alan Banks, "Labor and the Development of Industrial Capitalism in Eastern Kentucky, 1870–1930" (Ph.D. diss., McMaster University, 1980); John Gaventa, *Power and Powerlessness: Quiescence and Rebellion in an Appalachian Valley* (Urbana: Univ. of Illinois Press, 1980); David Corbin, *Life, Work, and Rebellion in the Coal Fields: The Southern West Virginia Miners, 1880–1930* (Urbana: Univ. of Illinois Press, 1981); Ronald D Eller, *Miners, Millhands, and Mountaineers: Industrialization of the Appalachian South, 1880–1930* (Knoxville: Univ. of Tennessee Press, 1982); Altina L. Waller, *Feud: Hatfields, McCoys, and Social Change in Appalachia, 1860–1900* (Chapel Hill: Univ. of North Carolina Press, 1988).

7. See articles in Robert D. Mitchell, ed., *Appalachian Frontiers: Settlement, Society, and Development in the Preindustrial Era* (Lexington: Univ. Press of Kentucky, 1991); and in Mary Beth Pudup, Dwight B. Billings, and Altina L. Waller, eds., *Appalachia in the Making: The Mountain South in the Nineteenth Century* (Chapel Hill: Univ. of North Carolina Press, 1995).

8. William H. Turner and Edward Cabbell, eds., *Blacks in Appalachia* (Lexington: Univ. Press of Kentucky, 1985); Ronald L. Lewis, *Black Coal Miners in America: Race, Class, and Community Conflict, 1780–1980* (Lexington: Univ. Press of Kentucky, 1987); and Joe William Trotter Jr., *Coal, Class, and Color: Blacks in Southern West Virginia, 1915–1932* (Urbana: Univ. of Illinois Press, 1990).

9. John C. Inscoe, *Mountain Masters: Slavery and the Sectional Crisis in Western North Carolina* (Knoxville: Univ. of Tennessee Press, 1989).

10. Low in comparison with the state of Kentucky as a whole (in which 21 percent of the population was enslaved), this was the highest rate of slaveholding in the Kentucky mountains. Although their number was small, free African Americans were a larger proportion of Clay County's African American population than that of the southern Appalachian region as a whole. At the onset of the Civil War, Clay County's free African Americans represented 25 percent of the entire free African American population of Appalachian Kentucky. See James B. Murphy, "Slavery and Freedom in Appalachia: Kentucky as a Demographic Case Study," *Register of the Kentucky Historical Society* 80 (1982): 151–69; Robert P. Stuckert, "Black Populations of the Southern Appalachian Mountains," *Phylon* 48 (1987): 141–51.

11. Dwight B. Billings and Kathleen M. Blee, "Agriculture and Poverty in the Kentucky Mountains: Beech Creek, 1850–1910," in Pudup, Billings, and Waller, *Appalachia in the Making*, 233–69.

12. We begin with 1850, the first census to enumerate all household members. Analysis of property holding draws most extensively from the 1850–1870 federal population censuses, which recorded property values and can be linked to records in the federal agricultural census. The reliability of the 1870 census has been questioned, especially for the southern states, so results from this census should be regarded with caution.

13. This method produces a changing population base over time. See Steven H. Hahn, "The Unmaking of the Southern Yeomanry: The Transformation of the Georgia Upcountry, 1860–1890," in *The Countryside in the Age of Capitalist Transformation: Essays in the Social History of Rural America*, ed. Steven H. Hahn and Jonathan Prude (Chapel Hill: Univ. of North Carolina Press, 1985), 179–203; Robert C. Kenzer, *Kinship and Neighborhood in a Southern Community: Orange County, North Carolina, 1849–1881* (Knoxville: Univ. of Tennessee Press, 1987).

14. Murphy, "Slavery and Freedom in Appalachia"; Stuckert, "Black Populations"; and Ronald L. Lewis, "From Peasant to Proletarian: The Migration of Southern Blacks to the Central Appalachian Coalfields," *Journal of Southern History* 55 (1989): 77–102.

15. Eller, *Miners, Millhands, and Mountaineers*.

16. There are problems with interpreting the absence of persistence over time in census data. People disappear from census pages when they die as well as when they move. Moving can be across country or simply over the county line. The lack of persistence in the census also may be an artifact of poor enumeration, particularly of African Americans. We checked whether any African Americans missing in one census reappeared in Clay County in a subsequent census but found none.

17. See for example Orville Vernon Burton, *In My Father's House Are Many Mansions: Family and Community in Edgefield, South Carolina* (Chapel Hill: Univ. of North Carolina Press, 1985).

18. Stephan Thernstrom, *The Other Bostonians: Poverty and Progress in the American Metropolis, 1880–1970* (Cambridge: Harvard Univ. Press, 1973); Laurence Glascoe, "Migration and Adjustment in the Nineteenth-Century City: Occupation, Property, and Household Structure of Native–Born Whites, Buffalo, New York, 1855," in *Family and Population in Nineteenth-Century America*, ed. Tamara K. Hareven and Maris Vinovskis (Princeton, N.J.: Princeton Univ. Press, 1978): 154–78.

19. See also Stewart E. Tolney and E.M. Beck, "Racial Violence and Black Migration in the American South," *American Sociological Review* 57 (1992): 103–16; George C. Wright, *Racial Violence in Kentucky, 1865–1940: Lynchings, Mob Rule, and Legal Lynchings* (Baton Rouge: Louisiana State Univ. Press, 1990).

20. In contrast, Burton, *In My Father's House*, found land-ownership associated with higher rates of persistence among African Americans in Edgefield, South Carolina.

21. Burton, *In My Father's House*.

22. Juliet E.K. Walker, "The Legal Status of Free Blacks in Early Kentucky," *Filson Club Historical Quarterly* 57 (1983): 382–95, suggests that natural increase accounted for a large proportion of Kentucky's free African American population. Birth and death records, which would provide more definitive insights into the African American population decline, are highly unreliable for rural Appalachia.

23. Luther P. Jackson, "Free Negroes of Petersburg, Virginia," *Journal of Negro History* 12 (1927): 365–88; Stuckert, "Black Populations"; Loren Schweninger, *Black Property Owners in the South, 1790–1915* (Urbana: Univ. of Illinois Press, 1990); Loren Schweninger, "Property Owning Free African-American Women in the South, 1800–1870," *Journal of Women's History* 1 (1990): 13–44.

24. Schweninger, *Black Property Owners*.

25. Jacqueline Jones, *The Dispossessed: America's Underclasses from the Civil War to the Present* (New York: Basic Books, 1992).

26. However, several African American property owners lent money and gave mortgages to African American and white farmers in antebellum Clay County.

27. As the 1850 census failed to record any occupation for 68 percent of the primarily rural African American–headed households in Clay County, it is difficult to estimate farm ownership with any precision. If we assume that most rural African Americans were engaged in agricultural pursuits, the actual number of African American household heads working on land owned by someone else may have been as high as 78 percent.

28. This rate of tenancy is only slightly lower than Lewis's (1989) estimate that 85 percent of southern rural African Americans in 1890 were tenant farmers or sharecroppers.

29. Based on Clay County tax rolls, 1871 and 1879; Bureau of the Census, *U.S. Census of Agriculture* (manuscripts), 1870 and 1880.

30. Sharon Holt, "Making Freedom Pay: Freedpeople Working for Themselves, North Carolina, 1865–1900," *Journal of Southern History* 60 (1994): 229–62, especially 267.

31. See also Dwight B. Billings and Kathleen M. Blee, "Family Strategies in a Subsistence Economy: Beech Creek, Kentucky, 1850–1942," *Sociological Perspectives* 33 (1991): 63–88.

32. The average livestock holdings of white tenants were $355 in 1860 and $153 in 1870. One of the two permanent white tenants had livestock worth $200 in 1860 and $60 in 1870, and the other owned livestock worth $240 in 1860 and $100 in 1870.

33. In 1860, for example, stable African American tenants averaged $357 in livestock. The average in that year for all African American tenants was $285; owners averaged $309. In 1870 one African American farmer, William Walker, who had been a tenant in every census year from 1850 to 1870, had an astonishing $800 in livestock, including 30 cattle, 4 milk cows, 8 oxen, and 45 pigs, figures far above the average holdings of either tenants or owners of either race.

34. Jones, *The Dispossessed*.

35. Holt, "Making Freedom Pay," cautions that some African Americans listed in the census as servants were simultaneously working as small proprietors, generating income and resources

through gardening and other forms of household economies, but the census did not collect information on secondary occupations.

36. Schweninger, "Free African American Women."

37 Civil court records indicate no divorce proceedings for Nancy Andrews, but no comparable death records exist.

38. The 1870 census specifically distinguished paid domestic wageworkers ("housekeepers") from unpaid family members who did housework ("keeping house").

39. Sara McLanahan, "Family Structure and the Reproduction of Poverty," *American Journal of Sociology* 90 (1985): 873–901; Schwarzweller, Brown, and Mangalam, *Mountain Families;* Carol Stack, *All Our Kin: Strategies for Survival in a Black Community* (New York: Harper and Row, 1974); S. Phillip Morgan, Antonio McDaniel, Andrew T. Miller, and Samuel H. Preston, "Racial Differences in Household and Family Structure at the Turn of the Century," *American Journal of Sociology* 98 (1993): 798–828; Steven Ruggles, "The Origins of African-American Family Structure," *American Sociological Review* 59 (1994): 136–51; Steven Ruggles, "The Transformation of American Family Structure," *American Historical Review* 99 (1994): 103–28.

40. See also Barbara F. Agresti, "The First Decades of Freedom: Black Families in a Southern County, 1870 and 1885," *Journal of Marriage and the Family* 40 (1978): 697–706; and Linda Gordon and Sara McLanahan, "Single Parenthood in 1900," *Journal of Family History* 16 (1991): 97–116.

41. Agresti, "First Decades of Freedom," found the reverse in a study of a nonplantation farming community in early postbellum Florida.

42. As Steven Ruggles, in "Availability of Kin and the Demography of Historical Family Structure," *Historical Methods* 19 (1986): 93–102; "Family Demography"; and "African-American Family Structure," points out, focusing on elderly persons or children also provides a different picture of racial differences in family structure from analysis at the household level. Also see Miriam King, "All in the Family? The Incompatibility and Reconciliation of Family Demography and Family History," *Historical Methods* 23 (1990): 32–40.

43. See also Ruggles, "Transformation of American Family Structure."

44. Daniel Scott Smith, Marchel Dahlin, and Mark Friedberger, "The Family Structure of the Older Black Population in the American South in 1880 and 1900," *Sociology and Social Research* 63 (1979): 544–65.

45. This finding contrasts sharply with the ability of white-headed households to expand or contract in the face of economic hardship. See Billings and Blee, "Family Strategies in a Subsistence Economy."

46. This rate is higher for white women than the rate that Smith, Dahlin, and Friedberger, "Family Structure of the Older Black Population," found overall for the South in 1880 and 1900.

47. Philippe Ariès, *Centuries of Childhood: A Social History of Family Life,* trans. Robert Baldick (New York: Knopf, 1962); Glen H. Elder, *Children of the Great Depression: Social Change in Life Experience* (Chicago: Univ. of Chicago Press, 1974); Lloyd DeMause, ed., *The History of Childhood* (New York: Harper and Row, 1975).

48. See also, Walker, "Legal Status of Free Blacks," 392; and Holt, "Making Freedom Pay."

49. For example, see Schwarzweller, Brown, and Mangalam, *Mountain Families.*

50. Billings and Blee, "Family Strategies in a Subsistence Economy."

11

SLAVERY'S END IN EAST TENNESSEE

JOHN CIMPRICH

Say the words "southern slavery," and most people imagine blacks picking cotton on a large Deep South plantation. One does not ordinarily think of slavery on the small, diversified farms of upland East Tennessee. Yet 9 percent of the region's population in 1860 consisted of slaves. The subsequent war years changed their lives as much as it changed the lives of those in the Cotton Belt. Slavery ended in East Tennessee in a manner very similar to that in other Federally occupied parts of the Confederacy, unraveling from within. Its normal operation was disrupted by war, and by 1863 Union forces actively encouraged the institution's deterioration.[1]

Two factors had a distinct effect on this process in East Tennessee. First, slaves were owned mostly in units of nine or fewer, contrary to the lower South's general pattern in which most slaves lived in larger plantation communities. A mere 3 percent of all East Tennessee masters held twenty or more slaves; only one owned more than two hundred. The dominant pattern of small slave holdings made personal master/slave relationships likely, something that was not necessarily to a slave's benefit. While it might lead to an intimate, warm relationship, it could also result in suffocating, constrictive supervision and cruel treatment. Slave disloyalty during the war aroused much white hostility partly because masters felt rejected in a personal way. Yet, at the same time, the small slave population limited the black dissidents' economic and political power. The other distinguishing factor in the death of East Tennessee slavery was the region's reluctance to support the Confederacy. Unionists originally wanted to preserve slavery and the Union, but the Federal government's gradual shift to an emancipation policy forced most of its southern allies to follow suit. So, slavery's end in East Tennessee involved a very personalized struggle within the institution and the reluctant conversion of most voters to emancipation.[2]

Shortly after the war began, East Tennessee's obvious Unionism led to a two-year period of Confederate military occupation. The small number of slaves in the region did not motivate the rebel regime to make extraordinary efforts to keep them under control. Chattanooga's municipal government, for example, simply set a stricter evening curfew for blacks, and a Confederate commander in Washington County ordered rigid compliance with the existing pass system for slaves. The army decided to open a central depot in Knoxville for the return of recaptured fugitive slaves, but probably never implemented the plan.

In 1863, retreating troops moved such a depot from middle Tennessee to Chattanooga for a short time before withdrawing into Georgia.[3]

Although no unusual problems in maintaining slave discipline occurred before Federal occupation, the situation did frighten some civilians. In 1861, fears of an insurrection in Hawkins County caused more intense patrolling than usual, and two blacks were sentenced to hang. No uprising occurred; East Tennessee slaves in all probability understood the foolhardiness of violent resistance in a society dominated by whites. Insurrection was also impractical, for, even though masters fleeing the Federal advance brought more slaves into the region, the slave population remained small and scattered. A few individuals murdered their masters in isolated acts of personal revenge, but the bold ones generally preferred to escape to Federal lines.[4]

During the fall of 1863, as Federal invaders took all of East Tennessee except its northeasternmost corner, slavery began to break down. Some fleeing secessionists abandoned their bondsmen. Many slaves ran away from secessionist and Unionist masters in search of freedom. One master's inhumanity pushed a slave named Richard into flight from Jonesboro during the depths of winter. The effort ended tragically with severe frostbite, surrender, and the eventual amputation of his feet. Martha, of Loudon County, asked her owner to start paying her the relatively low sum of fifty dollars a year. When he refused, she left to work for someone else who would provide compensation. Jourdan, a runaway from Big Spring, renounced servitude not only because he had received nothing in return for his labor, but also because his masters had forced his daughters into having sexual intercourse with them.[5] Thus desires to escape cruel treatment, to gain new opportunities, or to accomplish both goals motivated slaves to flee.

In their efforts to retain control over slaves, masters resorted to several tactics. Ebenezer Johnson of Loudon County called in his slave Henry for a very emotional meeting in which both men reaffirmed their obligations to each other under the institution's paternalistic ideals: Johnson promised to provide subsistence and protection while Henry vowed to serve faithfully in return. This personalized approach succeeded with Henry but not with his wife, who deserted her master and her husband after several bitter arguments. Some slaveholders used force, although not always with success. One of Johnson's neighbors recaptured several runaway women and children only to find himself confronted by angry male fugitives, who released the recaptured slaves and severely beat their captor. The only sure method for keeping blacks in bondage was to move them behind Confederate lines. One slave, taken deep into rebel territory in the state's mountainous northeast corner, was completely removed from the war until its end.[6]

Successful runaways, called contrabands by the Federals, concentrated in Knoxville, Chattanooga, and other occupied towns. A white resident of Chattanooga wrote, "The town is so crowded with them we have but a slim showing. . . . It is so diffrant [sic] from what it used to be." Military officials allowed some contrabands into quarters established for white Unionist refugees, but most had to live in tents, abandoned buildings, or shanties of their own construction. In late 1864 the army built a large camp for refugees of both colors, but a few months later authorities segregated blacks into a camp across the Tennessee River from Chattanooga. A lumber shortage forced many of the blacks to build and live in sod huts. Federal authorities began construction of a similar camp across the river from Knoxville but abandoned the project. Most black refugees there remained in a shantytown on the western side of the city, although they cultivated a large communal garden at the site of the unfinished camp. In Knoxville and Chattanooga, the wartime influx of fugitive slaves significantly increased black urban populations.[7]

Town life created new religious, educational, and economic opportunities for runaways. A Chattanooga contraband told a northern reformer that what he wanted most and had obtained from town life was the ability to attend black religious meetings without white regulation or supervision. Northern freedmen's aid societies and several Knoxville blacks opened schools. Alfred Anderson, a free black preacher, compensated for his inadequate education with hard work: "I fealt that this pepel must be traind for I knew tha wair humans. I sacrafised my bisness [to teach]." Besides a chance for personal development, towns offered job opportunities with private employers and the Federal government.[8]

From the perspective of their changing status, the most important contraband occupation was soldiering. Motivated by military expediency and antislavery feelings, Union officials opened recruiting stations at Pikeville and Chattanooga in December 1863. Almost as soon as a runaway arrived in those towns a recruiter tried to talk him into enlistment. A Knoxville station opened a month later with a different strategy: conscription of slaves and contrabands. The practice later spread throughout Federally occupied East Tennessee.[9] Slaveholders stiffly opposed voluntary and involuntary enlistment of their chattel. The pro-Confederate Ebenezer Johnson promised to do everything possible to keep his slave Henry out of the army, while another secessionist unsuccessfully tried to bribe an enlisted runaway into deserting. East Tennessee Unionists, many of whom were opposed to emancipation and black soldiering, used their political power to limit the amount of recruiting in the Knoxville area. Unionist and secessionist masters knew that arming former slaves marked a big step from bondage to freedom and raised the possibility of a higher social status for blacks.[10]

Enlistment made a difference in a contraband's life. He could now bear arms without obtaining the permit required by the slave code. The Union army built up the recruit's pride in his military appearance and performance. As a member of occupation forces, he held a certain amount of power, unlike a slave. A black sergeant from Jefferson County chose to prevent his men from sacking his former owner's plantation. Another soldier took his former mistress to bid her sister farewell at the Knoxville train station, a place that civilians could enter only with a military escort. Blacks benefited from the service in other ways as well. Many had an opportunity to build up small savings in company banks or to acquire some education in schools taught by chaplains and officers.[11]

Despite some improvement in status, black troops had great difficulty winning respect. White soldiers frequently insulted or attacked them. One white officer removed two of his men from a post jail because black sentries guarded it. Until June 1864, the army paid blacks less than it did whites. During the first half of the year, a black brigade at Chattanooga protested by refusing to accept any pay. Nevertheless, it continued to carry out the duties assigned to it. The unit built fortifications and hauled supplies because Maj. Gen. George H. Thomas, commander of the Department of the Cumberland, believed that blacks lacked the courage necessary to fight in battle. Col. Thomas J. Morgan, the brigade's commander, filed an official complaint about the denial of field service, but General Thomas refused to budge and even threatened Morgan with dismissal if he continued to protest. Thomas Cole, a private in the unit, perceived the matter in personalized terms: "When dey wents to battle I was always left in camp ter helps take care of de supplies. General Thomas calls me a coward."[12]

Events during the second half of 1864 brought black troops into field service, although they rarely clashed with Confederate troops. The Fourteenth U.S. Colored Infantry from Morgan's brigade fruitlessly pursued Maj. Gen. Joseph Wheeler's Confederate raiders through East Tennessee. The rest of the brigade fought in northern Georgia or middle Tennessee against Maj. Gen. John B. Hood's Confederate offensive. Fearing that Hood would attack Chattanooga, Federal officials mustered all able-bodied men from both races into active militia duty. As the southerners bypassed the town, the militia did nothing more than hold drills.[13]

The amount of damage done to slavery in the region by Federal recruitment, employment, and protection of runaways cannot be precisely determined, but by the end of the war the institution probably suffered some damage everywhere. Only after slavery had deteriorated did some Unionist politicians seriously begin to consider emancipation. The matter lay in their hands because they had convinced President Abraham Lincoln to exempt Tennessee from his famous Emancipation Proclamation. During 1863 continuing pressure from Lincoln moved the state's two leading Unionists, military governor Andrew Johnson and *Knoxville Whig and Rebel Ventilator* editor William G. Brownlow, to call for the institution's end. Rev. William B. Carter of Elizabethton led the unequivocally proslavery portion of East Tennessee Unionists. Hamilton County's Col. Daniel C. Trewhitt briefly spearheaded a compromise movement, advocating gradual and compensated emancipation for the slaves of Unionists and pardoned secessionists, but he soon switched to Johnson's side. During 1864, Trewhitt, Johnson, and Brownlow became leaders in the state's Union (later Republican) party, while Carter figured prominently in the Conservative (later Democratic) party.[14]

In April 1864, a convention of Unionist leaders, who had met twice in 1861, reconvened in Knoxville. Proslavery men tried to pack the meeting, and

William G. "Parson" Brownlow. (From Brownlow, *Sketches of the Rise, Progress, and Decline of Secession* [1862])

Carter succeeded in getting a majority of the business committee to propose resolutions against emancipation. A bitter debate over the subject deadlocked the convention until it decided to adjourn without passing any resolutions. To save face, Johnson and Brownlow two days later engineered a mass meeting in Knoxville that endorsed their position.[15]

Emancipation also received support from the only Unionist newspapers in East Tennessee, Brownlow's *Knoxville Whig and Rebel Ventilator* and James Hood's *Chattanooga Gazette*. Both held that slavery had broken down beyond repair, that slaveholders had caused secession, and that slave owners had maliciously lorded it over poor whites. Proslavery Unionists replied that the institution benefited both races and that its abolition would "turn loose millions of ignorant negroes to riot over their freedom and to devour the land."[16]

The issue deeply divided Unionists, but support for emancipation slowly grew. An observer at one of Johnson's antislavery speeches reported that "the citizens concurred most enthusiastically with him." A Bradley County resident recorded that many of his neighbors believed "slavery has played out and they would rather have the American Republic than all the negroes in Africa." In a state constitutional referendum on February 22, 1865, East Tennesseans cast almost half the ballots and voted 12,962 to 31 for emancipation, a wider margin than in the rest of the state. Restriction of the franchise to Unionists, who swore support for all of Lincoln's war policies, predetermined the outcome.[17]

The referendum resulted in slavery's legal end in Tennessee, although compliance followed very slowly in remote areas. The institution survived past the war's end and at least through the summer in some eastern counties. The Unionist majority had not turned antislavery because of egalitarianism, and now antiblack sentiment swelled in East Tennessee. Slave disloyalty, viewed in deeply personal terms as impudence and ingratitude, had greatly offended masters. Also, because blacks did not make up a major part of East Tennessee's labor force, class antagonism worked more fiercely against them. As one critic observed, "If Mr. A had no negroes to hire at half price he would let us have some of his good land to work, then we could soon begin to thrive." For these reasons some East Tennesseans demanded the forced colonization of freedmen abroad. One of the region's delegates tried to commit the legislature to the idea but failed because parts of middle and west Tennessee suffered from a labor shortage.[18]

To deal with several postwar problems, including the transition from slavery, a new Federal agency, the Freedmen's Bureau, opened a district office in Knoxville during the summer of 1865. By the fall, subordinate agents had started work in Hamilton and Washington Counties.[19] The freedmen's economic problems required immediate attention, for job opportunities with the Federal army sharply declined as it demobilized. Night riders terrorized blacks who rented land appropriated by the Federal government from Confederate owners. In addition, Knoxville and Chattanooga enforced prewar laws prohibiting blacks from selling groceries or dry goods. Increasingly freedmen had only one economic option—private employment with whites. The unwillingness of some former masters to treat black laborers fairly caused many headaches for the Freedmen's Bureau. Capt. David Boyd, the bureau's agent at Knoxville, repeatedly offered to settle labor disputes by creating arbitration boards. He tried to stop farmers from driving off laborers without pay by threatening to confiscate their farms. Actually he had no such power, and, because few of his efforts succeeded, Boyd soon viewed his task as impossible.[20]

Freedmen also had much trouble with the legal system. With the blessing of the local Freedmen's Bureau agent, Chattanooga municipal officials enforced a prewar law against the sale of liquor to blacks. When, however, Knoxville began to enforce an old ordinance against black possession of firearms, the bureau and the army halted the town's action. The most serious problem throughout the region, according to a Madisonville lawyer, was that "free persons of color cannot get what I call a fair and impartial trial." The bureau had authorized its agents to assume judicial jurisdiction over cases involving East Tennessee blacks, but during 1865, for unknown reasons, they did so only in the black village across the river from Chattanooga.[21]

The Freedmen's Bureau generally sought to aid the black community's development. Although it could offer neither funding nor protection at first, it did encourage the establishment of more schools for freedmen. In 1865 new ones appeared in Chattanooga, Cleveland, Athens, Clinton, Knoxville, Greeneville, Jonesboro, and other towns, although local whites closed a school in each of the last three places through threats or arson.[22] Freedmen organized several schools and churches completely through their own efforts. They sought to reunify families separated during slavery or the war by sending messages throughout the network of bureau offices in the South.[23]

The freedmen's major effort to extend and defend their freedom took the form of political action. In April 1865, East Tennessee black men sent the state legislature a petition for full civil and political rights, especially stressing that "without our political rights, our condition is very little better than it was before." Explaining that they sought legal not social equality, the document also urged the legislature to make it impossible to repeal the existing law against interracial marriage. The Knoxville black community, which probably originated the petition, sent Alfred Anderson and William Scott to Nashville to work for their rights. Anderson served as a lobbyist at the capitol, while Scott edited the state's first black newspaper, the *Colored Tennessean*. In August 1865, Scott helped organize the state's first black convention, which included East Tennessee delegates from Hamilton, Bradley, McMinn, Meigs, Knox, Blount, Washington, and Hawkins Counties. Like the East Tennessee petition, the convention called for full civil and political equality. However, 1865 ended without the passage of any significant legislation to clarify or expand the freedmen's rights.[24]

Whenever freedmen demanded better status, friction resulted. Brownlow wrote an angry editorial after being bumped into a gutter by blacks who refused to follow traditional racial etiquette and get off the sidewalk in the presence of whites. In a Knoxville restaurant a customer hailed a black waiter with "Here, boy!" Much to the patron's ire, the waiter replied, "My name is Dick."[25]

The worst conflicts occurred between black and white soldiers. One Confederate parolee, on seeing his first black troops at Greeneville, commented that they "looked exceedingly black, tall, and war-like." Another reported that they "taunted us with our loss of 'Southern rights, etc.,' and several bloody collisions were narrowly averted." At the same time, Captain Boyd of the Freedmen's Bureau observed that discharged white Federals were "armed to the teeth and in a state of intoxication, breathing violence alike against rebel and negroe [sic]." When a black soldier at Athens urged freedmen to stop the deferential practice of raising their hats to whites, a white Union veteran killed him for it. Just as in the rest of the state, rising racial antagonism led to murders of black soldiers by whites and vice versa.[26]

Post-emancipation tensions came to a high point throughout the South with the insurrection scare of Christmas 1865. The Federal commander at Chattanooga reported, "There is a bad disposition exhibited toward the negroes at this place[;] the whites affect to believe that an insurrection is intended[;] there is no truth in it." The town's civil officials petitioned for the removal of all black troops, but the army agreed only to disarm and confine unemployed civilian freedmen until jobs could be found for them. The holidays ended quietly, and East Tennessee entered 1866 with much still left to settle about the freedmen's future.[27]

The Civil War had made it possible for many slaves to throw off their servitude, but without help they could do little else to change their status. White Unionists, the dominant group in East Tennessee, had turned against slavery mostly for political reasons, and they made little effort to assist freedmen in their struggle for postwar change. Despite slavery's limited significance in East Tennessee, its legacy of racial, class, and personal conflict did not die easily or quietly.

NOTES

An earlier version of this essay was published in *East Tennessee Historical Society Publications* (1980–1981): 78–89, and is reprinted here with the permission of the East Tennessee Historical Society.

1. Bureau of the Census, *Eighth Census of the United States, 1860: Population* (Washington, D.C.: 1861), 466–67. General studies of slavery's end are Bell I. Wiley, *Southern Negroes, 1861–1865* (New Haven, Conn., 1938); and Leon F. Litwack, *Been in the Storm So Long: The Aftermath of Slavery* (New York, 1979). Works that deal with the process in Tennessee are David W. Bowen, "Andrew Johnson and the Negro" (Ph.D. diss., University of Tennessee, 1976); Charles F. Bryan Jr., "The Civil War in East Tennessee: A Social, Political, and Economic Study" (Ph.D. diss., University of Tennessee, 1978); John Cimprich, "Slavery amidst Civil War in Tennessee: The Death of an Institution" (Ph.D. diss., Ohio State University, 1977); Bobby L. Lovett, "The Negro in Tennessee: A Socio-Military History of the Civil War Era" (Ph.D. diss., University of Arkansas, 1978); Bobby L. Lovett, "The Negro's Civil War in Tennessee, 1861–1865," *Journal of Negro History* 61 (1976): 36–50.

2. *Eighth Census, 1860: Population*, 238–39; James W. Patton, "Unionists and Reconstruction in Tennessee, 1860–1869" (Ph.D. diss., University of North Carolina, 1934), 67–68; *Knoxville Whig*, June 8, 1861; LeRoy P. Graf and Ralph W. Haskins, eds., *The Papers of Andrew Johnson*, 6 vols. to date (Knoxville, Tenn., 1967–), 4: 160–62. The situation in East Tennessee closely resembled that in West Virginia and northwest Arkansas.

3. Gilbert E. Govan and James W. Livingood, *The Chattanooga Country, 1540–1962: From Tomahawks to T.V.A.*, 2d ed. (Chapel Hill, 1963), 183–84; *Jonesborough Union*, May 24, 1861, p. 1; U.S. War Department, *The War of the Rebellion: A Compilation of the Official Records of the Union and Confederate Armies*, 2d. ser., vol. 5 (Washington, D.C., 1880–1901), 844, 959.

4. Bryan, "Civil War in East Tennessee," 304–5, 318–19; Catherine Watterson to W.H. Watterson, May 20, 1861, Watterson Family Papers, McClung Collection, Knox County Library, Knoxville, Tenn.; Charles W. Cansler, *Three Generations: The Story of a Colored Family of East Tennessee* (n.p., 1939), 888–97; *Athens Post*, March 7, 1862; *Knoxville Register*, March 21, 1863. Together the *Knoxville Register* and *Chattanooga Rebel* ran an average of four new fugitive slave advertisements per month from April 1862 through September 1863.

5. *New York Tribune*, Oct. 21, 1863; S.E. Griffith to Clinton B. Fisk, Sept. 18, 1865. Registered Letters Received by the Assistant Commissioner for Ky. and Tenn., Records of the Bureau of Refugees, Freedmen, and Abandoned Lands (BRFAL), RG 105, National Archives; Mary Reynolds to Simeon Reynolds, Feb. 10, May 1, 1864, Mary Reynolds Papers, Special Collections, University of Tennessee Library, Knoxville; Lydia Maria Child, *The Freedman's Book* (Boston, 1865), 265–67.

6. Mary Reynolds to Simeon Reynolds, Feb. 16, May 1, 1864, Reynolds Papers; George P. Rawick, ed., *Tennessee Narratives*, vol. 11 of *The American Slave: A Composite Autobiography*, 41 vols. (Westport, Conn., 1972–79), 9.

7. E.P. Tiner to J.S. Tiner, Aug. 1, 1864, Andrew Johnson Papers, Library of Congress;

Chattanooga Gazette, Nov. 25, 26, Dec. 4, 11, 1864; Lyman W. Ayer to M.E. Strieby, Feb. 18, 1864, American Missionary Association Archives, Amistad Research Center, Dillard University, New Orleans; *Cincinnati Gazette*, Feb. 17, 1864; R.D. Mussey to T.J. Morgan, April 26, 1864, Letters Sent by the Commissioner for the Organization of U.S. Colored Troops, vol. 220/227, DC, 81, Records of the U.S. Army Continental Commands, 1821–1920 (USACC), RG 393, National Archives; Howard Rabinowitz, *Race Relations in the Urban South, 1865–1890* (New York, 1978), 128–29, contends that the contraband programs of the Federal army and of northern philanthropists began southern segregation.

8. Elvira J. Powers, *Hospital Pencilings* (Boston, 1866), 112; R.W. McGranahan, ed., *Historical Sketches of the Freedmen's Missions of the United Presbyterian Church, 1862–1904* (Knoxville, 1904), 22; Alfred Anderson to W.E. Whiting, April 25, 1865, American Missionary Association Archives.

9. *Nashville Union*, Dec. 5, 1863; *Knoxville Whig and Rebel Ventilator*, Jan. 16, 1864; *Nashville Press*, April 21, 1864; *Chattanooga Gazette*, Nov. 23, 1864.

10. Mary Reynolds to Simeon Reynolds, Feb. 16, 1864, Reynolds Papers; John A. Shannon to H.H. Deane, May 27, 1864, First U.S. Colored Artillery Letterbook, 26–27, Records of the Adjutant General's Office (AGO), RC 94, National Archives; J.R. Putnam to R.D. Muxsey, July 18, 1864, Forty-Second U.S. Colored Infantry Letterbook (unpaged), AGO.

11. *Chattanooga Gazette*, March 14, 1864; Thomas J. Morgan, *Reminiscences of Service with Colored Troops in the Army of the Cumberland, 1863–1865* (Providence, R.I., 1885), 20–24; Rawick, *American Slave*, Supp. Series 1, vol. 5, p. 315; Martha L. Mitchell Memoir, Tennessee State Library and Archives (TSLA), Nashville.

12. Henry Romeyn, *With Colored Troops in the Army of the Cumberland* (n.p., 1904), 12–14; Austin O. Lynn to a survivor, Aug. 14, 1865, Register of Letters Received by the District of First Tennessee, vol. 2, DET, 244, USACC; Morgan, *Reminiscences*, 22–24; T.J. Morgan to Lorenzo Thomas, July 20, 1864, Letters Received by the Colored Troops Division, ACO; W.D. Whipple to T.J. Morgan, Aug. 9, 1864, Letters Sent by the Department of the Cumberland, vol. 9, DC, 442–43, USACC; Rawick, *American Slave*, Supp. Series 2, vol. 3, p. 818.

13. Romeyn, *With Colored Troops*, 14–16; *Chattanooga Gazette*, Dec. 17, 20, 1864.

14. John Cimprich, "Military Governor Johnson and Tennessee Blacks," *Tennessee Historical Quarterly* 39 (1980): 462–67; *Knoxville Whig and Rebel Ventilator*, Feb. 6, 1864; *Cincinnati Gazette*, April 17, 1863, April 22, 1864.

15. Bryan, "Civil War in East Tennessee," 312–13; *Nashville Times and True Union*, April 23, 1864; John Baxter to William B. Campbell, Sept. 28, 1864, David Campbell Papers, Duke University Library, Durham. N.C.; Oliver P. Temple, *Notable Men of Tennessee* (New York, 1912), 407–8; *Knoxville Whig and Rebel Ventilator*, April 23, 1864.

16. *Knoxville Whig and Rebel Ventilator*, Nov. 23, 1864; *Chattanooga Gazette*, April 22, 1864; John Baxter to William B. Campbell, Sept. 28, 1864, Campbell Papers.

17. Paul E. Rieger, ed., *Through One Man's Eyes: The Civil War Experiences of a Belmont County Volunteer* (Mt. Vernon, Ohio, 1974), 93; John Hambright to J. Hambright, June 17, 1864, Johnson Papers; Tally Sheets of Elections, TSLA.

18. *Nashville Times and True Union*, Feb. 27, 1865; C.R. Hall, *Three Score Years and Ten* (Cincinnati, 1884), 227; Mary Reynolds to Simeon Reynolds, Jan. 6, June 20, 1864, Reynolds Papers; *Cleveland Banner*, Oct. 21, 1865; Clinton B. Fisk to O.O. Howard, Dec. 19, 1865, Letters Sent to the Commissioner, vol. 15, p. 128, BRFAL; *Tennessee House Journal*, 1865 General Assembly, Adjourned Sess., 67–68; George M. Fredrickson, *The Black Image in the White Mind: The Debate on Afro-American Character and Destiny, 1817–1914* (New York, 1971), 130–33, argues that racial prejudices were harsher in populations with small proportions of blacks.

19. Clinton B. Fisk to F.M. Lester, Aug. 26, 1865, Telegrams Sent by the Assistant Commissioner for Ky. and Tenn., vol. 18, p. 442, BRFAL; S.E. Griffith to Clinton B. Fisk, Sept. 18, 1865, Registered Letters Received by the Assistant Commissioner for Ky. and Tenn., BRFAL; N.B. Lucas Order, Oct. 18, 1865, Unregistered Letters Received by the Chattanooga Superintendent, BRFAL.

20. William G. Rutlage to John A. Henry, Sept. 1, 1865, Unregistered Letters Received by

the Knoxville Subassistant Commissioner, BRFAL; Knoxville Board of Mayor and Aldermen, Minute Book, 297–98, Knoxville City Archives; Law Court of Chattanooga, Civil Record A, pt. 2. p. 460, TSLA; John A. Henry to William Brown, Dec. 13, 1865, Letters Sent by the Knoxville Subassistant Commissioner, BRFAL; David Boyd to Ransom Badgett, Sept. 18, 1865, Registered Letters Sent by the Knoxville Subassistant Commissioner, BRFAL; David Boyd to W.T. Clarke, Oct. 5. 1865, Registered Letters Received by the Assistant Commissioner for Ky. and Tenn., BRFAL.

21. N.B. Lucas Order, Oct. 18. 1865, Unregistered Letters Received by the Chattanooga Superintendent, BRFAL; George Stoneman to the mayor of Knoxville, Nov. 22, 1865, Unregistered Letters Received hy the Knoxville Subassistant Commissioner, BRFAL; George Brown to William G. Brownlow, Nov. 13, 1865, Brownlow Gubernatorial Papers, TSLA; H. Doc. 70, 39th Cong., 1st sess., pp. 46, 108–11; J.T. Trowbridge, *The South: A Tour of its Battlefields and Ruined Cities* (Hartford, Conn., 1866), 252. Pressure from President Johnson may have limited bureau activities in East Tennessee. See J.S. Fullerton to Clinton B. Fisk, Aug. 19, 1865, Registered Letters Received by the Assistant Commissioner for Ky and Tenn., BRFAL.

22. Henry L. Swint. ed., "Reports from Educational Agents of the Freedmen's Bureau in Tennessee, 1865–1870, *Tennessee Historical Quarterly* 1 (1942): 55; David Boyd to W.T. Clarke, Oct. 5, 1865, Registered Letters Received by the Assistant Commissioner for Ky. and Tenn., BRFAL; John Tate to John Ogden, Dec. 1, 1865, American Missionary Association Archives; Trowbridge, *The South*, 239.

23. Anthony Carter to Clinton R. Fisk, Oct. 12, 1865, Registered Letters Received by the Assistant Commissioner for Ky. and Tenn., BRFAL; *Freedmen's Bulletin* 2 (1865): 35; Records of the Second Presbyterian Church of Knoxville, vol. 1, pp. 153, 191, McClung Collection, Knox County Library; Chattanooga Superintendent's Log, Dec. 21, 1865, BRFAL; Peter Barrett to his wife, Dec. 3, 1865, and David Boyd to Samuel Thomas, Oct. 5, 1865, Unregistered Letters Received by the Knoxville Subassistant Commissioner, BRFAL.

24. *Nashville Dispatch*, April 15, 1865; Robert Hamilton to S.S. Jocelyn, April 2, 1865, American Missionary Association Archives; *Nashville Colored Tennessean*, Aug. 12, 1865.

25. *Knoxville Whig and Rebel Ventilator*, Sept. 27, 1865; Trowbridge, *The South*, 239.

26. R.M. Collins, *Chapters from the Unwritten History of the War between the States* (St. Louis, 1893), 305; Hampton J. Cheney File, Civil War Questionnaires, TSLA; David Boyd to W.T. Clarke, Oct. 5, 1865, and David Boyd to F.M. Lister, October 8, 1865, Registered Letters Received by the Assistant Commissioner for Ky. and Tenn., BRFAL; *Nashville Dispatch*, Sept. 17, 1865; *Knoxville Whig and Rebel Ventilator*, Aug. 30, 1865.

27. Dan T. Carter, "The Anatomy of Fear: The Christmas Day Insurrection Scare of 1865," *Journal of Southern History* 42 (1976): 345–46; Alvan C. Gillem to Joseph Fowler, Dec. 19, 1865, Joseph Fowler Papers, Southern Historical Collection, University of North Carolina Library, Chapel Hill, N.C.; *Nashville Press and Times*, Dec. 30, 1865; William H. Gaw, General Order 36, Dec. 29, 1865, Chattanooga Post Records, vol. 377/10, DMT, USACC.

12

SOUTHERN MOUNTAIN REPUBLICANS AND THE NEGRO, 1865–1900

GORDON B. MCKINNEY

The mountain Republicans of the upper South have been a riddle to southerners for more than a century. Located primarily in eastern Kentucky and Tennessee, northwestern West Virginia, southwestern Virginia, and western North Carolina, they are the only part of the white population of the South that has consistently supported the party associated with Reconstruction. During the period between the end of the Civil War and the beginning of disfranchisement of black voters around 1900, the coalition of blacks and mountain whites in the Republican party was a powerful political force in these five states.[1] The resulting conflicts and accommodations between the two racial groups reveal much about politics and race in the South during the Gilded Age. Two factors shaped their relationship: the relative lack of racial hostility between mountain whites and blacks and the dependence of the Republican party of the upper South on black votes. This biracial alliance proved to be more pragmatic than idealistic. Although mountain Republican leaders could proclaim, "We want no white man's party or colored man's party, but a party of principle; a party on whose banner is inscribed Liberty, Union and Equality before the law; a party that proposes to elevate mankind of all races and colors," the presence of a racially conscious lowland white population made this goal unattainable.[2] The Republican strategy became one of offering their black following just enough to ensure their continued support while emphasizing issues that would attract greater numbers of white voters.

The mountain Republican parties of the upper South were created during the turmoil of Reconstruction. A few Republican votes were recorded in eastern Kentucky and northwestern Virginia in 1860, but the party did not really emerge as a potent force in the mountain regions until the end of the Civil War.[3] In West Virginia and Tennessee the mountain politicians found themselves in control of the state government, and several of their leaders were elected governors and congressmen. North Carolina and Kentucky mountain Republicans had a voice in determining policy in their state organizations but were unable to dominate them to any extent. The mountain leaders in these two states were strong enough, however, to ensure that they controlled the party in their regions. Only in Virginia did the mountaineers fail to play a significant role in the Reconstruction party.[4] There were so few Republican voters in the area that the party leaders from counties and cities with large black populations dictated party policy.

The bitterness left by the war encouraged many mountain Republican politicians to support Congressional Reconstruction. The war had left the mountains devastated, and many mountaineers had opposed the Confederacy and wanted revenge on the lowland populations of their states for causing the war.[5] They enthusiastically supported measures that disfranchised former Confederates in order to ensure continued Republican control.[6] It soon became obvious that these measures alone would not be sufficient and that a new source of support was needed. The only available alternative was the Negro.

The decision to accept blacks as political allies was an agonizing one for mountain Republicans. Blacks were regarded as inherently inferior, and this attitude had been formed and accepted long before the Reconstruction period.[7] John Brown's raid on Harpers Ferry had had a great impact on the mountaineers, indicating that many of them shared the South's fear of servile revolt.[8] In politics most mountain whites undoubtedly agreed with future Tennessee Republican leader William G. Brownlow when he stated in 1861 that "if we were once convinced in the border Slave States that the Administration at Washington . . . contemplated . . . the abolishing of slavery, there would not be a Union man among us in twenty-four hours."[9] Although mountaineers may have disliked slavery as an economic system, they accepted and supported it as a means of social control.[10]

Despite their racial prejudice, mountain Republicans soon found that they had to deal with black voters. Negro suffrage was introduced into Virginia and North Carolina by the Reconstruction Acts of 1867, and by 1869 Kentucky and West Virginia mountain Republicans were forced to accept blacks as voters. Only in Tennessee did the Republicans enfranchise blacks voluntarily despite the protest of many East Tennessee Republicans, including future governor DeWitt Clinton Senter.[11] Mountaineers in other states were also upset by Negro suffrage, and some were angry enough to start the Civil War again.[12]

These sentiments changed significantly as the first elections were held in the upper South under the new suffrage arrangements. The black voter proved to be a staunch Republican, allowing the party to win state elections in Tennessee, West Virginia, and North Carolina. Though blacks did not help the Republicans gain control in Kentucky or Virginia, they at least made the party competitive and gave it hope for the future. In addition, there was little indication that blacks would challenge the white leadership of the party. This was particularly true in the mountain counties. One group of western North Carolina blacks told a Republican leader, "We . . . wish to express to you our grateful thanks for the gratifying and praiseworthy way in which you spoke to us. Having so lately escaped from slavery, we know that our state and condition are backward, yet we are not so far back as to be ungrateful for kindness. We hope that 'ere long we may rise upward and testify to the friends of the colored

Freedmen registering to vote in Asheville, North Carolina. (From *Harper's Weekly*, September 28, 1867)

man we are and have improved sufficiently to merit their praise. We venture to promise, that should you be nominated for Congress, we will not only give you our own humble support, but also that we shall make strenuous efforts to secure that of every other colored man in the County."[13] This passive type of Negro Republican voter was an acceptable junior partner for most mountain Republicans.

Despite the general satisfaction with the Negro as a voter, his presence caused a major split within the mountain Republican parties. In West Virginia, Tennessee, and Virginia, black suffrage came at a time when many ex-Confederates still could not vote. To the mountain Republicans this was unthinkable, and they started movements for complete manhood suffrage in their states.[14] Mountain Republicans in many cases could not justify denying the ballots to whites, even to their political enemies, while blacks voted. There was editorial support for the movement in a black paper, indicating that some black politicians had joined the universal-suffrage movement.[15]

Though each of the state parties had somewhat different experiences with this movement, the result was always the same. In Virginia the Republican party split into radical and liberal wings, and each ran a candidate for governor. The liberal, or universal suffrage, wing ran Gilbert C. Walker in 1869 with the backing of the Conservative-Democratic party and some railroad interests. The mountaineers of southwestern Virginia, including the Republicans, were enthusiastic supporters of Walker, and he carried the region with over 70 percent of the vote.[16] Essentially the same thing happened in Tennessee. DeWitt Senter, interim governor, supported and implemented universal suffrage in the gubernatorial election of 1869 to help him defeat another Republican candidate, William B. Stokes. Once again the universal suffrage candidate carried the mountain counties.[17] In West Virginia the universal suffrage men seized control of the party and allowed all white males to vote.[18]

The mountain Republicans of North Carolina and Kentucky faced a different set of circumstances. In North Carolina the local Republicans had not disfranchised any of the former Confederates, and less than 10 percent of the white voters were prevented from registering by the Reconstruction laws passed in March 1867. Thus, it was dissatisfaction with Gov. William Woods Holden's administration, rather than the question of suffrage, that led many mountain Republicans to support Democrats for the state legislature in 1870. The resulting Democratic victory brought the impeachment of Holden and the elevation of conservative mountain Republican Tod R. Caldwell to take Holden's place. North Carolina Republicans now adopted a more conciliatory attitude toward the opposition and welcomed the Amnesty Act of May 1872 that restored full rights to most North Carolina Confederates.[19] As Kentucky had not been reconstructed, universal suffrage already prevailed in that state. There was, however, a noticeable shift in party tactics in 1870 and 1871 that resulted in a virtual repudiation of Congressional Reconstruction. Avoiding race-related issues, Kentucky Republicans began to campaign on a platform of improved education and internal improvements. The response of mountain Republicans to the change was very favorable.[20]

The reaction against Reconstruction proved to be a political disaster for the mountain Republican parties. In each of the five states, the Democrats were now in control of the state governments. It was equally important that the Republican party in these mountain areas split badly into competing factions.[21] By 1874 the Republicans were so disorganized that they failed to win a majority of the votes in any of the mountain regions, including formerly safe East Tennessee. Only the unexpected victory of John Daugherty White in a Kentucky mountain congressional district seemed to offer any hope for the future.[22]

At this point the mountain Republicans in each of five states seemed to reassess their situations and to make dramatic changes in the party. Abandoning all issues, the mountain Republicans began to concentrate on organizational structure to save the party. The structure drew on the extensive Civil War experience of the mountaineers and resulted in a party organized much like the Union and Confederate armies. Each member of the party was assigned a military rank, from private for the ordinary voter to general for leaders like Nathan B. Goff and William Mahone.[23] The voters were then organized into squads of ten with a captain to direct their voting on election day. The Houk machine in East Tennessee, for example, was so well organized that it had personal information on every voter in the Second Congressional District and could place two thousand squad leaders in the field to ensure that every Republican voted.[24] Clear lines of authority were established; there was a careful structuring of personnel within the party; and power was centralized, usually in the hands of one man for the entire region.[25] These organizations, often resembling big-city machines, proved to be quite effective, and by 1880 the mountain Republican parties were ready to win campaigns again. They did not do so immediately, but there was no chance that the mountain Republican parties would disappear.

One reason for their failure to be more successful in the late 1870s was a major shift in the national Republican party's southern policy. Starting with President Rutherford B. Hayes in 1877, the national party searched for a formula to win more southern white support.[26] Hayes attempted to attract former Whigs by appointing them to office, and this action deprived mountain Republicans of a large part of the federal patronage they expected to be theirs. West Virginia politician George W. Atkinson complained that this would "kill" the party in the southern mountains.[27] The situation did not improve much when Chester A. Arthur became president in September 1881. He supported Independent Democratic movements such as the Readjusters in Virginia and the liberal antiprohibitionists in North Carolina, and like Hayes, gave members of these groups federal positions that the mountain Republicans expected to control.[28] All of this forced the mountain Republican politicians to depend on the resources that the party had in the immediate area.

The most significant of these local resources was the black Republican. As Leonidas Houk, an East Tennessee Republican leader, observed, "The more I have studied the matter, the more convinced I have become, that it would not only be good politics, but good Civil Service, and equitable Republicanism to distribute the appointments among all classes [of] Americans, Germans, Irish, and Colored people."[29] In the lowland regions of every state except West Virginia blacks formed the major portion of the party's voters. This meant that even if the mountain Republicans had wanted to ignore the blacks they could not have done so. Electoral failures, party reorganization, and political necessity required that the white mountain Republicans work with black Republicans.

Much to their dismay, mountain Republican politicians found that they were no longer dealing with a docile black voting population. Knoxville black Henry Casper spoke for the new black political leaders when he announced, "We not only want to be nominated, but we want some assurance, that those who help nominate us are sincere and intend voting for us at the polls. We will not suffer that trick any longer. There are enough colored voters in Knox County to demand one or two good county offices every year if the Republican Party would but give us what our numbers entitle us to."[30] Not only did the black Republicans make demands, but they did something about the discrimination that they felt. William Yardley, an East Tennessee black leader, shocked the party in his state by running as a gubernatorial candidate in 1876.[31] Although he concentrated his campaign in west and middle Tennessee, with their large black populations, white East Tennessee Republicans were quite upset by his audacity. In the 1880s, black protest meetings in Tennessee, Kentucky, and North Carolina demanded more equal treatment from the party leaders.[32]

Two incidents involving blacks and mountain Republicans during this period illustrate the problems that the more aggressive black leadership created for white Republicans in the mountains. One problem was that blacks could act as the balance of power between competing white factions of the party. In 1882 in Tennessee's Second District a power struggle between Congressman Leonidas Houk and newspaper editor William Rule resulted in desperate bargaining for black votes by both men. In 1881 Houk had induced blacks to protest Rule's appointment as postmaster of Knoxville.[33] This protest proved successful, and Rule was replaced with a Houk man. Rule was incensed by this action and announced that he was going to unseat Houk in 1882. His campaign was based in part upon an attempt to control the black vote.[34] Houk reacted to this quickly by making an alliance with black leader William Yardley. Later a campaign worker reported to Houk, "Yardley and Sam Anderson got all the colored people together at night and with locked doors, they passed resolutions endorsing you."[35] The response of the Rule forces was that "Yardley . . . is a notoriously cheap piece of marketable material in every election."[36] The bitterness of the last remark clearly indicated that Rule had not been able to win the black vote and would be easily defeated by Houk. The significant point was that blacks were acting independent of white control in the mountain Republican party in East Tennessee.

West Virginia Republicans also encountered much dissatisfaction among black voters. Many black supporters seemed willing to leave the party in 1888 because they did not feel that they were receiving fair treatment. The Colored Independent party made its appearance in July of that year. At that time one spokesman observed that there was increasing dissatisfaction with the Republican party among blacks.[37] Republican papers demonstrated a close connection between the new party and the Democrats, and this apparently negated most of its appeal.[38] Nevertheless, blacks had once more shown themselves willing to break from a mountain Republican organization, and they thereby forced the mountaineers to make adjustments.

The increasing black demands were being made on a group of men who still retained strong racial feelings. The editor of a West Virginia Republican paper probably expressed most mountain Republican sentiment in the assertion that "they are just emerging from a purely animal existence and have their future to make out of very indifferent raw material."[39] Mountaineers expressed their prejudice in more than words. Throughout the late nineteenth century, mountain men, like other southern whites, found lynching to be a suitable means of social control.[40] One East Tennessee Republican even justified the practice: "However deplorable lynch law may be I say that negroes lynched in the South for assaulting white women are not lynched because they are negroes but because of the crime they have committed. . . . I say it is the unwritten law of the South to lynch a brute who assaults a woman without regard to his race or color. If more negroes are lynched for this crime than white men it is not because they are negroes but because in the South more negroes commit the crime than whites in the North."[41]

This would seem to raise the question of how the mountain whites could work with the more aggressive black politicians. One answer appears to be demographic. There were few blacks living in the mountain counties, apparently freeing the mountain whites of the fear of "Negro domination." The percentage of blacks in 1870 in the mountain regions ranged from a high of 14 percent in southwestern Virginia and western North Carolina to a low of less than 3 percent in northwestern West Virginia.[42] The average for the mountain counties in all five states was less than 9 percent. A more detailed statistical study of the relationship between white Republican voting in 1876 and the proportion of blacks in the population produced a correlation coefficient of -70.[43] The negative correlation indicates an inverse relationship between the variables. As the percentage of blacks in the population rises, the percentage of whites voting Republican decreases; as the proportion of blacks in the population drops, the Republican share of the white vote increases. Thus the small black population in the mountain counties made it easier for mountain Republicans to overlook their prejudice and work with blacks politically.

Despite the rapid increase in mining in the Appalachians in the upper South after 1880 and the increased presence of black miners, Republicans not only retained but increased their support among mountain whites. Table 12.1 helps to explain why this does not represent a conflict with the previous analysis. Although the number of blacks living in the mountain counties was increasing rapidly during this period, they actually were declining in proportion to the rest of the population. In only 33 of the 147 mountain counties did the percentage of blacks increase faster than that of the total population.[44] Even this figure is misleading because the number of blacks involved was so small. For example, the percentage increase in Clay County, West Virginia, between 1870 and 1900 was 450 percent, but in actual numbers the change was from four blacks in 1870 to a total of eighteen in a population of 8,248 in 1900.[45] In those few counties where there was a substantial increase in percentage and numbers, like Hamilton County (Chattanooga), Tennessee, there was a noticeable decrease in Republican voting among whites.[46] Thus, this demographic variable was constant throughout the period. There were few blacks in the mountain counties, and this fact apparently allowed the mountaineers enough freedom to ignore racist appeals and to work successfully with blacks in politics.

Another persuasive reason why white Republicans in the mountains were willing to work with blacks was that the arrangement was becoming increasingly successful. The southwestern Virginia Republican party, in fact, more than doubled its vote after Reconstruction. In the mid-1870s the Republican vote had nearly disappeared. Then in 1879 mountain Republicans, black Republi-

Table 12.1. Comparison of Negro Population and Total Population of Mountain Counties of the Upper South, 1870 and 1900

	1870		1900	
	Negro	Total Population	Negro	Total Population
Kentucky	8,621	211,232	11,178	449,975
West Virginia	7,715	324,440	16,154	695,363
Tennessee	36,238	327,035	65,387	625,971
North Carolina	29,673	207,318	53,145	424,579
Virginia	25,938	182,068	42,469	360,233
Total	108,185	1,252,093	188,333	2,556,121
Percent Negro		8.64%		7.37%

Sources: *Compendium of the Eleventh Census: 1890*, 1, 487-89, 499-501, 506-7, 512-14; Twelfth Census of the United States, 1900: Population, pt. 1, 540-41, 550-51, 556-57, 561-63.

cans, and poor Democratic farmers combined in a political coalition and formed the Readjuster party. Led by former Confederate general and railroad promoter William Mahone, the new party attacked the inequitable Virginia tax system. The issue was a popular one, and the Readjusters won at the state level and in the mountain counties in the elections of 1879, 1881, and 1882.[47] Happy to be winning elections at last and to be sharing in the federal patronage that Mahone distributed, the Virginia mountain Republicans worked effectively with black Republicans. Their willingness was undoubtedly increased by Mahone's policy of placing black politicians in an obviously subordinate position.[48]

The 1883 local elections in Virginia provided a clear test of the mountain Republican's loyalty to his black allies. The revitalized Virginia Democrats ran a heavily racist campaign directed particularly at mountain Republicans.[49] Three days before the voting a widely publicized race riot took place in the city of Danville, and increased pressure was placed on white voters in the mountains.[50] The result was an increase in the Readjuster total in the mountain counties of more than five thousand votes over the party's returns in 1882.[51] The reason for this somewhat unexpected result was, as one mountain politician reported, "The Republicans, I am proud to say, stood to their guns like men never saw them more determined, or united."[52] After surviving this experience, the mountain Republicans of southwestern Virginia were a potent political force.

Republicans in the other four mountain regions also enjoyed substantial successes as the party-army provided them with strengthened organizations.

Not only were Republicans winning in the mountains, in 1888 eight mountain Republican congressmen were elected, and they were threatening Democratic hegemony at the state level as well. In North Carolina in 1886 Republicans and Independent Democrats won control of the lower house of the legislature.[53] This victory was a profound shock to the Democrats and led to the extension of outside aid from the Republican National Committee to North Carolina Republicans two years later.[54] Although the party failed to carry the state for presidential candidate Benjamin Harrison, three Republican congressmen were elected. This represented the party's best showing since Reconstruction. Kentucky Republican leader William O. Bradley was the party's gubernatorial candidate in 1887, and his energetic campaign reduced the normal forty-thousand-vote Democratic majority to seventeen thousand. The next year these gains resulted in the election of three Republican congressmen from Kentucky. Tennessee mountain Republicans were cheered by the fact that businessman Henry Clay Evans carried the state's Third Congressional District for the Republicans, the party's first victory in that district in two decades.[55]

West Virginia Republicans in 1888 were even more successful, electing half of the state's four congressmen and a governor. Popular Republican congressman Nathan Goff had been persuaded to be the gubernatorial candidate, and he proved to be such an effective campaigner that the Democratic candidate refused to debate him.[56] When the returns were counted Goff had won by the slim margin of 110 votes. There were immediate protests of fraud, and an election contest conducted by a Democratic legislature eventually deprived Goff of his victory.[57] Still, West Virginia Republicans believed that they were on the verge of a great breakthrough.

Virginia mountain Republicans continued to enjoy success under Mahone's leadership. In 1886 the Republicans won six of Virginia's ten congressional seats, and in 1888 Harrison lost by only fifteen hundred votes out of more than three hundred thousand cast in the state.[58] The Republican party in the upper South was doing well, then, and was looking for some way to win control of their states.

Because the major barrier to Republican success had been Democratic control of the election machinery, most mountain Republicans eagerly supported the idea of a federal election law.[59] They were significant leaders in trying to secure this legislation. Most mountain Republicans were positive that a federal election law would ensure party success in their states, as it would guarantee black voting as well as accuracy in the counting of votes.[60] Veteran mountain Republican congressman Leonidas Houk of Tennessee was the chief spokesman for the region in favor of the measure. During his first month in Congress in 1879, Houk endorsed the idea of federal control of elections, and he introduced a piece of legislation to do this in November 1889.[61] Although his own bill was dropped in favor of one proposed by Henry Cabot Lodge, Houk continued to support the idea. His position is stated clearly in a speech delivered in 1890: "In conclusion he urged that the colored people of the South should be given a fair chance. If the white people of the South would not take their hand off the Government must take it off. Let no man hold a seat on this floor who was returned by means of Winchester rifles, clubs and fraudulent ballot boxes."[62] In the floor debate on the Lodge bill, Houk continued his enthusiastic support of the concept of federal intervention.[63]

Although Houk was probably the leading spokesman for a federal election law, there were many other mountain Republicans who supported Lodge's ideas. Congressman George W. Atkinson of West Virginia proposed that criminal penalties be enforced if anyone interfered with federal elections.[64] Along the same lines, East Tennessee Republican congressman Alfred Taylor thought that the final version of Lodge's bill should be strengthened to ensure compliance with the law.[65] Kentucky mountain Republican congressman Hugh Finley was quite satisfied, saying, "I most cheerfully endorse the bill as the best election bill that has ever been offered to any Congress in this country."[66] Republican voters in the mountain regions also seemed to accept the measure according to Republican newspapers and meetings endorsing the Lodge proposal.[67] When the vote was taken in the House, seven of the eight mountain Republicans supported it and thereby allowed the measure to pass by a narrow margin.[68]

There was, however, another opinion of the legislation among mountain Republicans, and the leader of this point of view was Congressman Hamilton C. Ewart of North Carolina. Ewart maintained that "this election bill is as damnable, illogical, inequitable, and vicious a piece of legislation as was ever attempted to be placed upon the statute-books of this Republic."[69] He went on to explain his stand in the following terms: "Every year the Republican party in the States of Tennessee, North Carolina, and the two Virginias is becoming stronger and more aggressive. It is not acquiring this strength by making morbid appeals to the negro and by exciting their passions and prejudices, but by appealing to the sober judgement of the white voters of the South on the great issue of protection."[70] Nor was Ewart alone in this feeling. The Republican gubernatorial candidate in Tennessee opposed the bill, and Republican congressional candidates in North Carolina, Tennessee, and Virginia also attacked the Lodge proposal.[71]

When the Lodge bill did not pass in the U.S. Senate, mountain Republicans found themselves in a difficult position. The legislation had alienated many white voters in their districts, and since it had failed, blacks had no more protection than before. As a result the congressional elections of 1890 were a real setback for mountain Republicans. In the elections they lost five of the eight seats that they had held.[72] It is difficult to assess exactly how significant the election-law issue was in defeating the party. The Republicans were badly defeated everywhere in 1890, and it seems clear that mountain voters, like other voters across the nation, reacted to issues other than the Lodge bill. The election in the First Congressional District of Tennessee offers the best illustration of mountain Republicans' reactions to the Lodge bill. There, Alfred Taylor, a strong backer of the bill, was opposed by former congressman Roderick Butler for the Republican nomination. After a hotly contested primary campaign both men claimed to be the regular party nominee.[73] The Democrats in this strongly Republican district decided not to run a candidate and to allow the two men to split their own party. In September Butler, in an obvious political maneuver, attacked the Lodge bill and federal control of elections.[74] Thus, the Republican voters of the district had a choice of candidates from their own party who took opposite positions on the issue. The election returns gave Taylor a narrow victory and indicated that he had won about 80 percent of the Republican vote.[75] It would be safe to conclude, then, that although there was substantial opposition to the Lodge bill among the mountaineers, it was backed by a majority of mountain Republicans.

The failures of the 1890 campaign and further defeats in the 1892 election prompted a serious reevaluation of the party's position.[76] The Lodge bill was proving to be a serious political liability, and more and more mountain Republicans began to reject federal intervention in southern elections as a viable means of adding voters to the party.[77] The disenchantment with this approach to winning voters coincided with dissatisfaction with the bosses who had directed the party in the mountains during the 1880s. Between 1890 and 1894 all the old leaders were replaced by politicians who brought a new perspective to the party.

In each state the power struggle between the old and new leaders was relatively brief. John D. White, the eastern Kentucky mountain boss, was defeated by David Colson in an attempt to win a congressional seat in 1894. Although the party was divided after Colson's election, White's reign was over.[78] In East Tennessee the powerful Houk machine disintegrated quickly after the death of Leonidas Houk in 1891, and by 1894 H. Clay Evans had become the dominant Republican.[79] The Mahone machine simply lost control of the Republicans in southwestern Virginia. Mahone ordered the party not to run candidates in the elections of the early 1890s, but the mountain Republicans disobeyed, and twice-elected congressman James A. Walker became the new leader of the party in the region.[80] Probably the quietest and least bitter change came in West Virginia. Machine leader Nathan Goff was being pressed by wealthy businessman Stephen B. Elkins for control of the organization. In 1891 Elkins arranged to have President Benjamin Harrison offer Goff a federal judgeship, giving him a face-saving way to leave politics.[81] Elkins quickly took advantage of Goff's withdrawal and by 1892 had consolidated his hold on the party in West Virginia.

The same process occurred in North Carolina, but there were two separate stages to it. In 1889 and 1890 the boss, John J. Mott, lost control of federal patronage to John Baxter Eaves, who used his position as collector of internal revenue in the mountain region to take control of the party.[82] Eaves maintained this position until 1894, when he resisted attempts to fuse the Republicans and the Populists for electoral purposes.[83] At the state convention of that year Eaves was deposed, and a new group of Republican leaders emerged, led by mountain Republican Jeter C. Pritchard.[84] The immediate success of fusion at the polls and the election of Pritchard to the Senate ensured that the change in leadership would be permanent. Despite strenuous racist opposition from the Democrats in 1896 the fusion arrangement worked again, and the Populists and Republicans continued to control North Carolina.

The new leaders shared a common goal of bringing more white voters into the Republican party. They believed that the strategy of relying exclusively on blacks and former Unionists, as the bosses had done, could never make their party into the majority party in the upper South. The emphasis now would be exclusively on economic issues.[85] The advent of the "Democratic" depression of the 1890s made this a most fortuitous decision. In 1894 and 1896 the Republicans elected most of the congressmen from the mountain districts, they elected governors in four of the five upper South states in the same period, and for the first time since the Readjuster period in Virginia, four Republican senators represented the upper South in Washington, D.C.[86]

This successful new mountain Republican leadership tended to ignore the older groups in the party, particularly the blacks. Another significant factor was pushing the Republican leadership in the same direction: the rise of southern Negrophobia as a conscious intellectual and social movement.[87] Lynching continued at an ever-increasing rate, and rigid segregation became the goal of many white southerners. Ominously for the Republican party, the program of the southern racial purists demanded an end to Negro suffrage. The mountain Republican politicians thus were caught between their need to retain black votes and the need to appeal to white, racist Democrats. The Democrats offered blacks so little that Republican politicians for the most part believed it safe to ignore the blacks.

Mountain Republican leaders now thought that they had to convince whites that "the Republican party is not the negro party."[88] The result was an effort to construct a "lily-white" movement. Mountain politicians tended to avoid blacks in their campaign appearances and to deny them federal patronage, but their statements and campaign strategies contradict the idea that they wanted to end Negro suffrage. Black voters, despite their occasional challenges to the party leadership, were too valuable as allies to be disfranchised.

The new mountain leaders tried to ensure that black Republican voters had only a minimal voice in the party organization while they also sought to preserve the black right to vote. All white Republicans in the mountains seemed to agree that federal patronage should be distributed to whites only. One North Carolina black politician accurately observed that "the Republicans themselves don't think it wise for colored citizens to . . . fill state [or] federal positions."[89] Still, blacks were appointed or promised appointments by mountain politicians when it was deemed necessary. The Elkins machine in West Virginia delayed giving patronage to black applicants in some cases to test their loyalty to the organization.[90] These tactics were quite successful in ending a revolt by blacks in West Virginia against Elkins in 1900.[91]

Even if a black did manage to secure a political job from mountain Republicans, he still had to contend with Republicans who thought he should not have the position. In March 1892 many white Republican Internal Revenue

Service employees in the mountain counties in North Carolina refused to work with a recently appointed black worker and seriously disrupted the agency's operations.[92] A black deputy marshal in eastern Kentucky also found he had great difficulty performing his job because of the hostility of the mountaineers.[93] The dilemma faced by black appointees is well explained in the following letter from Charles M. Cansler, future educator and civil rights leader in East Tennessee: "I have recently been appointed to a position as substitute in the Railroad Mail Service for the line centering in Chattanooga Tenn. from the Civil Service examination of last August. Because of the existing prejudice on the part of the white clerks on these lines I have been unable to get such work as will enable me to secure a livelihood from this position."[94] It appears that for some mountain Republicans the assignment of even one office to a black Republican was too many.

Blacks were increasingly passed over as potential candidates for public office and were even discouraged from attending party conventions. The Kentucky Republican gubernatorial candidate in 1895, William O'Connell Bradley, was apparently willing to make patronage commitments to blacks before he was nominated to ensure that blacks would not demand a spot on the state ticket.[95] Blacks were excluded from Republican state conventions as early as 1888, and by 1900 North Carolina Republicans could boast that their state meeting "was a convention not only dominated by white men, but composed of white men."[96] Moving increasingly toward segregation within the party, mountain Republicans became enthusiastic supporters of social segregation in churches, schools, public facilities, and on public transportation.[97]

Mountain Republicans used other means to give the appearance of eliminating the black man from politics while still striving to preserve his right to vote. One of the more effective ways to accomplish this was to gerrymander black voters to prevent their candidates from winning in local elections. In Knoxville, Tennessee, for example, black voters made up 35 percent of the electorate, but they made up a majority of only one of the city's nine wards. The contrast between Wards 4 and 7 is particularly instructive. In the former only 165 white voters formed a majority, while in the latter 678 blacks were in the minority.

Another trick resorted to by mountain Republicans in an effort to minimize black participation in campaigns was to run candidates that seemed hostile to black interests. Southwestern Virginia mountain Republicans ran James A. Walker for Congress four times in the 1890s, although his record as a Confederate general and former Democrat made him unappealing to blacks.[98] North Carolina mountain Republicans, reacting to the increasing racism of the opposition, supported Daniel L. Russell for governor in 1896. He was quoted as saying that "the negroes of the South are largely savages."[99] The strategy behind Russell's nomination was explained by the candidate himself: "The Democrats will try the old dodge of trying the 'Color line' but it worries them to discover just how to do it. They been preaching . . . that Russell is dead against the negroes, that he favors white supremacy and that he is opposed to even the mildest form of negro government. Now they will proceed to prove that he is in favor of compelling every white woman to marry a negro, and that he himself is a mulatto. This is a rather heavy job for them, but not too big for them to attempt."[100] North Carolina black Republicans were so outraged by Russell's nomination that they called a convention to protest and to demand a new candidate.[101]

Two other techniques were used to deemphasize the presence of blacks in the Republican party. Kentucky Republicans in the gubernatorial and state campaign of 1895 simply refused to acknowledge the existence of black Republicans. The party's campaign committee would not work with blacks and forbade candidates to mention racial matters.[102] The advice seems to have been generally followed. Harvey S. Irwin, a candidate for state railroad commissioner, was asked in an open letter if he would vote to repeal the separate-but-equal railway coach law. Irwin refused to answer and continued his campaign as if the question had never been asked.[103] Gubernatorial candidate William O. Bradley withdrew from a series of joint debates with his Democratic opponent when racial issues began to dominate the discussions.[104] Blacks, angered by these snubs, formed the Kentucky Colored Democrat Club to force a change in the Republican campaign. Tennessee mountain Republicans developed the novel idea of voluntary black disfranchisement. In 1894 H. Clay Evans, the gubernatorial candidate, and his campaign manager, Newell Sanders, persuaded many blacks not to vote, in the expectation that this strategy would reduce the racial excitement and fraud perpetrated by the Democrats.[105] All of these elaborate strategies were aimed at convincing white voters that the Republican party was a white man's party while at the same time preserving the Negro's right to vote.

White mountain Republicans seemed willing to accept this solution to the racial situation within the party. The 1898 election in North Carolina offered the greater test of the willingness of white mountain Republicans to be identified with blacks as political allies. In this campaign the Democrats made a special effort to convince mountain voters of the evil results of black political advances made under the fusion government in that state.[106] Democratic state chairman Furnifold M. Simmons and *Raleigh News and Observer* editor Josephus Daniels directed the attack against black officeholders who had been elected since 1894. The two men launched a racist cartoon campaign in western North Carolina newspapers to ensure that even the illiterate would receive the message.[107] The climax of the bitter attack on fusion was a white man's convention at Goldsboro attended by more than eight thousand voters.[108] The mountain Republicans launched an equally racist counterattack that stopped short of demanding an end to black voting.[109] The percentages in table 12.2 indicate that mountain Republican voters accepted their leaders' position. Although the Republican percentage of the vote did decline in western North Carolina in 1898, the decrease was relatively small and followed the general four-year pattern of the entire mountain region. North Carolina mountain Republicans simply refused to be frightened by continued Negro participation in politics.

Table 12.2. Percentages of the Republican Vote in the Mountain Counties of the Upper South, 1896, 1898, and 1900

	1896	1898	1900
North Carolina	51.1	49.3	52.2
Virginia	51.7	48.1	49.2
Kentucky	59.7	50.2	57.8
Tennessee	65.8	57.9	56.7
West Virginia	53.5	51.9	55.1

Source: Computed from ICPR data.

Despite the efforts by mountain Republicans to conceal their dependence on black voters, Democratic attempts to disfranchise Negroes were successful in North Carolina and Virginia. The North Carolina legislature had framed a suffrage amendment to the state constitution in 1899 that would effectively eliminate most black voters. When the proposal was submitted to the voters in August 1900 the mountain Republican leaders vigorously opposed its approval.[110] Senator Pritchard and others concentrated their attack on the fact that despite the "grandfather clause" many poor whites would lose the right to vote.[111] So effective was this approach that the Democrats had to call the legislature into special session a few weeks before the voting and modify the amendment to answer Republican criticism.[112] Nor did the mountain Republicans abandon the black voter. The leading Republican newspaper in the western part of the state printed an article written by black editor Timothy Thomas Fortune opposing the amendment.[113] Mountain Republicans were willing to allow Democrats the right to prevent blacks from holding office, thereby ending the chance of "Negro domination," but were unwilling to lose their Negro support at the polls.[114] This position apparently satisfied white Republicans in the mountains, who voted overwhelmingly against the suffrage changes.[115] Virginia Democrats saved themselves the trouble of a public debate and vote by having a constitutional convention declare that a new suffrage amendment was valid without popular ratification.

In the other three states of the upper South, blacks remained as voters, and the working relationship between mountain Republicans and blacks continued. In West Virginia the Republican party maintained control of the state until the depression of the 1930s, with the black voter remaining a relatively loyal member of the party. Although the Republicans as a whole were in the minority in Kentucky and Tennessee, mountain Republicans prospered in the years after 1900. Consistently winning congressional races in both mountain regions, mountain Republicans, blacks, and Progressive Democrats combined to elect Progressive Republicans Benjamin W. Hooper of Tennessee and Augustus E. Willson of Kentucky governors of their respective states. Even in the now lily-white electorate of southwestern Virginia, Republicans enjoyed some success. Campbell Slemp and his son, Campbell Bascom Slemp, constructed a Republican machine in the Virginia mountains that controlled the Ninth Congressional District for nearly two decades. In Virginia and North Carolina, however, the old relationship between black and white Republicans was destroyed. With blacks no longer voters and still competitors for federal patronage, mountain Republicans in both states read them out of the party.

The general position of white mountain Republicans on race relations within the party in the last third of the nineteenth century was determined by the power of the black man as a voter. The relationship that developed in each state was deeply influenced by two factors that remained relatively constant throughout this period. In comparison to other white southerners, mountain whites did not live with a large black population, and this geographic and demographic fact made it possible for them to determine political affiliation on the basis of issues other than race. In addition, Negro voters proved to be extremely loyal to the Republican party and were too valuable as political allies to abandon. This did not mean that mountain Republicans viewed blacks as equals or that blacks necessarily had the right to run for and be appointed to office. But mountain Republicans did maintain that blacks had the basic right to vote Republican. The men who had proposed to "elevate mankind of all races and colors" clearly had forsaken that goal and had turned instead to the elevation of their own political ambitions.

NOTES

This essay first appeared in the *Journal of Southern History* 41 (1975): 473–95, and is reprinted here with the permission of the *Journal of Southern History*.

1. There have been no studies dealing exclusively with mountain Republican racial policies, but the following accounts offer some useful information on the topic: Vincent P. De Santis, *Republicans Face the Southern Question: The New Departure Years, 1877–1897* (Baltimore, 1959); Helen G. Edmonds, *The Negro and Fusion Politics in North Carolina, 1894–1901* (Chapel Hill, N.C., 1951); Stanley P. Hirshson, *Farewell to the Bloody Shirt: North Republicans and the Southern Negro, 1877–1893* (Bloomington, Ill., 1962); Ross A. Webb, *Benjamin Helm Bristow: Border State Politician* (Lexington, Ky., 1969); Charles E. Wynes, *Race Relations in Virginia, 1870–1902* (Charlottesville, Va., 1961); Carl N. Degler, "Black and White Together: Bi-Racial Politics in the South," *Virginia Quarterly Review* 47 (summer 1971): 421–44.

2. Thomas Settle Jr., speech, March 1867, Thomas Settle Jr. and Thomas Settle III Papers, Southern Historical Collection, University of North Carolina Library, Chapel Hill, N.C.

3. F.H. Pierpoint to Waitman T. Willey, March 29, 1866; H. Hagan to Willey, April 11, 1866, Waitman Thomas Willey Papers, West Virginia Collection, West Virginia University Library, Morgantown, W.Va.: R.F. Walker to William Mahone, Dec. 10, 1867, McGill-Mahone Papers, University of Virginia Library, Charlottesville, Va.; W.C. Ken to B.S. Hedrick, March 22, 1867, Benjamin Sherwood Hedrick Papers, Perkins Library, Duke University, Durham, N.C.

4. F.B. Hart to William Mahone, April 22, 1869, McGill-Mahone Papers.

5. Old soldier to ——, July 24, 1865, Thomas A.R. Nelson Papers, McClung Historical

Collection, Lawson McGhee Library, Knoxville, Tenn.; Leonidas C. Houk, To the Voters of the 17th Judicial Circuit of Tennessee, Feb. 14, 1866, Leonidas Campbell and John Chiles Houk Papers, McClung Historical Collection; G.M. Humphreys to W.T. Willey, March 7, 1867, Willey Papers; *Statesville American*, April 15, 1876; *Winston (N.C.) Union Republican*, Aug. 10, 1876.

6. Leonidas C. Houk, To the Voters of the 2nd Congressional District of Tennessee, Aug. 1, 1865, Houk Papers; Alexander H. Jones to Thaddeus Stevens, Jan. 4, 1867, James A. Padgett, ed., "Reconstruction Letters from North Carolina," *North Carolina Historical Review* 18 (April 1941): 191–92; William E. Stevenson to Arthur I. Boreman, March 8, 1869, William E. Stevenson Papers, West Virginia Department of Archives and History, Charleston, W. Va.; O.G. Schofield to William H.H. Flick, June 19, 1869, William Henry Harrison Flick Papers, West Virginia Collection, West Virginia University Library; William E. Stevenson to Francis H. Pierpoint, Sept. 20, 1869, Francis Harrison Pierpoint Papers, West Virginia Collection, West Virginia University Library; James W. Patton, *Unionism and Reconstruction in Tennessee, 1860–1869* (Chapel Hill, N.C., 1934), 101–2; E. Merton Coulter, *The Civil War and Readjustment in Kentucky* (Gloucester, Mass., 1966), 326.

7. Recent historical scholarship has demonstrated that while there was some opposition to slavery in the mountain regions of the South, it was not accompanied by sympathy for blacks as persons. George M. Fredrickson, *The Black Image in the White Mind: The Debate on Afro-American Character and Destiny: 1817–1914* (New York, 1971), 20; Gordon E. Finnie, "The Antislavery Movement in the Upper South before 1840," *Journal of Southern History* 35 (Aug. 1969): 331–39.

8. Frank Aglionby to [Mrs.] Aglionby, Oct. 30, 1859, Frances Yates Aglionby Papers, Perkins Library, Duke University.

9. *Knoxville Brownlow's Weekly Whig*, May 18, 1861 (cited hereinafter as *Knoxville Whig*).

10. Bryan Tyson to S.F.B. Morse, Nov. 16, 1863; Bryan Tyson, To His Excellency President Lincoln, Aug. 28, 1863, Bryan Tyson Papers, Perkins Library, Duke University; Arthur I. Boreman to Francis H. Pierpoint, Feb. 27, 1863, Pierpoint Papers; H. Hagans to Waitman T. Willey, Feb. 28, 1863; "Junious" to Willey, March 25, 1864; H. Dering to Willey, May 31, 1864, Willey Papers.

11. John B. Brownlow to Leonidas C. Houk, Feb. 8, 1867, Houk Papers.

12. "Several gentlemen have said to me 'rather than permit free negroes to vote and hold office, we are ready for another war.' I tell them, 'no.' Let us have peace. The last war nearly ruined us.—another will finish the job." R.M. Pearson to William L. Scott, July 16, 1868, William Lafayette Scott Papers, Perkins Library, Duke University.

13. Alexander Gates et al., to William L. Scott, May 31, 1871, Scott Papers.

14. R.F. Walker to William Mahone, May 16, 1869, William Mahone Papers, Perkins Library, Duke University; B.M. Kitchin et al., To the Republicans of Berkeley County, 1870, American Political Broadsides Collection, Rare Book Collection, Perkins Library, Duke University; Spencer Dayton to William H.H. Flick, July 6, 1870; William P. Hubbard to Flick, April 19, 1871, Flick Papers; *Knoxville Whig*, June 13, 1869; *Wheeling Intelligencer*, Sept. 1, 1869; *Louisville Commercial*, July 4, 1871.

15. *Maryville (Tenn.) Republican*, Oct. 23, 1869.

16. *Enquirer Manual and Political Register for 1870* (Cincinnati, 1870), 109.

17. *Congressional Globe*, 41 Cong., 2 Sess., 138 (Dec. 15, 1869).

18. S.H. Corn to William H.H. Flick, Dec. 18, 1870, Flick Papers.

19. William A. Russ Jr., "Radical Disfranchisement in North Carolina, 1867–1868," *North Carolina Historical Review* 11 (Oct. 1934): 281; *Tribune Almanac and Political Register for 1872* (New York, 1871), 69; *Asheville (N.C.) Pioneer*, Sept. 7, 1871; J.G. de Roulhac Hamilton, *Reconstruction in North Carolina* (New York, 1914), 537–48; *Wilmington (N.C.) Daily Journal*, May 23, 25, 1872.

20. *Tribune Almanac and Political Register for 1876* (New York, 1875), 81; John D. White to John M. Harlan, June 2, 1875, John Marshall Harlan Papers, Law School Library, University of Louisville, Louisville, Ky.

21. Jacob M. Thornburgh to Oliver P. Temple, Aug. 21, 1874, Oliver Perry Temple Papers, University of Tennessee Library, Knoxville, Tenn.; Charles G. Manning to Thomas Settle Jr., Nov. 22, 1875, Settle Papers; J.C. Ramsay to J.W. Douglas, Dec. 4, 1874; Ramsay to U.S.

Grant, Jan. 8, 1875, James Graham Ramsay Papers, Southern Historical Collection, University of North Carolina; *Maryville (Tenn.) Republican*, Sept. 22, 1874, supplement; *Statesville (N.C.) Landmark*, Nov. 21, 1874, March 1, 1875.

22. *Tribune Almanac*, 74, 82; *London (Ky.) Mountain Echo*, April 30, May 7, 14, 1875.

23. *Richmond Daily Whig*, Oct. 13, 1882; George R. Underwood to John C. Houk, Nov. 12, 1891, Houk Papers; P.H. McGill to Mahone, Oct. 17, 1886, Mahone Papers; Alfred Dockery to Thomas Settle Jr., Sept. 29, 1886, Settle Papers.

24. John C. Houk to H. Clay Evans, March 28, 1892; J.M. Homer memorandum, Sept. 22, 1894, Houk Papers.

25. The most powerful of these men were John Daugherty White of eastern Kentucky, Leonidas Campbell Houk of East Tennessee, John J. Mott of western North Carolina, and Nathan Goff of northwestern West Virginia.

26. De Santis, *Republicans Face the Southern Question*, 71–85.

27. Atkinson to William H.H. Flick, April 2, 1877, Flick Papers.

28. Arthur hoped to attract Independent Democrats to the party to offset Blaine's strength among regular Republicans in the South. For a more complete discussion of this point see Vincent P. De Santis, "President Arthur and the Movements in the South in 1882," *Journal of Southern History* 19 (Aug. 1953): 346–63.

29. Houk to Oliver P. Temple, April 30, 1883, Temple Papers.

30. *Memphis Appeal*, Aug. 28, 1882.

31. Ibid., Oct. 11, 1876.

32. *Knoxville Tribune*, Sept. 5, 1876; *Louisa (Ky.) Big Sandy News*, May 19, 1887; *London (Ky.) Mountain Echo*, May 19, 1882; *Memphis Weekly Appeal*, March 30, 1881; *Nashville Daily American*, March 9, 1884; *Statesville (N.C.) Landmark*, May 27, 1881, March 17, May 26, 1882; J.D. Alston et al., minutes of meeting, April 2, 1881, William Woods Holden Papers, Perkins Library, Duke University.

33. *Memphis Weekly Appeal*, March 30, 1881.

34. J.L. Randle to Houk, June 29, 1882; W.H. Dietz to Houk, July 20, 1882, Houk Papers.

35. Oliver P. Temple to Houk, July 12, 1882, Houk Papers..

36. Clipping, 1882, William Rule Papers, McClung Historical Collection.

37. *Wheeling Intelligencer*, Sept. 13, 1888.

38. *Weston (W.Va.) Republican*, Oct. 12, 1888.

39. *Wheeling Intelligencer*, March 28, 1876.

40. Typical lynchings of blacks in mountains are reported in *Knoxville Whig*, Feb. 14, 1866; *Wheeling Intelligencer*, Aug. 23, 1876, Aug. 31, Sept. 17, 1889, April 13, 1891; *Statesville (N.C.) Landmark*, Oct. 19, 1883, Sept. 19, 1889, Oct. 1, 1891; *Clinton (Tenn.) Weekly Gazette*, Aug. 4, 1892; *Big Stone Gap (Va.) Post*, Feb. 2, Sept. 28, 1893; *Louisa (Ky.) Big Sandy News*, Feb. 10, 1893; *Chattanooga Daily Times*, Feb. 12, 1894.

41. John B. Brownlow to Oliver P. Temple, Jan. 1, 1894, Temple Papers.

42. *Compendium of the Eleventh Census: 1890*, 3 vols. (Washington, D.C., 1892–1897), vol. 1: 487–89, 499–501, 506–7, 512–14.

43. Gordon B. McKinney, "Mountain Republicanism: 1876–1900" (unpublished Ph.D. diss., Northwestern University, 1971), 30, 58. This dissertation was subsequently published as *Southern Mountain Republicanism, 1865–1900* (Chapel Hill, N.C.: Univ. of North Carolina Press, 1978).

44. The mountain counties that had an increase in the percentage of blacks from 1870 to 1900 were: West Virginia: Barbour, Brooke, Cabell, Calhoun, Clay, Hancock, Harrison, Marion, Marshall, Ohio, Pocahontas, Randolph, Tucker, Tyler, Webster, Wetzel; Kentucky: Bell, Boyd, Harlan, Whitley, Wolfe; Tennessee: Cumberland, Hamilton, Morgan, Scott, Sullivan; North Carolina: Buncombe, Cleveland, Jackson, Rutherford, Transylvania; Virginia: Alleghany, Tazewell. *Compendium of the Eleventh Census*, vol. 1: 487–89, 499–501, 506–7, 512–14; Bureau of the Census, *Twelfth Census of the United States: 1900, Population*, pt. 1 (Washington, D.C., 1901), 540–41, 550–51, 556–57, 561–63.

45. *Compendium of the Eleventh Census*, vol. 1: 514; Bureau of the Census, *Twelfth Census: Population*, pt. 1, 563.

46. The white Republican share of the vote declined in Hamilton County from 35 percent in 1880 to 21 percent in 1900. These figures were computed using a method popularized by Allen W. Trelease in "Who Were the Scalawags?" *Journal of Southern History* 29 (Nov. 1963): 445–68.

47. The election returns for 1881 and 1882 were obtained from the Inter-University Consortium for Political Research, University of Michigan, Ann Arbor, Michigan (hereinafter referred to as ICPR). The author wishes to acknowledge aid that the consortium extended to him and the permission to use these data. The relationship between Readjusters and Virginia Republicans is demonstrated in William D. McIver to Mahone, Dec. 3, 1882; Fred G. Rogers to Mahone, Nov. 3, 1882; B.W. Clark to Mahone, March 28, 1882, Mahone Papers; *Woodstock Virginian*, May 19, 1882; *Richmond Whig*, Oct. 13, 1882.

48. John A. Brown to Mahone, March 29, 1888; Mahone interview, Jan. 18, 1889, Mahone Papers; *Richmond Whig*, April 1, 1881; *Memphis Weekly Appeal*, Aug. 10, 1882.

49. Coalition Rule in Danville, scrapbook, no. 31, p. 25, Mahone Papers.

50. C.S. Wingfield to Mahone, Nov. 2, 1883, Mahone Papers; John T.S. Melzer, "The Danville Riot, November 3, 1883" (unpublished M.A. thesis, University of Virginia, 1963), passim.

51. ICPR election data; scrapbook, no. 32, p. 7, Mahone Papers. The percentage of Republican vote did decline as many peripheral voters were drawn to the polls by the sensational campaign.

52. J.H. Ballard to Mahone, Nov. 8, 1883, Mahone Papers..

53. *Statesville (N.C.) Landmark*, Jan. 6, 1887.

54. Journal, J. Granville Leach Papers, North Carolina Division of Archives and History, Raleigh, N.C.

55. ICPR election data; *Wheeling Intelligencer*, Feb. 4, 28, 1890.

56. T.S. Riley to W.J.W. Cowden, Sept. 13, 1888, Nathan Goff Papers, West Virginia Collection, West Virginia University Library.

57. *Wheeling Intelligencer*, Feb. 2, 12, 23, March 5, 13, Sept. 9, 1889; *Weston (W.Va.) Republican*, March 16, 1889; February 8, 1890.

58. ICPR election data.

59. *Winston (N.C.) Union Republican*, April 25, 1889; *Wheeling Intelligencer*, Dec. 31, 1889.

60. *Cong. Record*, 51 Cong., 1 Sess., 6771 (June 30, 1890).

61. Houk, "Freedom of Election in the South," April 3, 1879, Houk Papers; *Wheeling Intelligencer*, Nov. 7, 1889.

62. *Wheeling Intelligencer*, March 6, 1890.

63. *Cong. Record*, 51 Cong., 1 Sess., 6769–71 (June 30, 1890).

64. *Wheeling Intelligencer*, May 24, 1890.

65. *Cong. Record*, 51 Cong., 1 Sess., 6929 (July 2, 1890).

66. Ibid., 6774 (June 30, 1890).

67. *Weston (W. Va.) Republican*, June 7, Aug. 2, 1890; *Johnson City (Tenn.) Comet*, Aug. 7, 1890; *Wheeling Intelligencer*, Aug. 21, 1890; *Winston (N.C.) Union Republican*, Sept. 4, 1890.

68. *Cong. Record*, 51 Cong., 1 Sess., 6940–41 (July 2, 1890).

69. Ibid., 6688 (June 28, 1890).

70. Ibid., 6689 (June 28, 1890).

71. D.C. Kelley to Will A. McTeer, Sept. 29, 1890, Will H. McTeer Papers, McClung Historical Collection; John C. Houk to Leonidas C. Houk, Aug. 4, 1890, Houk Papers; *Winston (N.C.) Union Republican*, Jan. 16, Oct. 2, 1890; *Asheville (N.C.) Asheville Landmark*, July 10, Oct. 9, 1890; *Big Stone Gap (Va.) Post*, Aug. 22, Sept. 26, 1890; *Wheeling Intelligencer*, Sept. 15, 1890; *Johnson City (Tenn.) Comet*, Sept. 25, 1890.

72. Outspoken supporters of the Lodge bill, Taylor and Houk were reelected despite racist opposition. *Clinton (Tenn.) Weekly Gazette*, Oct. 30, 1890; *Chattanooga Daily Times*, Nov. 1, 1890.

73. *Johnson City (Tenn.) Comet*, April 17, 1890.

74. Ibid., Sept. 25, 1890.

75. ICPR election data. Using Lewis Baxter's vote as the Republican gubernatorial candidate and assuming that no Democrats would vote for the advocate of the Lodge bill, the Republicans divided approximately as follows: Taylor 11,500; Butler 2,200.

76. For a description of this process at the national level see Hirshson, *Farewell to the Bloody Shirt*, 236–58.

77. Augustus E. Willson, circular letter, Nov. 4, 1892, Augustus Everett Willson Papers, Collections of the Filson Club, Louisville Ky.; D.M. Furches to Thomas Settle III, July 29, 1892, Settle Papers; *Weston (W.Va.) Republican*, Jan. 24, 1891; *Winston (N.C.) Union Republican*, June 11, 1891; *Louisa (Ky.) Big Sandy News*, Oct. 21, 1892.

78. J.K. Watkins et al., circular letter, Oct. 8, 1894, scrapbook, David Grant Colson Papers, Southern Historical Collection; ICPR election data.

79. *Chattanooga Daily Times*, Aug. 23, 1894.

80. *Big Stone Gap (Va.) Post*, Dec. 6, 1894.

81. *Wheeling Intelligencer*, Dec. 17, 1891.

82. *Statesville (N.C.) Landmark*, Sept. 4, 1890.

83. Eaves to Richmond Pearson, April 10, 1894; Marion Butler to Pearson, Richmond M. Pearson Papers, Southern Historical Collection; Eaves to the Republicans of North Carolina, June 8, 1894; H.L. Grant, circular letter, July 12, 1894, Settle Papers.

84. *Winston (N.C.) Union Republican*, Sept. 6, 1894.

85. John W. Mason to Thomas E. Davis, Aug. 6, 1892, Letterbook, John W. Mason Papers, West Virginia Collection, West Virginia University Library; Charles F. Ballard to Augustus E. Willson, Feb. 29, 1892; Willson, circular letter, Nov. 4, 1892, Willson Papers; *Wheeling Intelligencer*, June 4, 1891; *Winston (N.C.) Union Republican*, June 11, 1891; *Clinton (Tenn.) Weekly Gazette*, Dec. 1, 1892; *Louisa (Ky.) Big Sandy News*, Feb. 23, 1894; *Big Stone Gap (Va.) Post*, Aug. 13, 1896.

86. The Republican governors included Henry Clay Evans of Tennessee in 1894, who would eventually be denied his victory by the highly partisan work of a Democratic legislature; William O'Connell Bradley of Kentucky in 1895; Daniel Lindsay Russell of North Carolina and George Wesley Atkinson of West Virginia in 1896; William S. Taylor of Kentucky in 1899, who like Evans would be unseated by a Democratic legislature; and Albert Blakeslee White of West Virginia in 1900. The Republican senators included Jeter Connelly Pritchard of North Carolina, elected in 1894 and 1896; Stephen Benton Elkins of West Virginia, elected in 1894 and 1900; William Joseph DeBoe of Kentucky, elected in 1897; and Nathan Bay Scott of West Virginia, elected in 1898.

87. Fredrickson, *Black Image*, 256–82.

88. Clipping, 1879, scrapbook, Willson Papers.

89. M.N. Corbitt to Thomas Settle III, July 26, 1892, Settle Papers.

90. S.B. Avis to Elkins, April 27, 1900, Stephen Benton Elkins Papers, West Virginia Collection.

91. H.F. Gamble to Albert B. White, Feb. 7, 1900; Daniel W. Shaw, *The Second Emancipation of the Negro*, Aug. 16, 1900, Albert Blakeslee White Papers, West Virginia Collection; H.C. Duncan to A. Brooks Fleming, March 10, 1900, Aretas Brooks Fleming Papers, West Virginia Collection; H.M. Adams to Stephen B. Elkins, March 20, 1900; L.R. LeSage to Elkins, March 20, 1900; Phil Waters to Elkins, March 22, 1900, Elkins Papers.

92. John W. Mason to W.W. Rollins, March 20, 1892, Letterbook, Mason Papers.

93. *Mt. Vernon (Ky.) Signal*, July 16, 1897.

94. Cansler to Leonidas C. Houk, Jan. 2, 1891, Houk Papers.

95. *Louisa (Ky.) Big Sandy News*, Aug. 2, 1895.

96. *Asheville Citizen*, July 29, 1888; *Winston (N.C.) Union Republican*, May 10, 1900.

97. Clipping, Aug. 27, 1895, scrapbook, William O'Connell Bradley Papers, University of Kentucky Library, Lexington, Ky.; *Wheeling Intelligencer*, Feb. 20, 1892; *Big Stone Gap (Va.) Post*, Oct. 18, 1894; *Louisa (Ky.) Big Sandy News*, Aug. 30, 1895.

98. *Big Stone Gap (Va.) Post*, Sept. 6, 1894.

99. *Winston (N.C.) Union Republican*, July 26, 1888.

100. Russell to J.H. Ramsay, May 27, 1896, Ramsay Papers.

101. James E. Shepard to Thomas Settle III, May 19, 1896; M.N. Corbitt to Settle, May 27, 1896; To the People of North Carolina, June 6, 1896, Settle Papers.

102. "The Republican Campaign of Kentucky, 1895," unpublished manuscript, George Davidson Todd Papers, Collections of the Filson Club.

103. Clipping, June 30, 1895, scrapbook, Bradley Papers.

104. "Republican Campaign of Kentucky, 1895," Todd Papers.

105. Rufus Terral, *Newell Sanders: A Biography* (Kingsport, Tenn., 1985), 81–82; Benjamin W. Hooper, *The Unwanted Boy: The Autobiography of Governor Ben W. Hooper*, ed. Everett R. Boyce (Knoxville, Tenn., 1963), 28.

106. *Statesville (N.C.) Landmark*, Oct. 4, 25, 28, Nov. 1, 1898.

107. Ibid., Nov. 1, 1898.

108. Ibid., Nov. 3, 1898.

109. *Winston (N.C.) Union Republican*, Sept. 1, 8, 29, Oct. 13, 20, 27, 1898.

110. Ibid., Jan. 11, 25, March 1, April 19, May 17, 24, 1900.

111. Ibid., March 11, May 24, 1900.

112. Ibid., June 21, 1900.

113. Ibid., April 26, 1900.

114. Ibid., Jan. 25, 1900.

115. *Statesville (N.C.) Landmark*, Aug. 15, 1900.

13

NEGOTIATING THE TERMS OF FREEDOM

The Quest for Education in an African American Community in Reconstruction North Georgia

JENNIFER LUND SMITH

When the long anticipated "Day of Jubilo" arrived in Lumpkin County, Georgia, fewer than five hundred African Americans were living in the area. Because of their small numbers, freedmen and freedwomen in Lumpkin County were not fawned over by the bevy of missionary groups that headed south after the war, nor were they the intense focus of Reconstruction politicians. Unlike freed people in Georgia's cities, like Atlanta and Savannah, or its low country, where slaves had been numerous, African Americans in Lumpkin County could not rally in large numbers to attempt to force change. They could not even boast an established antebellum elite; in 1860 the free black population consisted of thirty-seven illiterate farmers who owned almost no land and little personal property.[1]

Despite their small numbers and lack of experience, the freed people in this small mountain community used the resources available to them and skillfully negotiated with Lumpkin County's leading white citizens as they sought to define their freedom. Rather than challenging the social and economic structure of their time and place, they used the paternalistic ethos of the white elite to their advantage.

Located at the southern end of the Blue Ridge Mountains, the area that became Lumpkin County had become famous for its gold deposits in the early 1830s. To facilitate and ensure the success of the nascent mining industry in the area, the federal government mounted a massive and lethally effective campaign to remove the Cherokees from the land in the 1820s and 1830s. The effort enabled wealthy speculators and starry-eyed hopefuls alike to tear into the mountains to extract its precious metals.

Gold was Lumpkin County's raison d'être. Its discovery in 1828 and an elaborate land lottery designed to redistribute Cherokee lands attracted a population of independent miners, land speculators, and large-scale investors. Mines such as the Calhoun Mine, the Findley Mine, and the Free Jim Mine forever changed the landscape of the mountains. Enough settlers had flooded into the area by 1832 that the state legislature formally recognized the organization of Lumpkin County. The terrain of the new county encompassed mountainous peaks and valleys covered with dense foliage, as well as more hospitable and fertile areas in the lower elevations. Soon after Georgians embraced Lumpkin County as an official sector of the state, Dahlonega was designated the county seat. The village exemplified the "boomtown" atmosphere of so many mining towns. In this remote area, inhabitants found entertainment in courting "fancy ladies," inebriation, and the saloons that catered to both. Three years later Congress named Dahlonega the site of a branch mint.[2]

In 1875 an old miner fondly recalled the atmosphere of the county's mining heyday. He reminisced, "Scarcely a stream in the whole country but what was thronged with miners, delving after the precious metal, while the hills and valley were made to reverberate with the busy rattle of machinery, and clinking of the pick and shovel."[3]

African Americans arrived in Lumpkin County, then Cherokee lands, along with other hopefuls of the 1829 gold rush who swarmed into the area with fantasies to rival that of Hernando Cortés's "El Dorado." Contemporaries included African Americans in their descriptions of these "twenty-niners," descriptions that also included adjectives like "drunken" and "malicious" and nouns like "thieves, gamblers and murderers."[4] Certainly, some free black people did join this "lawless, ungovernable community" to try their luck at mining, but most African Americans who came to the area were brought as slaves.[5]

Mining could be profitable, but it was grueling work. The job entailed digging with picks and shovels through "five to ten feet to the gravel, which was about one foot thick." The gravel and dirt was then "shoveled into a trough . . . with holes in it" that was "rocked like a cradle, under a stream of water, till only the black sand and gold were separated from the gravel and dirt." Only then could the gold be "panned out."[6]

To perform the more arduous labor-intensive tasks that mining required, many operators turned to slaves. John Calhoun, the U.S. senator from South Carolina and erstwhile vice president of the Union, who owned one of the most productive mines in the area, transported his own slaves from South Carolina to work in his mines during the plantation's off-season.[7] Other miners likewise came to the area, bringing with them varying numbers of slaves. Mine owners were soon placing announcements in the newspapers for "negro men" to work in the mines; one newspaper ran an advertisement offering ten dollars a month for "strong negro men." These offers enticed many slave owners from the cotton belt to rent their slaves to the mines when they were not needed at home.[8]

The labor needs of the mines created a relatively transitory slave population in Lumpkin County until the 1840s, when the use of slaves declined. By then, slave owners began to realize that sending their slaves into the dangerous conditions in the mines for profit led to diminishing returns. Poor treatment by mine owners who had no vested interest in their workforce and the dangers of collapsing tunnels caused an increasingly high death rate for leased slaves. Additionally, David Williams, author of *The Georgia Gold Rush*, notes that "local residents were uncomfortable with the presence of a large slave population in the vicinity, and mine operators usually preferred free labor."[9]

A small number of free black people lived in Lumpkin County during the antebellum period. A few worked in the mines during the 1840s and 1850s. One exceptional free black man, James Bosclair, prospered and became fairly wealthy during this period. He had come to Dahlonega from Augusta and had opened a modest cake and fruit shop, but by 1845, "Free Jim," as he was called, owned one thousand dollars in bank stock and eight hundred dollars in town property. He had discovered a vein on some property in town, and through his guardian, J.J. Singleton, a politician, fellow miner, and the first superintendent of the U.S. Mint in Dahlonega, Bosclair purchased the land and, later, several other lots as well. In addition to mining, Bosclair owned a general store, an icehouse, and a saloon. Despite his relative wealth for a black man in Georgia, California, with its tales of gold veins and its new status as a "free" state, lured him away in 1850.[10]

Of the thirty-seven free black people living in Lumpkin County in 1860, only three of the men owned any land. The heads of household all farmed. Farming was an exhausting profession anywhere, but the mountain soil that yielded a crop only reluctantly made it an even more difficult occupation in Lumpkin County. In addition to subsistence farming these men may have grown some cotton, but primarily for household use. Certainly less common in the mountains was rice cultivation, although 219 pounds of rice were produced in Lumpkin County in 1860. One Lumpkin woman whose parents had been slaves recalled that in the postwar era she and her family continued to "raise rice" in a "swampy area" near their home. Whatever crops these farmers planted, they probably panned a bit of gold or spent time in the mines as well, as did many farmers in the gold region. The few free black women in Lumpkin County "kept house," as the census recorded, working on behalf of their own families in their homes.[11]

As elsewhere in Georgia, the majority of black people who lived in Lumpkin County were slaves. In 1860 the slave population in the county was 431. The majority of the residents of the mountain county owned no slaves at all. Among those who did, most possessed fewer than six slaves, although four individuals claimed more than twenty slaves and hence could officially be considered "planters."[12]

Despite their small numbers, black residents of Lumpkin County developed a sense of community. As with many slave "communities," their community centered on the church. Before the Civil War, slaves and free black people in Lumpkin County attended church in the gallery of the white Dahlonega Baptist Church. James Bosclair was one of its members, as were Hannah Bosclair and Hannah Grant. Bosclair lost his membership for a time for "selling goods and liquor" at his saloon on Sundays, but he was invited back into the fold about a year later.[13] On Sunday afternoons, after the morning service, slaves and free people observed the Sabbath in their own fashion, led by a black minister. The law required that a white person be present during this ceremony, which no doubt tempered the proceedings, but the service was still quite distinct from the morning ritual. The black preachers were men like Nicholas Chubb, a freeman and a blacksmith by trade, who was ordained in the Baptist church in 1847.[14] A white observer recorded that in these ceremonies the black ministers exhibited their "own way and style" and indicated that the black Baptists responded with a great deal more "singing and shouting" than did their white counterparts.[15]

In 1852, the members of the Baptist African Church received a rather unusual endowment. That year, Alexander Duncan, a white carpenter residing in Dahlonega, deeded in trust a piece of land to the "members of the Baptist African Church," provided they build a church on the property, which they did.[16] While possession of their own church building offered the members of the Baptist African Church a significant amount of autonomy, restrictions placed on them provided a constant reminder that white men retained ultimate control. To keep the church land they had to comply with the stipulations of the trust, set by Alexander Duncan, that a white person monitor their service and that church memberships remain with the white-controlled Dahlonega Baptist Church.[17]

It is not surprising then that following emancipation, African Americans chose to separate themselves from the Dahlonega Baptist Church to form the Baptist African Church. This decision created friction among the African American Baptists and between the white and black parishioners. The white Baptists were reluctant to relinquish their supervision of the Baptist African Church and refused to surrender the letters of membership that would signify complete separation. In reaction, the members of the Baptist African Church split on how to proceed with creating an independent church. One faction, led by Rev. Sam Burt, appealed to Gen. F. Prince Salm in Atlanta to intervene on their behalf. Salm, a Prussian-born professional soldier who had offered his services to the Union army during the Civil War and who was later stationed in Atlanta as an agent of the Freedmen's Bureau, agreed to use his authority to order the Dahlonega Baptist Church to release its African American members. But upon returning to Dahlonega with Salm's order, Burt met with some skepticism.[18]

Daniel Keith was one of the church members concerned with Burt's actions. Offering an alternative to Burt's antagonistic approach, Keith emerged as one of the leaders of the African American community in Dahlonega. Before emancipation, Keith had been the slave of Harrison W. Riley, one of the wealthiest men in the region.[19] After the war, Keith, a mulatto, served the community as a minister, in addition to supporting his large family as a farm laborer. In 1870 Keith owned no land, but his personal property amounted to $200, making him one of the wealthier black men in Lumpkin County. By 1878 he had acquired forty acres of land worth $250.[20] In many ways Keith fit

A black prayer service in Clarkesville, Georgia, 1870. (From Edward King, *The Southern States of North America*, vol. 3 [1875])

the profile of African American leaders during the Reconstruction era: though illiterate, he was a minister, and he was a man of relative means and light skin.

Keith took a copy of Salm's order to Dahlonega native William P. Price, a white lawyer and a member of the Dahlonega Baptist Church. In the years after the war Price served in the Georgia state House and Senate, and in 1870 north Georgians sent him to the U.S. Congress.[21] On the issue pertaining to the church, Price counseled restraint and arranged for those who were "worthy" to receive their letter of transfer. He also persuaded a "presbytery of white preachers and deacons" to "constitute them into a separate body." The bulk of the congregation agreed to follow Keith and Price's plan of conciliation.[22]

In the matter of establishing an independent church, freed people in Lumpkin County set a precedent for how they would achieve their collective goals. They wisely chose a course that did not alienate their white neighbors. By including William Price in the process, they soothed the anxieties of white Baptists who felt uneasy about an independent African American church. Keith and his faction indulged the white men's paternalistic posturing, and in return they not only realized their objective but also received the blessing of influential white citizens in the county. By intuition or by design, Keith and his adherents realized the value in allowing the existing white elite a voice in their former slaves' actions; this fostered a perception of participation that made the white elite less likely to resist the changes initiated by emancipation. And occasionally it flattered them into assisting the African American community to achieve its aims.

While the freed people fought for control of the spiritual body of the church, they were simultaneously involved in a struggle for the physical "body" of the church and the land on which it stood. Following the war, Alexander Duncan decided that he wanted his land back. He based his postbellum right to the land on the fact that the congregation had abandoned the church "as a house of worship" during the war, and hence they had defaulted on the terms of the trust. He took possession of the church building and refused the members entry. Not willing to accept his claim, the members of the church used the courts to challenge Duncan's title to the land. The struggle to keep the land engaged the freed people in a costly (for them) court battle, and the efforts they underwent to retain the land demonstrate how important it was to them.

Duncan left no explanation for why he deeded the land to slaves, but his reasons may have stemmed from his close relationship with Hannah Grant, a free black woman and a member of the Baptist African Church. One contemporary referred to her as his cook, but he allowed that the relationship was more intimate than that, and it seems that two children resulted from their union. Hannah Grant was also James Bosclair's sister, and in the 1870s her daughter Mary Ann is referred to as Bosclair's heir in the deed books. What is clear is that although Duncan's generosity extended to the black people in the county while they were slaves, he was not as sanguine about allowing them to own the property as freed people.[23]

To represent them, the freed people once again turned to William Price, who agreed to take the case for a fee of fifty dollars. Ultimately, the Superior Court of Lumpkin County awarded the land to the freed people.[24] Before making its decision, the jury was treated to the judge's enigmatic observation that "the negro had lost nothing by his emancipation; that he not only kept whatever rights had been given him during his enslavement, but reaped the benefit of everything that came to him by emancipation." Judge Harrell then demanded that the jury make its decision right in the jury box, without the benefit of further discussion.[25] To secure their church land, the freed people had exploited accessible resources: in this case, William Price and the court system. To be sure, they took the case to court after Congressional Reconstruction was in motion, which increased the likelihood that they would win. Although they had won their case, their inability to pay the solicitor's fee would once again put their claim to the land in jeopardy.

The church and the land surrounding it represented a potent manifestation of freedom not only in regard to land-ownership and autonomy, but also as a symbol of education. Soon after the war ended, the church building began to serve as a schoolhouse. The impetus to establish a school arose from freedmen who were employed by the mining companies. Recognizing that few, if any, African Americans in the county had the expertise to organize a school and teach in it, a group of miners approached Amory Dexter, a superintendent for the Dahlonega Mining Company at the time, to request formal schooling for their children. Dexter, a Massachusetts-born ex-Confederate, took up their cause.[26] Acting on the appeal of the mine laborers, Dexter turned to W.J. Wooten, a white Baptist minister in his late twenties who had already established Sabbath schools for the freed people in Dahlonega. Encouraged by Dexter's confidence that they would be able to solicit outside assistance, Wooten opened a day school, offering morning classes for children and evening classes for adults. By the summer of 1867 he claimed that eighty students filled his school.[27]

Dexter and Wooten pushed hard to establish the school in Dahlonega and to procure funding. Dexter appealed to some "Friends at the North" for donations apparently with some, if limited, success. They sent a box of books and, eventually, three hundred dollars. Dexter and Wooten hoped to maintain the school free of charge for their students, but by the summer of 1867 they had expended their funds. In an attempt to keep the school afloat, Wooten began to charge adult students; he asked one dollar a month from males and fifty cents from females. He noted wryly that they were "very eager to register but slow in paying."[28] Dexter confirmed the students' inability to pay tuition, explaining "the times are dull + their wages low." [29]

After Dexter and Wooten had exhausted the three hundred dollars from Dexter's northern connections, they turned to the Freedmen's Bureau. When Congress divided the South into military districts in the spring of 1867, Gen. John D. Pope, head of the Third District, comprising Georgia, Alabama, and Florida, chose six cities in Georgia as important bases; Dahlonega was one of these. He stationed troops at the U.S. Mint building there. In August Federal troops began to appoint civil officers in Lumpkin county. Though they chose local persons for the posts, the presence of the troops caused tension. But it may also have been the proximity of the troops that emboldened African Americans in the mines to consider asking for a school and that prompted Amory Dexter to ask for the Freedmen's Bureau's support.[30]

In a letter to G.L. Eberhart, the Freedmen's Bureau's state superintendent of education until the summer of 1867, Dexter explained that the African Americans required only forty to forty-five dollars a month to pay a teacher, rent a schoolhouse, and provide lights for the night school. He asked the Freedmen's Bureau to provide aid to pay a teacher and to eventually build an inexpensive schoolhouse. The building in which African American children in Dahlonega received their education was less than optimal. It was a twenty-five-by-thirty-foot edifice with no windows. In August 1868, fifty-seven students attended the school.[31] Ultimately, Dexter hoped to build a school on some land in town where the abandoned U.S. Mint stood. In the fall he began laying plans to petition the government for a half-acre of U.S. Mint lands on which to build the school.[32]

Dexter also attempted to engage the support of the local population. In September 1867, after receiving notice that the Freedmen's Bureau could not lend any aid that year, he attempted to create a board of education in the county, apparently on the advice of E.A. Ware, Georgia's state superintendent of education. Whether or not Dexter included the freed people in this endeavor he did not specify, but he noted that "these things have to be arranged slowly + cautiously up here, as in this section the whites are far the most numerous."[33] He claimed that his goal was to "see a large public school here for all colors." Shortly thereafter, however, he abandoned the project and left Dahlonega to follow a "new branch of business," taking his organizational and fund-raising expertise with him.[34]

Sustaining the school was a time-consuming affair, and after Dexter's departure, Wooten undertook the responsibility on behalf of his students, who lacked the skills and the time. They relied on Wooten to plead their case on paper to the Freedmen's Bureau, and while they struggled to feed their families, Wooten contended with the difficulties involved in the upkeep of the school: insufficient funding, meager supplies, sporadic attendance, an inadequate building, and the lack of a permanent location.

Wooten seems to have taken a genuine interest in the freed people. John D. Wilkens wrote to E.A. Ware on Wooten's behalf, describing him as a "clergyman zealous in his work for the colored people," and he added that Wooten had been "ostracised [sic] by his former friends for such zeal."[35] To be sure, Wooten earned his livelihood from his position as a teacher, but it was not a particularly secure one. In 1867 he began writing numerous letters to the Freedmen's Bureau asking for assistance; much of the text describes his inability to support his family on the money he was able to collect from his students.[36] In August 1867 he was able to raise only sixteen dollars, a far cry from the forty dollars that Dexter had estimated as their costs. By February of the next year his pupils were collectively two hundred dollars in arrears; and Wooten and his wife had just added another child to their family. Yet he persevered in his work; at the beginning of 1869 he reported to the Freedmen's Bureau that he would be starting the winter term despite the lack of financial support.[37]

Wooten claimed to be more than just a temporal guide for the ex-slaves. He reported that at the war's end he began "acting as spiritual leader" of the freed people of Lumpkin County. M.R. Archer, the Freedmen's Bureau agent in Dahlonega, reported that Wooten preached to the freed people every Sunday.[38] It seems doubtful, however, that after taking the pains to separate from the white Baptist church the freed people considered Wooten their spiritual leader; it may be that he perceived himself as a sort of adviser to the nascent Baptist African Church. And while he may have been ostracized by some white Dahlonegans, he was elected minister of the Dahlonega Baptist Church in 1867, at which time he was "knee deep" in actively promoting education for the freed people.[39]

The dilapidation of the school building and its maintenance costs were constant themes in Wooten's letters to the Freedmen's Bureau. Before the courts had settled the dispute involving the church land, Wooten had rented the church building from Alexander Duncan for nine dollars a month. The building, which had been stripped during the war, was drafty, and as winter approached Wooten informed the Freedmen's Bureau that he would have to close the school unless "other arrangement about a school room" could be made.[40]

The court's ruling on the church land, while a legal victory, had been materially hollow; a lawyer's lien had been placed on the land to ensure payment.[41] In an attempt to keep the land the freed people concentrated their economic attention on paying off that lien and "exerted themselves very much to raise the money to pay off the Lawyers claim on the house." Their best efforts yielded only five dollars. Their focus on retaining the land rather than on paying for schools suggests how important that church and owning the piece of land were to them. Their inability to raise more than five dollars illustrates the extent of their poverty.[42]

In 1868 M.R. Archer turned his attention to establishing more schools in Lumpkin County, as well as in contiguous Dawson and White Counties. The poverty that he encountered among black and white people astonished him. He asked his superiors to send books, because none of his prospective pupils either owned or could afford any. He remarked, "I was not aware of the extent of this destitution until the effort was made to organize schools."[43]

In Lumpkin County the freed people's economic situation continued to worsen. In 1868 and 1869 a number of mining ventures failed, leaving many freed people jobless and even less able to pay for education. Wooten explained to the Freedmen's Bureau that the freed people had "a mind to [pay] but they are not able the most of them even to get a living. This is owing to the failure of the mines throwing a great many of them out of employment."[44] By the fall of 1869 Wooten reported that "most of the heads of families have had to go to the RR for work," probably in Gainesville, an entire day's journey from Dahlonega at the time.[45] The next year, he asked the Freedmen's Bureau if there were not any benevolent societies that could help the African American families "in and around this place suffering for bread," adding, "It is *alarming* to see them in this condition."[46]

While focusing their assets on the church land, the freed people gambled that the Freedmen's Bureau would offer assistance for their education. And in 1868 the Bureau did begin to aid the school in Dahlonega. It contributed twenty-five dollars to Wooten's salary, which was also subsidized by a charitable organization in Pittsburgh. William Price had also contacted the Freedmen's Bureau on the freed people's behalf. He described their financial plight and asked the bureau to pay off the lien on the school to avoid the "judicial sale of [the] property." The bureau seems not to have acquiesced, but it did contribute five dollars a month to rent school space from William Price, money that Wooten felt could be better used to subsidize tuition.[47]

Wooten's school was not the only school available to African Americans in the county. Following the war, at least one school existed outside of the town limits. In 1949 Amanda Green recalled that, when she was ten years old, the war ended and she began to attend a school at Cavender's Creek, on the eastern side of the county. An older white man, who Amanda claimed "didn't know so much," taught classes in an "old log house with a big fireplace in it."[48] Her reminiscence also alludes to the existence of other schools.

In addition, by 1868 three Sabbath schools existed in the county, encompassing twenty-four teachers and 225 students. No information about these Sabbath schools exists, which is unfortunate; judging by their large student bodies, they reached and influenced many more people than did Wooten. The records are also frustratingly silent on the identities of the teachers. As reports to the Freedmen's Bureau indicated that white sentiment about education for African Americans ranged from indifference to hostility, it must be assumed that they were written by African Americans.[49]

By the beginning of 1869 attendance at Wooten's school had dwindled to thirty students, and by the spring he was asking J.R. Lewis, then head of the Freedmen's Bureau in Georgia, if he knew "any other field where the colored people need a School and would Support a teacher?"[50] Just when it seemed he would have to close his school forever, Wooten found the perfect school building, the old U.S. Mint. The bulk of the Federal troops had abandoned the post in the spring of 1869, leaving the building vacant for a school.[51] Unfortunately, Wooten's students enjoyed their new location for a brief time only. The mint was slated for auction at the beginning of 1870. The lack of a reasonable bid granted Wooten and his scholars a temporary stay, but Wooten began to search for other options.[52]

The Freedmen's Bureau had offered to help build a schoolhouse if Wooten and his students could obtain land. Once again it was William Price who intervened. In February 1870, Price offered a piece of land for the school in an area east of town known as Crane's Hill. Excitedly, Wooten informed the Freedmen's Bureau that he planned to deed the land to the American Baptist Missionary Society, with which he had recently aligned himself.[53] Instead, Price deeded it to three African American trustees whom he charged to use the land "for the education of freedmen, and children irrespective of race or color," by which he meant it was to be a school for black children.[54] The arrangement suited Price, who was by this time a member of the U.S. Congress and aspiring to establish a college on the grounds of the former mint.[55]

Price named Daniel Keith as one of the trustees, as he also did Henry Castleberry. Like Keith, Castleberry was a mulatto, a property owner, and one of the wealthier African Americans in the county. By 1878 he, too, owned forty acres of land, contiguous to Keith's, on the western edge of the county. The other trustee was Thomas Samuels. Considerably less information exists about Samuels, but he was not a wealthy man, and he owned no land. While only Wooten's correspondence with the Freedmen's Bureau survives, surely these three gentlemen, who had an established relationship with Price, and whose names appear on the deed, played a large role in the negotiations regarding the property transfer.[56]

Price's offer did not come free: it cost the freed people fifty dollars and the promise that they would "never make any claim to, or seek to enter any colored pupils, in the event the mint" became the college of Price's vision. The trustees accepted these terms in order to obtain the much needed school building for African American children.[57]

With the land secured, the Freedmen's Bureau approved nine hundred dollars for the erection of the school building, which doubled as the First Baptist Church.[58] Wooten arranged for the contractors and monitored the building's progress. He had hoped to secure an African American reported to be a "splendid carpenter" to build the school for six hundred dollars, but the Freedmen's Bureau's requirement of a "bond and security &c." precluded the employment of any black carpenter. Instead, Gilbert Parker erected the school at a cost of $825.[59]

Wooten was probably the first person to teach in the building, but by 1875 he had left the field and was working as a colporteur for the American Tract Society.[60] Amanda Green remembered that when she started attending the school in town a white woman was employed as the teacher. But Cora Harris probably only taught because she was desperate. She had married a northerner who had withheld from her the information that he was already married. Green commented that when "he went back North and left her with a little girl . . . she had to do something for a living."[61]

Between 1870 and 1886, the number of schools in Lumpkin County vacillated between one and four, then stayed at four until after the turn of the century. During the same period, the number of schools available to white students was between twenty-nine and thirty-seven.[62] In 1875, 1,620 white children and 148 African American children attended school in Lumpkin County. But the number of illiterate white people between the ages of ten and eighteen was 224; it was 35 for black children of the same age. Roughly 14 percent of white, school-aged children were illiterate; the corresponding number for African American children was about 24 percent.[63] But, in Lumpkin County, these figures may exaggerate the difference between education for black and white children. In fact, in Lumpkin County, the parity in education may actually have been greater than in other places in Georgia.

Because of the general poverty in the mountain area, schools for black as well as white children suffered. In Lumpkin County, the collapse of the mining industry further depressed the economy. In 1874 William Price made a tour of several northeastern counties, including Lumpkin, to assess why illiteracy was so high in the region. While he returned from that tour optimistic, he found himself making, for the same reasons, a similar study of Lumpkin County at the turn of the century. He found in 1902 that most schools for white children were taught in poorly located churches or "wretched-looking shacks or barns" with leaky roofs that were unfit for "school purposes." Moreover, he also encountered many white people who had had to defer their education to work on the farm or to take care of sick family members and then were too embarrassed to return to school as older students. Several of those he interviewed replied that "they knew several men elected to office in Lumpkin County who could not read and write," and hence they reasoned that education was unnecessary.[64]

Illiterate white men may have been elected to office in Lumpkin County, but no black man, regardless of his education, was elected to office during the nineteenth century. African Americans simply did not have the numbers to influence elections. For example, in 1878 forty-eight black men paid the poll tax that, theoretically, enabled them to vote. Obviously these men felt that voting was an important act despite their impotence at the polls. And the actions of African Americans in the county suggest that they were well aware of the political climate around them. Before elections in 1874, African Americans held meetings in their church; one reportedly lasted two days. Many were members of, or at least receptive to the message promoted by, the Union League. The local newspaper reported in May 1874 that African Americans had been "carrying on a Union meeting at this place. Several colored preachers from a distance officiated, while a large crowd was in attendance."[65]

The white men who controlled politics and the social order in Lumpkin County did not appear threatened by the Union League meeting attended by a "large crowd" of recently emancipated slaves. In fact, in 1874 the local newspaper confidently announced, "We have an orderly, law abiding colored population. The threatened war between the races will not effect [sic] us here."[66] Not all the African Americans in Lumpkin County were law abiding, and the newspaper printed the infractions of those who were not, but these cases were infrequent. The local African American population was just too small to concern those in power. Generally, the *Mountain Signal* printed stories that either ridiculed the efforts of local African Americans or displayed a paternalistic attitude toward those it referred to as "our colored populace." Some African Americans were singled out for their "industry" and "honesty." In his obituary in 1873 Nelson Singleton, a carpenter, was lauded for these qualities. Two others who didn't have to die before winning the praises of the *Mountain Signal*'s editors were Henry Castleberry and Daniel Keith, two of the trustees of the land that William Price had donated for the school.[67]

This appreciation of Henry Castleberry and Daniel Keith, two men involved in promoting education for African Americans, by the white elite suggests that white people in Lumpkin County came to terms with education for black children in their county. During the last quarter of the nineteenth century, three schools were established in three African American "settlements" outside of town. Hickory School held classes in a Methodist church in the southeastern part of the county, Lowry School was located a little more than three miles northeast of Dahlonega, and Keith School, named after Daniel Keith, was situated four miles outside of town in the southwestern part of the county. The county board of education paid the teachers in these schools and "such school appliances as [it] could supply."[68] In 1883, the only year for which there is an extant list of teachers, three black men taught in these schools.[69] The school in Dahlonega, which also served as the First Baptist Church, fell under the domain of the city board of education and continued to operate until the middle of the twentieth century. In 1945 the original building burned.[70]

To achieve their aims during Reconstruction, African Americans in

Lumpkin County negotiated with and used the resources of their white neighbors, such as Amory Dexter, W.J. Wooten, and William Price. To be sure, the freed people did not negotiate on equal terms with the white men in this Blue Ridge community. Nevertheless, they did accomplish a great deal: they created an independent church, won a court decision that awarded them a piece of town property—albeit only a partial victory—and arranged to preserve educational opportunities for their children. By appealing to their white neighbors' sense of paternalism, they achieved all this without inciting the racial tension and violence that accompanied such actions in many other areas of Georgia during this period.

NOTES

1. Bureau of the Census, *Eighth Census of the United States, 1860:* Population Schedules, Georgia, (hereafter cited as *Eighth Census*).

2. Andrew W. Cain, *History of Lumpkin County for the First Hundred Years, 1832–1932.* (1932; reprint, Spartanburg, S.C.: Reprint Company, 1984), 7–81. Auraria was the first settlement in the county, established in 1832, but the courthouse was moved to Dahlonega the next year because "the 'lot' on which the principal part of Auraria was located had been fraudulently drawn in the land lottery and . . . the title was defective." Ibid., 42–46; William P. Price, *Sixty Years of the Life of a Country Village Baptist Church, Dahlonega, Georgia, 1838–1897, by a Member Who Joined It Fifty Years Ago* (Atlanta: Franklin Printing and Publishing, 1897), 44.

3. Old citizen, "Dahlonega in 1838 and 1875," *Mountain Signal,* Jan. 30, 1875.

4. Maj. Phillip Wagner to Maj. Gen. Alexander Macombe, Sept. 30, 1830, in "Letters from the Georgia Gold Regions," James W. Covington, 407–8, quoted in David Williams, *The Georgia Gold Rush: Twenty-Niners, Cherokees, and Gold Fever* (Columbia: Univ. of South Carolina Press, 1993), 26.

5. David Williams, "Georgia's Forgotten Miners: African-Americans and the Georgia Gold Rush," *Georgia Historical Quarterly* 75 (spring 1991): 86. That essay is reproduced in this volume.

6. Cain, *History of Lumpkin County,* 122.

7. Ibid., 111.

8. E. Merton Coulter, *Auraria: The Story of a Georgia Gold-Mining Town* (Athens: Univ. of Georgia Press, 1956), 14. He quotes the *Western Herald* newspaper but offers no dates. The ads request the labor of "negro men," implying that these men were not necessarily slaves. Some were probably free black men, but census records of Lumpkin County indicate that free blacks in the area were extremely few in number.

9. Williams, *Georgia Gold Rush,* 86–87.

10. Cain, *History of Lumpkin County,* 402; Lumpkin County Tax Digest, 1845, Madeline K. Anthony Collection, Lumpkin County Heritage Center, Lumpkin County Library, Dahlonega, Georgia (hereafter cited as MKA); Williams, "Forgotten Miners," 96; W.S. Yeates, S.W. McCallie, and Francis P. King, *A Preliminary Report on a Part of the Gold Deposits of Georgia,* Bulletin 4–A, Geological Survey of Georgia (1896; reprint, Atlanta: Franklin Printing and Publishing, 1989), 438–39; Sylvia Gailey Head and Elizabeth W. Etheridge, *The Neighborhood Mint: Dahlonega in the Age of Jackson* (Macon: Mercer Univ. Press, 1986), 33.

11. *Eighth Census;* Williams, *Georgia Gold Rush,* 83; "Fannie Whelchel Remembers Being the Daughter of Slaves," in *"I Remember Dahlonega": Memories of Growing Up in Lumpkin County as Told to Anne Dismukes Amerson,* ed. Anne Dismukes Amerson (Alpharetta, Ga.: Legacy Communications, 1990), 43; *Agriculture of the United States in 1860: Compiled from the Original Returns of the Eighth Census* (Washington, D.C.: Government Printing Office, 1864) (hereafter cited as *Agriculture: Eighth Census*).

12. *Eighth Census,* Slave Schedules, Lumpkin County; *Agriculture: Eighth Census,* 227.

13. Williams, "Forgotten Miners," 96.

14. Price, *Sixty Years*, 23–24; Cain, *History of Lumpkin County*, 212; Bureau of the Census, *Manuscript Population Schedules for the Seventh Census, 1850* (hereafter cited as *Seventh Census*).

15. Price, *Sixty Years*, 23; Lumpkin County Tax Digest, 1848, MKA.

16. *Seventh Census; W.P.* Price, Dahlonega, to M.B. Archer, March 3, 1868. Records of the United States Bureau of Refugees, Freedmen, and Abandoned Lands, Record Group 105, Records of the Superintendent of Education for the State of Georgia, 1865–1870 (hereafter cited as FB Education); Price, *Sixty Years*, 23–24.

17. Price, *Sixty Years*, 24.

18. Ibid., 25–27.; *Official Records of the War of the Rebellion*, ser. 1, vol. 45, pt. 2, 162, 459–60.

19. *Mountain Signal*, Nov. 7, 1874.

20. Bureau of the Census, *Manuscript Population Schedules for the Ninth Census, 1880* (hereafter cited as *Ninth Census*); Lumpkin County Tax Digest, 1878–1882, MKA; William Price, *Lumpkin County and her Public Schools* (Atlanta: Franklin Printing and Publishing, 1902), 31.

21. Madeline K. Anthony, untitled biographical sketch, ser. 2, box 22, folder 21, MKA.

22. *Mountain Signal*, Nov. 7, 1874; Price, *Sixty Years*, 25–27.

23. *Seventh Census*, Lumpkin County; Price, *Sixty Years*, 24, 27. It would seem that Duncan's relationship with Hannah Grant ended some time between 1860 and the end of the war. In December 1866, apparently with the knowledge that he was seriously ill, he married Ritta Tinsley. She must have had children that he adopted; when he made his will the next month, he left most of his property to Ritta and "my children" or "her children." The will did provide, however, for Mary Ann and Martha Duncan, two mulatto women. He stipulated that they be allowed to live on a lot of land contiguous to the contested church property until they should build a house or vacate the property, at which time his wife would gain possession of the land. Lumpkin County Wills, Administrations, Guardianships, bk. 2, 1852–1933, Lumpkin County Courthouse, Dahlonega, Georgia (hereafter cited as LCCH); Lumpkin County Marriage Records, bk. B, 1857–1884, LCCH; Yeates, McCallie, and King, *Preliminary Report*, 440n.

24. W.P. Price to M.B. Archer, March 3, 1868, FB Education.

25. Price, *Sixty Years*, 27–28. It seems that Alexander Duncan died before the final verdict. See Superior Court Minutes, Lumpkin County, September Term 1867, LCCH.

26. Yeates, McCallie, and King, *Preliminary Report*, 379; *Ninth Census*.

27. W.J. Wooten to Col. C.C. Sibley, Aug. 9, 1867, FB Education.

28. W.J. Wooten to M.R. Archer, March 8, 1868, FB Education.

29. Amory Dexter to G.L. Eberhart, Aug. 9, 1867; Amory Dexter to E.A. Ware, Sept. 25, 1867, FB Education.

30. Paul A. Cimbala, "The Terms of Freedom: The Freedmen's Bureau and Reconstruction in Georgia, 1865–1870" (Ph.D. diss., Emory University, 1983), 363–65; Monthly Returns of the U.S. Army Detachments at Dahlonega, Ga., Jan. 14, 1867–May 16, 1869. See especially, Aug. 26, 1867, Sept. 26, 1867, Feb. 27, 1868, MKA.

31. Sub-Assistant Commissioner's Monthly Report, M.R. Archer, January and February 1868, May and June 1868; District Superintendent's Monthly Report, C.A. de las Mesa, August 1868, FB Monthly School Reports.

32. Amory Dexter to G.L. Eberhart, Aug. 8, 1867; Amory Dexter to E.A. Ware, Sept. 25, 1867, FB Education.

33. Amory Dexter to E.A. Ware, Sept. 25, 1867, FB Education.

34. Ibid.

35. John D. Wilkens to E.A. Ware, March 29, 1868, FB Education.

36. Examples are W.J. Wooten to E.A. Ware, Sept. 19, 1867, Oct. 29, 1868, FB Education.

37. Wooten to E.A. Ware, Sept. 19, 1867, Jan. 1, 1869, Wooten to M.R. Archer, March 8, 1868, FB Education.

38. W.J. Wooten, Dahlonega, to Col. C.C. Sibley, Aug. 9, 1867; M.R. Archer to E.A. Ware, Sept. 25, 1868, FB Education.

39. Carl W. Southwell, *History of Dahlonega Baptist Church, 1838–1983* (Gainesville, Ga.: Brewer Printing Services, 1983), 1.

40. W.J. Wooten to E.A. Ware, Sept. 9, 1867; W.J. Wooten, to M.R Archer, March 8, 1868, FB Education.

41. W.P. Price to M.R. Archer, March 3, 1868, FB Education.

42. Ibid.; M.R. Archer to E.A. Ware, May 8, 1868, FB Education.

43. M.R. Archer to C.C. Sibley, Feb. 18, 1868, FB Education.

44. W.J. Wooten to E.A. Ware, Jan. 1, 1869, FB Education.

45. W.J. Wooten to J. Lewis, Sept. 30, 1869, FB Education.

46. Ibid., April 1, 1870.

47. W.J. Wooten to E.A. Ware, Oct. 29, 1868; W.J. Wooten to J.R. Lewis, April 6, 1869, FB Education; District Superintendent's Monthly Report, C.A. de las Mesa, August 1868, FB Monthly School Reports; W.P. Price to M.B. Archer, March 3, 1868, FB Education.

48. Mary Abercrombie, "Ex-Slave of Lumpkin Tells Happiness Code," *Gainesville Daily Times*, April 17, 1949.

49. Sub-Assistant Commissioner's Monthly Report, M.R. Archer, January and February 1868, May and June 1868, District Superintendent's Monthly Report, C.A. de las Mesa, August 1868, FB Monthly School Reports.

50. W.J. Wooten to J.R. Lewis, Feb. 27, 1869, May 18, 1869, FB Education.

51. Monthly Reports of the U.S. Army Detachments at Dahlonega, Ga., Jan. 14, 1867–May 16, 1869, May 14, 1869, MKA.

52. W.J. Wooten to J. Lewis, Dec. 29. 1869, FB Education.

53. Ibid., Feb. 23, 1870.

54. W.J. Wooten to J. Lewis, Dec. 29, 1869, Feb. 23, 1870, FB Education; Lumpkin County Deed Book Q, 790–91, LCCH; Cain, *History of Lumpkin County*, 262.

55. Anthony, untitled sketch, MKA.

56. *Ninth Census;* 1878 Lumpkin County Tax Digest, 1878, MKA.

57. Price, *Sixty Years*, 28. The mint did indeed become North Georgia College in 1872.

58. Virstee Howell, "Virstee Howell Remembers Cooking at the Smith House," in Amerson, *"I Remember Dahlonega,"* 238.

59. W.J. Wooten to J. Lewis, March 23, 1870; J. Lewis to O.O. Howard, March 25, 1869; W.J. Wooten to J. Lewis, April 1, 1870, FB Education.

60. *Mountain Signal*, March 20, 1875.

61. *Gainesville Daily Times*, April 17, 1949.

62. *Fourth Annual Report of the State School Commissioner Submitted to the General Assembly at Its Session in January, 1875* (Savannah, Ga.: J.H. Estill, Public Printer, 1875) (hereafter cited as State School Commissioner's Report); Cain, *History of Lumpkin County*, 246.

63. *State School Commissioner's Report.*

64. W.P. Price, "Education in the Mountains," *Mountain Signal*, June 11, 1874; Price, *Lumpkin County and Her Public Schools*, 10–11.

65. Lumpkin County Tax Digest, 1878–1882, MKA; *Mountain Signal*, May 28, 1874, Oct. 31, 1874.

66. *Mountain Signal*, Sept. 26, 1874.

67. Ibid., Aug. 7, 1873, Oct. 30, 1873, Aug. 22, 1874.

68. Price, *Lumpkin County and Her Public Schools*, 31–32.

69. From a document labeled "Exhibit D" in ser. 3, box 24, folder 1, MKA.

70. Price, *Lumpkin County and Her Public Schools*, 31–32; "Virstee Howell Remembers Cooking," in Amerson, *"I Remember Dahlonega,"* 238.

14

The Salem School and Orphanage

White Missionaries, Black School

Conrad Ostwalt and Phoebe Pollitt

The academic focus on multiculturalism in the late twentieth century gives the impression that society was homogeneous until very recently. In particular, and despite the efforts of numerous scholars, the myth persists that the Appalachian region is a static and uniform society made up of poor white mountaineers. But the social and cultural makeup of the region is much more complicated than some are willing to admit, and its history is replete with examples of multicultural encounters and incidences of cooperation.[1]

One of the most ecumenical and complex of those was undertaken by the nineteenth-century religious and social reformers who established the Salem School and Orphanage in Elk Park, North Carolina. In this relatively isolated mountain community, Presbyterian, Congregationalist, and Mennonite missionaries identified and attempted to address the needs of an African American community.

The Salem School and Orphanage was an anomaly in the mountain reform movements of the late nineteenth and early twentieth centuries. Mission work on behalf of blacks in Appalachia was rare because of entrenched racism and because of the relatively low percentage of African Americans in the region but, more important, because of a general perception that the greater need was to uplift poverty-stricken mountain whites. James Klotter has argued that the poverty among white mountaineers "allowed some reformers to turn with clear conscience away from blacks" to aid an Appalachia that was characterized by its "whiteness."[2]

Klotter's thesis does not account for the Salem School and Orphanage. Its story is all but forgotten and provides a counterpoint to those dominant white-oriented missionary trends. The story of the Salem School can best be understood in the context of the broader missionary educational reform movements of the late nineteenth century and the unique contribution of the Mennonite Brethren Church.[3]

In the late nineteenth century, many Protestant churches sent workers into the Appalachian mission field to establish churches and schools and more generally to work for the betterment of mountaineers through the establishment of church schools and institutions of religious education. Helping mountaineers to realize "a more abundant life" describes the mission of a 1924 Lutheran Training School in Virginia and sums up the goal of religious education in southern Appalachia.[4] For the most part, this movement began with northern Protestant churches wanting to educate Appalachia's poor white mountaineers and followed other paternalistic attitudes that grew out of the history of religious education in the South.

Although education had been a part of the religious enterprise since colonial America, the religious education movement that most affected southern Appalachia is a product of nineteenth-century revivalism. During the 1790s and the early part of the nineteenth century revivals swept the country, including the southern highlands, and spawned what is commonly referred to as the Second Great Awakening. This revivalist era produced many changes in American religion, including an evangelistic interest in transforming society and Christianizing culture.[5]

Toward the end of the eighteenth century, Samuel Hopkins wrote that sin "consists in self love," while "holiness consists in disinterested benevolence."[6] Hopkins reasoned that Christians have a duty to work for the happiness and self-fulfillment of others and that this selflessness would result in good works directed toward one's neighbors and toward society in general.[7] From this philosophical stance issued a proliferation of religious reform, mission, and educational societies. Some of these, such as the American Education Society of 1816, were interdenominational, while others, such as the Presbyterian United Domestic Missionary Society of 1826, had a vested denominational interest. Nevertheless, these societies sought to provide educational opportunities where none existed, and during the nineteenth century, they made great strides in providing such opportunities in the West and South.[8] Of course, in practice this benevolent outreach was not as disinterested as it was in theory; however, the educational thrust did at least begin with the idea of providing a service where a need existed.

Organized education on a large scale was nonexistent in Appalachia in the early nineteenth century. Although by mid-century there were state-supported schools for white children, public funds came late to the mountains, and most early efforts at education were the products of missionary enterprises.[9] Following the Civil War, some reform, which had originally focused on the problem of slavery,[10] began to turn attention toward the problem of education in the Appalachian high country.[11] Specifically, reform-minded societies recognized the absence or scarcity of public funds for education in the mountain regions and turned their sights toward providing educational opportunities. Naturally, denominations viewed the mountains as a needy place and as a foothold for the expansion of their churches. By 1880, the practice of founding church-related mission schools had begun in earnest; by 1920 seventeen separate denominational mission schools existed in southern Appalachia.[12]

Following the general theme of reform, these mission schools for the most part were dominated by their own paternalistic attitudes. Their goal was to educate and to "save" the mountain children from illiteracy and ignorance. For example, the Konnarock Training School of Virginia was a 1920s project of the Woman's Missionary Society of the United Lutheran Church. The school was organized to throw "light upon [the] great problem of rural education" and to help untutored mountain girls overcome their impoverished backgrounds.[13] This same emphasis is clearly illustrated in a set of 1912 photographs taken at the Oneida Institute, an early twentieth-century Baptist mission school in Kentucky. The first photograph pictures five young girls as "they enter school" poorly dressed, disheveled, and completely lacking in refinement. The second picture shows seven young ladies "after about a year at Oneida"; they are well dressed, properly groomed, and more refined.[14] The implication is obvious. The mission schools were seeking to civilize what their founders perceived to be untutored natives of a backwoods area.

This civilizing process always meant Christianization, for the missionaries who came to the mountains to found schools and churches viewed the area as brutal and heathenish, a place ripe for "God's work."[15] For "disinterested benevolence" to succeed, Christianity had to be considered the solution to social ills, so the job of educating children never completely superseded the job of winning souls. In fact, missionaries saw the two tasks as mutually dependent; educating children and pursuing other reform projects were merely the results of evangelism. This attitude was summed up by James Anderson Burns, the cofounder and president of the Oneida Institute: "Religious education solves our mountain problems as nothing else can do. As teachers we do not preach less than missionary pastors. We preach every Sunday and our teaching all the week is to the same effect . . . our mission schools are missionary enterprises [and] are training schools for our churches and communities."[16]

Against this backdrop, the work of Emily Prudden in Elk Park might seem to fit this model of mission school development. After all, Prudden was a woman from the Northeast, the product of a liberal Protestant tradition who moved to the South to improve life or, at the very least, in David Whisnant's terms, to intervene culturally in a seemingly alien society.[17]

Prudden was the daughter of a reform-minded family from Connecticut. She was nearly deaf for most of her adult life. As she approached her fiftieth birthday, she was left without family and was evidently growing restless. In 1882 an old friend asked her to help with educational mission work at the Brainard Institute in Chester, South Carolina. Brainard was established by the New School Presbyterian Church to educate former slaves. Prudden's experience at Brainard echoes the predominant paternalism that Whisnant described, yet Prudden's own assessment of her work lacks the hard edge found in the memories of some religious educators of that day: "The girls in this home were taught in the public school . . . so for six hours daily I was free to visit the poor cabins, both colored and white. . . . [The children were] without advantage, no school, no church, no society. . . . I thought of my own school days, still a joy to remember and would say to myself, You could build a home in some lovely place where every influence is pure and uplifting and take fifteen girls and train them as your own, and send them out to live useful lives."[18]

Even though much of Prudden's experience resembles Whisnant's description of white liberal paternalism in Appalachia, her work differs from that pattern. Of the fifteen schools that Prudden established in rural North and South Carolina, seven were for African American children at a time when schools were segregated by law and when most other missionary reformers, almost always white themselves, worked with white people, especially in southern Appalachia, and built white institutions. And the subsequent evolution of Prudden's work at the Salem School under the influence of the Mennonites departed even further from the traditional pattern of paternalistic cultural intervention. The Mennonite Brethren made the Salem School a forum for cultural interaction, bringing the mountain African American community, described as a "neglected minority within a neglected minority," into contact with Kansas missionaries who were Russian émigrés and who had memories of religious persecution.[19]

In the late nineteenth century, Elk Park, nestled deep in the Blue Ridge Mountains just a mile from the Tennessee border, was a very small rural settlement. Most families lived on small farms and hunted and fished in the surrounding mountains. There were no schools, newspapers, or central governing body. Public schools were plagued by inadequate facilities; ludicrous classroom conditions, such as a single teacher responsible for forty pupils ranging in age from six to twenty-one; makeshift curricula that covered little more than the three Rs, plus history and geography; teachers who were paid little and who were often hired on the basis of family and political connections rather than competence; and the absence of mandatory attendance laws.[20] Under such conditions the coming of the mission schools and educators like Emily Prudden seemed a godsend.

But around 1890, before the arrival of Emily Prudden, Rev. Robert Payne Pell, a white Presbyterian minister, arrived in Elk Park.[21] Pell was the first link in the chain of events that would lead to the founding of the Salem School and Orphanage, and his first task was to build a Presbyterian church. Given the dismal condition of education there, Pell and many of his new congregation soon decided to sponsor and build a school, following the typical settlement-school pattern of the time.[22] Familiar with the work of Emily Prudden, Pell asked her to come to Elk Park to help with a school for white children. She agreed, and soon more than three hundred white children were attending the Elk Park Academy, funded through the cooperative efforts of the Presbyterian and Congregational missionary movements.

Prudden was soon joined by five missionary workers from Cleveland, Ohio, all of whom worked diligently at the school and among the residents around Elk Park. For example, teachers held "Mothers' Meetings" to teach basic concepts of nutrition, child rearing, and sanitation; they began a religious youth group, offering activities and fellowship to local teenagers; and they passed out or sold clothing and household items donated by northern supporters. Prudden wrote that these activities alone were enough to keep five teachers busy. However, something else continued to nag at Prudden. She felt the need to heed the Bible's call to "do for the least of these," and she interpreted this call to mean help for the children of the small African American community around Elk Park.[23]

This decision was predictable given Prudden's exposure to Reconstruction experiments such as the Brainard Institute and her own efforts at establishing African American schools such as the Lincoln Academy near Gastonia in 1886 and her possible exposure to African American education at Berea College in 1878.[24] Nevertheless, her decision to educate mountain blacks is remarkable for its Appalachian setting because it marks a departure from the normal settlement-school pattern within the region, to provide "a more abundant life" for poor white mountaineers only. In fact, given the times and the context, Prudden's experiment seems no less than phenomenal.[25]

In 1894, Prudden bought four acres of land and built a school in Elk Park for the African American children of the surrounding area, which included Avery, Mitchell, and Watauga Counties. Only one of the Cleveland missionaries who had been working with white mountain children chose to teach in the new school, and local attitudes soon made it difficult to attract teachers, as explained by the later writings of Mennonite missionaries: "When she [Prudden] bought the piece of land for the school for the colored people, no one knew for what purpose it was intended. Therefore she was able to select a lovely hillside which overlooked the whole town of Elk Park. The fine building and location for the colored people caused so much hatred and jealousy among the white people that they succeeded in frightening away the early occupants and Miss Prudden could no longer get teachers for the school."[26]

There is no record of the abuses suffered by the early teachers. Prudden, in her autobiographical sketch, glosses over this period, saying that the suffering and distress in their work would appear in their "tear book," if it were ever written. Deeds recorded at the Mitchell County courthouse indicate that in 1897 Prudden gave the land and the school building to the American Missionary Association (AMA), the home mission branch of the Congregational Church, and that the AMA deeded it back to Prudden in 1900.[27] Presumably, the local resistance to educating African American children was so strong that the AMA could not recruit teachers (or chose not to). Committed to providing schooling for the African American children around Elk Park, Prudden "sent a call westward" for Christian teachers who could be financially supported by their home churches to come and teach in her school.

Peter Wiebe, a Russian-born Mennonite missionary working in Flat Lick, Kentucky, heard about Prudden's plight and informed the Krimmer Mennonite leadership of the need for teachers in Elk Park. The Krimmer Mennonite Conference decided to expand their missionary program in the southern Appalachians and asked for a married couple to teach and preach in the North Carolina mountains.[28] Peter Wiebe's son, Henry, and his wife, Elizabeth Wiebe, both also born in Russia and both recent émigrés to the Mennonite commu-

Teachers and pupils at Salem Orphanage at Elm Park, North Carolina. (Courtesy of the Center for Mennonite Brethren Studies, Tabor College, Hillsboro, Kansas)

nity in Kansas, had met and married there in 1898. They answered the call to work in the North Carolina mountains, and they set out for Elk Park in the spring of 1900. Unfortunately, by the time they arrived, the schoolhouse had been rented to a white family, and Prudden had to arrange for the Wiebes to teach summer school near Hudson in Caldwell County, about forty miles to the east.[29]

A former student at the Elk Park African American school, Rev. Rhonda (Rondo) Horton, who died in 1986, remembered the Wiebes:

They came first to a place near Hudson. . . . I don't remember how long they were there, but not very long. . . . They started a mission and they opened this little school down there. They opened the school and the [Mennonites], they never segregated black people. . . . And then they went over to [Elk Park] and started a school over there. There was a lady that had a school, a church school. I forgot her name. And the Krimmer Mennonites bought her school and started a school there for white and black children. And [white people] told them they couldn't run it, that it was against the law. The law wouldn't allow them to run the school that way, that they would have to take one group; they couldn't mix them. And they felt that the black children needed school worse and they took the black children and started this school.[30]

The Wiebes returned to Elk Park in the fall of 1900, ready to start a new school term with the African American children from the surrounding community. On the second morning of school a note was attached to Wiebe's door: "We the citizens of Elk Park will not allow for a white man to stoop so low as to teach the niggars, they have enough of their own color to teach them. Your time is up! After this day."[31] The Wiebes and their students persisted even as tension built; however, no serious episodes of violence occurred. After that first year of operation, the Wiebes returned to Kansas, planning to seek a new mission field. When a petition arrived from African American citizens in Elk Park asking them to return and to reopen the school, the Wiebes consented. The Krimmer Mennonites bought the schoolhouse and eight acres of land; the Wiebes and their students built outbuildings, including a chicken house, granary, and barns. Together, the Wiebes and their students started to farm, in addition to doing school work.[32]

During the second year of the school, the Kansas missionaries faced a new challenge. Mrs. Wiebe recalled, "After we had been back for a few days a colored boy, twelve years of age came to our place and begged to stay with us. He was sick, poorly clad and homeless. We didn't know just what to do, but we couldn't turn him away, for judging from appearances he had not long to live. . . . Before long another homeless child arrived. . . . The homeless children kept coming."[33]

After conferring with the mission board, the Wiebes started an orphanage that could care for twenty children. The Kansas Mennonites supported the work with food, grain, clothing, and household items, and the school and orphanage expanded during that year. This expansion probably increased local hostility to the institution, for Mrs. Wiebe reported that during the second year, "there still were some people who tried to scare us out by bombarding the place with giant firecrackers at night."[34] Still the missionaries and the children persisted.

The third year brought more challenges to the Salem Mission when another Kansas Mennonite family, Rev. Jacob Tschetter and his wife and children, joined the Wiebes in Elk Park. A large addition was made to the house to accommodate the Tschetters and the growing number of homeless children; a chapel was constructed; and two local African American women, Alice Garnett and Gertrude Sapp, began teaching at the school. Despite the missionaries' work in improving relations with the local community, acceptance was rare. Mrs. Wiebe remembered, "During the third year one evening Brother Wiebe was asked to come outdoors, as there was someone to see him. We knew who he was and from his reputation we judged that he had no good intentions. I persuaded Brother Wiebe to stay in the house and felt that it had been the right thing, when in the morning we found the lower front steps loaded with fist size rocks. This was the place where the man stood and waited for Brother Wiebe the night before."[35]

Sentiment ran high against Tschetter as well, as evidenced in the musings of a white Mitchell County citizen: "We boys would often decide that we would run him [Tschetter] out of town, but you can't hurt a man who prayed like he did."[36]

The Wiebes left Elk Park in 1908, though the Tschetters stayed until around 1912. Nevertheless, the remote location and enduring local hostility took their toll, and the Salem Mission closed in 1912. After this closing, the Krimmer Mennonite Conference maintained a presence in the area but changed its focus to establishing Mennonite churches throughout the region.[37] Eventually several African American Mennonite churches were established in western North Carolina. Alice Garnett and Gertrude Sapp continued to teach the Salem children in a segregated public school. The old school grounds, consisting of eight acres and several buildings, were sold to a white family and later became the first hospital in Elk Park. Today one original building in very poor repair remains standing on the site, and there are no African American citizens in Elk Park.[38]

The story of the Salem Mission inspires sadness. The links between a North Carolina Presbyterian minister, a Connecticut Congregationalist, and Russian immigrant Mennonites demonstrate a unique experiment in multicultural interaction and ecumenical cooperation. "Courage" and "devotion" describe not only Emily Prudden, the Wiebes, and the Tschetters, but also the children who attended the Salem School or who lived at the orphanage. In the end, racism played a role in ending the Salem Mission, but its short life demonstrates an important departure from the norm that we have come to expect of missionary-inspired education efforts in the Appalachian mountains.

NOTES

An earlier version of this essay, titled "The Salem School and Orphanage: White Missionaries, Black School," was published in the *Appalachian Journal* 20 (spring 1993): 265–75, and is reprinted here with the permission of the *Appalachian Journal*.

1. A number of scholars have dealt with racial matters and multiculturalism in Appalachia. See Michael C. Cooke, "Race Relations in Montgomery County, Virginia, 1870–1990," *Journal of the Appalachian Studies Association* 4 (1992): 94–104; John C. Inscoe, *Mountain Masters: Slavery and the Sectional Crisis in Western North Carolina* (Knoxville: Univ. of Tennessee Press, 1989); Ronald L. Lewis, *Black Coal Miners in America: Race, Class, and Community Conflict, 1780–1980* (Lexington: Univ. Press of Kentucky, 1987); Conrad Ostwalt, "Crossing of Cultures: The Mennonite Brethren of Boone, North Carolina," *Journal of the Appalachian Studies Association* 4 (1992): 105–12; Robert P. Stuckert, "Black Populations of the Southern Appalachian Mountains," *Phylon* 48 (summer 1987): 141–51; Joe William Trotter, *Coal, Class, and Color: Blacks in Southern West Virginia, 1919–1932* (Urbana: Univ. of Illinois Press, 1990); William H. Turner and Edward J. Cabbell, eds., *Blacks in Appalachia* (Lexington: Univ. Press of Kentucky, 1985); Margaret Ripley Wolfe, "The Appalachian Reality: Ethnic and Class Diversity," *East Tennessee Historical Society Publications*, nos. 52 and 53 (1980–81), pp. 40–60.

2. James C. Klotter, "The Black South and White Appalachia," *Journal of American History* 66 (March 1980): 849.

3. Unfortunately, this reconstruction is based largely on sources from white missionaries and educators. With the exception of the Rhonda Horton interview, which is cited below, there is no direct testimony from African Americans concerning this episode.

4. See Catherine Cox Umberger, "Konnarock: An Experiment in Education," *Mountain Life and Work* 6 (April 1930): 6.

5. See Winthrop S. Hudson, *Religion in America: An Historical Account of the Development of American Religious Life*, 4th ed. (New York: Macmillan, 1987), 143–45.

6. Samuel Hopkins, "Disinterested Benevolence," in *American Christianity: An Historical Interpretation with Representative Documents*, ed. H. Shelton Smith, Robert T. Handy, and Lefferts A. Loetscher , vol. 1 (New York: Charles Scribner's Sons, 1960), 542. For the doctrine of "disinterested benevolence," see Samuel Hopkins, *The System of Doctrines Contained in Divine Revelation Explained and Defended*, vol. 1 (Boston: n.p., 1811), 465–77.

7. See also "Nathaniel W. Taylor" in Smith, Handy, and Loetscher, *American Christianity*, 28–36.

8. See Hudson, *Religion in America*, 143–48.

9. See H.E. Everman, "The Early Educational Channels of Bourbon County," *Register of the Kentucky Historical Society* 73 (1975): 13–49, and Neal O'Steen, "Pioneer Education in the Tennessee Country," *Tennessee Historical Quarterly* 35 (1976): 199–219. For the history of public funds and education in North Carolina (particularly the Literacy Fund), see Edgar W. Knight, *Public Education in North Carolina* (New York: General Education Board, 1916), 140–44. See also the State Superintendent's Reports for 1840, 1850, 1853, and 1855 by Calvin Wiley, U.S. Bureau of Education, *Beginnings of the Common School System in the South* (Washington, D.C.: Government Printing Office, 1888), 1442–46.

10. Richard B. Drake, "The Mission School Era in Southern Appalachia: 1880–1940," *Appalachian Notes* 6 (1978): 3.

11. See David E. Whisnant, *All That Is Native and Fine: The Politics of Culture in an American Region* (Chapel Hill: Univ. of North Carolina Press, 1983), 9, for an explanation of this pattern. See also Klotter, "Black South and White Appalachia."

12. Drake, "Mission School Era," 2–3. See also John C. Campbell, *The Southern Highlander and His Homeland* (New York: Russell Sage, 1921), 271.

13. Umberger, "Konnarock," 3.

14. See Samuel W. Thomas, ed., *Dawn Comes to the Mountains* (Louisville, Ky.: George Rogers Clark Press, 1981), 44–45.

15. Drake, "Mission School Era," 4.

16. J.A. Burns, *The Baptist Argus*, June 23, 1904, p. 2, as reprinted in Thomas, *Dawn Comes to the Mountains*, 37. See also E.V. Tadlock, "Church Problems in the Mountains," *Mountain Life and Work* 6 (1930): 6ff.

17. Whisnant, *All That Is Native and Fine*, 13. See also pp. 7–8 for the pattern of mission school settlement.

18. Emily C. Prudden, "An Autobiographical Sketch," *The American Missionary*, April 1914, 737–43.

19. Edward J. Cabbell, "Black Invisibility and Racism in Appalachia: An Informal Survey," *Appalachian Journal* 8 (fall 1980): 48–54; Turner and Cabbell, *Blacks in Appalachia*, 3.

20. See Daniel Whitener, *History of Watauga County* (Boone, N.C.: Souvenir of the Watauga County Centennial, n.d.). See also Robert Woodside, "The Educational Development of Avery County" (master's thesis, Appalachian State University, 1952).

21. Correspondence with Diana Ruby Sanderson, Presbyterian Study Center, Montreat, N.C., Jan. 26, 1989.

22. Prudden, "Autobiographical Sketch," 739.

23. Ibid.

24. Church records from the First Congregational Church of Milford, Conn., indicate that Emily Prudden and Jane Jeanette Colton, her niece, were dismissed to the Congregational Church in Berea, Kentucky, in 1878. Presumably they went to Berea to teach, although there are no records of the two either at Berea College or at the Congregational Church in Berea.

25. See John L. Bell, "Lawrence Augustus Oxley: The Beginnings of Social Work among Blacks in North Carolina Counties," *Journal of the Appalachian Studies Association* 4 (1991). Prudden also attempted to run an integrated school in Caldwell County around 1895.

26. Elizabeth Pauls Wiebe, "The Founding and Pioneer Work of the K.M.B. Mountain Mission in N.C.," *The Christian Witness*, March 15, 1950, 5.

27. Deeds recorded in the Mitchell County courthouse in bk. 28, pp. 64, 66.

28. See Katherine Siemens Richert, *Go Tell It on the Mountain* (Fresno, Calif.: Jet Print, 1984).

29. See Joel A. Wiebe, Raymond F. Wiebe, and Vemon R. Wiebe, *The Groening-Wiebe Family, 1768–1974* (Hillsboro, Kan.: Mennonite Brethren Publishing House, 1974).

30. Rev. Rhonda Horton, interview by Cheryl Claassen, tape recording, July 31, 1984, Appalachian Collection, Appalachian State University, Boone, N.C.

31. Wiebe, "Founding of K.M.B. Mountain Mission," 6.

32. Correspondence with Raymond F. Wiebe, August 12, 1991. See also Richert, *Go Tell It on the Mountain*, 6.

33. Wiebe, "Founding of K.M.B. Mountain Mission," 6.

34. Ibid.

35. Ibid.

36. Woodside, "Educational Development of Avery County," 53.

37. See Conrad Ostwalt, "The Junaluska Community of Boone," *Watauga County Times Post*, no. 26, June 1991.

38. Bureau of the Census, *Census of the United States, 1990*.

15

"WHAT DOES AMERICA NEED SO MUCH AS AMERICANS?"

Race and Northern Reconciliation with Southern Appalachia, 1870–1900

NINA SILBER

Sometime in the late nineteenth century, middle-class and upper-class northerners "discovered" the people and culture of southern Appalachia. North-ern magazines filled their pages with descriptive and fictional accounts of the mountain people, missionaries and educators showed a new concern for uplift-ing the southern Appalachians out of their degradation and poverty, theatergoers attended plays in which the mountaineers feuded and "moonshined" their way toward a romantic ending, and readers readily bought the novels of writers such as John Fox Jr., who made the little mountain boy a classic hero of fin de siècle fiction.[1]

To some extent, this "discovery" demanded that northerners reckon with a seemingly unusual and regionally distinctive population within their national borders. Consequently, northern audiences in the late nineteenth century learned to identify Appalachian otherness and to spot the features and charac-teristics that made the people of this locale different and unique. But the new awareness of Appalachia was only partly the product of late nineteenth-cen-tury local coloring. It also came amidst a process of cultural reconciliation and especially a growing tendency in northern culture to promote the cause of sectional healing, particularly with southern whites, in the post–Civil War era. Thus, by the end of the nineteenth century, northerners had begun to mini-mize the strangeness of the southern mountain region, celebrating this area and its inhabitants for supposedly "American" characteristics. Through the stories they told, most drawn more from myths than from reality, Yankees found new reasons to shake hands across the bloody chasm. And while they did not necessarily embrace white Appalachians as their brothers, they did wel-come them as a distant (albeit slightly backward) branch of the national family.

This new Yankee appreciation for the white mountaineers is part of a larger story of northerners' reassessment of poor southern whites. By the 1880s, northerners had begun to reevaluate this group, long described as the most degraded people of southern society, in somewhat more complimentary terms.

Encouraged by the optimistic forecasts of the New South movement, northern enthusiasts often suggested that the poor white may have risen above his
prewar degradation and become a chief beneficiary of economic growth in the
South. Writing as early as 1875, northern journalist Charles Nordhoff found
that the daughters of poor whites "make excellent factory operatives" and that
the Georgia factories, filled with "cracker" employees, exuded an "air of comfort and contentment." By the turn of the century, some believed that industrial progress and the New South movement had transformed the poor whites
into a middle class. "The grandsons and granddaughters of the Crackers of
antebellum days," explained a writer for *Arena* magazine in regard to southern
industry's civilizing influence, "form the mass of what might be called the
'middle class' of the South to-day."[2]

One feature that northern observers stressed repeatedly in their new assessments of the poor southern whites was the native and indigenously American qualities of these people. "The third estate of the South," explained Rev.
A.D. Mayo, in a reference to southern crackers, "is chiefly of good original
stock." In the eyes of observers such as Reverend Mayo, while immigrants
from strange European and Asian countries overran the North and made the
laboring class there almost completely foreign, the southern white population,
including the poor, remained free of any foreign tainting. "I think I can claim,
without egotism," explained travel writer Stephen Powers in the 1870s, "that I
sought out the poor whites in their homes more faithfully than most travellers
in the South have done." Powers painfully recounted the "saddening ignorance and apathy of that class," yet still rejoiced "that these were Americans all,
and not foreigners." And Charles Dudley Warner agreed that the South's racial purity and isolation from immigration made it "more homogeneous than
the North, and perhaps more distinctly American in its characteristics." Behind this classification of American stood the vague and generally ill-conceived
racial assessments of the era that not only defined Americans in terms of English descent but also tied this racial lineage to the rise of more "advanced"
civilizations. In the misused language of the era, most southern whites qualified as bona fide "Anglo-Saxons."[3]

The Anglo-Saxonism of the southern white people, including the poor
whites, gave added significance to northerners' conciliatory efforts at the turn
of the century. As many writers explained, northerners could no longer reject
the South, steeped in its proud racial heritage, while opening the gates to the
strange and alien immigrants who flooded into northern cities and supposedly
diluted American traditions. Joshua Caldwell expounded on this theme in an
article explicitly titled "The South Is American," written for *Arena* magazine
in 1893. "The war ended twenty-eight years ago," Caldwell wrote, "but it is
still the habit of the North to think of the people of the states which attempted
to secede as enemies of the Union and of the Constitution." After tabulating
the percentage of foreign-born in the total populations of various southern
states, Caldwell found that it would be difficult to find a population more
American than in the South. Moreover, the principles of freedom and union

could safely be trusted with the people of such a noble stock, certainly more so than with those who descended from alien cultures. For the Anglo-Saxons of the South, Caldwell explained, "no life but one of freedom is possible, and I can never believe that the hybrid population of Russians, Poles, Italians, Hungarians, which fills so many Northern cities and states, has the same love for our country, the same love of liberty, as have the Anglo-Saxon southerners, whose fathers have always been free." Others implicitly agreed with Caldwell's contention that the racial purity of the white South, including the poor whites, undercut the region's earlier rebellion against the Union, making the move toward conciliation more critical than ever before.[4]

In keeping with the conciliatory trend of uniting the whites and isolating the blacks, northern culture celebrated the southern poor white precisely because he was not black. Northern reformers, often with the encouragement of southern whites, consciously cultivated an interest in the crackers as a way to replace earlier philanthropic efforts for the freedmen. Even when discussing the South's "Negro problem," northerners often paid more attention to southern whites. At the Lake Mohonk Conference on the Negro Question, held in June 1890, Roeliff Brinkerhoff, an Ohio banker and a former Union general, revealed the new northern preoccupation with southern white people. "I want this Conference and these Northern people," explained Brinkerhoff, "to look at this question from the standpoint of the white men of the South." Implicitly comparing the native American qualities of southern white people with the foreign strain of the North, he continued, "Let us remember that the white people of the South are a noble people, that there is nowhere in the United States a purer strain of American blood than in the Old South." Northern humanitarians, missionaries, and educators also discovered in the poor whites a new impoverished and degraded group in the South especially deserving of attention because they were white and native-born. In an 1880 editorial, the *Nation* urged Republicans to switch from the black to "The White Side of the Southern Question": "Hitherto the Southern question has been treated by the organs of the party . . . as if it were simply and solely a Black question, whereas it is a combination of two questions, one black and the other white. The whites are more numerous than the blacks, and more energetic and able, and are far more potent for good and evil." For northerners seeking to uplift the South, southern blacks had become the "undeserving" poor, doomed to political and moral degradation for years to come. But poor southern whites, who came from a more "respectable" stock, had become the region's "deserving" poor. Missionary worker Ellen Myers thus advocated a redirection in the racial focus of the American Missionary Association. "'Our brother in black' has been held up to the view of two continents for the last fifty years," Myers explained. But, she noted in an implicit reference to the white people of the Tennessee and Kentucky mountains, "there is an unnoticed class of people dwelling almost in the very centre of the settled portion of the United States . . . another class as needy perhaps as any."[5]

If the crackers had become the South's deserving poor, then, as Ellen

Myers implied, one group among the poor whites became the region's most deserving of all. The white people of the southern mountains, especially in what came to be known as "Appalachian America," became northern culture's cause célèbre in the late nineteenth century. Northerners discovered this segment of southern white society in the writings of northerners who had visited the region as well as in those of southerners who wrote largely for a Yankee audience. Initially stressing the strange and alien qualities of this isolated population, northerners, by the 1890s, wrote of, read about, and helped to cultivate the truly American qualities of the southern mountain people. To a great extent, they helped to initiate and foster a pervasive mythology of southern Appalachia in which unadulterated Unionism, pure and upstanding patriotism, and undiluted racial purity became the hallmarks of the region's inhabitants. At the same time, these myths of southern mountain life opened a new path for northern humanitarianism that was far removed from the disturbing racial and social conflicts that held the South in its grip during this troubling period of economic and political turmoil.[6]

To a great extent, northerners remained virtually ignorant of the people of Appalachia until the 1880s. Unaware of the various and subtle social distinctions that lay between the poor white and the planter aristocrat, most northerners showed little understanding of the unique characteristics that distinguished the mountain white from the generic poor white designation used for every white person in the South who had never owned a grand plantation and hundreds of slaves. As late as 1898, William G. Frost, the northern-born president of Berea College in Kentucky, found it necessary to remind the readers of *Outlook* that the mountain white and poor white should not be confused. The mountaineers' "homespun garb, often in tatters, rude speech, and shuffling gait," Frost warned, "might lead us to classify them with the 'poor white trash.' But there could be no greater mistake." Aided by the advice of Frost and other writers and observers, northerners gradually learned to distinguish the unique characteristics of the southern mountain people and to identify the common set of characteristics that united the inhabitants of the mountainous regions of several different states. To some extent, they did so by pointing to the "primitive" traditions of Appalachia, including the traditions of feuding and "moonshining." But, gradually, they also learned to identify the noble qualities of racial vigor and patriotism that set the mountaineers apart.[7]

Northerners first met the inhabitants of southern Appalachia through the work of the writers of the local color movement whose ever-widening literary sweep had drawn in the quaint and peculiar peoples from regions throughout the United States. For the most part, the early local colorists of the southern mountains stressed the strange and alien qualities that set the mountain people apart from all others. Kentucky writer James Lane Allen thus found his home state divided into "two Kentuckys"—the mountain region and the bluegrass region—so different from each other that they comprised two distinct identities. Tennessee writer Mary Murfree, initially writing under the pseudonym Charles Egbert Craddock, described the lives of the mountain people of her state in numerous tales of romantic fiction during the 1870s and 1880s. Like Allen, she impressed upon northern readers a sense of Appalachian strangeness. "I was early familiar with their primitive customs, dialect, and peculiar views of life," Murfree explained to *Atlantic* editor Thomas Aldrich regarding her descriptions of the mountaineers, and she undertook to show her readers just how peculiar the people of Appalachia were.[8]

While local colorists were discovering the "peculiar" qualities of Appalachia, northern capitalists and investors had begun to make their own discoveries in this region at precisely the same time. Initially, the railroad opened up Appalachia to investment, bringing in tourist promoters, who set up the new mountain spas and resorts, and speculators interested in the mining and timber capabilities of the region. The New South movement came to Appalachia in the late nineteenth century with a vengeance, prompting observers to exude over the economic potential for the region and its inhabitants. "This mountain region alone," one railroad publication noted, "can furnish permanent employment, when fully developed, for a population twice as great as that of the United States today." In the 1890s, many were still marveling at the economic potential of the region, a point that the promoters of the 1895 Atlanta Exposition hoped to exploit. "The store of wealth that lies buried in the hillsides and mountains of the Southern states," noted an article in the exposition's newsletter, "will be a revelation to the Northern and Western miners and capitalists." Closely aligned with the region's industrial growth, according to the economic promoters and investors, was the development of the region's population into a class of capable employees. "What the Piedmont district and the Cumberland plateau may be capable of doing," remarked northern capitalist Edward Atkinson, "can only be developed when there is a sufficient density of population possessing modern aptitudes to prove by experience their potential. That mountain, valley and plateau section of the great Appalachian chain may hereafter become the richest part of the country, measuring riches by its potential."[9]

The advent of the New South in Appalachia encouraged observers to reassess the qualities of the peculiar mountain people, highlighting their economic potential as sturdy contributors to a capable middle class. Although observers still found much that was odd, peculiar, and even degraded about the mountaineers, they also stressed the positive features that made this group deserving of northern assistance. The mountaineers may have possessed many "primitive" characteristics, northerners believed, but they also possessed qualities that made them capable of uplift and improvement. Hence, the literature on Appalachia that appeared between the 1880s and the turn of the century turned away from its initial bewilderment over the strange and unusual qualities of the mountain people to a celebration of their strong, vigorous, patriotic, and racially pure characteristics. In this spirit, the economic promoters at the 1901 South Carolina Exposition commended the transformation of the mountain people into a capable industrial workforce. "Many of the mill people," the exposition advocates observed, "are drawn from the mountains of North Carolina, where the principal occupation is hunting and moonshine. . . . The people have come from the fields, the farms and the mountains to work in the cotton mills and are doing well. They are frugal and industrious, and above all have the native instinct of fidelity which is essential to the successful operation of a cotton mill." And William Frost could barely contain his excitement regarding the economic and racial potential of the mountaineers. They "are a glorious national asset," he wrote. "They are the unspoiled and vigorous reserve forces. They will offset the undesirable foreign elements, and give the South what it has always lacked, a sturdy middle class."[10]

As these and other observers suggested, the mountaineers, despite some primitive tendencies, had the potential for uplift and improvement. In particular, the mountain whites' alleged racial purity gave northern observers cause for optimism. In the last years of the nineteenth century it was this feature more than any other that northern and southern whites cherished about Appalachia's inhabitants. And, in the search for American Anglo-Saxonism in the late nineteenth century, many believed that they had found the purest and most concentrated expression of this racial strain in the remote southern mountains. Once the racial wholesomeness of the southern mountaineers had been established, northern whites could embrace them, no longer excluding them as strange and alien but instead bringing them into their national heritage at precisely the same moment when northern culture had begun to cast southern black people aside. Northerners never embraced the mountain folk as their equals; but, by stressing their perception of racial purity in Appalachia, they established a bond through which the mountaineers became worthy of northern attention and assistance. "Nowhere will be found purer Anglo-Saxon blood," claimed William Brewer, writing in the pages of the northern magazine *Cosmopolitan* about the mountain people in Georgia. Other writers agreed that the southern mountaineers epitomized racial purity, largely because the mountains had kept these people isolated from the waves of immigration that had polluted the racial stock, and thus the civilized tendencies, of the rest of the nation. The mountaineers, in effect, embodied the same racial makeup of the early settlers in America and the hardy frontier people who had pushed their way up the mountain range two hundred years earlier. Writing about the Appalachian people of the early twentieth century, one author for another northern periodical, *World's Work*, explained in 1902 that "these people have not changed in any essential respect since the days of the pioneer."[11]

Impressed by the racial purity of Appalachia, observers, travelers, and folklorists in the 1890s and early 1900s reevaluated many of the same characteristics that had formerly been a sign of the mountaineers' barbarity. The American Folklore Society, for example, established in 1889, became enthralled with the study of the Appalachian people, finding in the mountains a guide to the traditions and values of the American past. In time, educators, missionaries, and travelers also turned with a new interest to the southern mountains. And, in this regard, although many agreed that the feuding and moonshining in the mountains pointed to the region's primitive nature, they found that even this primitiveness contained distinctively American and Anglo-Saxon quali-

ties. In effect, because they were "backward" and "primitive," the mountaineers demanded uplift; but, because their primitiveness revealed Anglo-Saxon
roots, they would likely benefit more than others—and also benefit a reunified
nation from whatever assistance they received. "The mountaineer is to be regarded as a survival," explained William Frost in his attempt to establish tenu-
ous and questionable racial links. "In his speech you will soon detect the flavor
of Chaucer. . . . His very homicides are an honest survival of Saxon temper."
Folklorists rhapsodized over the American roots of the mountain people's "peculiar" musical traditions. "The music of the Southern mountaineer is not
only peculiar," wrote one mountain scholar, "but, like himself, peculiarly American." Even what seemed to be inbreeding among mountain families could be
construed as a sign of the Appalachian people's rich racial and historical legacy.
"The men and women of this region," commented travel writer Leon
Vandevort, "unlike those of the Adirondacks, are a community so old that its
various branches interweave until the whole family is firmly united. . . . The
root of the family tree is invariably in Virginia or the fertile sections of Eastern
North Carolina. Here in the mountains are many of the names that stand for
all that men consider honorable and distinguished in those old lands."[12]

It was this spirit of celebrating the primitive but truly American qualities
of the mountain people that guided the work of William Goodell Frost during
his tenure as president of Berea College from 1892 until his retirement in
1920. After leaving his post at Oberlin, Frost came as an outsider to Appalachia, determined to prove to the rest of the world the worthiness of the Appalachian cause. The college's efforts in the mountain district extended back to
the antebellum period, but Frost gave a new emphasis and direction to the
school's work. Most notably, Frost redirected the institution away from biracial education and undertook a focused campaign of white recruitment, especially among mountain residents. During the 1890s and early twentieth century,
Frost became the leading interpreter of the white mountaineers and their culture, writing scores of articles for northern magazines and delivering countless
speeches in his efforts to elicit humanitarian funds for his project to educate
the people of this mountain district. In his eagerness to uplift and improve
mountain life, Frost noted those "primitive" and "backward" characteristics of
the people that required the civilizing tools of the outside society. Yet, unlike
earlier observers, Frost did not assume that this Appalachian primitiveness
demanded the isolation and ostracism of the region. Rather, Frost sounded the
theme, which others echoed, of lauding the mountaineers' ancient, albeit un-
tamed, traits as primitive indicators of the true American spirit. "We will not
teach them to despise the log-cabin," Frost wrote of his educational efforts,
"but to adorn it. And . . . we respect their sturdy independence and endeavor
only to help them to help themselves." The mountaineers combined all of the
sturdy and commendable characteristics of the original settlers and of the pioneers, possessing the same strength and independence as America's ancestors, traits that needed only to be updated to present conditions. In this sense,
Frost identified the Appalachians as a "simple, primitive people, showing the

strong traits of their race—independence, respect for religion, family affection, patriotism."[13]

Moreover, Frost also assumed that among the Anglo-Saxon people of the mountains lay the key to civilizing and uplifting the entire South. As Frost saw it, once the Appalachians had been uplifted, their influence could extend to other impoverished populations in the region. It is important to consider, Frost explained, the mountaineers' "central location in the heart of the South. When once enlightened this highland stock may reinforce the whole circle of Southern states." In this way, Frost helped to broadcast the concerns of the southern mountains throughout the United States, identifying the unique position of Appalachia as a critical component in the reinvigoration of the entire South. And, in this way, he also made it clear that the uplifting of Appalachia could contribute to the broader process of sectional reunion. By developing this nucleus of Anglo-Saxon strength in the heartland of Dixie, Frost suggested that the Anglo-Saxon bonds of the entire nation, of North and South, would also be strengthened.[14]

Frost believed that the people of Appalachia represented the best hope of the South because, as he and others never tired of explaining, not only did the mountaineers embody a pure racial heritage, they had also proved repeatedly their patriotic attachment to the American nation. "What does America need so much as Americans?" Frost queried. "And here they are—vigorous, unjaded of nerve, prolific, patriotic— full of the blood and spirit of Seventy-six." Indeed, in the realm of patriotism, mountain whites apparently excelled where other southern whites had failed, or so claimed the unfolding myth of the region. While recent scholarship on the Civil War paints a much more complicated picture of divided and even changing loyalties in various parts of the southern mountains, journalists and novelists in the 1880s and 1890s repeatedly emphasized Appalachians' overwhelming attachment to the Union and identified this as a signpost that set the Appalachians apart from the rest of the white South. As early as the Reconstruction period, northerners had tried to establish the unqualified Unionism of the mountain region. "It is certain that the majority of the able-bodied men of the mountains," wrote Union officer John DeForest during his postwar stint in South Carolina, "were eventually bullied or dragged by main force into the Confederate army. They sought to remain loyal." During the 1880s and 1890s, other publicists and missionaries expanded this theme of the patriotic and therefore deserving mountain people in scores of fictional and nonfictional accounts of Appalachia. Some hesitated to generalize about the Unionist sentiments of all the southern mountain people, although they accepted the argument that the mountain region was, for the most part, an enclave of Union support. According to some, the mountain feuds received a new stimulus from the divisions of the Civil War, suggesting that while some feuding families supported the North, others fought for the Confederacy. During the war, William Frost explained, "the mountain people were divided." Still, as Frost maintained, the patriotic spirit prevailed as "the greater part [of the mountain population] were steadfast in loyalty to the old flag."[15]

Crucial to the mountaineers' pro-Union stance was their assumed ignorance of the system of slavery. The mountaineers, wrote missionary writer Mrs. S.M. Davis, "would have no complicity with slavery, and hence the slaveocracy would have nothing to do with them." According to the historical accounts, the slave system left many poor whites with little choice but to escape the control and domination of the slaveholders' economy by retreating to the isolated mountain regions. In the "mountain valleys of the Blue Ridge and the Alleghenies," explained Harvard geology professor Nathaniel Shaler, the poor whites "formed independent and singularly isolated communities, in which no negroes were ever seen." The mountain white's distance from the degradations and sectionalism engendered by the slave system made him unreceptive to the Confederate cause and thus more inclined to support the boys in blue.[16]

But this separation from slavery implied much more than the mountaineers' immunity to sectionalism; perhaps more significant, it also revealed their racial isolation, even racial "innocence," with respect to slavery and the slaves themselves. Northern observers, missionaries, and educators, actively looking for "the white side" of southern race relations, needed to look no further than this racially pure and definitively nonblack population. Here, amazingly, was a group of southern white people who, it could be argued, had virtually no contact with the unwholesome influences of slavery—the devaluation of free labor, the extremes of wealth and impoverishment within the white population, and the racial hostility that beset many poor whites, not to mention familiarity with the degraded characteristics of southern blacks. Indeed, what began as an explanation of the mountaineers' isolation from the sectional politics of slavery and the slaveholder became a tribute to the Appalachian people's detachment from African Americans. "The landless, luckless 'poor white,'" argued William Frost, "degraded by actual competition with slave labor, is far removed in spirit from the narrow-horizoned but proud owner of a mountain 'boundary.' The 'poor white' is actually degraded; the mountain man is a person not yet graded up." Suddenly, the Appalachians had become a people defined by their distance from southern blacks, a point of considerable significance in a period when many suspected that the lowland poor whites did much to exacerbate the region's racial turmoil. Unlike other poor whites, the mountain whites would seem to have no cause to lynch southern blacks, as many had never even seen them. "Men and women would ride twenty miles to see the black men and stare them out of countenance," explained Nathaniel Shaler, thereby suggesting that the mountaineers, although curious about African Americans, lacked the racial anxiety that supposedly preoccupied the poor white people of the lowlands.[17]

Likewise, in contrast to earlier writers who had described the mountaineers as suffering from depravities similar to those of southern blacks, turn-of-the-century observers commented on the noteworthy absence of African American peculiarities, something which other poor whites did not possess. "These mountaineers," explained one writer for a New England publication, "are by no means as superstitious as the people of the southern lowlands who have been brought up surrounded by a negro population." In the same spirit, this author also criticized Mary Murfree's renditions of mountain dialect claiming that "the speech of the better class of mountaineers contains far fewer noticeable peculiarities than that of the uneducated people of the southern lowlands," a characteristic that he attributed in part "to the absence of the black population in the mountains." In many ways, then, the southern mountain whites captured the imagination of northern observers in the late nineteenth and early twentieth centuries for their remoteness from the region's racial turmoil. Their culture embodied distance and separation from southern blacks and from poor whites' racial hysteria. And perhaps to a certain extent, the mountaineers' distance from southern blacks allowed northerners to establish and enhance their own detachment from this troublesome race. By aiding and celebrating the white, and racially innocent, people of the southern mountains, northerners decisively retreated from their earlier intrusions into the "negro question."[18]

And, in this regard, the mountain whites had again proven themselves superior to other poor southern whites. According to the then-prevalent view of race relations in the South, as discussed by northerners and southerners at the turn of the century, racial antagonism was most acute between southern blacks and whites from the lower classes. Believing southern gentlemen to be refined and civilized and possessed of an intuitive grace in handling the region's racial dilemmas, northern whites believed that the worst violations of the South's racial code occurred in the interactions between poor whites and African Americans. As early as 1885, Carl Schurz found that outrages were committed against blacks "partly because there is still a larger class of whites in the South who feel so little confident, and therefore so restless, concerning their superiority over the negro." Other northerners explicitly condemned southern crackers for fomenting the disfranchisement and lynching movement against southern blacks. "The movement to disfranchise the negro has not been engineered by the high-bred whites," wrote an author for *Arena* magazine. "They, as a class, are the most friendly to the negro, as they feel their dependency on them; but with the cracker class it is different." In contrast, the mountain whites lacked this racial animosity because they apparently had had little contact with southern blacks. In this way, they again proved themselves worthy of northern concern because of their isolation from not only the degrading influences of the black population but also from the disturbing pattern of racial violence that concerned northern whites in the late nineteenth century.[19]

Turn-of-the-century fiction writers championed the proud and patriotic mountain people without dwelling on the oddities of mountain culture as earlier local colorists had done. Perhaps no work better captured the new celebration of Anglo-Saxonism, patriotism, and racial isolation in Appalachia than John Fox's *The Little Shepherd of Kingdom Come* (1903). Fox, as a Kentucky native, had taken up the literary tradition of James Lane Allen in his tales of bluegrass and mountain society. But Fox moved beyond an examination of Allen's "two Kentuckies," exploring the unique and specific characteristics of the people of the Cumberland Mountains. Although Fox was not a product of that society, he was aware of a growing cultural preoccupation with poor southern white people, and mountain people in particular. As a southerner, Fox responded to northerners' interest in this subject by producing several novels and short stories, many of which appeared in a variety of northern magazines. None, however, achieved the success of *The Little Shepherd*, a work that quickly became a best-seller after its publication in 1903 and remained extremely popular during the first half of the twentieth century.[20]

The Little Shepherd of Kingdom Come chronicled the adventures of a Kentucky mountain boy, Chad Buford, who, at the outset, was left without a home and family when cholera killed his aunt and uncle. In the midst of this initial tragedy, Fox described Chad's noble American heritage. Resolving to depart from his forlorn surroundings, Chad was moved by that "restless spirit that had led his unknown ancestor into those mountain wilds after the Revolution." Chad left his isolated, mountain home for the somewhat more civilized valley where he met the Turner family, who promised to nurture and care for the orphaned boy. But, as he approached the settlement in the valley, Chad also met two black slaves, a strange and unusual sight for the naïve mountaineer. Chad's newfound companions from the valley expressed amusement at his racial ignorance. "Lot's o' folks from yo' side o' the mountains nuver have seed a nigger," explained one of Chad's new friends, apparently as much for the reader's understanding as for Chad's. "Sometimes," the friend said, "hit skeers 'em." Chad, however, lacked any clear-cut racial code or philosophy and replied, "Hit don't skeer me." Like many other mountaineers, Chad was a blank slate when faced with questions of race relations.[21]

Eventually, Chad traveled with the Turners to the aristocratic bluegrass region where he met old Maj. Càlvin Buford, who saw in Chad "shades of Dan'l Boone." The major also saw in Chad a potential relation, the descendant of a long-lost great uncle. Thus, Fox explained that Chad not only sprang from sturdy American stock, but might also have descended from a noble aristocracy as well. The major invited Chad to live with him, and Chad agreed. The mountain boy slowly won the respect and friendship of his new bluegrass friends and family, even the black servants who were at first bemused by his appearance but gradually came to revere him. Acting in part out of his own unfamiliarity with racial etiquette and his unswerving commitment to justice, Chad even defended a helpless black "pickaninny" who had been tormented by his young master.[22]

Predictably, Chad's personal turning point coincided with the turning point for the nation. Resisting the Confederate sympathies of the Turners and of Major Buford, Chad enlisted in the Civil War on the side of the Union. In doing so, Chad responded to the sentiments and traditions that he had learned or, more precisely, that he had remained ignorant of in the mountains. In the Kentucky hills, John Fox explained, "unionism was free from prejudice as nowhere else on the continent save elsewhere throughout the southern mountains. Those southern Yankees knew nothing about the valley aristocrat, nothing about his slaves, and cared as little for one as for the other." This much Fox had drawn from long-standing tales of southern mountain Unionism. But Fox also added a new twist to the story. Explaining the mountaineers' stand in the Civil War, Fox noted that Chad's ignorance of slavery made his commitment to the Union cause noble and pure, untainted by seemingly extraneous causes and issues. Fox implicitly compared Chad's Unionism to that of the abolitionist, who was fired and presumably sidetracked by a vision of racial cruelty and oppression. Chad, however, who saw the slaves as "sleek, well-fed, well-housed," remained untouched by "the appeal of the slave." He was moved by the cause of nationalism itself, making him and his mountain compatriots "the embodiment of pure Americanism." Fox's book thus stood on the side of the Union while adopting the southern white and, increasingly, the northern white view of the kindly conditions of slavery. And, as Fox suggested, the isolation from slavery not only made the mountaineers dedicated Unionists, it also made their Union spirit more lofty and noble than that of the abolitionist who, apparently, had been dragged down by his more mundane concern for the slaves. Finally, Fox showed that Chad, who remained untainted by any feelings of sectionalism, was able to respect the North and the South, even paying tribute to the latter by naming his horse "Dixie." In this way, Chadwick Buford, the Anglo-Saxon mountain boy who rejected the extremism of slaveholder and abolitionist and who embraced the Union cause without condemning southern slavery, became the human embodiment of reconciliation and the national spirit.[23]

By creating racial and political myths of the Anglo-Saxonism and unqualified patriotism of Appalachia, northerners learned to view the white people of the southern mountains as unique among the mass of poor whites throughout the South. True, even the lowland population had begun to attract the attention of northerners for their sturdy racial heritage. Yet, to a great extent, the stereotype of the lazy and untidy cracker clung to the poor white during the late nineteenth and early twentieth centuries. And, unlike the mountain people, the company that the poor white kept and the political sympathies that he professed during the Civil War made him suspect to most northerners.

In contrast, southern highlanders, who were isolated from southern black people and from the strange, foreign breeds invading northern cities, seemed to be a unique refuge for white Anglo-Saxonism. Here, in Appalachia, isolation had bred patriotism, a continuation of pioneer traditions, and a sturdy and vigorous nature. The mountaineers exuded a potential for uplift and industry, especially in light of their purer racial heritage and their minimal exposure to the degradations of slaves and the slave system. And, in the age of reunion, when reconciliation rested on a reunification of white people from all the sections, northerners found in Appalachia a people worthy of their humanitarian and conciliatory gestures.

NOTES

1. The best accounts of the discovery of Appalachia are Henry Shapiro, *Appalachia on Our Mind: The Southern Mountaineers in the American Consciousness* (Chapel Hill, N.C., 1978), and James Klotter, "The Black South and White Appalachia," *Journal of American History* 66 (March 1980): 832–49. While I am indebted to the ideas of Klotter and Shapiro, I also depart slightly from their emphasis on Appalachian "otherness."

2. Charles Nordhoff, *The Cotton States in the Spring and Summer of 1875* (New York, 1876), 108; S.A. Hamilton, "The New Race Question in the South," *Arena* 27 (April 1902): 357.

3. A.D. Mayo, "The Third Estate in the South," *New England Magazine*, n.s., 3 (Nov. 1890): 307; Stephen Powers, *Afoot and Alone: A Walk from Sea to Sea by the Southern Route* (Hartford, Conn., 1872), 106; Charles Dudley Warner, *Studies in the South and West with Comments on Canada* (New York, 1889), 20. Most historians agree that the term "Anglo-Saxon" was used with little precision in this period of intense racial scrutiny. The majority of commentators, including those who wrote about "Anglo-Saxonism" in Appalachia, probably saw it mostly as a reflection of English roots. On this, see, for example, Thomas G. Dyer, *Theodore Roosevelt and the Idea of Race* (Baton Rouge, 1980). On the linkage between Anglo-Saxonism and notions of civilization, see Gail Bederman, *Manliness and Civilization: A Cultural History of Gender and Race in the United States, 1880–1917* (Chicago, 1995).

4. Joshua Caldwell, "The South Is American," *Arena* 8 (Oct. 1893): 607–17.

5. Gen. Roeliff Brinkerhoff, quoted in Leslie H. Fishel and Benjamin Quarles, eds., *The Negro American: A Documentary History* (Glenview, Ill., 1967), 339; "The White Side of the Southern Question," *Nation* 31 (Aug. 19, 1880): 126; Myers quoted in Klotter, "Black South and White Appalachia," 842. This tendency to focus on southern whites at the expense of southern blacks also characterized the work of the Southern Education Board in the early twentieth century. For a discussion of this development, see Louis Harlan, "Southern Education, the Race Issue, and Intersectional Cooperation," in *The South and the Sectional Image*, ed. Dewey Grantham (New York, 1967), 79–87.

6. Henry Shapiro, in *Appalachia on Our Mind*, credits Berea College president William G. Frost for isolating this distinct mountain region and identifying it as "Appalachian America" (115–16).

7. William G. Frost, *University Extension in the Southern Mountains* (New York, 1898), 5.

8. My understanding of northern culture's "discovery" of Appalachia has been greatly influenced by Shapiro, *Appalachia on Our Mind*. While I think Shapiro correctly pinpoints a tendency to isolate the problem of Appalachian otherness during the 1870s and 1880s, he fails to stress the ways in which northern culture worked to obliterate that sense of otherness, especially at the turn of the century, and the extent to which the southern mountaineers were brought into a national culture from which southern blacks were excluded. For an analysis of the early local color literature of Allen and Murfree, see Shapiro, *Appalachia on Our Mind*, 3–31. Mary Murfree, Sept. 30, 1884, to Thomas B. Aldrich, Houghton-Mifflin Papers, Houghton Library, Harvard University.

9. Jacquelyn Dowd Hall et al., *Like a Family: The Making of a Southern Cotton Mill World* (Chapel Hill, N.C., 1987), 9–10; Exposition Notes, May 3, 1895, in folder 1, box 46, Exposition Records, R.U. 70, Smithsonian Archives; Frank Presbrey, *The Empire of the South: An Exposition of the Present Resources and Development of the South, 1899* (Washington, D.C., 1898), 9; Edward Atkinson to J. Sterling Morton, Dec. 26, 1893, Edward Atkinson Papers, New York Public Library.

10. "The Cotton Mills of Spartanburg," *The Exposition* (May 1901), in folder 15, box 60, Exposition Records, R.U. 70, Smithsonian Archives; [William] G. Frost, "Our Southern Highlanders," *Independent* 72 (April 4, 1912): 714.

11. William Brewer, "Moonshining in Georgia," *Cosmopolitan* 23 (June 1897): 132; "The Real Southern Question Again," *World's Work* 4 (May 1902): 2068, 2072.

12. Frost, *University Extension*, 5; Emma Bell Miles, "Some Real American Music," *Harper's Monthly* 109 (June 1904): 119; Leon Vandevort, "A National Playground in the South," *Outing* 42 (Sept. 1903): 680.

13. Shapiro reviews Frost's work as Berea College president in *Appalachia on Our Mind*, 113–32, but overemphasizes the degree to which Frost projected Appalachia as a problem. Frost, *University Extension*, 10; William Frost, "Our Contemporary Ancestors in the Southern Mountains," *Atlantic Monthly* 83 (Feb. 1899): 315–16; Frost, "Our Southern Highlanders," 714.

14. Frost, "Our Contemporary Ancestors," 318.

15. The myth of Appalachian Unionism is challenged, most notably, in Kenneth Noe and Shannon Wilson, eds., *The Civil War in Appalachia: Collected Essays* (Knoxville, 1997). Frost, *University Extension*, 11; John DeForest, *A Union Officer in the Reconstruction* (New Haven, Conn., 1968), 161; Shapiro, *Appalachia on Our Mind*, 86–97; Frost, "Our Contemporary Ancestors," 316; Frost, *University Extension*, 8.

16. Mrs. S.M. Davis, quoted in Shapiro, *Appalachia on Our Mind*, 97; Nathaniel Shaler, "The Peculiarities of the South," *North American Review* 106 (Oct. 1890): 483.

17. Frost, *University Extension*, 5; Shaler, "Peculiarities of the South," 484.

18. Frank Waldo, "Among the Southern Appalachians," *New England Magazine*, n.s., 24 (May 1901): 246, 243.

19. Carl Schurz, *The New South* (New York, 1885), 25; S.A. Hamilton, "The New Race Question in the South," *Arena* 27 (April 1902): 357.

20. Shapiro, *Appalachia on Our Mind*, 30; Frank L. Mott, *Golden Multitudes: The Story of Best Sellers in the United States* (New York, 1947), 214.

21. John Fox Jr., *The Little Shepherd of Kingdom Come* (1903; reprint, Lexington, Ky., 1987), 7, 24.

22. Fox, *Little Shepherd*, 69.

23. Ibid., 188–92.

16

African American Convicts in the Coal Mines of Southern Appalachia

RONALD L. LEWIS

The industrial transition that gripped many sections of southern Appalachia during the late nineteenth and early twentieth centuries triggered a dramatic population growth in the region's coalfields. Local farmers, black southerners, white northerners, and newly arrived foreigners all converged in the single-industry coal mining towns and centers that seemed to sprout overnight in this mountainous rural countryside. Scholars now recognize the diversity of the Appalachian economy and its labor force; they also recognize that the region probably never was as uniformly isolated and homogeneous as it is in the popular imagination. Considerable scholarship has documented the development of this heterogeneous workforce in the Appalachian coalfields, but the important role played by tens of thousands of convicts leased to private mining companies has remained unexplored within Appalachian studies. Although the analogy is easily strained, the model for convict labor in the New South was slave labor in the Old South. Under the convict-leasing system, a white power structure benefited financially from forcing black prisoners against their will to labor under physical and psychological conditions that were all too reminiscent of slavery.

Emancipation terminated slave labor in the southern Appalachian coal industry as it did throughout the South, but some of the economic benefits derived from forced labor were preserved, at least for a few mine operators, in the new bondage of convict leasing. Although leasing convicts to private contractors was common in the South, it became prevalent in the coalfields of Georgia, Tennessee, and Alabama. Other southern states with significant coal reserves did not use prison labor in mining. The manifold rewards derived from convict leasing prompted charges that the system was merely an attempt to reinstate slavery in new form, but the motives underlying its development were far more complex. During the period of economic and political instability immediately after the war, neither capitalists nor political officials had a comprehensive awareness of the economic potential in convict leasing. Once instituted, however, the system rapidly developed into a hydra-headed monster that corrupted politics and business and undermined public morality in the New South.

Coalfields in southern Appalachia. (Map produced by University of Georgia Cartographic Services)

Before the Civil War, most black lawbreakers were slaves who were disciplined by their masters. Impoverished state governments were not eager to take on the responsibility and the expense of providing prisons for thousands of black criminals after the war. A few state prisons were damaged during the war, but most simply suffered the ravages of neglect. Convict leasing was initially seen as a way to shift one of the many financial burdens to private entrepreneurs. Provisional military governments began leasing convicts as a temporary expedient, and the practice was continued with the Radical Republicans and then institutionalized by the Redeemer Democrats.

Projecting themselves as the protectors of individual property owners, the Democrats regained political power by attacking the Republicans for extravagance, corruption, and excessive taxation. Consequently, "cheapness, even niggardliness, under this tutelage became widely accepted as the criterion of good government," as C. Vann Woodward has observed.[1] The convict-leasing system was remarkably adaptable to the retrenchment policies of the

Democrats. With the prisoners leased to the private sector, the necessity for additional taxes to expand and maintain prison facilities was eliminated. Moreover, the revenues generated from leasing could be substantial, and they helped to reduce financial pressures on the heavily indebted state treasuries. In 1880, Enoch Cobb Wines, the father of the prison reform movement, stated that about one-half of the expenses of operating prisons in non-convict-leasing states came from income derived from the labor of inmates. By comparison, the U.S. commissioner of labor reported in 1886 that where leasing was practiced the average revenues constituted 372 percent of the costs for operating those prisons.[2]

The convict-leasing system also suited the new criminal codes of the Redeemer administrations, which were designed to protect property owners from petty crimes that had also been controlled by local planters before the war. Stiff sentences for petty offenses were leveled primarily at freedmen at the same time that their protection in court was being weakened. With prisoners leased to the private sector, additional convictions meant additional revenues for the empty state treasuries.[3] George Washington Cable, an arch opponent of the system and the leading convict-lease reformer of the day, denounced the system for its banal economic motivations: "Without regard to moral or mortal consequences, the penitentiary whose annual report shows the largest case balance paid into the State's treasury is the best penitentiary." In effect, there was no "human right that the State is bound to be at any expense to protect." It was this characteristic that led governors to congratulate their legislatures for making convicts "into a shameful and disastrous source of revenue" from lessees whose only motive was to make money.[4]

Cable's critique of convict leasing was a modified version of the antislavery argument and demonstrates a continuity in the mentality that informed the opposition to forced labor before and after emancipation. Indeed, the continuities between slavery and convict leasing also were striking. Leasing, which evolved out of the heritage of slavery as an adaptation to the needs of a nascent industrial capitalism in its aggressively exploitative stage, may have sprung from habits of thought and attitudes rooted in agricultural slavery, but it took nourishment and flourished in the New South's most dangerous labor-intensive industries, especially mining. Slaves had, after all, worked in the region's coal mines, so it was an easy progression to send convicts into them after the war. Just as slave owners desired a cheap and tractable labor force, so did industrialists.[5] For decades, therefore, the most powerful coal operators of Georgia, Tennessee, and Alabama exerted political influence and their considerable financial resources to secure convict labor.

The desire for the steady labor that convicts offered mine operators was intensified by an inadequate supply of free industrial labor. T.J. Hill, who worked convicts in Alabama and Tennessee mines, informed delegates at the 1897 convention of the National Prison Association that in the 1870s a strong effort was made to develop the iron and coal resources of the southern states, but it was "a practical impossibility to get our native free people, either white or

Banner Mine prison buildings that housed black convicts. (Courtesy of the Birmingham Public Library, Birmingham, Ala.)

black, their training having been principally of an agricultural tendency, to
work in the mines." The acquisition of convicts, however, made possible the
rapid development of the coal reserves in Alabama and Tennessee and "gave an
impetus to the manufacturing interests of the entire South, which could not
otherwise have been possible, for at least many years."[6]

Convict leasing was, however, more than a means by which state governments alleviated financial pressures on their depleted treasuries or industrialists secured cheap, tractable labor. Leasing also was an important pillar of the
South's racial hierarchy.[7] Whites who were afraid that the hierarchy of the Old
South was beginning to crumble took aggressive action to reinforce the edifice
of white supremacy through the now familiar mechanisms of segregation. Although the black codes were disallowed by the federal government, the use of
vaguely worded laws relating to vagrancy and loitering remained on the books
for a century and allowed white authorities to arrest blacks for any behavior
that they deemed inappropriate and then sentence offenders to excessive jail
terms. Consequently, the prison population became overwhelmingly black, and
disproportionately, blacks were leased to do the hard, dirty, and dangerous
work of mining coal.[8]

Critics such as George Washington Cable insisted that the racism that
permeated southern society lay behind the disproportionate impact that the

system exerted on African Americans. Blacks served longer sentences for lesser crimes against property at an alarmingly disproportionate rate.[9] In this context, the brutality that became characteristic of convict leasing may be understood as part of a more comprehensive system of racial intimidation and subjugation. The flagrant racial injustice of the lease system, one scholar observed, presents "incontrovertible evidence of the New South's moral failure."[10] With the system generating revenues for the state treasury, taxpayers expressed their gratitude at the polls, and the coal companies extracted as much labor for as little expense as they could get away with. The cruelty that resulted from this unholy alliance between government and capital was a labor system with a mortality rate three times higher than the rate in northern prisons, and at certain mines ten times higher.[11] As one lessee observed in 1883, "Before the war we owned the negroes. If a man had a good nigger, he could afford to take care of him." Convicts were better than slaves, however, because "we don't own 'em. One dies, get another."[12]

Georgia was one of the first states to establish the convict-lease system after the Civil War. Confronted with an empty treasury and an increasing number of convicts for a prison that had been destroyed during the war, the General Assembly instituted leasing in 1866 as a practical expedient.[13] In 1876 the legislature enacted a comprehensive convict-lease plan that remained in force for the next three decades. Under this plan, the state entered twenty-year contracts with three private companies for a total of $500,000. The vast majority of the convicts were leased to industrial establishments, such as brick factories, sawmills, railroads, and especially coal mines.[14] From its inception Georgia's convict-lease system was deeply enmeshed in political corruption. Between 1868 and 1908, when the system was abolished, dozens of well-connected public officials supped at the convict-lease trough. Until an act in 1874 extended the leases to five years, the system was relatively honest; the state received forty thousand dollars annually between 1868 and 1874 from leasing. A decade later, however, the number of convicts had doubled, but the state received less than sixteen thousand dollars per year because public officials flagrantly ignored the law requiring that convicts be let to the highest bidder.[15]

No politician was as adroit as Joseph E. Brown in manipulating the system to his own advantage. So adept was he, in fact, that Brown was known as Georgia's "convict king." After serving as a Democratic governor during the Civil War, he became a Republican and advocated acceptance of Radical Reconstruction. As a reward he was appointed chief justice of the state supreme court by Radical governor Rufus Bullock. Following redemption he returned to the Democratic party and, proving that principle was not a prerequisite for high office, served as U.S. senator from 1880 to 1890.[16] Brown was the leading coal mine operator in Georgia and the principal contractor of convict labor for his own company, Dade Coal Company, and for the Walker Coal and Iron Company, both located in the mountainous northwestern corner of the state. Even though coal never became a major industry in Georgia, Brown was financially successful because each convict leased to mine his coal cost him only seven cents a day.[17]

The former governor used his political influence to ensure cheap and ready access to all the convicts he needed. Sometimes such access meant sharing the spoils. When Governor Bullock demanded a share in Brown's interests, for example, the lessee replied that he was perfectly willing that Bullock "be employed by our company in the capacity you mention at a reasonable compensation" and privately advised his partner that the arrangement was "not a matter that would do to write about."[18] It was this kind of political chicanery that enabled Brown to retain his lease in 1876 when other convict companies bid as high as 400 percent more than the former governor. Similarly, when a joint committee of the Georgia legislature inspected Brown's convict mine in 1881, he held an elaborate banquet in their honor. Subsequently, the committee reported favorably on conditions at the senator's prison, even though a minority report charged that the prisoners worked in sixty-degree temperatures with cold water dripping on them and then slept in the same wet, dirty clothing. No feast could eradicate that fact, the minority report declared, but apparently it did quell any hunger for reform among the committee's majority.[19]

In 1887, Rebecca Latimer Felton, the wife of a prominent Georgia congressman and a pioneer in the movement to abolish leasing, charged that the system was allowed to continue despite serious abuses because of this kind of collusion between politicians and contractors. She claimed that most of the convict revenues went to "a gang of supernumerary officials, who are generally 'go-betweens'" involved in the business of selling the poor and powerless to the highest bidder. Himself a contractor, Gov. James M. Smith lent credence to Mrs. Felton's charge by publicly declaring that "of the convicts in the penitentiary, five to one are colored persons, most, if not all of whom, by reason of their ignorance and former habits of life, can never be profitably employed in any of the mechanical arts." It was this aspect of leasing, not the inadequate food and cruel treatment, that reflected the most deplorable side of the system.[20]

Felton's criticisms, which were published in a widely circulated national magazine, sparked a major public controversy in Georgia. Just as the storm broke over the Felton article, a young prisoner still in his teens was beaten to death by former Governor Brown's whipping boss. The public outcry precipitated by these two events forced the governor to call on Brown to show cause why his lease should not be annulled. On October 2, 1887, Brown personally defended his conduct as a lessee and presented an elaborate justification of the system. This position paper was printed as a pamphlet and widely circulated at Brown's expense in an attempt to stem the rising tide of public sentiment against convict leasing.[21]

Brown's defense relied on the notion that the labor of prisoners should be expropriated to generate funds for the treasury. He claimed that if the leased men were returned to the walls, approximately $500,000 would be required to construct a new prison, the old one having been burned during the war by General Sherman. Then money would have to be raised in taxes from "honest laboring people" for the support of dishonest felons, who, under the current lease system, earned their own keep. The fifteen hundred convicts that would have to be housed in the penitentiary in 1887 would cost the taxpayers at least $4 million if the system were abolished, Brown argued. Under the lease system, however, the lessees paid into the treasury over a quarter of a million dollars between 1872 and 1886, and the state incurred no maintenance costs. In an argument reminiscent of the defense of slavery, Brown asserted that "the lessees would be fools" to maltreat their prisoners, for "every man of sense knows that the greatest aggregate of labor, during the year, may always be obtained from a man who is well fed and well clothed, and kindly treated, and his health carefully preserved."[22]

Brown's disclaimers about harsh treatment notwithstanding, conditions of life and work at Dade Coal mines earned the company its rank as one of the worst mine prisons in the southern Appalachian coalfields. Part of the reason was that Brown, like other contractors, complied with regulations only when it was expedient, as is amply demonstrated by the prison inspectors' reports. The report for 1886, for example, called attention to the wretched sanitary conditions at Brown's mines.[23] That same year, the U.S. commissioner of labor released a special report denouncing the conditions in Georgia as "very bad." All the convicts, including the miners, were "worked to the utmost and barbarously treated, from every point of view, moral, physical, and sanitary," resulting in a death rate described as "very high."[24] Similarly, a committee of the legislature reported in 1890 that at Dade mines the barracks, bedding, and clothing were filthy. Inside the mines the men worked "in such places as rendered it necessary for them to lie on their stomachs while at work, often in mud and water with bad ventilation, in order to get out the daily amount of coal that would save them from the punishment to be inflicted by the whipping boss."[25] On several subsequent occasions the Dade County grand jury committee on prisons reported on these same conditions. The committee noted that "the bed clothing was very filthy and infested with body lice. Window glass was broken, the barracks roof leaked, and the floor was too loose to keep an offensive odor from rising up through it." Moreover, the prisoners complained bitterly that the physician in charge was incompetent to judge whether the convicts were able to work.[26]

Physician incompetence was a potentially serious problem for convict miners. The act of 1876 stipulated that only able-bodied men were permitted to labor in the coal mines, and the state sent doctors to certify the health of workers. In 1883 the state-appointed physician, Dr. Thomas Raines, arrived at the Dade mines intoxicated. He remained in that condition for his entire stay and mistakenly certified twelve sick convicts as able-bodied men even though they could only be moved on stretchers. Such dereliction of duty was not sufficient to have Dr. Raines dismissed, however, for Acting Governor James S. Boynton reappointed him to another term the following year.[27]

Certainly, Dr. Raines did not protect the life of Lancaster LeConte. In his defense of the system in 1887 Governor Brown argued that the mortality rate was high at his prison because the jails sent "a class of aged and decrepit persons" to the mine who did not belong there, men "completely broken down in health, who linger in the hospital for months or possibly years, and die without ever doing a day's work."[28] Even as Brown spoke, however, seventy-five-year-old LeConte was sentenced to three years of hard labor at Dade mines for receiving stolen goods. Dr. Raines must have declared him an able-bodied man, for like the other three hundred convicts leased to the Dade Coal Company, LeConte was forced to work ten to twelve hours a day crawling in mud and water to dig Brown's coal. He wrote to his former master, the eminent scientist Dr. Joseph LeConte, for money to hire a lawyer, but his plea apparently was ignored. It was not long before Lancaster LeConte entered the prison hospital, ailing with "chronic rheumatism," and died there early in 1889.[29]

The dangers confronted by convicts in Georgia's coal mines are clearly revealed in the hospital records of the Dade Coal Company. During the twelve months from October 1888 to September 1889, twenty-six convicts were killed or injured. Two were killed by slate fall, and another died under the wheels of a railroad car. Of the remaining twenty-three whose injuries were identified, rock falls disabled seven, railroad cars injured seven more, explosions injured two, and a mule kick fractured one man's jaw. Twelve other men were injured at the hands of fellow convicts, their wounds variously described as "cut and carved all to pieces fighting," "abdomen ripped open with coal pick," and "eye knocked out fighting."[30] Such conditions undoubtedly reduced some men to a reliance on their most basic instincts for survival. Andrew Hargrove, for example, whose misbehavior verged on self-destructiveness, received eight vicious whippings between January 1885 and September 1886 for "rebelliousness."[31] Hargrove's case was exceptional, but in 1886, twenty-two other prisoners were flogged for "rebelliousness."[32] During the years 1888–1889, twelve others received the same punishment for the same charge, and two men were shot while attempting to escape from Brown's coal mines.[33]

Corruption and the cruel abuse of convicts did not go without public protest. A small but growing movement to abolish the system finally succeeded in swinging public opinion to its point of view by the turn of the century. During the summer of 1908, the *Atlanta Georgian and News*, along with such middle-class reformers as Rebecca Felton and the Atlanta clergyman John E. White, had exposed the many injustices of the system and had galvanized public opinion against leasing. Their strategy was to concentrate on atrocity stories involving white convicts (although more than 90 percent of the prisoners were black) in the belief that the populace would be less incensed by news of brutality against blacks. Mass meetings were staged throughout the state that summer, and the legislature, inundated with memorials and protests, was forced to act.[34] Against this background, the newly elected reform governor, Hoke Smith, seized the initiative and called a special session of the legislature to convene in late August 1908. Governor Smith recommended terminating the leasing system and assigning the prisoners to labor on the public highways. Confronted with an escalating spiral of popular indignation and a determined governor, the Georgia General Assembly abolished convict leasing in September 1908.[35]

In Tennessee, public officials also found it expedient to expropriate the labor of convicts by leasing them to private contractors in order to generate revenues for a war-depleted state treasury. And as in Georgia, the number of blacks in the prison population grew dramatically during the post–Civil War period. In October 1865, blacks accounted for 66 of the 200 convicts in the penitentiary (about 33 percent), but by November 1867, that proportion had increased to 283 of 551 (about 64 percent). Thereafter, the figure remained around 60 percent until the system was abolished in 1896. The percentage of black convicts in Tennessee coal mines, as we shall see, was much higher.[36]

A plan to lease the prisoners to coal mine operators received widespread public support on the grounds that such employment would reduce taxation, lower the cost of fuel, make the penitentiary self-sufficient, and alleviate convict competition with free labor.[37] These were the chief arguments of the state's New South proponents as well, who were in full accord with the plan. The foundations of economic expansion in Tennessee were the basic industries of coal and iron, and many of the state's Redeemer oligarchy had direct business ties with these industries.[38]

Tennessee's first Democratic governor was John C. Brown, former Whig and brother of the antebellum Whig governor Neill S. Brown. He became president of the Bon Air Coal Company and chief executive in the Tennessee Coal, Iron, and Railroad Company (TCI). Democrat James D. Porter, who succeeded Brown in the governorship, left that office and also became a TCI director. Albert S. Marks, who succeeded Porter, was a relative and former law partner of Col. Arthur S. Colyar, another mine owner and the undisputed leader of the industrial wing of the state Democratic party.[39]

Colyar lost a campaign for the Democratic gubernatorial nomination in 1870, but a major plank in his platform for industrial development was leasing convict labor to the coal mines in the eastern section of the state.[40] Though he subsequently derived considerable personal wealth from leasing, he genuinely regarded the system as wise public policy. "The greatest work of my life," he told a convention of mechanics, "has been in turning convict labor from mechanical pursuits, and putting it where it helps the mechanic by furnishing him cheap coal."[41] With the support of groups such as the Nashville Mechanics' and Manufacturers' Association, he was able to apply sufficient political leverage to win a contract in December 1870. For one dollar a day per man, with the state providing all necessities except the prison facility, Colyar leased 102 black convicts for his Tennessee Coal Company mines at Tracy City, about forty miles west of Chattanooga.[42]

Labor difficulties arose almost immediately. The free men promptly went out on strike demanding removal of the prisoners and tried unsuccessfully to attack the convicts. The prisoners then refused to work, but a sound flogging persuaded them to return to their picks. After two weeks of unproductive demonstrations, the free miners also grudgingly returned to their workplaces.[43] These events were portents of the serious labor problems in the future.

From the beginning, conditions of life and work were just as deplorable in Tennessee convict mines as they were in Georgia. Even state officials found plenty to criticize. Dr. P.D. Sims, chairman of the state board of health's Committee on Prisons, reported excessively high mortality rates (95.2 convicts per 1,000 per year) at Tracy City, figures at which "humanity stands aghast and our boasted civilization must hide her face in shame."[44] George Washington Cable denounced the death rates in Tennessee as "startlingly larger" when compared with those of prison systems that did not lease convicts. The causes were not difficult to comprehend, Cable asserted: overwork, overcrowding, poor food, poor sanitation, and violent behavior on the part of prisoners and guards all shortened the life expectancy of convict miners. Moreover, living quarters were so cramped that prisoners slept in a space that approximated a "good sized grave," and medical facilities were "too revolting for popular reading." No wonder escapes from the mine camps were so high, he wrote. In northern state prisons containing 18,400 convicts, there were only sixty-three escapes in 1881. That same year, 49 Tennessee prisoners escaped from a leased population of only 630.[45]

Conditions did not improve over the next decade either.[46] One courageous prisoner testified in 1891 that conditions still had not changed significantly: "There is lots of water and sometimes I have to roll up my pants to wade through. The air is bad and while at work it hurts me in the chest, to sleep in it. We are only allowed one shirt, one pair of pants, and are not allowed any socks."[47] Neither the state nor the company were sufficiently stirred by these exposés to alter the lucrative arrangement, and TCI experienced no difficulty in securing another six-year lease in 1889.[48]

Convict-mined coal might have provided mechanics with an economic advantage, as Colyar had suggested, but free miners certainly were not included in his calculations. Tennessee Coal and Iron Company paid free miners daily wages of $2.50, but convicts cost the company only $0.24 a day. The company forthrightly admitted that its purpose in leasing convicts was to counter the "high cost of regular miners."[49] Just as important, TCI found that convict labor was extremely effective in defeating unionism, as convicts acted as strikebreakers. In fact, Colyar openly declared in 1883 that "one of the chief reasons which first induced the company to take up the system was the great chance it seemed to present for overcoming strikes."[50] TCI exploited another cost advantage when it worked convicts in the most productive sections of the mines, whereas free miners, who worked on a tonnage basis, were assigned to sections that required considerable "dead work" before they could begin producing coal.[51]

Free miners were not ignorant of the effects of convict leasing, and they complained bitterly. The *United Mine Workers Journal* (*UMWJ*) is filled with angry charges from correspondents that the Tennessee legislature and TCI were in collusion to enrich a few oligarchies at the expense of the free miners. No wonder TCI put up such a fierce struggle to retain the system, the United Mine Workers of America (UMWA) charged, when each convict miner earned the corporation a net profit of $9.80 a day, and 1,029 convicts produced a profit of more than $10,000 a day. At this rate, one work year of three hundred days yielded the company a bonus of $3 million. Meanwhile, the *UMWJ* noted, the four thousand white miners in the district were "compelled to compete with the East Tennessee Company miners on equal terms."[52]

TCI's use of convicts to cut labor costs and to curtail unionization precipitated a conflict of legendary proportion with the free miners in the early nineties. Labor militancy escalated dramatically during the winter of 1890–1891 as remnants of the Knights of Labor and locals of the newly founded UMWA began challenging the company's policies. On April 1, 1891, TCI closed down its Briceville operation, ostensibly for repairs, but when the mine reopened two months later the free miners were required to sign "iron-clad" oaths repudiating the union in order to regain their jobs. Those who refused were evicted from company houses, and a convict stockade for 150 additional convicts was erected. In retrospect, the rebellious protest that erupted into the "convict wars" seems to have been inevitable, a natural consequence of the company's systematic suppression of lawful, moderate opposition. The rebellion signaled, as C. Vann Woodward has suggested, that not all southern labor would accept the "Old-South labor philosophy of the New-South leaders."[53]

More than three hundred convicts, the overwhelming majority of them blacks, were imported into Anderson County mines along Coal Creek during the first two weeks of July 1891. Local public officials bitterly denounced the state and the company for shipping in "undesirables" to displace native citizens.[54] On July 14, a mass meeting of miners and their supporters met to condemn the Coal Creek importation. Early the next morning three hundred armed miners captured the convicts at Briceville and herded them onto a train bound for Knoxville, thirty miles away. When the miners appealed to Gov. John P. Buchanan to halt the influx, he responded by ordering out three more companies of state militia. H.H. Schwartz, a representative of the Chattanooga Federation of Trades, reported from the scene that the miners were outraged and that "whites and Negroes are standing shoulder to shoulder." He counted 840 rifles and a multitude of "pistol-toters" among one group of miners who marched through town that night.[55] The following week approximately fifteen hundred armed miners once again commandeered the prisoners who had replaced the earlier convicts at Briceville and put them aboard a train for Knoxville. In a nearby camp another 125 convicts, "only five being white," were captured and shipped to the same destination.[56]

In an attempt to avoid further turmoil, Governor Buchanan dispatched an emissary to negotiate a sixty-day truce while he called a special session of the state legislature to consider the future of the leasing system. Reluctantly, the miners accepted his proposal.[57] Meanwhile, the state commissioner of labor, George W. Ford, and the entire Board of Penitentiary Inspectors held a surprise on-site investigation of conditions at the mines that revealed multiple health and safety violations. Their reports became fuel for a heated debate over abolition of the system when the special session convened on August 31. Whatever hope that the antileasing forces held for the outcome of the session faded, however, before TCI's arguments that no adequate prison facility existed and that the state would lose considerable revenues if the system were abolished. Reluctant to raise taxes, the legislators saw the kind of wisdom they understood in TCI's position and voted to retain the leasing system.[58]

Upon hearing this news, the miners immediately resumed their attacks against the stockades, freeing the "zebras" and entraining them for Knoxville and Nashville. Fellow miners from Kentucky and Virginia supported the uprising, and the entire countryside seemed to have fallen to the forces of anarchy as armies of black and white miners challenged authorities and assaulted the convict stockades. Outraged public opinion in the rest of the state forced the governor to send in the National Guard armed with the latest weapons. Hundreds of Coal Creek miners were incarcerated by troops operating under orders to give no quarter to those who resisted. In one incident, soldiers riddled the body of Jake Whitson, a free black miner, with twelve bullets on the claim that he had resisted, but the several thousand miners who attended his funeral were convinced that Whitsen was murdered because of his leadership role in the revolt.[59] It was months before the state militia crushed the rebellion and returned the convicts to the mines. The free miners were forced to sign the detested iron-clad oath before returning to their old jobs, and those who refused were summarily fired and blacklisted as troublemakers. As for the convicts themselves, of the approximately 458 set free, two-thirds were recaptured, but 165 made good their escape.[60]

Despite the magnitude of the miners' protest, the convict wars of 1891–1892 were only indirectly responsible for the abolition of convict leasing. The arrangement between the state and TCI had been founded on mutual economic advantage, but heavy financial burdens incurred during the disturbances altered that relationship. The August 1891 outbreak alone cost the state over $125,000. With neither the government nor TCI willing to bear these expenses, it became impossible for politicians to support continuation of convict leasing in Tennessee.[61]

In January 1893, lame duck Governor Buchanan's farewell address recommended that the lease system be abolished and that the state purchase its own coal mine in which to employ the prisoners, as did newly elected Gov. Peter Turney in his inaugural speech. Negative reports presented by the superintendent of prisons, the prison doctor, and the chief warden reinforced the growing sense that the system must be abandoned. But the legislators were cautious and formed still another committee to investigate the mines. The investigation found that little had changed over the years; it finally concluded that all of the suffering had resulted from "petty meanness" and that the system itself was morally flawed for encouraging lessees "to make the last possible cent out of the flesh and blood bought with our money."[62] These remarks carried strong lineaments of wrath, but many inspections over the years had inoculated legislators against any potential shock induced by such unsavory details. The real difference was that the system was now costing the state money rather than making it. The legislature passed a bill in April 1893, therefore, abolishing the system when the lease with TCI expired on January 1, 1896.[63]

Some Tennessee convicts continued to mine coal after 1896, but only at the state-owned Brushy Mountain mine. That Tennessee prison officials still considered coal mining particularly suited for blacks is made clear by the fact that 85 percent of the Brushy Mountain convicts in 1898 were African Americans, and twelve years later they still constituted 82 percent of the 747 convict miners in the state.[64]

Convict leasing achieved its fullest development in Alabama, where economics, politics, and racist ideology converged in full support of the system. Alabama confronted financial exigencies similar to those of Georgia and Tennessee following Reconstruction. Saddled with a heavy bonded indebtedness and blaming Republicans for fiscal responsibility, Redeemers regained control of state government in 1874 and made frugality the hallmark of government in Alabama, reducing a $25 million debt to approximately $9 million by 1882.[65]

One new source of revenue was convict leasing, which brought into the treasury a modest $14,000 in 1877 and increased to $109,000 by 1890. This income placed Alabama first among all of the states in revenue earned from convict labor and next to the bottom in per capita taxation.[66] Convict labor came to play a more integral role in the political economy of Alabama than in Georgia or Tennessee. Between 1880 and 1904, Alabama's profits exceeded $2.3 million, an average of about $95,000 per year, or about 10 percent of the state's annual budget.[67]

The system was profitable for public officials also. Bulging jails and automatic convictions were to the financial advantage of nearly every public official in the criminal justice network. Paying sheriffs and the clerks of court out of fees, rather than a fixed salary, practically guaranteed a bountiful supply of convict labor. The Jefferson County sheriff, for example, received fees ranging from twenty-five cents to ninety dollars each for more than forty services. The sheriff's annual income in 1912, therefore, reportedly was between fifty thousand and eighty thousand dollars, and clerkships paid approximately twenty-five thousand dollars per year.[68]

Alabama's convict lease system also functioned as an agency for racial control and supervision. Certain broadly drawn statutes gave employers a mechanism for keeping workers on the job. For example, the vagrancy law empowered the police to arrest "any person wandering or strolling about in idleness, who is able to work, and has no property to support him; or any person leading an idle, immoral, profligate life, having no property to support him."[69] The public concern with idle blacks that lay behind such measures is evident in the press. A 1906 editorial in the *Birmingham News*, for example, remarked that "anyone visiting a Southern city or town must be impressed at witnessing the large number of loafing Negroes. . . . They can get work, but they don't want to work. The result is that they sooner or later get into mischief or commit crime."[70]

That racial control was an essential element in the lease system is amply demonstrated in the composition of the prison population itself. An Alabama prison official aptly observed that, judging from the prisoners, white men apparently "do not commit crime, or else they are safely insulated from the penitentiary by greenbacks or other penal non-conductors."[71] Although few blacks were detained in the state prison until after the Civil War, throughout more than half a century of leasing in postwar Alabama the prison population remained overwhelmingly black. In 1871, 78 percent of the 182 state convicts were African Americans. Between 1874 and 1877 the penitentiary population nearly trebled to 655, of which blacks made up 88 percent in 1874 and 91 percent in 1877. That percentage leveled off at about 90 percent throughout the 1880s and 1890s even as the total population doubled. Thereafter, the proportion of black convicts declined to 83 percent, where it remained until the leasing system was abolished in 1927. County prisons, over which the state exercised little control, roughly paralleled the pattern of the state prison.[72]

During Reconstruction, most of the state convicts were consigned to railroad construction crews. When J.G. Bass was appointed warden in 1875, he quickly earned the praise of the new Democratic administration by turning the penitentiary into a profitable institution. Nevertheless, the next governor, Rufus Cobb (1878–1882), expressed his dissatisfaction with Bass, who he felt could have negotiated better terms for the state than he had.[73] He was replaced in 1881 by a new warden, John H. Bankhead. Immediately after his appointment, Bankhead negotiated an agreement under which lessees paid twelve dollars per month for first-class hands sent to the mines, as opposed to eight dollars under Bass.

As revenues escalated, convict conditions deteriorated. Conditions at the mines in the Birmingham district, particularly at Coketon (which became Pratt Mines) and New Castle, were alarming when Bankhead took charge of the prison. Dr. John B. Gaston, president of the Alabama Medical Association, and Dr. Jerome Cochran, the state health officer, conducted an inspection of convicts working in the coal mines that year. Their report left little to the imagination, condemning the unsanitary conditions as "filthy and disgusting" and the treatment of prisoners as unnecessarily cruel. Blacks and whites were segregated into cramped and filthy quarters. The cells for blacks were slightly smaller than those for whites. They contained the same five-foot-seven-inch-by-three-foot bunks with straw mattresses, but three men were assigned to each, instead of the two in white cells, thus affording one foot of sleeping space for each occupant. The recommended space for prison cells without ventilation fans was four hundred to six hundred cubic feet per person, but whites had less than half that amount, and blacks less than one-third. Moreover, the mattresses were infested with bedbugs, and the blankets were caked with a mixture of coal dust, human sweat, and grease. The prisoners all worked with shackles on their ankles and were marched to and from the mines chained together. After a full shift, they were marched directly to the dining hall to eat the evening meal without even washing their hands. The main meal, usually consisting of fat bacon, peas, cornbread, and coffee, was often served cold in tin containers without utensils, forcing the men to eat with their fingers.[74]

The report sparked a bitter public controversy between Dr. Gaston and

John T. Milner, owner of the mine at New Castle. Milner published a rebuttal vehemently denying the charges, but Dr. Gaston, the inspectors, and Warden Bankhead uniformly persisted in their denunciation of these conditions.[75] In 1883, this controversy prompted a major legislative reform of the system. The reform created a board of inspectors and concentrated two-thirds of the convicts with the companies Comer & McCurdy and Pratt Coal. These two companies leased two hundred convicts and jointly operated the group of Birmingham District pits called Pratt Mines.[76] The legislature initiated another major reorganization in 1885 when it abolished the office of warden and reassigned his duties to the new board of inspectors.[77] R.H. Dawson, who was appointed president of the new board, favored a plan for concentrating all of the convicts at Pratt Mines, which had been taken over by the Tennessee Coal and Iron Company in 1886. When the previous contracts expired in 1888, therefore, a new ten-year lease was awarded to TCI, under which the company agreed to accept all able-bodied male convicts for between $9.00 and $18.50 per month, depending on their classification. The Pratt Mines division of TCI operated ten coal mines in 1895, with convicts concentrated at Shaft No. 1 and Slope No. 2, and free labor at the other eight. Together, numbers 1 and 2 contained nine hundred convicts, over 80 percent of them blacks, who worked 313 days that year producing over 1.5 million tons of coal.[78]

TCI's bid had not been the highest, but the company had agreed to take responsibility for all the prisoners. It never accepted more than three-quarters of the state's more than one thousand convicts, however, because of the economics of convict classification. For example, in 1889 first-class men (the most able-bodied) cost contractors $18.50 per month; second-class men, $13.50; third-class men, $9.00; fourth-class men, the cost of their maintenance. First-class convicts were tasked to cut and load four tons of coal per day; second-class, three tons; third-class, two tons; fourth-class, one ton. At fifty cents per ton for a twenty-seven-day month, a first-class convict earned the contractor $54.00; a second-class miner, $40.50. But the difference in the price paid per month between the two classes was $5.00, while the difference in earnings was $13.50 per month. Contractors, therefore, made $8.50 more per month on first-class men simply because of their classification.[79] Consequently, it was in the economic interest of TCI to accept only men of the soundest physical ability and to leave the less able behind walls.

One reason that the state permitted the contract to remain in force even though TCI had failed to comply with the lease was the company's promise to construct new prison facilities at Pratt Mines. TCI fulfilled this promise, and according to the board of inspectors, Pratt had the best facilities "ever erected by any convict contractor in the South." The facilities at Shaft No. 1 had accommodations for 420 inmates with six hundred cubic feet of space for each, and a similar prison was erected at Slope No. 2.[80] A local newspaperman toured the mines in 1889 and reported that prison compartments were spacious, well-ventilated, and scrupulously clean. However, there was a "marked difference between the treatment of the convicts here and at Coalburg," the reporter observed. "While they are dying at the latter place like sheep with the rot," Pratt had only three of its five hundred inmates on the sick list.[81]

Conditions at nearby Coalburg were indeed poorer. Unable to obtain state convicts, independent producers, such as the company that operated Coalburg Mines, pooled the available county prisoners. Because these prisoners were sentenced to short terms, they cost operators much less, about eight dollars per month, but they were less disciplined and seldom became skilled miners. With little control from state penitentiary inspectors, county convicts generally toiled under the severest of conditions. Such was the case at Coalburg, which John Milner sold to the Sloss Iron and Steel Company in 1889. The state health officer, Dr. Jerome Cochran, that year charged Sloss officials with criminal negligence and cruelty. The doctor found the prison to be "dark, damp and loathsome" and so dirty as to be "offensive to the sight and smell." Punishments were excessive as well. During the first two weeks of June, 137 whippings were administered for failure to complete the required tasks, even though most of the men had been seriously weakened by a six-month epidemic.[82]

Conditions did not improve at Coalburg over the next several years. Dr. Thomas D. Parke, the health officer for Jefferson County, filed another disturbing report in 1895 on the high rates of sickness and mortality at the prison mine. During the previous two years, 105 men had died at the Sloss Company mine, the major causes being tuberculosis and the life-threatening infection erysipelas ("sore leg"). Parke concluded that the high incidence of tuberculosis was the natural result of too much time spent underground and prescribed more sunlight as the cure. But the company was concerned with production more than with the health of its convicts; consequently the death rate at Coalburg for 1893 and 1894 was an alarming ninety per thousand. To underscore his point, he compared Coalburg prison's annual death rate with the rate of nine per thousand for penitentiaries in Ohio and Pennsylvania. Even in other southern convict-lease systems rates were lower. Mississippi's deplorable death rate of forty per thousand was still dramatically better than Coalburg's.[83] As late as 1908 the Sloss Company mines still had serious problems in the proper handling of prisoners, even by the standards of southern white prison officials.[84]

The incredible inhumanity displayed by some mine operators gave new meaning to the old phrase "slave driving," and a sentence in the mines quite properly instilled fear in even hardened criminals. In fact, 90 percent of all the crippling accidents and nearly all deaths among Alabama convicts occurred in the coal mines.[85] The injury and death rate was so high that Dr. Shirley Bragg, president of the Alabama Convict Bureau, voiced grave doubts in 1907 about consigning convicts to labor in the mines at all. If the state wished to exterminate its convicts, he contended, it should do so directly, not through a third party.[86] Even a casual perusal of the local press discloses innumerable accidents involving convicts.[87] The most devastating accident to take the lives of Alabama convicts occurred on April 8, 1911, when an explosion at Pratt Consolidated's Banner Mine left 128 convicts dead, all but 5 of them black; 72

of the convicts were from Jefferson County jails, and 30 percent of them had been sentenced to twenty days or fewer for such misdemeanors as gambling, vagrancy, or illegal drinking. It was into the most hazardous occupation in America that these and one-half of the Alabama state and county prisoners were sentenced in 1911. The disaster dramatically focused public attention on the system of working convicts in the mines.[88]

Unsurprisingly, many convicts reasoned that the disparity between the threat to life and limb from working and the physical dangers inherent in attempting to escape was greatly diminished by such conditions. The longer the sentence, the greater the probability that a prisoner would be maimed or killed. Yet those who became fugitives, however temporarily, were likely to receive the severest punishment when their pursuers caught them. For example, one of two black escapees from the Pratt Mines was overtaken by bloodhounds, and when his pursuers arrived the hounds were mauling him. "He begged pitiably to have the dogs taken off him," but they were permitted to continue tearing the man's flesh for a short time while the party chased the other escapee. Failing to overtake him, they returned to interrogate the captured man. Wetting a strap and applying it to the escapee's naked back, one of the men whipped the fugitive until he begged for death. Afterward, it was reported, "they took the negro on the back of a mule and carried him about 3 or 4 miles. Finding he could go no further, they left him in a negro cabin, where . . . he died within a few hours."[89]

The practice of sending public prisoners into the privately owned mines of Alabama was more resistant to change than it was in Georgia and Tennessee only partly because the treasury had become so dependent upon the system as a source of revenue. This was more or less the case in the other two states as well. In Alabama, however, despite the periodic outcries against the most barbarous aspects of the system, leasing endured because it constituted the quid pro quo in a compromise between the two major wings within the state Democratic party: the conservative planters of the black belt and the "progressive" industrial promoters of the Birmingham mineral district. The party was dominated by the black-belt planters, who succeeded in turning out the Republicans in 1874 by campaigning against their financial extravagance in promoting industrial growth through railroad construction. Once in power, therefore, the conservatives were obliged to avoid the appearance of fostering industrial growth and yet accommodate the industrial wing of the party. This important schism within the party required vigilant management in order to prevent an outright rupture. In the interests of unity, the conservatives granted major concessions to the proponents of industry, and Democratic policy on convict leasing represented an important political concession with direct economic rewards for mine owners.[90]

In fact, mine owners believed that "they could not work at a profit without the lowering effect on wages of convict-labor competition," reported the U.S. commissioner of labor in 1886. One of the largest of all southern mine operators, Henry DeBardeleben, explained to an Alabama legislative committee that "convict labor competing with free labor is advantageous to the mine owner. If all were free miners they could combine and strike, and thereby put up the price of coal, but where convict labor exists the mine owner can sell coal cheaper."[91] Convict-mined coal benefited all mine operators in the region, even those who did not lease convicts, by depressing the wages of free miners. Coal could not be loaded into cars for less than $2 per ton with free miners, but that same coal cost only 80 cents with convicts. The average daily cost for the six hundred prisoners at Pratt Mines in 1888–1890, including maintenance, amounted to not more than 87.5 cents. Free miners received 50 cents per ton and, at five tons per day, cost the employer $2.50. At the lowest average whole-sale price of $2.50 per ton, therefore, each convict earned the company an additional $1.625 per day.[92]

Another important, although immeasurable, cost advantage derived from forced labor was its regularity and predictability. The mostly black farmers who were induced to enter coal mining lacked the proper socialization for the routines of industrial labor traditionally found among many northern or im-migrant miners. J.S. Sloss, president of Sloss Iron and Steel, testified before a U.S. Senate committee that "as to the character of the labor employed by this company, . . . I will state that as a general thing they are mostly negroes, and in the main unreliable." Few of these workers were "disposed to settle down to regular, systematic work," and they labored an average of only fourteen days per month instead of the usual twenty-seven. Explaining the unreliability of free black labor, another employer claimed that "a colored boy growing up is apt to feel that if he is controlled by his employer he is a slave." A Pratt Mines executive informed investigators that a great number of black workers floated from job to job. "On our roll we have an average of one hundred and thirty-six that make only ten days' time a month."[93] Against the background of a rapidly expanding industry, the predictability of convict labor took on added signifi-cance. A reporter testified before a U.S. House committee in 1912 that, while in Birmingham, mine operators informed him time and again that the reason that they preferred convict labor was its regularity. "Three hundred men go to work in the morning, for 310 days a year. There are no picnics, no general laying off to attend funerals of fellow workers, no excursions. Practically a constant number of men are certain to be on duty every day."[94]

The inevitable progression of this reasoning led some operators to con-clude that a sentence in the mines was beneficial for blacks, an argument remi-niscent of that made for slavery. Warden T.J. Hill believed that prison discipline helped the "ignorant negro" adapt to the status of free man. Indeed, "a term in the penitentiary was without question the best lesson he could obtain in citi-zenship, as it brought him to a realization of the fact that the blessing of citi-zenship also had its responsibilities." A survey conducted by the U.S. commissioner of labor confirmed that most southern mine managers held simi-lar convictions.[95]

Alabama mine operators argued, with greater merit, that the system func-tioned as a sort of vocational school for retraining redundant black farm laborers for a trade that was in high demand. As evidence they cited the fact that over 50 percent of the black coal miners in the Birmingham mineral district learned their trade as convicts.[96] This view was found in all quarters of the Alabama mining community, although not everyone regarded this development favorably. J.R. Tankersly, a white miner at Pratt Mines, testified to a congressional committee that convicts generally remained in the mines after they were released. In the vicinity of Coketon, he observed, "there are about 250 ex-convicts. They have got their families there and seem to be at home." Upon completion of their sentences, the company provided each of the men with a good suit of clothing, eight to twenty dollars in cash, tools, and a month's rations to get them started. The state warden confirmed Tankersly's comments when he testified that the former convicts at Pratt Mines "who have been discharged from here with a good record for good conduct, nearly all have staid in the mine; hardly any of them have gone away." After all, a man who knew nothing but farming could earn only eight or ten dollars a month on a plantation, the warden asserted, but after learning the miner's trade that same man could earn two or three dollars a day by staying in the pits.[97]

Forced labor also provided coal companies with a powerful weapon against labor unions, for convicts could be compelled to keep the mines open when free miners went on strike.[98] This was a particularly obnoxious point for free miners, who found it difficult to earn a living in the face of convict competition. An editorial in the *Birmingham Labor Advocate* by free miner Bo Jerkins expressed the frustration that emanated from bargaining with operators who used prison labor. If miners demanded a wage increase, he said, the companies "tell us they can work the convicts longer hours, and obtain all the coal they want." But if the companies demanded a reduction in miners' wages, they would "sing the old song again" about removing the prisoners from the pits.[99] Another free miner sarcastically editorialized that it meant "something to be an American citizen" after all: "If you don't like common labor or farming you can go to the State warden of the prison and get a suit of striped clothes and be appointed a coal miner, provided the judge and grand jury are favorable."[100]

For their part, the operators could not have been more forthright in declaring their intention to use convicts to prevent unionization. As one operator declared in 1894, prison labor might appear detrimental to free workers, but actually it was "beneficial to free labor, as it prevents strikes, keeps the free miners employed and insures the running of the industries of the State that use coal."[101] James Bowron, a TCI official in Birmingham, rejected the free workers' demand that convicts be eliminated from the mines because he considered it "not right" that the coal industry of Alabama "be placed under the control of arbitrary and inconsiderate union leaders."[102]

Alabama continued to send its convicts into the coal mines, nevertheless, and operators such as T.G.I. president G.G. Crawford continued to seek their labor because the system was so advantageous for both parties. Economic imperatives continued to triumph over considerations of social justice. It would take a dramatic turn of events, a public storm so furious that political survival would require politicians to correct their course, before the system could be abolished. Just such a storm arose in 1926 with the death of James Knox, an African American from Ravenswood, West Virginia, who was imprisoned in 1924 for forging a thirty-dollar check. On August 14, 1924, less than a week after his transfer to Flat Top coal mine, Knox was dead, allegedly from swallowing bichloride of mercury. The true cause of his death did not come to light until a prominent professor of medicine and a score of witnesses testified to the actual cause of death more than a year afterward.

Knox was an unusually heavy man for his five-foot-five-inch frame, and his weight made it impossible for him to meet the ten-ton task required at Flat Top. Consequently, he was whipped every day. Weakened from the beatings, he collapsed on August 14. In this state, Knox was virtually dragged out of the mine by his heels and dumped into a laundry vat, where hot and cold water were turned on him alternately until he died from shock. After this story became public, a special grand jury indicted the warden and several of his assistants for murder, but they were summarily acquitted. Nevertheless, the scandal stirred the citizens of Alabama to such a pitch that in 1927 the legislature bowed before their wrath and passed a bill abolishing the system on June 30, 1928. Several days before the deadline, all the white prisoners were removed from Flat Top. Then on July 1, 1928, more than a half-century after the Emancipation Proclamation and the end of the Civil War, 499 black convicts turned in their lamps and picks, singing "Swing Low, Sweet Chariot," and "All My Troubles Are Over." One convict exclaimed, "Boss, I'm no longer in slavery."[103]

NOTES

An earlier version of this essay first appeared as chapter 2 in Ronald L. Lewis, *Black Coal Miners in America: Race, Class, and Community Conflict, 1780-1980* (Lexington: Univ. Press of Kentucky, 1987), and is reprinted here with the permission of the University Press of Kentucky.

1. C. Vann Woodward, *Origins of the New South, 1877–1913* (Baton Rouge, 1971), 58–59.

2. Enoch Cobb Wines, *The State of Prisons and of Child-Saving Institutions in the Civilized World* (Cambridge, 1880), 94; *Second Annual Report of the Commissioner of Labor, 1886: Convict Labor* (Washington, D.C., 1887), 381.

3. Woodward, *Origins*, 212–13

4. George Washington Cable, *The Silent South, Together with the Freedman's Case in Equity and the Convict Lease System* (New York, 1889), 126, 128.

5. James C. Cobb, *Industrialization and Southern Society, 1877–1984* (Lexington, Ky., 1984), 68–69; W. David Lewis, *Sloss Furnaces and the Rise of the Birmingham District: An Industrial Epic* (Tuscaloosa, Ala., 1994), 152–55; Blake McKelvey, *American Prisons: A History of Good Intentions* (Montclair, N.J., 1977), 197–98; Edward L. Ayers, *Vengeance and Justice: Crime and Punishment in the Nineteenth-Century South* (New York, 1984), 192, 194–95; Harold D. Woodman, "Sequel to Slavery: The New History Views the Postbellum South," *Journal of Southern History* 4 (Nov. 1977): 549.

6. T.J. Hill, "Experience in Mining Coal with Convicts," *National Prison Association Proceedings* (1897), 389–90.

7. Matthew J. Mancini, "Race, Economics, and the Abandonment of Convict Leasing," *Journal of Negro History* 63 (fall 1978): 339.

8. Daniel A. Novak, *The Wheel of Servitude: Black Forced Labor after Slavery* (Lexington, Ky., 1978); August Meier and Elliott Rudwick, *From Plantation to Ghetto* (New York, 1970), 154;

Lawrence J. Friedman, *The White Savage: Racial Fantasies in the Postbellum South* (Englewood Cliffs, N.J., 1970), 17; Walter Wilson, *Forced Labor in the United States* (London, 1935), 40; McKelvey, *American Prisons*, 180; Fletcher Melvin Green, "Some Aspects of the Convict Lease System in the Southern States," in his *Essays in Southern History* (Chapel Hill, N.C., 1949), 115–16.

9. Cable, *Silent South*, 198, 202; W.E.B. Dubois, *Some Notes on Negro Crime, Particularly in Georgia*, Atlanta University Publications, no. 9 (1904; reprint, New York, 1968), 4–5.

10. Ayers, *Vengeance and Justice*, 222.

11. McKelvey, *American Prisons*, 208–10.

12. Quoted in Hastings H. Hart, "Prison Conditions in the South," *American Prison Association Proceedings* (1919), 200.

13. A. Elizabeth Taylor, "The Origin and Development of the Convict Lease System in Georgia," *Georgia Historical Quarterly* 26 (June 1942): 113–18; "Report of the Principal Keeper of the Penitentiary of the State of Georgia, 1869," p. 5, Georgia Penitentiary Records, Georgia Department of Archives and History (hereafter GDAH); A.F. McKelway, "The Convict Lease System of Georgia," *Outlook* 90 (Sept. 5, 1908): 67.

14. Rebecca L. Felton, "The Convict System in Georgia," *Forum* 2 (Jan. 1887): 484–86; Taylor, "Origin of Convict Lease," 113–17; John Dittmer, *Black Georgia in the Progressive Era, 1900–1920* (Urbana, Ill., 1977), 82–83.

15. McKelway, "Convict Lease System of Georgia," 67; Rebecca Felton, *My Memories of Georgia Politics* (Atlanta, 1911), 439, 471.

16. Derrell Roberts, *Joseph E. Brown and the Politics of Reconstruction* (University, Ala., 1973); idem, "Joseph E. Brown and His Georgia Mines," *Georgia Historical Quarterly* 52 (Sept. 1968): 285–92.

17. Roberts, *Joseph E. Brown*, 94.

18. J.E. Brown to Gov. R.B. Bullock, April 14, 1877, Brown to W.T. Walker, April 18, 1877, and see Brown to Walker, March 28, 1877, Walker to Brown, March 29, 31, 1877, Joseph E. Brown Papers, Atlanta Historical Society (hereafter AHS).

19. Felton, *Memories of Georgia Politics*, 463; Dan T. Carter, "Prisons, Politics, and Business: The Convict Lease System in the Post-War South" (master's thesis, University of Wisconsin, 1964), 71.

20. Felton, "Convict System in Georgia," 485–87, 489.

21. Joseph E. Brown, *Senator Brown's Argument before the Governor in Defense of Dade Coal Company on the Convict Question*, Oct. 2, 1887, copy in Brown Papers, AHS.

22. Ibid.

23. Derrell Roberts, "Joseph E. Brown and the Convict Lease System," *Georgia Historical Quarterly* 44 (Dec. 1960): 405–6.

24. *Second Annual Report of the Commissioner of Labor, 1886*, 301.

25. Georgia *House Journal* (1890), 722, and (1892), 652; Taylor, "Origin of Convict Lease," 126.

26. Dade County Superior Court Minutes, Grand Jury Presentments, 1893, 1894, GDAH.

27. *Atlanta Constitution*, Sept. 1, 1883.

28. Brown, *Senator Brown's Argument*, Brown Papers, AHS.

29. Lester D. Stephens, "A Former Slave and the Georgia Convict Lease System," *Negro History Bulletin* 39 (Jan. 1976): 505–7; Weekly Register of Convicts in Prison Camp Hospitals, 1888–90, GDAH.

30. Weekly Register of Convicts in Hospitals, GDAH.

31. Whipping Reports for Dade Coal Company, 1885–1886, in Monthly Reports of Corporal Punishment, Diet, and Conditions of Convicts, 1884–1886, 1889, GDAH.

32. Roberts, "Joseph E. Brown and the Lease System," 403; Whipping Reports for Dade Coal Company, July 1886.

33. Weekly Register of Convicts in Hospitals; Whipping Reports for Dade Coal Company; Whipping Reports for Durham Coal and Coke Company, 1908–1909, GDAH.

34. McKelway, "Convict Lease System of Georgia," 67–72; Dittmer, *Black Georgia*, 114–15; Dewey W. Grantham Jr., *Hoke Smith and the Politics of the New South* (Baton Rouge, 1958), 173.

35. Grantham, *Hoke Smith*, 173–74; McKelway, "Convict Lease System of Georgia," 67–72; Dittmer, *Black Georgia*, 114–15; Taylor, "Origin of Convict Lease," 128. For an overview, see Jane Zimmerman, "The Penal Reform Movement in the South during the Progressive Era, 1890–1917," *Journal of Southern History* 17 (Nov. 1951): 462–92.

36. *Reports of the Tennessee Penitentiary* (1865), 102; (1867), 347; (1869), 195; Tennessee Division of Library and Archives. The overall percentages are tabulated in biennial reports. See also Bureau of the Census, *Prisoners and Juvenile Delinquents* (Washington, D.C., 1918), 288–90; Randall G. Shelden, "From Slave to Caste Society: Penal Changes in Tennessee, 1830–1915," *Tennessee Historical Quarterly* 38 (winter 1979): 465.

37. *Nashville Republican Banner,* June 10, 1870.

38. Constantine G. Belissary, "The Rise of Industry and the Industrial Spirit in Tennessee, 1865–1885," *Journal of Southern History* 19 (May 1953): 196–98.

39. Woodward, *Origins*, 3.

40. *Nashville Union and American*, Aug. 23, 1870. See also *Nashville Republican Banner,* Aug. 14, 23, 1870; Clyde L. Ball, "The Public Career of Colonel A.S. Colyar, 1870–1877," *Tennessee Historical Quarterly*, Part 1, 12 (March 1953): 44, and Part 2, 12 (June 1953): 106–7.

41. *Nashville Daily American*, July 14, 1876; Ball, "Career of Colonel Colyar," Part 2, 117–18.

42. Justin Fuller, "History of the Tennessee Coal, Iron, and Railroad Company, 1852–1907" (Ph.D. diss., University of North Carolina, 1966), 288–89; Ball, "Career of Colonel Colyar," Part 2, 118; *Nashville Republican Banner,* Jan. 25, 1872; Fuller, "History of TCI," 290; Cable, *Silent South*, 130.

43. Ball, "Career of Colonel Colyar," Part 2, 118; *Nashville Republican Banner,* Jan. 19, 20, 1871; Fuller, "History of TCI," 289–90.

44. Sims, quoted in Robert Mintz, "The Miners Who Tore Down the Walls" (Ph.D. diss., University of California, Berkeley, 1974), 43–44.

45. George W. Cable, "The Convict Lease System in the Southern States," *National Conference of Charities and Corrections Proceedings* (1883), 274.

46. *Second Annual Report of the Commissioner of Labor, 1886*, 302–3.

47. "Special Report of George W. Ford, Commissioner of Labor and Inspector of Mines of Tennessee, to the Special Session of the Legislature," quoted in *United Mine Workers Journal* (hereafter *UMWJ*), Sept. 17, 1891.

48. Fuller, "History of TCI," 293.

49. Ibid., 288–89.

50. *Nashville Daily American*, Aug. 23, 1883, Aug. 23, 1892.

51. *New York Times*, Aug. 15, 1892.

52. *UMWJ*, Nov. 12, 1891. Although the *UMWJ*'s analysis was otherwise accurate, the editor incorrectly assumed that the free men were white. Actually, in 1891 there were a total of 4,595 free miners in Tennessee, and 840, or 18 percent, of them were black. The *UMWJ* was essentially correct when it presumed that the convicts were black, however, for 593 of the 858 prisoners (69 percent) working in the mines were black. George W. Ford, *Special Report of the Commissioner of Labor and Inspector of Mines* (Nashville, 1891), 73–74, portions reproduced in Mintz, "Miners Who Tore Down the Walls," App. D, 361.

53. *UMWJ*, Nov. 1, 1938; Woodward, *Origins*, 234. The most thorough account of the Tennessee convict wars is Karin A. Shapiro, *A New South Rebellion: The Battle against Convict Labor in the Tennessee Coalfields, 1891–1896* (Chapel Hill, N.C., 1998).

54. *Knoxville Journal*, July 31, 1891; *New York Times*, July 22, 23, 1891.

55. "Tennessee Coal, Iron, and Railroad Co.," *Engineering and Mining Journal* 52 (July 25, 1891): 104; *New York Times*, July 22, 1891; Schwartz quoted in a long article by Walter Wilson, "Historic Coal Creek Rebellion Brought an End to Convict Miners in Tennessee," *UMWJ*, Nov. 1, 1938, 10–13.

56. *UMWJ*, Nov. 5, 1891; Pete Daniel, "The Tennessee Convict War," *Tennessee Historical Quarterly* 34 (fall 1975): 279.

57. Daniel, "Tennessee Convict War," 281.

58. "Special Report of George W. Ford," p. 42, in Mintz, "Miners Who Tore Down the

Walls," 111–12, 116; Daniel, "Tennessee Convict War," 282–84; *Knoxville Journal,* Aug. 12, 14, 18, Sept. 11, 17, 19, 22, 1891; "Tennessee," *Engineering and Mining Journal* 52 (Sept. 12, 1891): 317–18.

59. Daniel, "Tennessee Convict War," 286–87; *UMWJ,* Nov. 1, 1938; and Shapiro, *New South Rebellion,* 209–10.

60. *UMWJ,* Nov. 1, 1938; *New York Times,* Aug. 15, 1892. The literature on the "Coal Creek Troubles" is surprisingly extensive. My account comes primarily from Shapiro, *New South Rebellion;* Daniel, "Tennessee Convict War," 273–92; Archie Green, *Only a Miner: Studies in Recorded Coal-Mining Songs* (Urbana, Ill., 1972), 155–92; Philip S. Foner, *The History of the Labor Movement in the United States: From the Founding of the A.F.L. to the Emergence of American Imperialism* (New York, 1975), 219–29. See also George Korson, *Coal Dust on the Fiddle: Songs and Stories of the Bituminous Industry* (Philadelphia, 1943), 353–70; A.C. Huston Jr., "The Coal Miners' Insurrections of 1891 in Anderson County, Tennessee," *East Tennessee Historical Society Publications,* no. 7 (1935); "The Overthrow of the Convict Lease System in Tennessee," *East Tennessee Historical Society Publications,* no. 8 (1936); Wilson, "Historic Coal Creek Rebellion," 10–13. See also James Dombrowski's notes (1930s) and manuscript, "Fire in the Hole," on deposit at Tuskegee Institute. The best contemporary account is Ford, *Special Report of the Commissioner of Labor and Inspector of Mines.* Ford was sympathetic to the miners' cause. The Nashville and Knoxville newspapers were filled with detailed accounts. The violence was reported in most of the labor papers, particularly the *National Labor Tribune* and *UMWJ.* For other contemporary accounts see the letter of Welsh miner Howell Davies from Jellico, Tennessee, Jan. 11, 1892, in Alan Conway, ed., *The Welsh in America: Letters from the Immigrants* (Minneapolis, 1961), 201–4; Albert Roberts, "Iniquity of Leasing Convict Labor," *Engineering Magazine* 1 (Sept. 1891): 749–57; *Engineering and Mining Journal* 52 (July 25, 1891): 104, and 52 (Sept. 12, 1891): 371–78. At least one novel has been written about these events, Myra Page, *With Sun in Our Blood* (New York, 1950).

61. *UMWJ,* Aug. 15, 1892; *New York Times,* Aug. 16, 17, 23, 1892; Tennessee *House Journal* (1895), 378–97; Mintz, "Miners Who Tore Down the Walls," 328, 331–32.

62. "Report of the Sub-Committee to Visit the Prisons," in Tennessee *House Journal* (1893), 334–36, 344, 347; Appendix to Tennessee *Senate Journal* (1893), 63.

63. Daniel, "Tennessee Convict War"; Mintz, "Miners Who Tore Down the Walls," 323–24.

64. Shapiro, *New South Rebellion,* 243–46; Chris Evans, *United Mine Workers of America* (Indianapolis, n.d.), 2:612–14; Bureau of the Census, *Prisoners and Juvenile Delinquents,* 286, 288–90.

65. Allen J. Going, *Bourbon Democracy in Alabama, 1874–1890* (University, Ala., 1951), 62–65, 76–77, 80–82.

66. Ibid., 79, 86–87, 120.

67. Message of the Governor, Alabama *House Journal,* 1884–85, pp. 20–21; Carter, "Prisons, Politics, and Business," 92–93; David Alan Harris, "Racists and Reformers: A Study of Progressivism in Alabama, 1896–1911" (Ph.D. diss., University of North Carolina, 1967), 274–75. See also p. 376. Critics charged that that these figures were far too low. For example, the *Birmingham Labor Advocate,* the official organ of the Alabama Federation of Labor, claimed that revenues from the convict department actually grossed over $759,000 for fiscal year 1905–1906 and netted the state $368,000. *Birmingham Labor Advocate,* Jan. 11, 1907.

68. Shelby M. Harrison, "A Cash-Nexus for Crime," *Survey* 27 (Jan. 6, 1912): 1553–54; *UMWJ,* March 28, 1912; *National Prison Association Proceedings* (1897), 314; Message of the Governor, Alabama *Senate Journal,* 1886–87, pp. 25–26; Carter, "Prisons, Politics, and Business," 94–95.

69. William Cohen, "Negro Involuntary Servitude in the South, 1865–1940: A Preliminary Analysis," *Journal of Southern History* 42 (Feb. 1976): 48, 31–60; Dewey W. Grantham, *Southern Progressivism: The Reconciliation of Progress and Tradition* (Knoxville, 1983), 137.

70. Quoted in Carl V. Harris, "Reforms in Government Control of Negroes in Birmingham, Alabama, 1890–1920," *Journal of Southern History* 38 (Nov. 1972): 567.

71. R.M. Cunningham, "The Convict System of Alabama in Its Relation to Health and Disease," *National Prison Association Proceedings* (1889), 137.

72. The demographics of the state prison population can be obtained from the biennial

Convict Inspectors' Reports, Alabama Division of Archives and History (hereafter ADAH). For a less detailed summary, see Going, *Bourbon Democracy in Alabama*, 176, 180. See also Bureau of the Census, *Prisoners and Juvenile Delinquents*, 204; *Birmingham Post*, March 27, 1926; Harris, "Racists and Reformers," 285–87.

73. Going, *Bourbon Democracy in Alabama*, 176–77.

74. *Report of Inspectors of the Penitentiary* (1882), 3–5, 13–15; Fannie Ella Sapp, "The Convict Lease System in Alabama, 1846–1895" (master's thesis, George Peabody College for Teachers, 1931), 28–32.

75. *Report of Inspectors* (1882), 3–5; *Montgomery Daily Advertiser*, Jan. 28, Feb. 8, 1883.

76. Sapp, "Convict Lease System," 38; *Report of Inspectors* (1884), 24.

77. Going, *Bourbon Democracy in Alabama*, 173.

78. U.S. Senate, *Report of the Committee of the Senate upon the Relations between Labor and Capital, and Testimony Taken* (Washington, D.C., 1885), 4:437–38; Cable, *Silent South*, 30; clipping dated Jan. 4, 1888, in Thomas D. Parke Papers, Birmingham Public Library Archives (hereafter BPLA); *Report of Inspectors* (1886–1888), 23, (1888–1890), 61; "Pratt Division Statistics: Calendar Year 1895," Jan. 4, 1896, Erskine Ramsay Papers, BPLA; *Report of Inspectors* (1902–1904), 8, 13.

79. Going, *Bourbon Democracy in Alabama*, 178; clipping dated Feb. 4, 1889, in Parke Papers. See also Warden John Bankhead's comments in U.S. Senate, *Relations between Labor and Capital*, 4:437–48.

80. *Montgomery Daily Dispatch*, Feb. 4, 1889.

81. *Pratt Mines Advertiser*, July 26, 1889. The reporter noted that "the same system observed here is carried out at prison No. 2."

82. Report summarized in *Pratt Mines Advertiser*, July 19, 1889; *UMWJ*, Nov. 26, 1891. See also Robert David Ward and William Warren Rogers, "Racial Inferiority, Convict Labor, and Modern Medicine: A Note on the Coalburg Affair," *Alabama Historical Quarterly* 45 (fall-winter 1983): 203–10.

83. "Report on Coalburg Prison, 1895," in Parke Papers, BPLA. For Dr. Parke's response to the denunciation of his report by the lessees, see Thomas D. Parke to the Board of Convict Inspectors, n.d., and Parke Diary, unpublished manuscript, both in Parke Papers, BPLA. See also, Lewis, *Sloss Furnaces*, 214–15.

84. W.A. Burns, M.D., to B.B. Comer, Aug. 29, 1908, Braxton Bragg Comer Papers, ADAH.

85. "After Florida, Alabama," *Nation* 117 (June 11, 1923): 31.

86. *Birmingham Labor Advocate*, Jan. 11, 1907.

87. See, for example, *Pratt Mines Enterprise*, May 22, 1891; *Birmingham Labor Advocate*, March 26, 1898, March 4, Oct. 7, 1899; *Montgomery Daily Dispatch*, April 8, 1889.

88. H.B. Humphrey, *Historical Summary of Coal-Mine Explosions in the United States, 1880–1958*, Bulletin 586 (Washington, D.C., 1960), 45–49; Harrison, "Cash-Nexus," 1541; *Birmingham Labor Advocate*, April 14, 1911; *UMWJ*, April 13, 1911, March 28, 1912. See also *UMWJ*, April 13, 20, 1911; *New York Times*, April 9, 10, 1911; *New York Herald Tribune*, April 9, 10, 1911. The most thorough study of convict labor and the Banner disaster is Robert David Ward and William Warren Rogers, *Convicts, Coal, and the Banner Mine Tragedy* (Tuscaloosa, Ala., 1987).

89. "Deposition of John D. Goode, Fall 1879" and "Report of the Joint Committee to Inquire into the Treatment of Convicts Employed in the Mines, Feb. 9, 1881," Legislative Files, ADAH. For additional examples of escapes see *National Labor Tribune*, Oct. 1, 1908; *Birmingham Age-Herald*, July 12, 1908; *Birmingham Labor Advocate*, July 23, 1915.

90. *Birmingham Chronicle*, Oct. 4, 1885; Going, *Bourbon Democracy in Alabama*, 67, 110, 116–17; Jonathan M. Weiner, *Social Origins of the New South: Alabama, 1860–1885* (Baton Rouge, 1978), 162–85. For a contradiction of Weiner's interpretation see Lewis, *Sloss Furnaces*, 476–78.

91. *Second Annual Report of the Commission of Labor, 1886*, p. 301; Henry DeBardeleben, *Testimony before the Joint Committee of the General Assembly Appointed to Examine the Convict System of Alabama* (Montgomery, 1888–89), 39. On DeBardeleben, see Justin Fuller, "Henry F. DeBardeleben, Industrialist of the New South," *Alabama Review* 39 (Jan. 1986): 3–18.

92. Alabama *House Journal*, 1888–89, p. 463; Jesse Stallings to Emmett O'Neal, Nov. 15, 1911, Jesse Stallings Papers, Southern Historical Collection, University of North Carolina.

93. U.S. Senate, *Relations between Labor and Capital*, 4:278–83, 394, 49–50, 404. See also John A. Fitch, "The Human Side of Large Outputs," *Survey* 27 (Jan. 6, 1912): 1527.

94. Hearings reported in *UMWJ*, March 28, 1912; Harrison, "Cash-Nexus," 1546.

95. Hill, "Experience in Mining Coal with Convicts," 391; *Second Annual Report of the Commissioner of Labor, 1886*, p. 301.

96. U.S. Senate, *Reports of the Immigration Commission, Immigrants in Industries*, 61 Cong., 2 Sess., Doc. 633, pt. 1, vol. 2 (Washington, D.C., 1912), p. 218.

97. U.S. Senate, *Relations between Labor and Capital*, 4:434, 437–38.

98. Harris, "Racists and Reformers," 379; Daniel Letwin, *The Challenge of Interracial Unionism: Alabama Coal Miners, 1878–1921* (Chapel Hill, N.C., 1998), 48–49; Lewis, *Sloss Furnaces*, 213–14.

99. Gregory Lewis McDonald, "Satisfying the Claims of Offended Justice: Politics, Profit, and Change in the Alabama Penal System, 1819–1928" (master's thesis, University of Southern Mississippi, 1998), 134–35; *Birmingham Labor Advocate*, July 24, 1897. For similar arguments, see also issues of Dec. 25, 1897, March 26, May 28, 1898, July 23, 1915; *Pratt Mines Advertiser*, June 7, 21, 1889.

100. Quoted in Herbert G. Gutman, ed., "Black Coal Miners and the Greenback-Labor Party in Redeemer, Alabama, 1878–1879: The Letters of Warren D. Kelley, Willis Johnson Thomas, 'Dawson,' and Others," *Labor History* 10 (summer 1969): 516–17.

101. Robert David Ward and William Warren Rogers, *Labor Revolt in Alabama: The Great Strike of 1894* (University, Ala., 1965), 46.

102. "Autobiography of James Bowron," 1:217, manuscript in the James Bowron Papers, University of Alabama, Tuscaloosa, Alabama. See also Robert J. Norrell, *James Bowron: The Autobiography of a New South Industrialist* (Chapel Hill, N.C., 1991).

103. *New York World*, Jan. 28, May 2, 1926; *Birmingham Post*, March 22–24, 27–28, 1926; *UMWJ*, April 1, Nov. 13, 1926, April 30,1927, and July 15, 1928. For a recent overview of the movement to abolish convict leasing in Alabama, see McDonald, "Satisfying the Claims of Offended Justice," chap. 5.

17

THE FORMATION OF BLACK COMMUNITY IN SOUTHERN WEST VIRGINIA COALFIELDS

JOE WILLIAM TROTTER JR.

The rise and expansion of the bituminous coal industry stimulated the emergence of a black proletariat in southern West Virginia. Blacks were largely excluded from the northern industrial labor force between 1880 and World War I. But the coal companies of Central Appalachia actively recruited blacks, along with "native whites" and European immigrants, to make up the labor force for their rapidly emerging industry.[1] The rise of the black coal-mining proletariat was nonetheless a complex process; it was rooted in the social imperatives of black life in the rural South as well as in the dynamics of industrial capitalism. In their efforts to recruit and control black labor, coal operators employed a blend of legal and extralegal measures reinforced by the racist attitudes and practices of white workers and the state. However, black workers, using their network of family and friends, organized their own migration to the region. In this way, they facilitated their own transition to the industrial labor force and paved the way for the rise of a new black middle class that helped to gradually transform the contours of African American community life in coal-mining towns.

Under the impact of the coal industry's rapid expansion, southern West Virginia underwent a dramatic transformation during the late nineteenth and early twentieth centuries. While the entire state produced only five million tons of coal in 1887, coal production in its southern region alone increased to nearly forty million tons in 1910, which made up 70 percent of the state's total output that year. The region's population increased just as dramatically, growing from about eighty thousand in 1880 to nearly three hundred thousand in 1910.[2] Immigrants from southern, central, and eastern Europe grew from only fourteen hundred in 1880 to eighteen thousand (6 percent of the total) in 1910. The black population's growth was even greater, moving from forty-eight hundred in 1880 to over forty thousand in 1910. With 6 percent of the total in 1880, by 1910 African Americans made up 14 percent of the populace thirty years later, over twice the proportion of immigrants in the southern part of the state.[3] West Virginia's concentration of African Americans shifted southward as well. Only about 21 percent of the state's blacks lived in the southern counties in 1880; by 1910, that figure had climbed to 63 percent. In order to cut costs and keep wages down, some coal operators preferred a mixed labor force of immigrants, blacks, and American-born whites.[4]

Coal mining transformed African American life and labor. As rural black men entered the coal mines in growing numbers, their seasonal rhythms of planting, cultivating, and harvesting gradually gave way to the new demands of industrial labor. The techniques of dynamiting coal, a variety of mine safety procedures, and the mental and physical requirements of hand-loading tons of coal all increasingly supplanted black workers' agricultural skills and work habits. Because coal mining evolved in semirural settings, the transformation was not as radical as it might have been; black coal miners regularly shifted back and forth between farming and work in the coal mines.[5]

At the same time that these transitions were taking place, black miners and their families also contributed to the formation of black community in southern West Virginia. Black religious, fraternal, and political organizations dramatically expanded. African American institution-building activities reflected growing participation in the coal economy, rapid population growth, and the effects of racial discrimination; they also reflected and stimulated the rise of a vigorous black leadership. As elsewhere, however, although the black community developed a high level of racial solidarity in the process, it failed to fully surmount internal conflict along class lines. Black congregations, fraternal orders, and state and local politics offer the most sensitive barometers of change in these areas within the black coal-mining community.

The independent African American churches in southern West Virginia had their roots in the early emancipation era. Until the Civil War, blacks had worshipped in the same congregations as whites, but on a segregated basis. Following the Civil War, as elsewhere in the South, African Americans increasingly separated from white religious institutions. Under the leadership of Rev. Lewis Rice, for example, the African Zion Baptist Church at Tinkerville (Malden) in Kanawha County spearheaded the independent black Baptist movement in the region. A member of the Providence Association of Ohio, formed in 1868, the African Zion Baptist Church stimulated the rise of new "arms of the African Zion Church" in West Virginia. By 1873, as a result of the church's vigorous organizing activities, West Virginia's black Baptists seceded from the Ohio conference and formed the Mt. Olivet Baptist Association. Until he left the region in 1880, Booker T. Washington was a member, a Sunday school teacher, and a clerk of the "mother church" at Malden.[6]

As the processes of black migration, proletarianization, and institutional racism converged during the late nineteenth and early twentieth centuries, black religious institutions dramatically expanded. Black membership in West Virginia churches more than doubled, from over seven thousand in 1890 to nearly fifteen thousand in 1906. Although blacks developed a thriving Presbyterian church in McDowell County, and although the number of African Methodist Episcopal churches increased to more than thirty-five at the turn of the century, Baptists dominated the region's black religious life. In 1906 the U.S. Census of Religious Bodies reported 148 black Baptist churches in the Mountain State. New congregations were initiated and new associations rapidly emerged in McDowell, Mercer, Raleigh, Fayette, Mingo, and Logan Counties. The Mt. Olivet Baptist Association was soon followed by the New River Baptist Association in 1884, the Flat Top Baptist Association in 1896, and the Guyan Valley Association in 1913. The Flat Top Baptist Association, located in the Pocahontas Field, became the largest and richest in West Virginia.[7]

Black religious life mirrored and stimulated the growth of an energetic black ministry. The number of black ministers increased from 93 in 1900 and to 150 a decade later. Black ministers played a major role in harnessing working-class financial resources to pay church debts, although some preached for months without pay. Sometimes their fund-raising efforts were quite successful. In May 1913, for example, under the pastorate of Rev. R.H. McKoy, the Bluestone Baptist Church at Bramwell, Mercer County, "closed one of the most successful [financial] rallies in its history," raising $330 over a two-week period. Under the pastorate of Rev. R.V. Barksdale, in July 1913 the First Baptist Church of Anawalt, McDowell County, raised $400 in a special rally.[8] When a fire destroyed the St. James Baptist Church in Welch, Rev. W.R. Pittard and his congregation launched a spirited rebuilding campaign. Within six months, they had raised nearly $500.[9] Coal companies often gave financial support to black and white churches, but their assistance was not enough to sustain black churches. Only the persistence of black coal miners, their families, and their ministers in contributing to the churches fully explains the churches' success in the coalfields.

If the resources of black coal miners underlay the material well-being of the church, their spiritual and cultural needs shaped patterns of church worship and participation. Rooted deeply in the religious experience of southern blacks, the black church in southern West Virginia helped to sustain and reinforce the black workers' spiritual and communal beliefs and practices through sermons, revival meetings, baptismal ceremonies, and funeral rites. At a May 1914 revival meeting, Rev. C.H. Rollins of the Slab Fork Baptist Church "preached two able sermons to an appreciative audience." Taking his texts from Matthew 7:7 and Zechariah 13:1, he "preached so powerful that we were made to say within ourselves as one of the apostles of old, 'Did not our hearts burn within us as he talked by the way.'"[10] At the Wingfield Baptist Church in Eckman, McDowell County, a huge crowd gathered at the river's edge to witness "the 'plunging under' or the 'Burial in Baptism'" of the new converts. "People from all over the county hearing of the occasion . . . came on every train, both east and west. A densely packed crowd of men and women, boys and girls . . . were there."[11] In mid-1913 a funeral for a black miner who died in a slate fall was conducted at the Mt. Ebenezer Baptist Church near Gilliam, McDowell County, where he was a member in good standing. Rev. L.A. Watkins preached the funeral sermon to a host of "friends and relatives," selecting his text from John 19:30, "When Jesus therefore had received the vinegar, he said, It is finished: and he bowed his head, and gave up the ghost." The choir sang the deceased miner's favorite hymn, "Will the Waters Be Chilly?"[12] Moreover, besides attending funerals and other local church functions, through frequent visits to their old southern homes, black workers renewed their ties with the established religious customs of their past.[13]

As blacks entered the southern West Virginia coalfields in greater numbers, although they retained important cultural links with their rural past, their religious beliefs and practices underwent gradual transformation. Although the evidence is quite sparse, an educated black ministry gradually emerged in the prewar years. Under its leadership, emotional services increasingly gave way to ones featuring rational and logical sermons often concerned with improving temporal, social, economic, and political conditions, and above all, with the proper attitude and behavior for racial progress in the new industrial age.[14] These emphases undoubtedly had antecedents in the southern black religious experience, but they emerged clearly within the socioeconomic, political, and cultural environment of southern West Virginia.

The growing pool of educated black preachers included schoolteachers who doubled as ministers, such as Rev. J.W. Robinson, principal of the Tidewater Grade School. In November 1913, Reverend Robinson was installed as pastor of the First Baptist Church of Kimball. "He is one of the best known and ablest men in the state, an advocator of note and a preacher of great ability," the *McDowell Times* reported. But perhaps the best example of the rising educated black ministry was Rev. Mordecai W. Johnson, who took the pastorate of the First Baptist Church of Charleston, West Virginia, in 1913. Born in 1890 in Paris, Henry County, Tennessee, Johnson received a bachelor of arts degree from Morehouse College in Atlanta in 1911, where he taught economics and history for a while, and another from the University of Chicago in 1913. In the postwar years he left the First Baptist Church for a position at Howard University, where, in 1926, he became its first black president. Before leaving, though, Johnson played an important role not only in the religious life of the community, but also in the civil rights struggle.[15]

Some influential ministers in southern West Virginia were self-taught. The pastor of several black churches in Kanawha County, Rev. Nelson Barnett of Huntington, Cabell County, was perhaps the most gifted. Born a slave in Buckingham County, Virginia, in 1842, Barnett migrated to West Virginia in 1873 and eventually became the pastor of churches in St. Albans, Longacre, and Raymond City. Upon his death in 1909, the *Huntington Dispatch* wrote: "He lacked the learning of the schools because he was born a slave. But he was of a studious turn of mind, gifted in speech, could expound the scriptures with an insight truly remarkable, and his preaching was wonderfully effective in bringing men to Christ."[16] The funeral sermon for Barnett, preached by the educated black minister Rev. I.V. Bryant of Huntington, was even more eloquent. "If by education we mean the drawing out of the latent powers and spreading them in glowing characters upon the canvas of the mind, if by education we mean the proper cultivation of all the faculties, the symmetrical development of the head, the heart, and the hand, together with those combined elements that make the entire man, I positively deny that he was uneducated. . . . He was taught by the Great God."[17]

Formally and informally educated black ministers helped to transform black workers' religious beliefs and practices. By appealing to the intellect rather than merely to the emotions of their congregants, they helped to rationalize black religious services. Reverend Barnett, his eulogizer stated, "preached industry as well as religion, and had accumulated considerable property, owning two or three houses and lots in the city. He was active in all interests for the betterment of his race, and took particular interest in the education of young people who regard him as a father."[18] In his sermon before the Seventeenth Annual Meeting of the Flat Top Baptist Association, Rev. G.W. Woody stressed "the fact that men must work for this world's goods." "In conclusion, Rev. Woody grew more forceful and urged upon the brethren to be patient in the small details of their life's work." Before World War I, Rev. J.H. Hammond of Jenkinjones became an agent of the *McDowell Times* and received praise for helping with the "educational uplift of his race." And in late 1914, the Baptist minister Rev. J.W. Crockett was elected to the Northfork District School Board of McDowell County.[19]

As black ministers broadened their interest in the here and now, their sermons before their coal-mining congregations underwent a gradual change. In two sermons at Giatto, a black Baptist minister was "forceful and practical." At the First Baptist Church of Kimball, Rev. R.D.W. Meadows "preached one of the most profound and scholarly sermons." Another sermon "showed much thought in preparation" and delivery. Still another Baptist minister "preached a strong and scholarly sermon." At a meeting of the Winding Gulf Ministerial and Deacons Union, Rev. T.J. Brandon "gave a high class lecture to preachers and congregation on how they should act in church." On the same occasion, another minister delivered an "able" and "instructive" sermon on the subject "Behave." When the "spirit" threatened to overcome him, another Baptist minister took "pains as to control his voice." Yet however rational and controlled their sermons may have become, black ministers worked to retain contact with the traditional black culture and consciousness of black workers. At the Baptist church in Keystone, Reverend Brown of Kimball preached "quite a deep sermon," but he nonetheless emphasized, "It matters not how much learning one may have, unless they have the Spirit of God they cannot have power to do the best work of life."[20]

The Methodist Episcopal and the African Methodist Episcopal churches were more hierarchical in their administrative structures than were the Baptist churches. Their hierarchies exercised greater control over ministers and congregations in particular, controlling the mandatory movement of ministers from one church to another, and vigorously promoted an educated black ministry. These two churches were nonetheless deeply enmeshed within the spiritual traditions of southern blacks. Utilizing Baptist ministers, for example, the Methodists often conducted revivals and engaged in spirited meetings similar to those of the Baptists. In April 1914 the Northfork Methodist Episcopal Church conducted a revival that resulted in fifty-one accessions, twenty-six new converts, and twenty-five more converts by letter. Under the pastorate of

Rev. W.R. Burger, the *McDowell Times* suggested, the Methodists, like the Baptists, understood how "to shout, sing, preach and pray."[21] Yet over time, black Methodists and Presbyterians in southern West Virginia, as elsewhere, shed the spiritual and emotional aspects of their religious traditions more rapidly than did the Baptists. Within three years of Rev. James Gipson's transfer from the AME Kentucky Conference to Williamson, West Virginia, Gipson developed a reputation as "a hard worker, constructive in mind and progressive in spirit." Under his leadership, the congregation grew from eight members to forty members and moved from an inadequate public hall near the railroad tracks to a new brick building in a previously all-white area. The church's assets grew from a mere forty-four cents to over eight hundred dollars, the minister's salary not included; and, starting with no church auxiliaries, a "flourishing" array of them was begun.[22]

Under the pastorate of Rev. R.P. Johnson, the small Presbyterian church of Kimball developed a more energetic social orientation. In December 1913, the church held a sacred concert. The program featured a variety of guest speakers who addressed a broad range of religious, political, and social issues. In his speech, attorney H.J. Capehart, the *Times* reported, emphasized the need to make "services so varied and instructive that they will appeal to all classes. He spoke of the gymnasium, the swimming pool, reading room, sewing circle and settlement work as examples of the work being done by adher[e]nts of the new school of thought in religious worship."[23] In an address titled "My Dream of the Future Church," attorney T.E. Hill looked forward to a church that practiced the principles of social justice and equality. "In this institution there will be no color line, the brotherhood of man will be a fact instead of a catch phrase and it will seek to save the bodies as well as the souls of mankind." In another example of the black church's growing social bent, the pastor Rev. R.P. Johnson developed a vigorous ministry among black convicts on the road crews of McDowell County and also a Sunday school relief department, which was designed to aid the working-class "poor of our town, especially children whose parents are not able to keep them in school and Sunday school."[24]

In addition to joining churches, black coal miners participated in an expanding network of fraternal organizations and mutual benefit societies. By World War I black fraternal orders included the Elks, the Knights of Pythias, the Odd Fellows, the Independent Order of St. Luke, and the Golden Rule Beneficial and Endowment Association.[25] The Golden Rule Association emerged as one of the most energetic of the prewar black fraternal orders. Formed in 1903 under the leadership of Rev. R.H. McKoy, the order established headquarters at Bramwell, Mercer County, and served blacks in southern West Virginia and parts of Kentucky and Virginia. Within one decade the organization proudly celebrated its success: fifty-four subordinate lodges, twenty-six nurseries serving young people aged three to sixteen, more than 5,280 members, and more than thirteen thousand dollars paid out in death and sick claims. In numerous churches in the coalfields, Reverend McKoy and officers of the Golden Rule Association publicly paid benefits in ceremonies replete with speeches, indeed, sermons, on the value of the order. In July 1913, for example, the organization paid the endowment of one member "before an overflowing congregation."[26] With God's help, McKoy said, "The continued progress of the Golden Rule Association means the actual progress of the race in a tangible form."[27]

Within the framework of black religious culture, the fraternal orders offered black coal miners an opportunity to protect their material interests. The obituary for John Panell, who lost his life in a slate fall at Gilliam, McDowell County, noted Panell's membership in the Grand United Order of Odd Fellows. Samuel Blackwell, who died of injuries sustained in a slate fall, belonged to the Shining Light Association of the Golden Rule Beneficial and Endowment Association. The 1913 obituary of A.H. Hudle described him as "a consistent Christian, a member of the A.M.E. Church . . . [and] a member of the Grand United Order of Odd Fellows and also a Knight of Pythias."[28] All these black fraternal orders offered mutual aid and insurance plans to their members that promised to cushion them and their families against hard times.

At the same time as fraternal orders addressed the material welfare of black workers, they repeatedly reinforced the communal and spiritual aspects of their culture. In company and noncompany towns, the fraternal parade, replete with marching band in full regalia, and the annual thanksgiving sermon emerged as prominent features of African American life in the coalfields. In May 1913, for example, at Keystone and Eckman, McDowell County, the Grand United Order of Odd Fellows held their Thirteenth Annual Thanksgiving Parade and Services. Led by Lord's Cornet Band, the order assembled at Lord's Opera House, in Keystone, marched up Main Street, and wound its way to Eckman, where the Odd Fellows then assembled at the Wingfield Baptist Church. There Rev. L.E. Johnson called the service to order, Rev. William Manns read the scripture, and Reverend Dabney "preached one of the most forceful sermons ever heard here." Taking his text from the 133rd Psalm, Reverend Dabney exclaimed, "Behold how good and how pleasant it is for brethren to dwell together in unity." More than one thousand people witnessed the parade and services.[29]

If the fraternal orders helped to reinforce the religious culture of black workers, they also helped to link black miners to the larger African American political and civil rights campaign. The fraternal orders invited major political figures to speak at the annual thanksgiving services and parades.[30] In 1913 the Keystone and Eckman Odd Fellows secured Republican governor H.D. Hatfield as their guest speaker. Similarly, at the Twenty-First Annual Meeting of the West Virginia Knights of Pythias, held at Charleston's First Baptist Church, Mayor J.F. Bedell addressed the gathering.[31] In this manner, blacks used the fraternal orders to subtly and not so subtly advance their political aims.

More important, unlike most of their counterparts in other southern states, African Americans in West Virginia received the franchise in 1870 and retained it throughout the period between Reconstruction and World War I.

During the 1890s and early 1900s, at a time when other southern blacks were being disfranchised, black coal miners in southern West Virginia exercised a growing impact on state and local politics. West Virginia blacks developed a highly militant brand of racial solidarity, marked by persistent demands for full equality, albeit on a segregated basis.[32] African American unity across class lines was most evident in protests against racial violence. When whites lynched a black man at Hemphill, McDowell County, in 1896, an aroused black community, workers and elite members alike, confronted local authorities with demands for justice and protection. Under the leadership of prominent middle-class blacks, an estimated five to eight hundred blacks held a mass meeting in the company town of Elkhorn, McDowell County. The group petitioned county and company officials and demanded an investigation. Although the guilty parties were never brought to justice, the blacks involved did secure public announcements from government and company officials promising an investigation to determine the guilty parties.[33]

Black coal miners and their elite allies supplemented their protest activities with electoral politics. As early as 1873, Charleston appointed its first black public official, Ernest Porterfield, who served as a regular policeman. In 1877 the former coal miner Booker T. Washington began his public speaking career as a Kanawha County Republican. According to biographer Louis R. Harlan, Washington played a major role in mobilizing the black vote in the successful campaign to relocate the state capital from Wheeling to Charleston. Washington not only supported the relocation of the capital, a change backed by powerful white Republicans in the state, but also joined other blacks in tying the capital campaign to the issue of equity for blacks within the party and the state. "Washington began his speeches for the capital on June 27, at a rally in Charleston of 'the colored citizens of Kanawha.'... A resolution of the meeting claimed 'the right to a fair portion of the public institutions' in their part of the state." Although Washington later abandoned this vigorous political tradition, most blacks in southern West Virginia did not. Even so, the state's powerful Democratic party, which called itself the "white man's party," reinforced by the Ku Klux Klan in the early post–Civil War years, kept black Republican influence at bay."[34]

For the next two decades Democrats controlled West Virginia's political machinery. The party's constituency included voters in counties that were predominantly agricultural, workers in the industrial centers of northern West Virginia, and, increasingly, the state's powerful industrialists. By the early 1890s the Democrats not only regularly returned their candidate to the governor's mansion, but also returned majorities to the state legislature.[35] The increasing migration of blacks into the region, however, set the stage for the resurgence of the Republican party during the late 1890s. By 1910 blacks made up over 17 percent of the state's voting-age (male) population. Immigrants made up 13 percent, but their voting potential was actually much lower, for only 11.5 percent of voting-age immigrants were naturalized and eligible to vote. Thus, the rise of the black coal-mining proletariat gave African Americans the decisive

A young Booker T. Washington (ca. 1873). (Courtesy of the Library of Congress)

balance of power in Mountain State politics. As early as the gubernatorial election of 1888, for example, the Republican candidate defeated his Democratic opponent by a narrow margin of 110 votes. Democrats contested the vote, arguing that several hundred black migrants in Mercer and McDowell Counties "had voted without the required period of residence and that many of them were, in fact, migratory or transitory workers with no fixed abode." More than a year later, a special session of the legislature awarded the office to the Democratic candidate by a margin of 237 votes. In the gubernatorial election of 1896, however, the Republican candidate, George W. Atkinson, courted black voters and won the governorship by more than twelve thousand votes. Although the Democratic party continued to control the legislature, Republicans made increasing inroads there as well.[36]

Despite the increasing role of black voters in Republican victories, blacks fought an uphill battle for recognition within the party. As one state historian has noted, in addition to courting the black vote, Republicans appealed to mountain whites for vital support by rejecting "unpopular national issues, especially federal intervention in racial matters." Thus they were able to "overcome identification with the black population and hated Reconstruction policies," which included the enfranchisement of blacks. For example, even as G.W. Atkinson campaigned for black votes, he loudly proclaimed his belief in white supremacy. In a letter to the *New York World*, Governor Atkinson affirmed his southern roots and racial beliefs: "I am a Virginian, and am therefore 'to the manor born.' . . . Southern people will not submit to negro rule. 'They will die first.' This is an old Southern expression, and they mean it when they say it." Within this racist framework, however, Atkinson and similar Republicans made room for an alliance with West Virginia blacks around the issue of education. Atkinson delivered a scathing attack on Mississippi senator James K. Vardaman, who sought to deprive blacks of the right to an education: "When he says it is folly to attempt to advance the negro race by education, and in any way qualify them for responsibility and power . . . because by so doing we spoil corn-field hands and make 'shyster' professional men, he simply loses sight of good judgment and fair dealing, and seeks to vent his narrowness, prejudice and spleen against his 'brother in black.'"[37]

In order to push for greater influence in the Republican party, forty-nine black delegates met in Charleston in 1888. They attacked the Republicans for "absolutely" refusing to give blacks "the recognition" to which they were "entitled, notwithstanding the fact that there are eleven thousand colored voters in the state, nearly all of whom are Republicans." These black voters were not merely Republicans; more fundamentally, they were coal miners. They added substance to the African American protests against racial injustice within the party of their allies. It was the black coal miners' vote that enabled middle-class black politicians to gain increasing access to public office in southern West Virginia.

Over the next decade the expanding proletarian electorate fueled the African American campaign for elective and appointive office. In 1896 Republicans elected Christopher Payne, the first African American, to the state legislature. Born in Monroe County, West Virginia, Payne was, in turn, a teacher, preacher, and attorney. Allied with Nehemiah Daniels, a powerful white Republican and county sheriff, Payne entered the statehouse from Fayette County, signaling the gradual rise of black power in southern West Virginia. Payne's election also inaugurated a long tradition of black Republican legislators in West Virginia. Attorney James M. Ellis of Oak Hill, Fayette County, succeeded Payne in the legislative sessions of 1903, 1907, and 1909, while the educator H.H. Railey of Fayette County served in the 1905 session.[38] In 1904 blacks in the Pocahontas District formed the McDowell County Colored Republican Organization (MCCRO). Over the next decade, the MCCRO claimed credit for a growing number of black elected and appointed officials. In November 1913 the organization celebrated its achievements: six deputy sheriffs, three guards on the county road, constables and justices of the peace in four districts, members of school boards in three districts, and the state librarian, a post first held by the influential schoolteacher and grand chancellor of the West Virginia Knights of Pythias L.O. Wilson. MCCRO was open to "All Negro Republicans"; in 1913 its officers included the deputy sheriff Joe E. Parsons, president; the attorney S.B. Moon, recording secretary; the educator E.M. Craghead, corresponding secretary; and the attorney A.G. Froe, treasurer.[39] Black coal miners were a powerful springboard for the political ascent of educated blacks in southern West Virginia.

Nowhere did the political alliance of black workers and black elites in the region produce greater results than in the educational system. African Americans ranked education as their first priority. In their expanding electoral activities, they increasingly demanded equal access to the state's educational resources. In rapid succession, during the 1880s and 1890s, the state funded black public schools in Fayette, McDowell, Mercer, and Kanawha Counties. In 1891 the state legislature established the West Virginia Colored [Collegiate] Institute, a Morrill land grant college for the training of blacks in "agricultural and mechanical arts." Four years later, the legislature created the Bluefield Colored [Collegiate] Institute by "an act to establish a High Grade School at Bluefield, Mercer County, for the colored youth of the State."[40]

Storer College was the earliest institution to offer West Virginia blacks an education "above the common school grades." Founded in 1867 at Harpers Ferry, Jefferson County, Storer would remain the only such school for the next twenty-five years.[41] Following the establishment of the Bluefield Colored Institute and the West Virginia Colored Institute, though, Storer declined as a major provider of educational services to blacks in southern West Virginia.[42] This decline was yet another indication of the shifting center of black life from northern to southern West Virginia as the black coal-mining proletariat expanded.

Although the educational strides of blacks in southern West Virginia proceeded on a segregated and unequal basis, they still symbolized a victorious black community. As suggested by Howard Rabinowitz in his study of race relations in the urban South, whites increasingly accommodated themselves to black access to, rather than exclusion from, fundamental resources and human services. Racial separation was not a static phenomenon; it was not entirely imposed by white racism, and it was not uniformly negative in its results. Within the segregationist framework, the rise of the black coal-mining proletariat spurred the African American struggle for racial equity, facilitated the winning of new concessions, and made racial discrimination in the institutional life of the region less demeaning than it might have been.[43]

Through membership in national black religious, fraternal, and political organizations, southern West Virginia's black coal miners and small black elites also participated in a larger national black community. The National Baptist Convention, the Colored Bureau of the Republican party, and the nationwide bodies of the Elks, Masons, Knights of Pythias, and Odd Fellows all helped to create bonds between the region's blacks and their southern and northern counterparts. Through black ministers like the self-educated Reverend Mr. Barnett of Huntington, blacks in southern West Virginia were intimately linked to blacks in northern West Virginia, Ohio, and parts of Kentucky. In addition to pastoring churches in West Virginia, such as the First Baptist Church in Huntington, Barnett also pastored a variety of black Baptist churches in southern Ohio, including the Tried Stone Baptist Church in Ironton as well as others in Gallipolis, Glouster, Providence, and other cities. Upon Barnett's death, the New Hope Baptist Church of Ashland, Kentucky, adopted a resolution expressing its "admiration of the many fine qualities of our departed leader." "For a hundred miles around," the *Huntington Dispatch* proclaimed, "Rev. Barnett's name is a household word in negro homes."[44]

Based upon their firm support within the black coal-mining community, black elites from southern West Virginia sometimes took prominent leadership positions in national organizations. At its 1913 annual meeting in Atlantic City, New Jersey, and for several years thereafter, for example, the Improved Benevolent Protective Order of the Elks of the World elected Charleston attorney T.G. Nutter as its Grand Exalted Ruler. In 1913 Nutter defeated the incumbent, Armand Scott, of Washington, D.C. It was the mass migration of working-class blacks to southern West Virginia, along with their rich pattern of visiting states farther south and north, that fundamentally underlay Nutter's victory and the growing participation of southern West Virginia blacks in the creation of a national black community. These national linkages were to intensify during World War I and its aftermath.[45]

Although extensive evidence attests to the strength of African American unity across class lines, this unity had its limits. The *McDowell Times* worked for African American solidarity, for example, and yet it also supported the class interests of coal operators and the small black elites. The editor encouraged black miners to provide regular and efficient labor and repeatedly warned them against joining unions. In a mid-1913 letter to the editor, one reader dropped his subscription, emphasizing the editor's antiunion position as the reason. The *Times* not only worked to mold workers' behavior to meet their employers' demands, but also worked to shape working-class behavior to fit middle-class cultural norms. In an editorial titled "Clean Up and Swat the Flies," the editor admonished black coal miners to keep their surroundings sanitary, downplaying the failure of operators to pay higher wages or to provide necessary repairs and sanitation facilities.[46]

As black coal miners faced the limitations of their alliance with the black elites, they developed distinct strategies of their own. While they did seek to endear themselves to employers by providing regular and efficient labor, they frequently shunned other elite injunctions. Seeking to improve the terms of their labor, black coal miners often moved from one mine to another, either within southern West Virginia or farther north and south, and often switched between coal mining and farming in nearby southern agricultural areas, especially Virginia. In the early 1890s, and again in the Paint Creek-Cabin Creek strike of 1913–1914, against the advice of middle-class leaders, numerous black miners joined white miners in organized confrontations with management. The Paint Creek-Cabin Creek confrontation produced the heroic exploits of "Few Clothes" Dan Chain, a black union man. Portrayed by James Earl Jones in the 1987 film *Matewan*, "Few Clothes" was a big man of over 250 pounds, according to available evidence. Labor historian Ronald Lewis claimed that "Dan Chain's size, nerve, and fighting ability made him a favorite among strikers." In 1887, however, when whites lynched a black man in Fayette County, black miners initiated their own mass march of some one thousand men, by some estimates three thousand, vowing to retaliate in kind. Although they disbanded without confrontation, James T. Laing noted, "Whites at the mines in the New River Valley were terrified, for the report was sent to them that the Negroes expected to 'clean out' every white person along the river."[47]

While cleavage along class lines was the most prominent division within the black community, gender inequality was also a significant problem. Emphasizing the home as women's proper sphere, *McDowell Times* editor M.T. Whittico sought to regulate the behavior of black women, endorsed the removal of married women from teaching positions, and opposed woman's suffrage. In an editorial titled "Split Skirts," the editor urged black women to shun the "split skirt" and maintain codes of "modesty." The injunction, however, was directed mainly at black women in coal-mining families: "Only a few of the vulgar variety have been seen in Keystone and none are worn at present by the better class of Colored [women]."[48] On another occasion, the editor threatened to publish a gossip list if black women failed to attend to their own "home work, social affairs and individual business and stop going from house to house, store to store carrying messages and . . . stirring up strife and generally making trouble."[49] On gender issues, the views of elite black men, expressed by the editor, converged with those of the black proletariat.

Yet, as with class conflicts within the black community, gender conflict tended to give way to the imperatives of racial solidarity. Black women perceived their class and gender interests in essentially racial terms.[50] Black Baptist, Methodist, and Presbyterian women, through their regional, state, and local auxiliaries, figured prominently in black religious activities, especially fundraising campaigns, sacred concerts, musicals, and literary programs.[51] Moreover, under the energetic leadership of Mrs. Malinda Cobbs, by World War I black women dominated the Independent Order of St. Luke, which diligently worked "to benefit the race."[52]

Although racial hostility, along with an expanding black consciousness, helped to forge African American unity across class and gender lines, substantial interracial cooperation went on as well. At elite and working-class levels, as discussed above, blacks and whites in southern West Virginia developed interracial alliances. As early as the 1880s, black miners in the Kanawha-New River Field joined the Knights of Labor. They served on integrated committees and, during strikes, helped to persuade black strikebreakers to leave the area.[53] As the United Mine Workers of America (UMWA) supplanted the Knights in the early 1890s, it attracted blacks from the Pocahontas Field as well as the Kanawha-New River area. Blacks soon gained recognition in the union, not only as members, but as officers too. In 1893 when the white president of District 17 died in office, the black miner J.J. Wren of Fayette County filled the position. At Freeman, Mercer County, a white official exclaimed, "The Colored miners have been in the lead in this district until they have shamed their white brethren."[54]

Despite the dramatic display of interracial working-class unity during the 1880s and early 1890s, interracial unionism declined during the mid-1890s and resurged only briefly during the 1914 coal strikes.[55] Even during periods of intense interracial organizing, black members and officers of local unions frequently complained that they were not accorded equal treatment with white unionists. During the 1880s, for example, the Knights of Labor established segregated units, while white members of the UMWA, formed later, some-times blatantly resisted black leadership. Such resistance led one black labor leader to complain, "If your vice president is a Negro . . . he must be treated the same as a white man and unless you do there is going to be a mighty earth-quake somewhere." Although interracial working-class unity remained highly volatile, it was nonetheless important in the lives of black workers.[56]

Black elites developed a corresponding relationship with white elites, mainly coal operators, within the political framework of the Republican party. As noted earlier, through alliances with black coal miners, on the one hand, and white Republicans, on the other, black professional and business people gained election to the West Virginia legislature, appointments to prestigious positions like state librarian, and membership on the board of regents of all-black colleges.[57] Likewise, in McDowell County, coal operators supported M.T. Whittico's black weekly, the *McDowell Times*, which became a preeminent pro-moter of the McDowell County Colored Republican Organization. No less than the alliance between black and white miners, however, the alliance be-tween black elites and the coal operators was inequitable, as indicated by the companies' demand that black leaders like Whittico help to discipline the black coal-mining labor force. In the hostile class and racial climate of southern West Virginia, neither black elites nor black workers could fully articulate their in-terests in class terms.

Linked to each other through color and culture, black workers and black elites forged their strongest bonds, across class lines, with each other. They developed a distinct African American community in the coalfields. In the on-going struggle between white capital and labor, however, African Americans developed their most consistent alliances with coal operators and their corpo-rate and political representatives rather than with organized labor. For example, Republican governor H.D. Hatfield, speaking in a local black church in 1913 before a gathering of black Odd Fellows, declared his "uncompromising pur-pose to see that every man gets a square deal."[58] Unfortunately, no corresponding white labor leader developed such a close bond with the black community.

As the black coal-mining proletariat expanded following the Civil War through the early twentieth century, it established the socio-economic and demographic foundation for the emergence and growth of the black middle class, the rise of black communities in coal-mining towns, and, most impor-tant, the emergence of viable political and civil rights struggles. These processes, rooted in the prewar rise of the black industrial working class, involved the complex dynamics of class, race, and region. Along with new developments, they would reach their peak during World War I and the 1920s.

NOTES

An earlier version of this essay appeared as chapter 2 in Joe William Trotter Jr., *Coal, Class, and Color: Blacks in Southern West Virginia, 1915–1932* (Urbana: Univ. of Illinois Press, 1990), and is reprinted here with the permission of the University of Illinois Press.

1. William H. Harris, *The Harder We Run: Black Workers since the Civil War* (New York: Oxford Univ. Press, 1982), 29–50; Philip S. Foner, *Organized Labor and the Black Worker, 1619–1973* (New York: International Publishers, 1974), 64–135; Sterling D. Spero and Abram L. Harris, *The Black Worker: The Negro and the Labor Movement* (1931; reprint, New York: Atheneum, 1968), 53–115.

2. Ronald D Eller, *Miners, Millhands, and Mountaineers: Industrialization of the Appalachian South, 1880–1930* (Knoxville: Univ. of Tennessee Press, 1982), 128–40; David A. Corbin, *Life, Work, and Rebellion in the Coal Fields: The Southern West Virginia Coal Miners, 1880–1922* (Urbana: Univ. of Illinois Press, 1981), 1–7; Darold T. Barnum, *The Negro in the Bituminous Coal Mining Industry* (Philadelphia: Univ. of Pennsylvania Press, 1970), 1–24; Spero and Harris, *Black Worker,* 206–45; Ronald L. Lewis, *Black Coal Miners in America: Race, Class, and Community Conflict, 1770–1980* (Lexington: Univ. Press of Kentucky, 1987), chap. 7; West Virginia Department of Mines, *Annual Reports, 1909, 1910* (Charleston, W.Va.).

3. For fuller figures on the population change in southern West Virginia, see table 1.1 in Joe William Trotter Jr., *Coal, Class, and Color: Blacks in Southern West Virginia, 1915–1932* (Urbana: Univ. of Illinois Press, 1990), 11.

4. Corbin, *Life, Work, and Rebellion,* 8, 43–52; Eller, *Miners, Millhands, and Mountaineers,* 129, 165–75; Barnum, *Negro in the Coal Industry,* 1–24; Randall G. Lawrence, "Appalachian Metamorphosis: Industrializing Society on the Central Appalachian Plateau, 1860–1913" (Ph.D. diss., Duke University, 1983), 224–28; Price V. Fishback, "Employment Conditions of Blacks in the Coal Industry, 1900–1930" (Ph.D. diss., University of Washington, 1983), 44–51; Lewis, *Black Coal Miners in America,* chap. 7; Kenneth R. Bailey, "A Judicious Mixture: Negroes and Immigrants in the West Virginia Mines, 1880–1917," *West Virginia History* 34 (1973): 141–61; Bureau of the Census, *Report on the Population of the United States, Eleventh Census of the United States, 1890* (Washington, D.C.: Government Printing Office, 1895), 435; Bureau of the Census, *Thirteenth Census of the United States, 1910* (Washington, D.C.: 1913), 3:1032–41.

5. For further discussion of these adjustments in the labor force and the genesis of a black working class, see Trotter, *Coal, Class, and Color,* chap. 1.

6. John R. Sheeler, "The Negro in West Virginia before 1900" (Ph.D. diss., West Virginia University, 1954), 256–57; Booker T. Washington, *Up from Slavery* (1901; reprint, New York: Bantam Books, 1967), 57–58; Louis R. Harlan, *Booker T. Washington: The Making of a Black Leader, 1856–1901* (New York: Oxford Univ. Press, 1972), 33–51, 84–85, and 137–38.

7. Bureau of the Census, *Religious Bodies, 1906* (Washington, D.C.: 1910), 140; Bureau of the Census, *Religious Bodies, 1926* (Washington, D.C.: 1929), 133, 998; "Sacred Concert," 5 Dec. 1913, "Services at Keystone" and "Locals," 15 May 1914, "The Presbyterian Sunday School Relief Department," 16 Oct. 1914, "The Mt. Olivet Baptist Ass'n," 18 July 1913, "The Flat Top Baptist Association," 9 May 1913, all in *McDowell Times;* Sheeler, "Negro in West Virginia," 251–74; Washington, *Up from Slavery,* 57–58; Harlan, *Booker T. Washington,* 33–51, 84–85, and 137–38.

8. Bureau of the Census, *Twelfth Census of the United States, 1900: Special Reports, Occupations* (Washington, D.C.: 1904), 410–14; Bureau of the Census, *Thirteenth Census* (Washington, D.C.: 1913), 4:529–30; "Bluestone Baptist Church Rally," 9 May 1913, "Rally at Anawalt," 4 July 1913, and "Welch News," 13 June 1913, all in *McDowell Times.*

9. "Welch News," *McDowell Times,* 13 June 1913.

10. "McAlpin Notes," 1 May 1914, "Locals," 23 May 1913, "Coalwood News," 22 May

1914, and "Slabfork," 11 Dec. 1914, all in *McDowell Times*. For insight into black religion during the industrial era, see Lawrence Levine, *Black Culture and Black Consciousness: Afro-American Folk Thought from Slavery to Freedom* (Oxford: Oxford Univ. Press, 1977), chap. 3; E. Franklin Frazier, *The Negro Church in America* (New York: Shocken Books, 1963), chaps. 3, 4, 5; and Elizabeth R. Bethel, *Promiseland: A Century of Life in a Negro Community* (Philadelphia: Temple Univ. Press, 1981), 69–91, 136–44.

11. "Baptizing at Wingfield Baptist Church: Fifteen Hundred People . . . Witness Ceremony," 9 May 1913, "Bramwell News," 28 Nov. 1913, "Giatto News," 12 Dec. 1913, "Kimball Notes," 23 Oct. 1914, all in *McDowell Times*.

12. "Death at Gilliam," *McDowell Times*, 4 July 1913.

13. See various issues of the *McDowell Times*, 1913–14; Lawrence, "Appalachian Metamorphosis," 13–35.

14. For works on black religion in the South, see note 10 above.

15. "The Flat Top Baptist Association Holds Successful Session in City," 25 July 1913, and "Pastor Installed at First Baptist Church," 14 Nov. 1913, both in *McDowell Times*; Joseph J. Boris, *Who's Who in Colored America*, vol. 1, *1927* (New York: Who's Who in Colored America, 1927), 108–9; Mary M. Spradling, ed., *In Black and White: A Guide to . . . Black Individuals and Groups* (Detroit: Gale Research, 1980), 517; Wilhelmina S. Robinson, *Historical Afro-American Biographies* (Cornwells Heights, Penn.: Publishers Agency, 1978), 215–16.

16. "In Memory: Rev. Nelson Barnett," and Rev. I.V. Bryant, "Funeral-Sermon of Rev. Nelson Barnett," both in private files of Capt. Nelson L. Barnett, U.S. Air Force (retired), Huntington, W.Va. (copies in author's possession).

17. Ibid.

18. Ibid.

19. "The Flat Top Baptist Association Holds Successful Session in City," 25 July 1913, "Rev. Coger Preaches Able Sermon," 25 July 1913, "Jenkinjones Notes," 8 Aug. 1913, and "Colored Member Elected," 30 Oct. 1914, all in *McDowell Times*.

20. "Giatto News," 12 Dec. 1913, "Rally at First Baptist Church, Kimball," 10 April 1914, "Services at Keystone," 1 May 1914, "Great Baptist Meeting at Tams," 24 July 1914, "Glen White," 2 Oct. 1914, "Religious Services at Keystone," 20 March 1914, all in *McDowell Times*.

21. For spirited revivals at African Methodist Episcopal churches, see "A Voice from the A.M.E. Church," 8 May 1914, "Locals," 15 May 1914, and "Great Revival at Landgraff," 16 May 1913, all in *McDowell Times*. Black Presbyterians in West Virginia also retained important links to the spiritual traditions of southern blacks. See especially "Back from Vacation," *McDowell Times*, 5 Sept. 1913.

22. "Successful Evangelistic Services Conducted at Northfork," 24 April 1914, and "Rev. Gipson and His Church Work," 25 Sept. 1914, both in *McDowell Times*.

23. "Sacred Concert," *McDowell Times*, 5 Dec. 1913.

24. T.E. Hill, "My Dream of the Future Church," reprinted in full in the *McDowell Times*, 12 Dec. 1913. Also see "The Prisoners' Friend," 5 June 1914, "The Presbyterian Sunday School Relief Department," 16 Oct. 1914, and "McDowell County Applies for 150 State Convicts," 20 June 1913, all in *McDowell Times*.

25. See the *McDowell Times*, 1913–1914 passim.

26. "Golden Rule News," 9 May 1913, "Address of Rev. R.H. McKoy, D.D.," 13 June 1913, "2000 Wanted," 16 Jan. 1914, and "Golden Rule Association: Hold 10th Annual Meeting in Tazewell," 12 June 1914, all in *McDowell Times*.

27. "Golden Rule News," "Address," and "2000 Wanted."

28. "John Panell Killed by Falling Slate," 5 Sept. 1913, "Death at Times. Gilliam," 4 July 1913, and "Landgraff Loses a Good Citizen," 25 July 1913, all in *McDowell Times*.

29. "Colored Odd Fellows Parade: Hold Great Thanksgiving Service," 16 May 1913, *McDowell Times*.

30. "Keystone Lodge A.F. and A.M. Hold Services," 27 June 1913, and "Pythian Anniversary Ceremonies Held," 3 April 1914, both in *McDowell Times*.

31. "Colored Odd Fellows Parade: Hold Great Thanksgiving Service," 6 May 1913, and

"Mayor: Delivers Address of Welcome to Colored Pythians of State," 8 Aug. 1913, both in *McDowell Times.*

32. Sheeler, "Negro in West Virginia," 191–94. For patterns of black disfranchisement in other parts of the South, see Joel Williamson, *The Crucible of Race: Black-White Relations in the American South since Emancipation* (New York: Oxford Univ. Press, 1984).

33. Lawrence, "Appalachian Metamorphosis," 183–86.

34. Sheeler, "Negro in West Virginia," 202–3; Washington, *Up from Slavery*, 64–65; Harlan, *Booker T. Washington*, 93–96.

35. Otis K. Rice, *West Virginia: A History* (Lexington: Univ. Press of Kentucky, 1985), 165–73, 204–16; John A. Williams, *West Virginia: A History* (New York: W.W. Norton, 1984), 115–29; Corbin, *Life, Work, and Rebellion*, 10–18.

36. Sheeler, "Negro in West Virginia," 207–12; Bureau of the Census, *Thirteenth Census* (Washington, D.C.: 1913), 3:1032–41; Rice, *West Virginia*, 172, 206, 208.

37. Rice, *West Virginia*, 207; Williams, *West Virginia*, 115–19; Corbin, *Life, Work, and Rebellion*, 10–18; quote in *New York World*, 23 July 1899, reprinted in *Public Addresses, etc., of Governor G.W. Atkinson*, courtesy of Gary L. Weiner, Clarksburg, W.Va.

38. Williams, *West Virginia*, 115–29; Corbin, *Life, Work, and Rebellion*, 10–18; Sheeler, "Negro in West Virginia," 207–12; Bureau of the Census, *Thirteenth Census* (Washington, D.C.: 1913), 3:1032–41; C.W. Swisher, ed., *Manual of the State of West Virginia, 1907–1908* (Charleston, W.Va.: Tribune, 1907), 114; "Great Meeting of the McDowell County Colored Republican Organization," 21 Nov. 1913, "Republicans Together," 31 July 1914, and "Prof. Sanders Promoted," 31 July 1914, all in *McDowell Times;* West Virginia Bureau of Negro Welfare and Statistics (WVBNWS), Biennial Report, 1921–1922 (Charleston, W.Va.), 67.

39. "Great Meeting of the McDowell County Colored Republican Organization," 21 Nov. 1913, "Republicans Together," 31 July 1914, "Prof. Sanders Promoted," 31 July 1914, all in *McDowell Times;* "State Librarian," in John T. Harris, ed., *West Virginia Legislative Hand Book* (Charleston, W.Va.: Tribune, 1916), 809.

40. Sheeler, "Negro in West Virginia," 223–26, 230–46; "The School Attendance," 9 May 1913, and "West Virginia Colored Institute," 27 June 1913, both in *McDowell Times;* John C. Harlan, *History of West Virginia State College, 1890–1965* (Dubuque, Iowa: Wm. C. Brown, 1968).

41. Sheeler, "Negro in West Virginia," 234–39; "Storer College" and "State of W.Va. Correspondence on Appropriations to Storer, 1914–1941," box 1, Storer College Papers, West Virginia Collection, West Virginia University.

42. See Storer College to Gov. H.D. Hatfield, Feb. 1915, box 1, Storer College Papers.

43. "Interracial Racial Relations," WVBNWS, Biennial Report, 1925–1926, pp. 118–20.

44. Sheeler, "Negro in West Virginia," 251–60, 207–13; "In Memory" and "Funeral Sermon," in private files of Capt. Nelson L. Barnett, Huntington, W.Va.; "Pythians Capture the City of Baltimore," 5 Sept. 1913, "National Baptist Convention," 26 Sept. 1913 and 25 Sept. 1914, and "Locals," 5 Sept. 1913, all in *McDowell Times;* Harris, *West Virginia Legislative Hand Book (1916)*, 809; Harris, *West Virginia Legislative Hand Book* (1928), 220; Harris, *West Virginia Legislative Hand Book* (1929), 201.

45. "Elks Hold Great Meeting" and "Nutter Elected Grand Exalted Ruler," 5 Sept. 1913, "Convention of Elks," 17 July 1914, " Elks Hold Big Meeting," 4 Sept. 1914, "Fifteenth Annual Session of the I.B.P.O.E. of the World," 11 Sept. 1914, all in *McDowell Times;* Louis R. Harlan, *Booker T. Washington: The Wizard of Tuskegee, 1901–1915* (New York: Oxford Univ. Press, 1983), 125–27; and Trotter, *Coal, Class, and Color,* chap. 2.

46. For the *Times'* antiunion position, see "We Still Adhere to Our Policy," 4 July 1913, "Illimitable as the Wind: We Blow on Whom We Please," 11 July 1913, "Unfair Attitude of Union Men toward the Negro," 18 July 1913, Rev. M.L. Shrum to M.T. Whittico, 20 June 1913, reprinted, 4 July 1913, and "Clean Up and Swat the Flies," 9 May 1913, all in *McDowell Times.* See also Corbin, *Life, Work, and Rebellion,* 75–79.

47. Corbin, *Life, Work, and Rebellion,* 41, 77–105; Lawrence, "Appalachian Metamorphosis," 63, 133–38, 184–85, 262–63, 288; Lewis, *Black Coal Miners in America,* chaps. 7 and 8, especially pp. 141–42; John Sayles, *Thinking in Pictures: The Making of the Movie "Matewan"* (Boston:

Houghton Mifflin, 1987); Spero and Harris, *The Black Worker,* chap. 7; James T. Laing, "The Negro Miner in West Virginia" (Ph.D. diss., Ohio State University, 1933) 493–96.

48. "Split Skirts," *McDowell Times,* 4 July 1913.

49. "Attend to Your Duties," *McDowell Times,* 25 July 1913.

50. "Literary Program," 13 March 1914, and "Woman's Auxiliar[y] National Baptist Convention," 5 Sept. 1913, both in *McDowell Times.*

51. "St. Luke News," 9 May 1913, "Mrs. Malinda Cobbs: A Successful Deputy," 10 Aug. and 31 Aug. 1917 (includes a photo and summary of Cobbs's lodge activities), "Woman's Auxiliar[y] National Baptist Convention," 5 Sept. 1913, all in *McDowell Times.*

52. "Bluefield Police," 18 July 1913, and "Brave Colored Woman Defends Her Honor and Home Shoots at Cops," 18 July 1913, "Colored Odd Fellows," 16 May 1913, "The Annual Thanksgiving Services," 30 May 1913, and "The Ninth Annual Meeting," 13 June 1913, all in *McDowell Times.*

53. Stephen Brier, "Interracial Organizing in the West Virginia Coal Industry: Participation of Black Mine Workers, 1880–1894," in *Essays in Southern Labor History,* ed. Gary M. Fink and Merle E. Reed (Westport, Conn.: Greenwood Press, 1977), 18–43; Lewis, *Black Coal Miners in America,* 136–40.

54. Brier, "Interracial Organizing in the West Virginia Coal Industry," 29.

55. For the upsurge of interracial unionism in 1913–14, see Corbin, *Life, Work, and Rebellion,* 87–101; Lewis, *Black Coal Miners in America,* 14–42; Richard D. Lunt, *Law and Order versus the Miners: West Virginia, 1907–1933* (Hamden, Conn.: Archon Books, 1979); Hoyt N. Wheeler, "Mountaineer Mine Wars: An Analysis of the West Virginia Mine Wars of 1912–13 and 1920–21," *Business History Review* 50 (spring 1976): 69–91.

56. Brier, "Interracial Organizing in the West Virginia Coal Industry," 32–33.

57. See note 36 above, especially Sheeler, "Negro in West Virginia," 207–12, and *McDowell Times,* 21 Nov. 1913, 31 July 1914, and 16 May 1913. See also "Editor Mr. Whittico," 23 Feb. 1917, and "Whittico Dead," 23 June 1939, both in *McDowell Times.*

58. "Colored Odd Fellows Parade: Hold Great Thanksgiving Service," 16 May 1913, *McDowell Times,*

18

RACIAL VIOLENCE, LYNCHINGS, AND MODERNIZATION IN THE MOUNTAIN SOUTH

W. FITZHUGH BRUNDAGE

In October 1891, in Clifton Forge, a mining town in southwestern Virginia, a mob of whites ceremoniously executed three black men and a black boy. The lynching avenged the wounding of several whites who earlier had engaged the black men in fatal gunplay. A year later, a well-organized group of vigilantes (or "whitecappers") in Whitfield County in north Georgia dragged Jack Wilson, a black man, from his home and, without evident cause, murdered him. In 1909, Richard Watson, one of two blacks living in Elliott County in eastern Kentucky, was murdered by his white neighbors for no apparent reason other than his business acumen. And during the "Red Summer" of 1919, whites in Knoxville, provoked by the murder of a white woman, randomly attacked blacks, destroyed the city jail and surrounding property, and killed at least one black man.[1]

The mountain South, as these examples indicate, was the setting for the full repertoire of southern collective and racial violence. Lynchings, "whitecappings," rioting, and all manner of violence erupted there. The history of that violence from Reconstruction to World War II offers scant evidence of either distinctive race relations or traditions of violence in the Appalachian South. Instead, it confirms the findings of a generation of scholars who have challenged the received wisdom about Appalachian exceptionalism. The mountain South was neither blessed by exceptionally benign race relations nor cursed by implacable race hatred. Rather, the pattern of antiblack violence in the mountains underscores John Inscoe's conclusion that racial attitudes and practices there fit seamlessly along the continuum of orthodox race relations in the Jim Crow South. What is most striking about the history of lynching in the mountain South is its congruence with that of mob violence elsewhere below the Mason-Dixon line. Lynching in Appalachia was simply and fundamentally, in a word, southern.[2]

The ebb and flow of mob violence between 1880 and 1940 was consistent throughout the Appalachian South. Although the history of lynching during Reconstruction remains obscure, it appears that as the turmoil following the Civil War eased, lynchings and extralegal violence diminished. The late 1870s and early 1880s were infrequently scarred by mob violence. But after roughly

1885, lynchings increased sharply and, as was true throughout the South, peaked during the 1890s. Mob violence then declined steadily after the turn of the century, although the region was never entirely free from racial violence, as the Knoxville riot of 1919 graphically demonstrated. This pattern of mob violence paralleled the broad trends of lynching evident throughout the South as a whole.[3]

The evolving distribution of lynching victims by race also coincided with broader southern tendencies. With each passing decade the proportion of mob victims who were black increased. Before 1900, mobs in the mountain region executed almost as many whites as blacks. Indeed, in eastern Kentucky before the century's end, white mob victims actually outnumbered black victims three to one. At first glance, this characteristic would seem to distinguish lynchings in the mountains from mob violence elsewhere in the South. But, just as the mountain regions of Tennessee and Kentucky were prone to white-on-white lynchings, so too were the parishes of northern Louisiana, the counties of central Arkansas, and the foothill border counties of Tennessee and Kentucky. A recent study concludes that the lynchings of whites by white mobs was most commonplace "in predominately white, rural counties of the South."[4] Thus, while notable, the frequency of lynching of whites in the mountain South paralleled patterns in other mostly white areas of the South. And, most important, after 1900, lynching in Appalachia and in the South in general became almost exclusively a form of antiblack violence.[5]

Whether deep in the plantation South or high in Appalachia, the alleged offenses that provoked mobs to inflict summary punishment were tragically consistent. Wherever mob violence occurred in the South, the precipitating causes of most lynchings were alleged murders and violent attacks. These two offenses provoked over twice as many lynchings as did ostensible sexual offenses, while minor offenses prompted few mob executions. In those areas of the mountain South where blacks were the mobs' targets, whites reacted to alleged sexual assaults and murders according to the brutal etiquette of southern race relations that justified the lynching of black rapists and murderers. Three lynchings in north Georgia are illustrative. In 1913, a mob of hundreds in Stephens County lynched two black tramps who had killed a popular town policeman who tried to arrest them for loitering. In 1915, another mass mob in Stephens County executed Sam Stephens, a convict serving time on the chain gang, who allegedly had raped a sixteen-year-old white girl. Finally, in 1916, in the last lynching in the region a mob of one hundred in Walker County lynched Henry White, a "floater" who was accused of raping a young white woman. (The black-owned *Chicago Defender* claimed that the black man and the white woman had actually been lovers.)[6]

Alleged murders and sexual offenses also precipitated the overwhelming majority of mob murders in eastern Kentucky, where two-thirds of lynching victims were white. When, on December 23, 1881, in Ashland, Kentucky, George Ellis and two other white men raped two white girls, murdered them and a young crippled boy with axes, and then set the mutilated corpses on fire, they aroused a communal fury that could not be assuaged by the courts. After being captured by the police, Ellis turned state's evidence, thereby securing the conviction of his partners in the murders. He too was convicted and sentenced to life in prison. Even so, on June 3, 1882, the night after his sentencing, a mob of several hundred men from Ashland traveled by chartered train to Catlettsburg, where Ellis was jailed, overpowered the jailer, and returned with Ellis to Ashland by train. Near the site of the murders, the mob hanged him from the limb of a sycamore tree.[7]

The public ritual of the Ellis lynching and most other mob executions in Appalachia was indistinguishable from the practice elsewhere in the South. Mountain lynchings were neither spontaneous affairs nor substitutes for distant or absent legal institutions. Some lynchings in the region were hue-and-cry affairs in which an outraged community rose up in the immediate aftermath of a crime to punish the perpetrator, but many were not.[8] Most lynchings were premeditated affairs that displayed at least a modicum of organization. Some planning was required simply for the mobs to wrest their victims away from the legal authorities. For instance, the mob that lynched Sam Stephens in 1915 displayed striking fortitude. After devoting more than five hours to breaking into the jail and being thwarted by the door of the black man's cell, the mob settled for firing hundreds of rounds through the cell door and into Stephens's body.[9] Similarly, the logistics involved in transporting the mob that captured and then lynched George Ellis demanded careful coordination. And, as in the Ellis and Stephens cases, the overwhelming majority of mob victims in the mountains of Virginia and Georgia were seized while in legal custody. Sometimes law officers vigorously resisted the mobs, but more often, like their counterparts throughout the South, they surrendered their prisoners with unbecoming haste to any threatening crowd.[10]

In Appalachia, as was common throughout the South, a mob's brutality escalated according to the race of its victim and in direct proportion to the perceived severity of the alleged precipitating transgression. Mountain mobs showed no more restraint than their flatland counterparts when they executed their victims. One scholar has suggested that the most brutal forms of extralegal execution, especially burning, were uncommon in the region.[11] It is more accurate to observe that the lynching of whites usually did not incorporate the full repertoire of brutality that whites reserved for the lynching of some black victims. Because whites comprised a large percentage of lynching victims in the mountain South, a corresponding percentage of lynchings there were free of the most extreme forms of torture and mutilation. The restraint of the mobs that executed whites was evident, for instance, in the lynching of George Ellis in Ashland, Kentucky. Despite the viciousness of the crimes that Ellis was convicted of committing, his executioners refrained from any mutilation of his corpse. The mob that murdered Dock Posey, a white man in Whitfield County, Georgia, accused of raping his stepdaughter, displayed similar discipline. After hanging Posey, an unidentified "captain" of the mob explicitly ordered that no shots be fired into the corpse.[12]

Such forbearance was almost unheard of when the mobs' victims were black. The lynching of Thomas Smith in Roanoke, Virginia, offers one vivid illustration of the capacity of mobs in the Appalachian South to erupt in almost uncontrollable violence. On September 23, 1892, Smith, a young black laborer, allegedly choked, beat, and robbed Mrs. Henry Bishop, a "respectable" white woman, in the downtown of the booming city of Roanoke. Within a short time, Smith was arrested and placed in jail. Throughout the afternoon a belligerent crowd milled in front of the jail and demanded the prisoner. The pleas from prominent public officials for the crowd to disperse were met with shouts and threatened violence. As conditions around the jail worsened, Mayor Henry Trout ordered the entire city police and local militia to protect the prisoner. Unintimidated by the gathered police and militia forces, an enormous crowd, variously estimated at between fifteen hundred and five thousand participants, hurled rocks at the militiamen and made a wild rush at the jail. Shooting broke out, and in the subsequent chaos seven mob members were killed and at least twenty-five members of the mob and the jail's defenders were wounded, including the mayor.[13]

Once the wounded and dead were cleared from the streets, the mob directed its fury against three targets: the mayor, who they believed had given the order to shoot; the militia, which they believed had fired without provocation; and Smith, whose alleged crime had sparked the crisis. The mob searched furiously for the mayor and ransacked his home and the hotel to which he had been moved for medical care. The mayor, meanwhile, had fled the city. Having failed to punish either the militia or the mayor, the mob set about locating Smith, who had been quietly removed from his cell by the police during the chaos surrounding the jail. Early the next morning, the mob finally discovered the hiding place of the alleged black assailant and lynched him. Only the timely intercession of a local minister prevented the mob from burying the body of Smith, which bore a sign with the caption "Mayor Trout's friend," in the front yard of the mayor's home. In the end, the mob satisfied itself by burning the body.

The lynching of Thomas Smith was an exception; rarely did lynchings anywhere in the South degenerate into comparable assaults on public authority. But, in some regards, Smith's execution was emblematic. In keeping with the pattern in the region, it was the work of a large mob, perhaps numbering in the hundreds.[14] Like most lynching victims in the mountain South, Smith was seized from law officers. His murderers, as was typical in the region, made no effort to disguise their identities. Instead, they relied upon the large size of the crowds that participated in and observed most lynching in the mountain South to provide whatever degree of anonymity they sought. In sum, few contemporary observers of the lynching of Thomas Smith in Roanoke, of Dock Posey in Dalton, Georgia, or of other instances of mob violence in Appalachia could have distinguished the practice of lynching there from the work of mobs elsewhere in the South.

Images of mob violence in the Appalachian South during the late nineteenth century may appear to mesh with the region's reputation for feuding and rampant violence. But, as Altina Waller has demonstrated, neither the myth of hillbilly feuding nor the notion of a distinctive Appalachian culture of violence withstands careful scrutiny. Violence in the region, she insists, cannot be traced to some purported genetic inheritance or received culture from Scotch-Irish ancestors. Nor did the violence simply reveal an irrational penchant for bloodshed among the region's residents. Such explanations obscure and trivialize the very real conflicts and tensions that burst forth in violence in the mountain South.[15]

The preconditions for collective racial violence seemingly should have been absent in the region. The large white majority faced little serious threat, economic or otherwise, from the small and vulnerable black population in the region. Plantation agriculture and its attendant traditions of violent and exploitative labor relations remained peripheral to the mountain economy.[16] Yet during the late 1880s and early 1890s mob violence in the mountains reached levels comparable to other regions of the South. How, then, can the history and magnitude of the bloodshed in the Appalachian South be explained?

The answer lies in the wrenching innovations and unwelcome immigrants that mountain folk confronted as the isolation of their region diminished. The steep ridges, shorter planting season, and seclusion of the mountain South had impeded the incorporation of the region into the plantation economy before the Civil War. Local elites, like their southern counterparts elsewhere, did invest in slaves, who in time comprised a small but important part of the labor force. Certainly, by the Civil War, the institution of slavery had touched virtually every county in the mountain South. Yet, for many of the largely self-sufficient white farmers who peopled the valleys and hollows of the region, slaves were an expensive luxury. And after emancipation the black presence in mountain hinterlands seemed destined to diminish after many longtime black residents deserted the countryside, flocking instead to the burgeoning cities of the mountain region.[17]

The growth of towns and cities was just one measure of the transformations that swept the Appalachian South during the postbellum era. For the first time, rail lines cut deeply into the mountains, simultaneously incorporating the region into the nation's expanding market economy and disrupting the prevailing subsistence economy. In southwestern Virginia, eastern Tennessee, and the western corner of north Georgia, improved transportation profoundly transformed the region; staple crop cultivation expanded, commercial activity increased, and mill towns, even cities, arose. Before 1870, for instance, a single rail line ran down the valleys of southwestern Virginia. By 1900, railroads and mining companies, lured by vast lumber and mineral resources, had penetrated virtually all of the region. New communities sprang up, often with astonishing speed. When the Norfolk and Western Railroad transformed Big Lick, a tiny village in 1880, into the city of Roanoke, with a population exceeding twenty-five thousand in 1890, it created one of the most celebrated boomtowns of the New South.[18]

Rural industrialization also was the catalyst for substantial population changes throughout the mountain South. Company recruiters brought foreign immigrants and blacks into the mushrooming mills, lumber camps, and coal mines, sometimes creating racially and ethnically mixed communities. The steady stream of black laborers who flowed from the plantation belt of the South to the mountain lumber camps and mining towns never assumed the proportions of a large-scale migration, but it still significantly increased the black population in the mountains. The number of blacks there grew from 175,000 in 1860 to more than 274,000 by century's end. Simultaneously, an ongoing redistribution of the black population within the region that had begun after emancipation continued. Two counties in Virginia are illustrative. Between 1880 and 1900, the black population of Wise County grew from 101 to 1,965, and in Alleghany County, from 1,132 to 4,013. In counties that were not undergoing rapid economic development, however, black populations either remained small or declined. Thus, the substantial growth of the black population between 1865 and 1900 actually represented a far more significant increase within certain portions of the region.[19] The region's modernization, in short, took place unevenly. While some counties underwent dizzying transformations others remained largely cut off from the most pronounced manifestations of change. This quilt-like pattern contributed to a similarly complex pattern of local responses to the developments sweeping over the region.

The racial tension that flared into mob violence in Appalachia was one consequence of the furious pace of these social and economic transformations. That the influx of black laborers into predominantly white communities, together with the social and economic effects of rapid development, spawned deep tensions is hardly surprising. Some longtime mountain residents fought the advance of industrialization with tactics ranging from lawsuits to outright violence, while others acceded to the transformations but retained grave concerns about the new immigrants. The editor of the Abingdon *Weekly Virginian* expressed the uneasiness of many locals when, after surveying the effects of the arrival of the railroad in his county, he complained that "along the tracks of the railroad there have congregated ex-convicts, robbers, cutthroats, and outlaws, the very scouring of the earth, until life and property are not safe." Elsewhere in the region, the fears of many whites focused specifically upon the influx of itinerant black laborers.[20]

At first glance, the mob violence of the 1890s may appear to have been the product of the collision of preindustrial values with the new industrial order and the shift of community life from stable self-sufficiency to dependency and exploitation. We may be tempted to assume that mountain residents, who watched as distant industrialists and their local lackeys wrested control over the region from them, struck out violently against diffuse targets. Anger, frustration, social instability, and economic disruption, the argument goes, ignited violence without bounds, ranging from so-called feuds, killings, and labor violence, to lynching.[21]

Certainly, more than coincidence explains the simultaneous phenomena of rural industrialization and frequent lynchings in the mountain South. But it is a mistake to assume that mob violence was an expression of the dedication of deeply traditional mountaineers to purge their society of the forces of modernity. The violence of the mountain lynchers was not an inarticulate, irrational reaction to inchoate fears but rather a concentrated effort to control, not stop or reverse, change. Like their counterparts in other rapidly changing regions of the South, such as the piney woods of south Georgia and Mississippi, the whites who lived in Appalachia used violence as a tool to define racial boundaries in a region where traditional racial lines were either vague or nonexistent. There is ample evidence that the frustration and anger of the white residents of the region found its target with brutal precision.

The settings for many of the lynchings are suggestive of the tensions that helped fuel mob violence in the region. Had raw competition between white and black workers been at the root of the violence, lumber camps and coal towns presumably would have been the sites of frequent lynchings and racial clashes. In these communities the conflict between the older preindustrial values of mountain whites and the new order represented by migrant black workers arguably was most marked; however, they were seldom the sites of mob violence. Until the full history of black and white workers in the mountain South is written, it is difficult to know precisely why the economic competition and rugged communal life in the mines and mills did not spark more racial violence. Nevertheless, there is growing evidence that suggests that a surprising degree of racial harmony existed between the races in many industrial communities. The nature of the labor in the mines and mills and the considerable sense of community that developed in some industrial towns seem to have mitigated against some of the harshest expressions of prejudice against blacks. Almost certainly, steady friction between the races was present, but it seldom escalated into outright mob violence.[22]

Lynching, rather than serving as a form of backwoods or mining camp justice, instead often occurred in the comparatively cosmopolitan towns of the mountain South. For instance, of the twenty-two counties in southwestern Virginia, only twelve counties had lynching incidents, and of these only six had more than one. The most mob-prone communities were the transportation, financial, and administrative centers for the surrounding countryside, and typically were—much more than company towns—dependent upon a single industry. Among the towns in which lynchings occurred were Wytheville, Bluefield, Richlands, Clifton Forge, and Roanoke. Lynching occurred in areas that tended to have a slightly higher percentage of black residents than was typical in the region and that also enjoyed a more rapid rate of population growth than the counties free of mob murders. Lynchings, then, occurred in precisely those communities that were the centers of change within the region.[23]

That explosive forces were at work in southwestern Virginia was evident in the concentration of mob violence in place and in time. The twenty-eight lynchings that occurred in the region reflected, more than in any other portion of the Old Dominion, the desperation of whites to define the status of blacks in a region where blacks were still uncommon and where rapid change was taking place. The explicit racial inspiration for the violence was evident in the targets of the mobs; in a region where whites outnumbered blacks by a margin of nine to one in 1900, the overwhelming majority of mob victims were black.

The motivations of the overtly racist mobs in southwestern Virginia went far beyond simple vengeance for some alleged crime and included blatantly prescriptive aims. In some instances, white lynchers tapped into inherited attitudes of "contempt, hostility and social superiority" toward all blacks.[24] The lynching of five black railroad hands in Tazewell County in February 1893, for example, was intended to convey in unmistakable form the indiscriminate desire of whites to rid their communities of all blacks. Four of the black men had spent the evening before the lynching with two white store owners carousing, drinking, and listening to "a disreputable white woman" play banjo. Later that night, as the white men stumbled home, the blacks allegedly robbed and beat them. On the following day, local law officers arrested and jailed one of the black men. A mob quickly formed, easily overpowered the jailer, and captured the prisoner. Within hours the sheriff arrived with the other three alleged assailants. The sheriff, who perhaps was intimidated by the mob of eighty men, or, more likely, was sympathetic to their aims because he was a cousin of one of the assaulted white men, readily surrendered his prisoners. The Tazewell County mob, which organized openly and made no effort to disguise its ranks, hardly represented a misdirected or veiled assault on the established order. At the front of the mob were James Hurt, a magistrate and a member of the Richlands town council, and James Crabtree, a prominent Richlands businessman. After hanging the four black men from the same tree, the lynchers murdered a fifth victim, an innocent black man, and posted signs throughout the county warning blacks to leave immediately or risk vigilante justice. In neighboring Buchanan County, whites also ordered blacks out, announcing "that Buchanan should be altogether a white county."[25]

Comparable racial tensions also flared in the northwestern corner and along the southern tier of counties in north Georgia, where economic development was most marked. Much of the violence expressed the rage and frustration of white tenants and sharecroppers. Landless whites, who chafed when they found themselves caught in a system of labor that they believed was fit only for blacks, insisted that they be in loftier positions than blacks on the agricultural ladder. But the direction of staple-crop agriculture almost certainly stripped most embattled poor whites of any hopes of acquiring land. They were left with the token advantages that they received from white landlords: modestly better land to till and a degree of latitude denied blacks. Their pent-up discontent periodically surfaced in terrorist racial violence against blacks.

Where mountain whites pressed down into the upper piedmont and, in turn, blacks pushed up from the cotton belt, white tenant farmers sporadically organized campaigns to drive black families off their landlords' land and to ostracize the white farmers who rented to them. In 1912, for example, white tenant farmers in Forsyth County, a county on the southern border of the region, determined to force all black landowners to sell their farms and to drive all black tenants out of the county. They whipped and murdered an undetermined number of blacks, burned their homes and barns, and warned them to leave. The white planters who depended upon black laborers tried to prevent the exodus of blacks by refusing to hire white tenants or to extend credit to the leaders of the terrorist campaign, but even so, almost all blacks were driven out of the county.[26]

More often, whites apparently intended for lynchings to communicate codes of acceptable black behavior rather than to purge the region of blacks. The targets of the violence, as was so often the case in the South, were young, itinerant, black workers whose raucous and sometimes violent lifestyles provoked considerable concern among whites. In the eyes of many whites, the behavior of blacks was doubly upsetting because it was unpredictable and posed a threat to life and property.

The lynching of four black miners in Alleghany County, Virginia, in 1891 is but one instance of savage white retaliation provoked by nothing more than foolhardy black bravado in a region where the definition of acceptable conduct by blacks had yet to be precisely etched. The events that culminated in the bloodletting began on October 17, 1891, in the boomtown of Clifton Forge. Six black miners from nearby mines came to town to carouse on their day off. Whites would later claim that the miners had a more sinister motive, namely, "to take the town."[27] Like most black miners in the region, the party was composed of men who had been lured from the fields of eastern Virginia by promises of good pay, new opportunities, and tempered racial discrimination. But as the men would discover, the tolerance of whites for any conspicuous behavior by blacks had limits.

The miners first relaxed at a bar, and then, with considerable hoopla, had themselves photographed. A surviving photograph records Charles Martin, the leader of the group, with a pistol in each hand, his arms crossed on his chest, and three additional pistols stuffed in his belt. Beneath a broad-brimmed cowboy hat, he stares from the photograph as if self-consciously adopting the appearance of a Wild West outlaw. One by one, the rest of the group followed Martin and adopted equally fierce poses for their photographs. After their visit to the photo studio, the men divided their time between shopping for flashy clothing and carrying out various pranks against convenient passersby on the street.[28]

Although Martin and his friends seem to have committed no specific crime beyond harassing a young black street vendor, their boisterous, intimidating behavior attracted attention. A town police officer attempted to arrest them but was forced to retreat when they announced that "they would die before they were taken." Actually, the men seem to have had no interest in trouble, and, sensing the danger that they faced, they abandoned the town and began the journey back to the mines. The officer, stung by his humiliation at their hands, gathered together a posse and set out after them. A short distance from the mines, the posse overtook the blacks and ordered them to surrender. The details of subsequent events remain vague, but there is no question that a lengthy gun battle took place and left two members of the posse wounded, one of them mortally. When news of the gun battle reached Clifton Forge, heavily armed white men poured from the town and scoured the mountains for the black miners. Within hours, four of the black "gang" had been captured and lodged in the jail in Clifton Forge.[29]

By early evening plans to lynch the black men were under way. At ten o'clock, a mob that may have numbered as many as three hundred surrounded the mayor's office and the jail that held the black "desperadoes." Ignoring the mayor's meek protests, the mob methodically broke into the jail and seized the black prisoners. After placing ropes around the necks of Miller, John Scott, and William Scott, the mob dragged them through the streets to a neighborhood known variously as Slaughter House Hollow or Butcher's Hollow. The lynchers allowed each man to pray and to confess before they yanked the victims up and fired hundreds of rounds into their swaying bodies. Despite three executions to their credit, the lynchers still were not appeased. They returned to the jail for Bob Burton, whose leg had been shattered by a bullet earlier, loaded him into a cart, and transported him to the tree where the mangled bodies of his three friends remained suspended. Despite his youth—he was only a teenager—and Miller's earlier confession that Burton had been forced to participate in the day's events against his will, the mob showed no pity. They hoisted him aloft beside the three corpses and riddled his body with shot.[30] There was little ambiguity in the intended meaning of the Clifton Forge executions. The mob used the murders to ensure that blacks were well aware that they remained in the region only with the sufferance of whites.

So extensive were the social and economic transformations in the mountain South that at times the vigilantes there sometimes appeared to lash out in all directions at once. The whitecappers of north Georgia, where terrorist violence was especially pronounced, vented concerns over economic dislocations and social disarray. Corn rather than cotton had been the region's staple, and the abundance of corn and the isolation of most farms had provided two of the essential ingredients to the moonshining industry that thrived there.[31] When federal revenue agents launched an aggressive campaign to stamp out moonshining during the late 1880s, many mountain men resisted by joining with other whitecappers in punishing revenue agents and their informants. Simultaneously, whitecappers worried that indolence and lasciviousness were invading the budding towns of the region. Some also apparently resented surrendering more and more local autonomy to the whims of the market autonomy. Finally, whites were troubled by the vexing problem of blacks, who did not always abide by the region's hardening code of white supremacy. Thus, the spasm of lynchings and whitecappings against prostitutes, wife-beaters, petty criminals, "uppity" blacks, and revenue informers was all part of a response to modernization and its attendant far-reaching economic and social changes.[32]

Even where whites and blacks averted violence, the threat of it often provided the pretext for the ongoing calibration of racial etiquette in the region. For instance, in 1909, in the town of Glen Wilton in southwestern Virginia, a murder allegedly committed by a black miner threatened to provoke a wholesale pogrom against all blacks in the community. Local blacks, including several ministers, met with concerned local whites and agreed on measures to relieve the crisis. By posting signs warning that "all bad negroes must quit town," the black community hoped to mollify white concerns about black lawlessness. Local officials moved the alleged murderer to a safe jail, and tensions subsided. As one white later observed, "What's the use of having race trouble when the good negroes want to be good?"[33] Taken together, the averted violence in Glen Wilton and the lynchings in Clifton Forge, Bluefield, and Forsyth County were all part of the unfolding of a regional racial etiquette. Each event was intended to teach blacks what forms of public and private behavior would and would not be tolerated in the new biracial communities of the Appalachia South. Each was part of the tense negotiation between longtime residents and newcomers, blacks and whites, workers and capitalists, over the direction, speed, and benefits of the region's transformation.

If mob violence in the mountain South was not a unique phenomenon rooted in a peculiar mountain culture, it still was inextricably bound up in the dislocations produced by the rapid and profound change there. It would be a mistake to explain the pattern of lynching by exaggerating the enduring impact of such social strains as economic depression and industrialization. These processes unquestionably generated serious racial friction. But they may explain, at most, only brief eruptions of mob violence. As profound as the shock of rapid change was for many residents of the mountain South, it did not create the preconditions for perpetually high levels of mob violence. The level of mob violence in the mountain South, after all, subsided after 1900. No precise explanation for this decline is apparent. The decline of lynching in the region, as noted earlier, paralleled broader southern trends. Yet, any explanation for the decline must take into account, in addition to regional trends, developments specific to the mountain South.

The eruption of widespread mob violence almost certainly marked an important but transitional stage in the social and economic modernization of the mountain South. The peak of lynching in Appalachia, like the pattern of collective violence in other areas undergoing rapid economic change, coincided with the period when industrialization was relatively new.[34] Rural industrialization, wherever it took place, was a catalyst for racial antagonisms. The combination of the footloose black workers in such rural industries as lumbering and mining and the challenge that the industrial labor practices posed to prevailing labor traditions predictably fostered ambivalence and hostility among many white residents in communities undergoing rural industrialization. And because rural industrialization did not require or encourage the expansion of local government or the development of anything that might be labeled civic culture, neither institutions nor individuals with any firm commitment to discourage categorically racial violence existed.[35]

The racial tensions generated by the industrialization of the Appalachian

South, however, were quickly subsumed by greater and more enduring strains within the white community. The flurry of mob violence during the early years of industrialization was an attempt by whites to define the status of blacks, an effort that took on significance only because of the transformations within the region. By the turn of the century, racial etiquette in the region was codified in law and practice. The racial geography of the region likewise was stabilized. After the initial dramatic influx of blacks into southwestern Virginia, eastern Kentucky, and eastern Tennessee, fewer and fewer blacks found employment in the mines there. Blacks seemingly preferred the coalfields of West Virginia, where they suffered less oppressive treatment at the hands of whites.[36] Only the coal mines of Alabama continued to employ large percentages of blacks. Throughout much of the region, whites, unchallenged by black laborers, retained for themselves the dubious privilege of eking out a living in the region's mines and mills. When racial antagonism flared in those settings, it was most often inflamed by mine and mill operators anxious to stymie unions and suppress strikes. As the effects of development became clear, residents of Appalachia allied themselves either in support of the changes or against them. The ebbing of mob violence and the ongoing, periodic eruption of labor unrest and violence in the Appalachian South during the twentieth century signaled the advent of increasingly politicized protest directed against the people who spearheaded change and the inequities of industrialization itself.

Even fewer catalysts for racial violence were evident in the areas of the mountain South untouched by industrialization. Unlike the transformations in the pine barrens of Louisiana or the Delta of Mississippi, two other areas marked by headlong change after the Civil War, the changes in the mountain South did not remake the region in the image of the plantation South. Only a small portion of Appalachia, specifically the area along the borders with the foothills, was devoted to monocultural agriculture with all of its attendant evils, including lynching. Mobs flourished within the boundaries of the plantation South where sharecropping, monocultural agriculture, and a stark line separating white landowners and black tenants existed. In regions characterized by these traits, mob violence became part of the very rhythm of life. Deeply rooted traditions of violent labor control, unhindered by any meaningful resistance from either institutions or individuals opposed unconditionally to racial violence, sustained a tradition of mob violence for decades. In rough proportion to the degree that a particular region diverged from the plantation South, the likelihood of habitual mob violence in that region shrank. Of course, neither the pursuit of economic justice nor the rejection of violence lay behind the absence of violence in agricultural labor relations in Appalachia. Mountain landlords simply devised instead a system of labor that was exploitative, stable, and lucrative but that did not rest upon the steady application of coercive methods. They showed little interest in mimicking their low country counterparts, who assumed the prerogative to regulate violently all aspects of black life. Thus, the enduring stimuli for lynching that were so abundant in the plantation districts of the South were largely absent from rural Appalachia. The point is that although the color line was etched into the day-to-day reality of race relations in Appalachia during the twentieth century, few whites believed that the up-heavals of the late nineteenth century required them to defend violently and habitually their property, livelihood, rights, or status from a black threat.

NOTES

1. *Clifton Forge Valley Virginian,* Oct. 22, 1891; *Savannah Morning News,* Oct. 25, 1892; *Dalton North Georgia Citizen,* Oct. 27, Nov. 3, 1892; George C. Wright, *Racial Violence in Kentucky, 1865–1940: Lynchings, Mob Rule, and "Legal Lynchings"* (Baton Rouge: Louisiana State Univ. Press, 1990), 128; *Knoxville Journal and Tribune,* Aug. 31, Sept. 5, 1919; Lester C. Lamon, *Black Tennes-seans, 1900–1930* (Knoxville: Univ. of Tennessee Press, 1977), 243–53.

2. For a cogent and concise discussion of race relations in the mountain South, see John C. Inscoe, "Race and Racism in Nineteenth-Century Southern Appalachia: Myths, Realities, and Ambiguities," in *Appalachia in the Making: The Mountain South in the Nineteenth Century,* ed. Mary Beth Pudup, Dwight B. Billings, and Altina L. Waller (Chapel Hill: Univ. of North Carolina Press, 1995), 103–31. Also see William H. Turner and Edward J. Cabbell, eds., *Blacks in Appala-chia* (Lexington: Univ. Press of Kentucky, 1985).

3. The ebb and flow of violence in the region did vary from state to state. For example, the level of mob violence in eastern Kentucky was constant from 1870 until the century's end, and then it declined sharply. In northern Georgia and southwestern Virginia, the dramatic rise and fall between 1885 and 1900 was more pronounced. On eastern Kentucky, see Wright, *Racial Violence in Kentucky,* esp. 72–73. For broader regional trends see Stewart Tolnay and E.M. Beck, *A Festival of Violence: An Analysis of Southern Lynchings, 1882–1930* (Urbana: Univ. of Illinois Press, 1995).

4. See E.M. Beck and Stewart E. Tolnay, "When Race Didn't Matter: Black and White Mob Violence against Their Own Color," in *Under Sentence of Death: Essays on Lynching in the South,* ed. W. Fitzhugh Brundage (Chapel Hill: Univ. of North Carolina Press, 1997), 132–54.

5. After 1900, 71 percent of the victims of mob violence in eastern Kentucky were black. In Virginia, 83 percent were black; in north Georgia, 80 percent were. Even so, it is important not to exaggerate the scale of antiblack violence in Appalachia. Statistically, blacks in Appalachia were more vulnerable than were blacks anywhere else in the South. But, the small black population of the region notwithstanding, generations of blacks in the mountains lived without suffering the ignominy of witnessing mob murder in their counties. In the last analysis, blacks in Gordon County, Georgia, or McDowell County, North Carolina, almost certainly would not willingly have surrendered a lifetime in a county free from the stain of lynching for the statistical safety of the Mississippi Delta or South Carolina piedmont. The mountain South may not have been a favorable environment for blacks to secure economic and social independence, but, if nothing else, they were relatively free from the threat of the noose and torch. The data for eastern Kentucky were derived from Wright, *Racial Violence in Kentucky,* 307–23, and for southwestern Virginia and north Georgia, from Brundage, *Lynching in the New South,* chaps. 4 and 5.

6. *Montgomery Advertiser,* March 1, 1913; *Toccoa Record,* March 6, 1913; *Atlanta Constitu-tion,* June 15, 1915; *Clarkesville Advance,* June 15, 1915; *Toccoa Record,* June 17, 1915; *Atlanta Con-stitution,* Sept. 21, 1916; *Chicago Defender,* Sept. 30, 1916.

7. *Louisville Courier Journal,* June 2–4, 1882.

8. Fourteen of the twenty-nine lynching victims in southwest Virginia were lynched more than a day after the alleged crime that precipitated the lynching. Seven of the nineteen lynching victims in north Georgia were lynched more than a day after the alleged crime that precipitated the lynching. In both states, several victims were lynched weeks and even months after their alleged crimes.

9. For the details of the Alonzo Williams lynching, see *New York Times,* July 30, 1908; *Atlanta Constitution,* July 30, 1908. On the Stephens lynching, see *Atlanta Constitution,* June 15, 1915; *Clarkesville Advance,* June 15, 1915; *Toccoa Record,* June 17, 1915.

10. Twenty-seven of the twenty-nine lynching victims in southwestern Virginia were seized

from law officers by the mob; thirteen of nineteen lynching victims in north Georgia were taken from law officers.

11. Robert P. Stuckert, "Racial Violence in Southern Appalachia, 1880–1940," *Appalachian Heritage* 20 (spring 1992): 35.

12. *Atlanta Constitution*, July 2, 1907; *Macon Telegraph*, July 2, 1907; *Savannah Morning News*, July 2, 1907; *Dalton Citizen*, July 4, 1907; *Savannah Tribune*, July 5, 1907.

13. The best contemporary discussions of the Roanoke Riot are in the *Roanoke Times*, Sept. 21–27, 1893; *Norfolk Virginian*, Sept. 21–23, 1893. The best account of the riot is Ann Field Alexander, "Like An Evil Wind: The Roanoke Riot of 1893 and the Lynching of Thomas Smith," *Virginia Magazine of History and Biography* 100 (April 1992): 173–206. Two other scholarly accounts are John A. Waits, "Roanoke's Tragedy: The Lynch Riot of 1893" (master's thesis, University of Virginia, 1972); and Gordon McKinney, "Industrialization and Violence in the 1890s," in *An Appalachian Symposium*, ed. J.W. Williamson (Boone, N.C.: Appalachian State Univ. Press, 1977), 131–44.

14. Seventeen of twenty-nine lynching victims in southwestern Virginia were executed by mobs numbering more than fifty members; seven of nineteen victims in north Georgia were lynched by mobs of fifty or more members.

15. Altina L. Waller, *Feud: Hatfields, McCoys, and Social Change in Appalachia, 1860–1900* (Chapel Hill: Univ. of North Carolina Press, 1988); Altina L. Waller, "Feuding in Appalachia: Evolution of a Cultural Stereotype," in Pudup, Billings, and Waller, *Appalachia in the Making*, 347–76.

16. On plantation agriculture and lynching, see Brundage, *Lynching in the New South*, esp. chap. 4; Terrence Finnegan, "At the Hands of Parties Unknown: Lynching in Mississippi and South Carolina" (Ph.D. diss., University of Illinois, 1993), 189–90, 199–202; Tolnay and Beck, *Festival of Violence*, esp. chap. 5.

17. John C. Inscoe, *Mountain Masters: Slavery and the Sectional Crisis in Western North Carolina* (Knoxville: Univ. of Tennessee Press, 1989), passim; Inscoe, "Race and Racism in Appalachia," 117–19; Frederick A. Bode, *Farm Tenancy and the Census of Antebellum Georgia* (Athens: Univ. of Georgia Press, 1986), 77–78.

18. Ronald D Eller, *Miners, Millhands, and Mountaineers: Industrialization of the Appalachian South, 1880–1930* (Knoxville: Univ. of Tennessee Press, 1982), 65–80; Douglas Flamming, *Creating the Modern South: Millhands and Managers in Dalton, Georgia, 1884–1984* (Chapel Hill: Univ. of North Carolina Press, 1992); Joseph T. Lambis, "The Norfolk and Western Railroad, 1881–1896: A Study in Coal Transportation" (Ph.D. diss., Harvard University, 1948), 54; Randall G. Lawrence, "Appalachian Metamorphosis: Industrializing Society on the Central Appalachian Plateau, 1860–1913" (Ph.D. diss., Duke University, 1983), 28–47; Paul Salstrom, *Appalachia's Path to Dependency: Rethinking a Region's Economic History* (Lexington: Univ. Press of Kentucky, 1994), esp. chap. 4.

19. Bureau of the Census, *Twelfth Census of the United States, 1900* (Washington, D.C.: U.S. Census Office, 1901), 1:561–62; Inscoe, "Race and Racism in Appalachia," 106–7.

20. *Abingdon Weekly Virginian*, April 11, 1889. See also Eller, *Miners, Millhands, and Mountaineers*, 170–72; Lawrence, "Appalachian Metamorphosis," 48–122.

21. McKinney, "Industrialization and Violence," 131-44. Contrast with Waller, *Feud*, 7–11, 235–49.

22. See Kenneth R. Bailey, "A Judicious Mixture: Negroes and Immigrants in the West Virginia Mines, 1880–1917," *West Virginia History* 34 (Jan. 1973): 141–61; Stephen Brier, "Interracial Organizing in the West Virginia Coal Industry: The Participation of Black Mine Workers in the Knights of Labor and United Mine Workers, 1880–1894," in *Essays in Southern Labor History*, ed. Gary M. Fink and Merl E. Reed (Westport, Conn.: Greenwood Press, 1977), 18–43; David A. Corbin, *Life, Work, and Rebellion in the Coal Fields: The Southern West Virginia Miners, 1880–1922* (Urbana: Univ. of Illinois Press, 1981), chap. 3; Ronald L. Lewis, *Black Coal Miners in America: Race, Class, and Community Conflict, 1780–1980* (Lexington: Univ. Press of Kentucky, 1987), passim; Crandall A.Shifflett, *Coal Towns: Life, Work, and Culture in Company Towns of Southern Appalachia, 1880–1960* (Knoxville: Univ. of Tennessee Press, 1991).

316 W. FITZHUGH BRUNDAGE

23. See appendix, table 16, "Average Population Growth in All Counties and in Counties with Lynchings in Southwestern Virginia by Decade, 1880–1930"; and table 17, "Percent Black Population in All Counties and in Counties with Lynchings in Southwestern Virginia by Decade, 1880–1930," in Brundage, *Lynching in the New South.*

24. On mountain traditions of racism, see Inscoe, "Race and Racism in Appalachia," 115–16.

25. *Richmond Planet,* July 23, 1893. See also Feb. 11, 1893; *Richmond Dispatch,* Feb. 2–3, 1893; *Baltimore Sun,* Feb. 2, 1893; *Washington Post,* Feb. 2, 1893.

26. *Atlanta Constitution,* Oct. 13, 1912; for other examples, Jan. 8, 1900, Nov. 20, 1900, Jan. 13, 1916, June 1, 1916; John M. Matthews, "Studies in Race Relations in Georgia, 1890–1930" (Ph.D. diss., Duke University, 1970), 163; Royal Freeman Nash, "The Cherokee Fires," *Crisis* 11 (March 1916): 265–70; Robert Preston Brooks, "A Local Study of the Race Problem," *Political Science Quarterly* 26 (June 1911): 193–221. For a discussion of the changes in race relations in the foothills, see Wallace H. Warren, "Progress and Its Discontents: The Transformation of the Georgia Foothills, 1920–1970" (master's thesis, University of Georgia, 1997).

27. *Clifton Forge Valley Virginian,* Oct. 22, 1891.

28. *Richmond Planet,* Oct. 31, 1891.

29. *Clifton Forge Valley Virginian,* Oct. 22, 1891. The events at Clifton Forge can be recon-structed from *Richmond Dispatch,* Oct. 17, 1891; *New York Times,* Oct. 18, 1891; *Lynchburg Virginian,* Oct. 18, 20, 1891; *Lynchburg News,* Oct. 20, 1891; *Lexington Augusta County Argus,* Oct. 20, 1891; *Lexington Gazette,* Oct. 22, 1891.

30. *Richmond Planet,* Oct. 31, 1891; *Clifton Forge Valley Virginian,* Oct. 22, 1891.

31. Edward L. Ayers, *Vengeance and Justice: Crime and Punishment in the Nineteenth-Century South* (New York: Oxford Univ. Press, 1984), 255–64; William F. Holmes, "Moonshining and Collective Violence: Georgia, 1889–1895," *Journal of American History* 67 (Dec. 1980): 589–611; and Dale E. Soden, "Northern Georgia: Fertile Ground for the Urban Ministry of Mark Matthews," *Georgia Historical Quarterly* 69 (spring 1985): 39–54.

32. Holmes, "Moonshining and Collective Violence," 608–11. For similar conclusions about whitecappers in Missouri, see David Thelen, *Paths of Resistance: Tradition and Dignity in Industrializing Missouri* (New York: Oxford Univ. Press, 1986), 88–99.

33. Richard W. Hale, "Lynching Unnecessary: A Report on Commonwealth v. Christian," *American Law Review* 45 (Nov.-Dec. 1911): 875–83; *Hampton Monitor,* March 26, 1909. Another example of attempts by blacks to define a social contract of race relations in the mountain South occurred following the execution of Will Harris, a black "desperado," by a posse in Asheville, North Carolina, in 1906. The local black community sought to reaffirm publicly a code of racial etiquette that applied to whites and blacks alike. See Eric J. Olson, "Race Relations in Asheville, North Carolina: Three Incidents, 1868–1906," in *The Appalachian Experience: Proceedings of the Sixth Annual Appalachian Studies Conference,* ed. Barry M. Buxton et. al. (Boone, N.C.: Appala-chian Consortium Press, 1983), 162–63.

34. Charles Tilly argues that communities undergoing rapid urbanization and industrial-ization have often endured less violence than stable communities. See Charles Tilly, "Queries on Social Change and Political Upheaval," cited in James B. Rule, *Theories of Civil Violence* (Berkeley: Univ. of California Press, 1988), 173. In contrast, Howard Zehr contends that crime peaked in Germany and France at the outset of modernization. See Howard Zehr, "The Modernization of Crime in Germany and France, 1830–1913," in *Readings in Comparative Criminology,* vol. 1, ed. Louise I. Shelley (Carbondale, Ill.: Southern Illinois Univ. Press, 1981), 20–140.

35. For a fuller discussion of the repercussions of rural industrialization, see Brundage, *Lynching in the New South,* esp. chap. 4.

36. The absence of the harshest manifestations of racism and discrimination in West Vir-ginia undoubtedly attracted blacks. Blacks in West Virginia also resisted white violence, whether from mobs or hired thugs from mining companies. See Corbin, *Life, Work, and Rebellion in the Coal Fields,* chap. 3; Lewis, *Black Coal Miners in America,* chaps. 7–8; and especially, Joe William Trotter Jr., *Coal, Class, and Color: Blacks in Southern West Virginia, 1915–1932* (Urbana: Univ. of Illinois Press, 1990), chaps. 5 and 9.

CONTRIBUTORS

DWIGHT B. BILLINGS is professor of sociology at the University of Kentucky. He is the author of *Planters and the Making of the "New South,"* the coauthor (with Kathleen M. Blee) of *The Road to Poverty: The Making of Wealth and Hardship in Appalachia,* and the coeditor of *Appalachia in the Making* and *Confronting Appalachian Stereotypes.*

KATHLEEN M. BLEE is professor of sociology at the University of Pittsburgh. She is the author of *Women of the Klan* and the coauthor (with Dwight B. Billings) of *The Road to Poverty: The Making of Wealth and Hardship in Appalachia.*

W. FITZHUGH BRUNDAGE chairs the history department at the University of Florida. He is the author of *Lynching in the New South: Georgia and Virginia, 1880–1930,* and the editor of *Under the Sentence of Death: Lynching in the South.*

JOHN CIMPRICH is professor of history at Thomas More College in Kentucky. He is the author of *Slavery's End in Tennessee, 1861–1865,* and a forthcoming study of Fort Pillow during the Civil War.

CECELIA CONWAY is a folklorist and professor of English at Appalachian State University. She is the author of *African Banjo Echoes in Appalachia: A Study of Folk Traditions.*

CHARLES B. DEW is the W. Van Alan Clark Third-Century Professor in the Social Sciences at Williams College. He is the author of *Ironmaker to the Confederacy: Joseph R. Anderson and the Tredegar Iron Works* and *Bond of Iron: Master and Slave at Buffalo Forge.*

RICHARD B. DRAKE is professor emeritus of history at Berea College. He is the author of the forthcoming *The Appalachian Experience* and of numerous articles and essays on Appalachian history.

WILMA A. DUNAWAY is assistant professor of sociology at Virginia Polytechnic Institute and State University at Blacksburg. She is the author of *The First American Frontier: Transition to Capitalism in Southern Appalachia, 1700–1860,* and a forthcoming book on the impact of the slave trade on Appalachian slave families.

JOHN C. INSCOE is professor of history at the University of Georgia. He is the author of *Mountain Masters: Slavery and the Sectional Crisis in Western North Carolina* and coauthor (with Gordon B. Mckinney) of *The Heart of Confederate Appalachia: Western North Carolina in the Civil War.*

RONALD L. LEWIS is Eberly Professor of History at West Virginia University. He is the author of *Black Coal Miners in America: Race, Class, and Community Conflict* and *Transforming the Appalachian Countryside: Railroads, Deforestation, and Social Change in West Virginia,* and is the coeditor of *The Black Worker: A Documentary History from Colonial Times to the Present.*

GORDON B. MCKINNEY is the Goode Professor of Appalachian Studies at Berea College and the director of its Appalachian Center. He is the author of *Southern Mountain Republicans, 1865–1900,* coauthor (with John C. Inscoe) of *The Heart of Confederate Appalachia: Western North Carolina in the Civil War,* and the coeditor of the microfilm edition of *The Papers of Zebulon B. Vance.*

KENNETH W. NOE is Draughan Associate Professor of History at Auburn University. He is the author of *Southwest Georgia's Railroad: Modernization and the Sectional Crisis* and the coeditor (with Shannon H. Wilson) of *The Civil War in Appalachia.*

CONRAD OSTWALT is professor of philosophy and religion at Appalachian State University and the coordinator of the university honors program. He has written widely on the Mennonite presence in western North Carolina.

PHOEBE POLLITT is a nurse in Boone, North Carolina, and a former student of history at Appalachian State University with a continuing interest in the religious history of southern Appalachia.

NINA SILBER is associate professor of history at Boston University. She is the author of *The Romance of Reunion: Northerners and the South, 1865–1900,* and the coeditor (with Catherine Clinton) of *Divided Houses: Gender and the Civil War.*

JENNIFER LUND SMITH teaches history at North Georgia College and State University in Dahlonega. She earned her Ph.D. at the University of Georgia with a dissertation titled "Twill Take Some Time to Study When I Get Over": Varieties of African American Education in Reconstruction Georgia."

JOHN E. STEALEY III is professor of history at Shepherd College in West Virginia. A native West Virginian, he is the author of *The Antebellum Kanawha Salt Business and Western Markets.*

MARIE TEDESCO is the archivist for the Appalachian Collection at the Archives of Appalachia at East Tennessee State University. She also teaches courses on Appalachian history and on Appalachian women. She is writing a history of workers and managers at two rayon factories in Elizabethton, Tennessee.

JOE WILLIAM TROTTER JR. is professor of history at Carnegie Mellon University. The son of a coal miner in West Virginia, he is the author of *Coal, Class, and Color: Blacks in Southern West Virginia, 1915–1932*, and of six other books dealing with the Great Migration of African Americans out of the South and their industrial and urban experiences in the North.

DAVID WILLIAMS is professor of history at Valdosta State University. He is the author of *The Georgia Gold Rush: Twenty-Niners, Cherokees, and Gold Fever* and *Rich Man's War: Class, Caste, and Confederate Defeat in the Lower Chattahoochee Valley.*

ACKNOWLEDGMENTS

A couple of years ago, I was approached by editors at the University Press of Kentucky about the possibility of a revised and expanded version of *Blacks in Appalachia*, a landmark collection edited by Bill Turner and Ed Cabbell and published by the Press in 1985. In looking at the recent scholarship on race relations in the southern highlands, I quickly realized that, as with so many areas of Appalachian Studies, an abundance of rich material on the subject has been produced over the last decade and a half, either in print or in progress, and that it would not be difficult to compile a second volume of new material rather than to merely expand the first. The pleasures of such collaborative projects lie in working with so many other scholars of like interest. I have the good fortune to count the majority of the contributors as friends as well as colleagues, which has made working with them all the more pleasurable an experience. Their support, enthusiasm, and cooperation in shaping their parts of the whole have made this a much smoother process than one has any right to expect in dealing simultaneously with nearly twenty authors.

A number of the essays originally appeared as journal articles or book chapters. While some authors have chosen to update their essays to reflect new work that has appeared, others have chosen to leave their pieces in the original form. The authors and/or the editor have condensed several articles to fit the confines of this volume and reshaped book chapters to stand as independent essays. While effort has been made to standardize citation form, some variables in note formats remain.

The contributors and I are all grateful for the valuable input of the two readers who provided us with good, sharp critiques of the whole and of its individual components, and we feel that this is a stronger volume because of their efforts. I am grateful, as always, for the support I enjoy in my department at the University of Georgia and, on this project particularly, for that of Bonnie Carey and Sheree Dendy.

INDEX